Darkness Descends

"The Roman world is falling. . . . The whole country between the Alps and the Pyrenees, between the Rhine and the ocean, has been laid waste by the hordes. . . . As the common saying goes, I forgot my own name."

St. Jerome
Letter to Ageruchia

Darkness Descends

From vicious beginnings a civilization is born

Clovis's son Clodomer falls in battle in 524, and his brothers (above right), Childebert and Clotar, covet his kingdom of Orleans. They resolve to kill Clodomer's three heirs, mere children, and divide Orleans between themselves. From such violent and treacherous origins, the Franks emerged. Guided by monks and bishops, they were gradually converted to Christianity and laid the foundations of the modern Western World.

Details from the illustration by John Smith, page 212.

A.D. 350 to 565

The Fall of the Western Roman Empire

The
Christians

THEIR FIRST TWO THOUSAND YEARS

Fourth Volume

CHP

CHRISTIAN HISTORY PROJECT

THE EDITOR:

Ted Byfield has been a journalist for fifty-five years and a western Canadian magazine publisher since 1973, the founder of *Alberta Report* and *British Columbia Report* weekly newsmagazines, and founding editor of *Alberta in the Twentieth Century*, a twelve-volume history of Alberta. A columnist for Canada's *Sun* newspapers and sometime contributor to the *National Post* and *Globe and Mail* national newspapers, he is active in evangelical journalistic outreach. He was one of the founders of St. John's School of Alberta, an Anglican school for boys where he developed a new method of teaching history.

THE ASSOCIATE EDITOR:

Calvin Demmon of Marina, California, has worked as an editor of *Alberta Report* newsmagazine; as city editor of the *Huntington Park Daily Signal* and of the *Daily Southeast News* in Los Angeles County; and as a columnist and editor for the *Monterey County Herald*. He has contributed articles and short stories to a number of magazines and to several books.

COVER:

The engraving on the cover, of a barbarian attack on a western city, is from Francois Guizot's *History of France*, published in Paris in the 1870s.

CHRISTIAN HISTORY PROJECT LIMITED PARTNERSHIP

President and CEO	Robert W. Doull
Controller	Terry White
Contact Center Manager	Kathy Therrien
Contact Center Administrators	Brian Lehr, Bheko Dube, Larry Hill
Marketing Manager	Leanne Nash
Credit Manager	Keith Bennett
Customer Service Manager	Lori Arndt
Customer Service	Grace de Guzman, Katrina Soetaert
Information Systems Manager	Michael Keast

Darkness Descends, A.D. 350-565, The Fall of the Western Roman Empire

Writers	Michael Byfield, Ted Byfield, Virginia Byfield, Calvin Demmon, Ed Keen, John Muggeridge, Steve Weatherbe, Joe Woodard
Art Director, Illustration/Photo Editor	Jack Keaschuk
Page Production and Graphics	Dean Pickup
Illustrators	Richard Connor, Jamie Holloway, Jim Nunn, Dale Shuttleworth, John Smith
Volume Planner and Director of Research	Barrett Pashak
Researchers	Louise Henein, Jared Tkachuk
Production Editor	Rev. David Edwards
Proofreaders	P. A. Colwell, Faith Farthing
Academic Consultants	Father Brian Hubka, Dr. Joseph H. Lynch, Dr. Eugene TeSelle

THE CHRISTIANS: Their First Two Thousand Years

© 2003 Christian History Project Inc.
© 2003 Christian History Project Limited Partnership
Chairman   Gerald J. Maier

NATIONAL LIBRARY OF CANADA CATALOGUING IN PUBLICATION

Byfield, Ted
Darkness Descends : A.D. 350 to 565, The Fall of the Western Roman Empire / Ted Byfield, Calvin Demmon.

(The Christians : their first two thousand years ; 4)
Includes bibliographical references and index.
ISBN 0-9689873-3-8

1. Church history—Primitive and early church, ca. 30-600. 2. Middle Ages—History. 3. Rome—History—Germanic Invasions, 3rd-6th centuries. I. Demmon, Calvin, 1942- II. Christian History Project. III. Title. IV. Series.

BR205.B93 2003   270.1   C2003-910969-0

PRINTED IN CANADA BY FRIESENS CORPORATION

CONTENTS

ILLUSTRATIONS

(*Artists*)

CHARACTER SKETCHES
Chapters 1, 2, 5 (*Jamie Holloway*)
Chapters 3, 7, 8 (*John Smith*)

The Christian History Project is deeply indebted to the work of Francois Guizot, a nineteenth-century French lawyer and historian, who on his retirement wrote with his daughter a history of France for his grandchildren. Since he knew the stories could be far better understood if the events were lavishly illustrated, he commissioned the artist Alphonse de Neuville to make dramatic woodcuts of the events in the story. Guizot's The History of France, *writes the veteran American senator Henry Cabot Lodge in an 1876 edition of* The North American Review, *"stoops down to the little children, takes them by the hand, and leads them to heights from which the wide horizon of history is displayed." The illustrations, 130 years after they were made, have lost none of their vigor. One appears on the cover of this volume; others throughout the text.*

CHP

For additional copies of this book or information on others in the series,
please contact us at:

The Christian History Project
10333 178 Street
Edmonton AB, Canada, T5S 1R5
www.christianhistoryproject.com

1-800-853-5402

The catastrophe that befell western Europe in the fifth and sixth centuries of the Christian era is beyond the experience of almost anyone living in the modern world, except perhaps the victims of the Pol Pot calamity in Cambodia, or of the periodic tribal and religious slaughters of central and east Africa. But it is not beyond our fantasy and imagination. The attempts of fiction writers, movie-makers and scientists to envision the depredation of a full-scale nuclear conflict give us some sense of what must have happened so many years ago.

To perceive the reality of those two calamitous centuries, we must imagine beautiful and sophisticated cities reduced to virtual ghost towns, magnificent buildings stripped of everything movable and standing like spectral witnesses above paved streets devoid of all human life. We must see whole counties, once lush with vineyards, gardens or waving grain, now returned to wilderness, their drained fields once again marshland, their barns charred ruins, the people fled. We must see bridges crumbling and collapsing, roads cracked and overgrown, magnificent aqueducts deliberately smashed to cut off the water supply to besieged cities, every facet of civilized life gone and replaced by a scene of utter prostration. To restore what is lost will require fourteen centuries of human endeavor. Such is the story that unfolds in this volume.

But there is another story as well. For while the Christian West was enduring the horrors of the barbarian invasions, a very different dynamic was unfolding, largely in the Christian East. It too was cataclysmic. In these same two centuries, the Christians produced their answer to the question that had perplexed them from the beginning: Who was, or is, Jesus Christ? For more than 125 years of bitter, sometimes violent argument, they debated all the answers they could think of, and finally came down to the only one that seemed to satisfy all the questions. Jesus Christ, they agreed, is "perfect God and perfect man, of reasoning soul and human flesh subsisting." The words are from the creed named for, although not written by, the man who stood against the world in this controversy and won: Athanasius of Alexandria, whose victorious struggle is described in this volume's first two chapters.

It is important to realize that what Athanasius established in the fourth century, and his successors safeguarded in the fifth, was the view of Jesus Christ that is still embraced today by almost all Christians—Catholic and Orthodox, Protestant and Evangelical. The decisions of the councils of Nicea, Constantinople, Ephesus and Chalcedon were endorsed by both Luther and Calvin, as they are endorsed today by spokesmen for nearly all major churches.

Such was the Christian conviction carried into the charred ruins of the West. There it would lay the foundation of a new civilization that would arise from the ashes of the old, and over the coming centuries, would create the world we live in today.

Ted Byfield

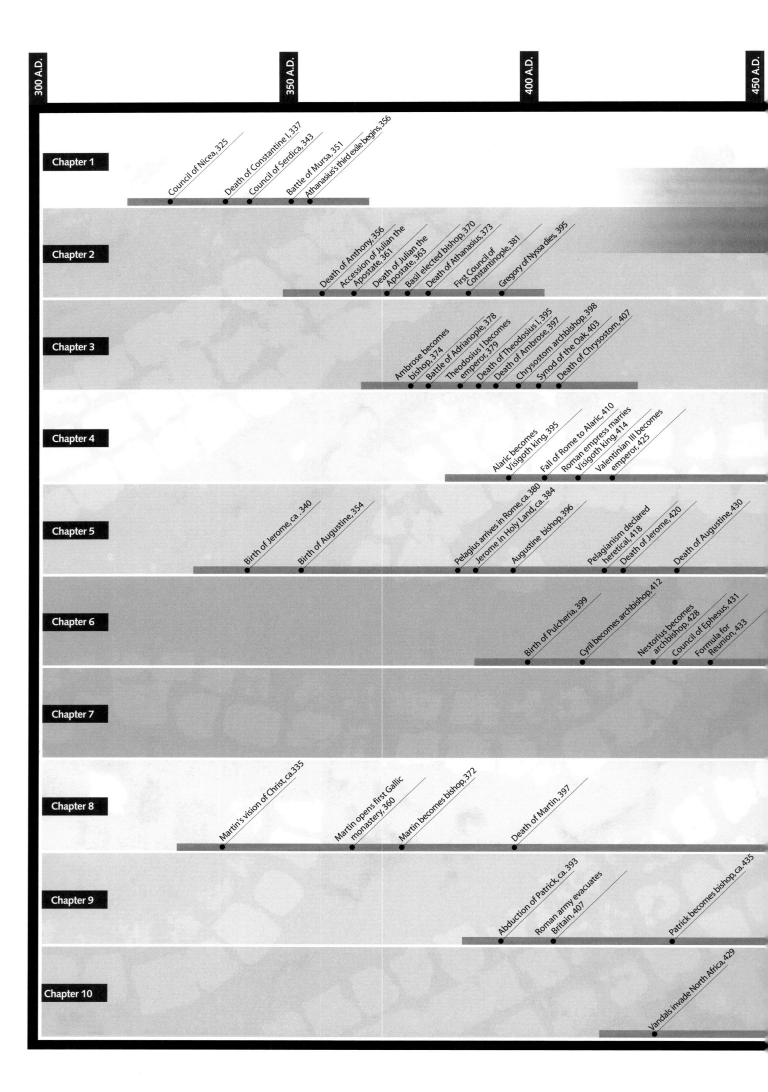

300 A.D. 350 A.D. 400 A.D. 450 A.D.

Chapter 1

Council of Nicea, 325
Death of Constantine I, 337
Council of Serdica, 343
Battle of Mursa, 351
Athanasius's third exile begins, 356

Chapter 2

Death of Anthony, 356
Accession of Julian the Apostate, 361
Death of Julian the Apostate, 363
Basil elected bishop, 370
Death of Athanasius, 373
First Council of Constantinople, 381
Gregory of Nyssa dies, 395

Chapter 3

Ambrose becomes bishop, 374
Battle of Adrianople, 378
Theodosius I becomes emperor, 379
Death of Theodosius I, 395
Death of Ambrose, 397
Chrysostom archbishop, 398
Synod of the Oak, 403
Death of Chrysostom, 407

Chapter 4

Alaric becomes Visigoth king, 395
Fall of Rome to Alaric, 410
Roman empress marries Visigoth king, 414
Valentinian III becomes emperor, 425

Chapter 5

Birth of Jerome, ca. 340
Birth of Augustine, 354
Pelagius arrives in Rome, ca. 380
Jerome in Holy Land, ca. 384
Augustine bishop, 396
Pelagianism declared heretical, 418
Death of Jerome, 420
Death of Augustine, 430

Chapter 6

Birth of Pulcheria, 399
Cyril becomes archbishop, 412
Nestorius becomes archbishop, 428
Council of Ephesus, 431
Formula for Reunion, 433

Chapter 7

Chapter 8

Martin's vision of Christ, ca. 335
Martin opens first Gallic monastery, 360
Martin becomes bishop, 372
Death of Martin, 397

Chapter 9

Abduction of Patrick, ca. 393
Roman army evacuates Britain, 407
Patrick becomes bishop, ca. 435

Chapter 10

Vandals invade North Africa, 429

CHAPTER TIME FRAMES

450 A.D.　　　500 A.D.　　　550 A.D.　　　600 A.D.

Attila defeated at Chalons, 451
Death of Attila, 453

Birth of Benedict, ca. 480
Benedict leaves Rome, ca. 500
Death of Benedict, ca. 550

Death of Cyril, 444
Death of Nestorius, 451

...avian archbishop, 446
Robber Council, 449
Council of Chalcedon, 451
Death of Pulcheria, 453

Clovis becomes king, 481
Clovis baptized, 496
Death of Clovis, 511
Clodomer killed, 524
Clotar becomes king of all the Franks, 558

...of Patrick, ca. 445
Columcille founds Iona, ca. 564
Columban lands in Gaul, ca.585

Vandals take Rome, 455
Death of Marcian, 457
Death of Vandal king Gaiseric, 477
Birth of Justinian, ca. 483
Theodoric becomes sole ruler of Italy, 493
Accession of Justin I, 518
Death of Theodoric, 526
Accession of Justinian I, 527
Nika Revolt, 532
Belisarius in North Africa, 533
Belisarius defeats Witigis, 540
Death of Theodora, 548
Second Council of Constantinople, 553
Death of Justinian, 565
Birth of Mohammed, ca. 570

In this detail from a stained glass window in St. Athanasius Episcopal Church in Brunswick, Georgia, artist Jon Erickson captures the iron resolution that made Athanasius of Alexandria an enduring model for lone crusaders against entrenched authority. The saying Athanasius contra mundum (Athanasius against the world) would become their lasting watchword.

CHAPTER 1

The man who stood against the world

Defying emperors, bishops, officialdom, fire and sword, Athanasius fights alone to save the creed Christians would recite for the next sixteen hundred years

In the intimate inner circles of the burgeoning new Christian capital of Constantinople, the operative word was *metaschematizo*. It meant change. But not merely surface change; it meant to rearrange the entire form of something. The year was 337 and in the last two decades much had changed. Constantinople was becoming the new Rome. More than that, though, it was becoming the capital of a whole new kind of empire, one whose senior officialdom increasingly spoke Greek rather than Latin. And at the center of the new empire was a new religion, Christianity—new, anyway, to official favor. But most important of all, declared those widely regarded as in touch with the times, Christianity itself must change. There must be a new Christianity.

Everyone close to the levers of power, those who considered themselves realistic and knowledgeable, regarded this as self-evident. The old literalist superstition of a god that died on a cross must go, they said. Cultured people, informed people—people like themselves—could not be expected to accept it. Whoever the man Jesus might be, the Christians must not claim he was of the same "essence" or "substance" as the Divine God, if they were to be taken seriously by serious-minded people. That this claim be unalterably repudiated, they were convinced, was the most important change of all.

Such, for example, was the view of the icily pragmatic Eusebius, bishop of Nicomedia, who stood for what he considered "realism." And along with this critical theological change, he believed, the old order of church governance would also have to go. The bishop of Rome, of course, must still represent a certain spiritual presence, but it would be largely a symbolic thing. Real ecclesiastical power, Eusebius was sure, must henceforth lie with the Christian emperor at Constantinople, who in turn would be advised by the Christian archbishop of Constantinople, a post to which Eusebius himself aspired, and which he would soon fill.

Naturally, there were problems. Chief among them was the massive church council that had been held twelve years ago at nearby Nicea.[1] There, the literalists, the urban traditionalists and the backcountry rubes, as Eusebius regarded them, led by old Alexander, archbishop of Alexandria, at a crucial juncture had somehow gained the ear of the newly Christian emperor Constantine. In an appalling backward step, they had most dubiously inserted a detestable clause into the church's official statement of belief. Jesus Christ, it said, was *homoousion*—"of

They accused him of murdering a priest and desecrating a church. The trial went badly. He produced the murder victim very alive, and proved the 'church' wasn't a church and wasn't desecrated.

one substance"—with the Father, meaning with God. The unregenerate old guard was now advancing this preposterous Nicene declaration as the formal "creed" of Christianity.

In adopting the clause, the Nicene council had rejected what had come to be called Arianism, named for the man who first espoused it. The Arian case was essentially negative. It said what Jesus was not, that he was *not* of the same essence as the Father. What he *was* instead, the Arians were not altogether clear about. But in the view of Eusebius and those in Constantinople's inner circle, the Arian cause was in no sense lost. They were sure that if they could make the right appointments, get rid of the old-liners, put sound, modern-thinking people in as bishops and dispose of the troublemakers who hewed to the old, dead theologies, then the Nicene decision could be reversed. Christianity, too, could then undergo metaschematizo and become the new faith for the new order, stripped of its central mythology—and intellectually respectable.

One major obstruction to their plan, they knew, was a singularly obstinate individual, the undoubted chief of the troublemakers. He was, in the Constantinople view, a sinister, clever and most objectionable man, dangerously facile with words, a hero of the mob, violent, defiant of proper imperial and ecclesiastical authority and a troublemaker born to the role. He could pour out prose, persuasive to the unedified masses, in torrents. It seemed to spread all over the empire, entrenching the old superstitions and impeding theological advance. His name was Athanasius.

1. The theological controversy over Arianism, the early life and career of Athanasius and the story of the Council of Nicea are covered in a previous volume, *By This Sign*, chapters 8 and 9.

Banishment to Trier did not necessarily entail hardship for Athanasius. The city was then, as it is now, a center of commerce and culture. The imperial baths (left) would have drawn citizens and visitors alike. The following centuries would enlarge upon the beauty achieved by the Romans, as for example in the exquisite "Peter's Fountain" (below), erected in 1595.

His enemies derided him as a cocky little upstart, who as a deacon had got himself made secretary to old Alexander and doubtless had helped pull the strings that caused the setback at Nicea. With Alexander dead, this Athanasius had contrived to have himself elected archbishop of Alexandria and metropolitan of Egypt and Libya. [2]

In the view of officialdom, therefore, every effort must be made to repudiate his election to such a high office. For that purpose, a council of dependably enlightened bishops had been convened at Tyre on the Mediterranean coast of Palestine, but he had walked out when he found it loaded against him. There had been a commission of inquiry into charges that he had murdered a priest and that one of his people had desecrated a church. This, too, had gone badly when he produced before the hearing the supposed murder victim, fully alive, and persuasively demonstrated that the desecrated property wasn't a church and wasn't desecrated. In the end, in his typical grandstand fashion, he had personally taken his case before the emperor, who, soft on him as he always was, had sent him into exile at beautiful Trier, a city that would one day advertise itself as the oldest metropolis in Germany. Some exile, scoffed his enemies. The place was a resort town, where the emperor himself often holidayed.

Trier was also, in fact, the permanent residence of the eldest of the emperor's three surviving sons, also named Constantine, whom the irrepressible Athanasius came to know well, thereby strengthening the prince's commitment to the Nicene Creed. An occasional visitor was the emperor's youngest son, Constans, who likewise fell under Athanasius's spell. Both sons lived and ruled as caesars in the far less populous west, where most Christians were conventionally Nicene anyway.

Meanwhile, the middle son, Constantius, as caesar in the powerful east, lived near Constantinople. His theology had been moving in a different direction. Eusebius of Nicomedia had seen to it that this young man was relieved of what Eusebius considered the baleful influence of the past, and that his mind was broadened into the thoroughgoing Arianism that was taking hold in major eastern cities, except in Alexandria.

2. In the fourth and fifth centuries, the title of archbishop was applied to bishops of distinguished sees (such as Alexandria). Metropolitans were bishops who exercised jurisdiction over a province, or a group of territorially linked dioceses, rather than just a single diocese. Later, the title archbishop and metropolitan would frequently become interchanged, particularly in the west.

3. Constantine's nephews were the children of his three halfbrothers, all sons of his father's second wife. The half brothers were: (1) Delmatius, whose sons Delmatius and Hannibalian were named in the emperor's will to share the succession with Constantine's own three sons; (2) Julius Constantius, whose sons, Gallus and Julian, were children at the time of Constantine's death and were not included in the succession, and (3) the youngest, the late Hannibalianus, who had died without issue.

As long as Constantine lived, however, the east's Arianism must remain covert. To the old emperor, universal acceptance of the Nicene Creed was essential to the unity of the whole empire. Any bishop departing from it risked immediate banishment. Many held their noses and signed the Nicene Creed anyway, confident that when the old emperor died they could become overtly Arian and Christian theology could be brought into step with the times.

On May 22, 337, that event occurred. Constantine the Great—whose ascent to power as the first Christian emperor had provided the opportunity for all this metaschematizo—died, having been baptized on his deathbed by Eusebius of Nicomedia. The city he had declared as the new capital of the Roman Empire, which would bear his name for the next 1,116 years, was still very much under construction. And so, in the opinion of the ecclesiastics who had surrounded him, was Christianity.

However, the emperor's death had created a profoundly unsatisfactory situation that the army proceeded to eliminate—with a bloodbath. Shrewd though Constantine had certainly been in other respects, his plan for the succession invited real trouble. He had actually left five imperial heirs—his own three sons and two grown nephews.[3] The great emperor was scarcely buried before a spurious document was produced in which the now-dead emperor complained that his two half brothers had poisoned him. This was on the face of it absurd, but it was enough to spur the army, fiercely loyal to Constantine, to execute without hesitation both of his half brothers, along with the two nephews and several other high officials. Only the two youngest sons of his half brother Julius Constantius, both still children, were spared. For an ostensibly Christian regime, it was an inauspicious start, but arguably preferable to the civil war which often followed in such circumstances.

With that problem cleared up, Constantine's three sons met fifteen weeks later at Viminacium (now Widin, Bulgaria) near the Danube, to determine who would rule what. The older brother, Constantine II, aged twenty-one, became augustus of the west, except for Italy and part of Illyricum, which were conferred on the youngest brother Constans, aged fourteen. The middle brother Constantius, at twenty years of age, became augustus of the east. Since this included Alexandria, it gave Constantius immediate responsibility for the Athanasius problem.

Before Constantius could act on that case, however, his oldest brother Constantine had already ordered his good friend Athanasius sent home to resume his post as bishop. But first, to persuade his brother of the fairness and sanity of this move, Constantine brought Athanasius to Viminacium, so that Constantius could meet the bishop himself. Athanasius was certainly impressive, though not physically. A slight man, his hair auburn, his face bearded, he walked with a noticeable stoop, or so

ATHANASIUS ON ORDER IN CREATION

When we see the creation, we conceive of God as the Creator of it; so when we see that nothing is without order therein, but that all things move and continue with order and providence, we infer a Word of God who is over all and governs all.

the only surviving physical description of him records. What won him such wide support, however, was his command of the Greek language. He could phrase his arguments for the God who died on a cross with a telling simplicity and lucidity, so that simple Christian laymen could grasp them, and unlettered men convincingly echo them, much to the discomfort of the more learned.

Constantius appears to have been convinced, but not for long. Even as the three emperors conferred, Eusebius and other Arian bishops complained that the man the emperors had just restored to Alexandria had in fact been deposed by the Council of Tyre. Moreover, they had a new charge against him. Supplies of grain, allocated by the late emperor Constantine for poor widows in Egypt and Libya, had been commandeered by Athanasius, they said. And even as cheering crowds greeted the returning bishop at Alexandria, his foes were assembling in yet another council at Antioch, reasserting the old charges of church desecration, and declaring him no longer Alexandria's bishop. Instead, they named one Pistus to take over the job and dispatched him to Alexandria, sending a notification of their decision to Julius, the bishop of Rome.

But Athanasius, dexterous as usual, could call councils of his supportive bishops at Alexandria as fast as Eusebius could assemble them elsewhere. His Alexandria council met, voted overwhelmingly to affirm him as bishop and dispatched this decision to Julius to counter the one from Antioch. It included a postscript. They had conclusive evidence, they said, that Pistus had been an Arian priest, ordained by an Arian bishop. So it was now up to Bishop Julius of Rome to decide.

At about this point, Athanasius received a formidable endorsement from an old friend whom he had visited as a young man at his wilderness hideaway. This was Anthony, the desert ascetic revered by both Coptic and Greek Egyptians, whose visit to the city during the Galerian persecution nearly three decades before had inspired Christians to sustain their faith. The Arians had apparently been circulating the report that Anthony himself was an Arian, an assertion that brought this determined old man, now close to ninety, into the city to denounce Arianism, and declare his support for Athanasius. Anthony's action had a profound effect, permanently uniting the general Christian populace to Athanasius.

All three sons of Constantine the Great, reigning in various parts of the empire, would have to deal with the "Athanasius problem." Constantine II (top) and Constans (bottom) would be the fiery bishop's friends and defenders. Second son Constantius (middle) became an unflagging adversary.

In the meantime, Eusebius gave up on the would-be bishop Pistus, called yet another council at Antioch, and this time named a certain Gregory, from the province of Cappadocia in Asia Minor, to the see of Alexandria. The council had help from the emperor Constantius, who, surrounded as he was by Arian advisers, had come to regard Athanasius as something akin to an ecclesiastical disease. He had already been irked, in fact enraged, a year before, when he returned to the capital from the three-brother conference at Viminacium. He had discovered that the Alexandrian bishop had taken part in the restoration of one Paul, notably orthodox, as bishop of the capital city itself and had failed to have Paul's election ratified by other local bishops. Back in the capital, Constantius called another council and this one ordered Paul banished. Unsurprisingly, the emperor named the diligent Eusebius as bishop of the capital city instead. Paul, meanwhile, took his case to Rome.

In any event, by March of 339, the time was at hand to deal with the obstreperous Athanasius on his home turf. Gregory, newly appointed to the Alexandrian see, was well aware that opinion in Alexandria ran strongly in Athanasius's favor, and that Alexandrians were renowned for backing their religious inclinations with violence—there had indeed been bloodshed and riots with the city's minority Arian group when Athanasius first came home. So, as the new shepherd of the Alexandrian flock,

Governor Philagrius, an ex-Christian reverted to paganism, looses a gang of local hoodlums on a church favorable to Athanasius.

Gregory prepared resolutely to head south and bring the wayward sheep under control. Ahead of him by several weeks went a new governor, Philagrius, and five thousand troops. Philagrius, an ex-Christian reverted to paganism, had been chosen by Constantius to succeed an appointee of his father's, who, it was decided, had been far too sympathetic and lenient with Athanasius.

Governor Philagrius wasted no time. After lining up a gang of hoodlums and vagrants from the surrounding district, he announced to the churches that Gregory had been chosen as their new bishop. He knew there would be protest and outrage, since Alexandrians had been accustomed for some two hundred years to electing their own bishops. So Philagrius didn't have long to wait, and in response, he unleashed a mob crackdown on one church and its congregation, as luridly described by Athanasius:

> The church and the holy baptistery were set on fire and straightway groans, shrieks and lamentations were heard through the city, while the citizens in their indignation at these enormities cried shame upon the governor and protested the violence used against them. For holy and undefiled virgins were being stripped naked and suffering treatment that is not to be named. If they resisted, they were in danger of their lives. Monks were being trampled underfoot and perishing; some were being hurled headlong; others were being destroyed with swords and clubs; others were being wounded and beaten.
>
> And oh, what deeds of impiety and iniquity have been committed on the Holy Table. They were offering birds and pinecones[4] in sacrifice, singing praises of their idols and blaspheming even in the very churches our Lord and Savior Jesus Christ, Son of the living God.

4. Pinecones were used in certain pagan rites. Some translators render this as meaning seashells, which were used in another pagan rite.

CONNOR

Athanasius goes on to recount "impious men" burning the Scriptures, removing their clothes, "and acting such a disgraceful part, even by word and deed, as one is too ashamed to relate." Is his description an exaggeration? Probably not. That mob frenzy should lead men into behavior exceeding in violence and depravity anything they might indulge individually is unhappily a common occurrence in human history. As the centuries would unfold, too often those mobs would be Christian. Some theologians attribute this phenomenon to the diabolical. Crowds, they say, can become devil-possessed, a peril for which Christians are far from ineligible.

The rising power of holy women

The idea of sanctified virginity draws so many adherents that the church has to defend sex within marriage, and scold those who look down on it

The fourth-century persecution of Athanasius and the Christians at Alexandria dramatically underlines the phenomenon of "holy virgins" or "holy women." Savagely abused during the vicious Arian conflicts, these dedicated women were playing an increasingly significant role in the spiritual life of the church. Christian care for and recognition of women goes back to apostolic times, and reverence for consecrated virginity emerged early. By the fifth century, as barbarian invasions disrupted the west and worldliness corrupted the faith in the east, this idea captivated more and more young women—just as thousands of men were joining monasteries.

Tertullian, in the second century, praised female virginity as an imitation of Christ, notes Jesuit historian James A. Mohler (*The Heresy of Monasticism*, New York, 1971), and virgins took a prominent part in liturgical processions. In the third century, Cyprian of Carthage placed them in honor behind only the martyrs. Indeed, notes British historian Joan M. Petersen in *Handmaids of the Lord* (Kalamazoo, 1996), female virginity seemed to acquire such exaggerated esteem as to admit scarcely any justification for marriage. "I praise marriage, I praise wedlock," wrote Jerome in the fourth century, in a famously controversial letter to his disciple, the virgin Julia Eustochium, "but only because they produce virgins."

However, this implied that the married state, if not actively sinful, was at best second-rate. Did it not cast doubt, some people wondered, on the essential goodness of God's creation? The question came to a head in the mid-fourth century, at the Council of Gangra in Paphlagonia in central Turkey, after one bishop actually denounced marriage as sinful. The council passed twenty canons to repudiate him, not only reaffirming the goodness of sex within marriage, but also anathematizing anyone who embraced virginity solely because he or she abhorred marriage. It further denounced any virgin who regarded the married state "arrogantly," or any woman who left a marriage because she abhorred the married state itself.

Similarly, the so-called Apostolic Canons, a series of eighty-five church laws written in the fourth century, and claiming to go back to the teaching of the apostles, spoke out categorically on the essential goodness of sex within marriage. For example, Canon 51 reads: "If any bishop, presbyter or deacon, or any one of the sacerdotal list, abstains from marriage, or flesh, or wine, not by way of religious restraint, but as abhorring them, forgetting that God made all things very good, and that he made man male and female, and blaspheming the work of creation, let him be corrected, or else be deposed and cast out of the church. In like manner a layman." The Apostolic Canons would become the basis of the church's canon law.

Female asceticism, whether solitary or monastic, virginal or simply celibate, nonetheless quickly spread through the Middle East, Europe, and eventually the world. The most powerful inspiration behind it, scholar Petersen suggests, was surely the same as that of male ascetics. Christ's call is always for total commitment. With Christianity an accepted state religion, the especially devout may have seen the ordinary, everyday church as requiring of them too little sacrifice. Conscious of the standard set by the martyrs only a generation or so earlier, they yearned for a similarly heroic expression of their devotion to Jesus Christ.

At first, many such women probably lived an ascetic life at home, dressing simply, eating frugally,

When Gregory arrived, he intensified the crackdown. Churches were turned over to Arian clergy, and all Christians were obliged to receive the sacraments from them. Those who refused were deprived of their property, whipped and imprisoned. Virgins were ordered to appear with heads scandalously uncovered. Members of the clergy loyal to Athanasius were fired, banished or imprisoned.

Meanwhile, Athanasius waited in the Church of St. Theonas for his own inevitable arrest and probable execution. Philagrius, the determined governor, didn't entrust this job to a mob. He surrounded the church with a contingent of troops in full battle order. Since a service was in progress, they decided to await

following a demanding prayer rule, and joining with like-minded friends within church congregations. But some came to believe, writes the Benedictine nun Laura Swan in *The Forgotten Desert Mothers* (New York, 2001), that achievement of inner peace was impossible amidst the pressures and crowding of city life. They felt they must abandon whatever else possessed their mind and heart, and seek God in the immense solitude of the desert.

Notable among these female solitaries is Mary of Egypt, subject of many popular legends and highly regarded in the Orthodox Church as an exemplar of extreme sin, followed by extreme repentance. Mary was no virgin. To the contrary, according to seventh-century sources, Mary of Egypt was a notorious prostitute in fifth-century Alexandria, but while plying her trade among pilgrims to Jerusalem, she was violently stricken with remorse on the threshold of the Holy Sepulchre. She then disappeared into the wilderness beyond the Jordan River to expiate her sins, reportedly seeing no one for the next forty-seven years. At last, a priest-monk named Zosimus,

chancing to encounter the practically skeletal woman, gave her communion. She asked him to return a year later; complying, he found and buried her body.

Among female desert dwellers, there soon appeared the figure of the *amma* (Aramaic for mother, equivalent to *abba*, father): a lone-woman ascetic tutoring disciples one by one in the life of solitude with God. As with their male counterparts, however, groups of female hermits took to gathering on occasion, and desert convents began to form.

They proliferated rapidly. Palladius, a much-traveled historian of fourth-century monasticism, encountered one in the Thebaid region on the Upper Nile, where some four hundred virgins followed a rule almost identical to that of the men's monasteries. Smaller communities were housed in caves, ruins, family tombs, or on islands. Within a half-century,

Today's nuns, in both the west and the east, are the inheritors of a long-established tradition of dedicated communal living for Christian virgins and widows. (Below) Orthodox nuns participate in the Easter Vigil in Jerusalem's Church of the Holy Sepulchre.

its conclusion before moving in. Toward the end of the service, the main doors opened and the congregation emerged, devoutly chanting a psalm in procession. Respectfully, the soldiers let it pass, then entered the building. The bishop was gone. He had left in the midst of the procession.

Soon Athanasius was en route to Rome, exiled for a second time. But while he might be deprived of his see, he could not be deprived of his pen, and the encyclical letter he wrote to the bishops of east and west, describing the misdeeds of Gregory and Philagrius at Alexandria, soon reached every corner of the empire, further garnering support for his cause and inflaming the determination of his enemies to stop him.

Led by Eusebius, those enemies were concentrated almost entirely in the east,

convents were opening all over Roman Europe, although those in the west tended to locate near cities for protection against barbarian attack.

They generally observed a communal rule regulating daily prayer (usually at eight stated hours between dawn and bedtime), Divine Liturgy, meals, and so on. Most expected their members to memorize the Psalter and diligently study the Scriptures. Work included weaving, gardening, household chores, and care of the sick and the aged. Personal possessions were limited to a few storage jars and books, plain clothing, and a sleeping mat. Some sisters slept on the ground with only a rough coverlet of goat's hair. Wine was taken for medicinal purposes, and only in small amounts.

Jerome, who founded numerous monasteries and convents, set out firm rules for girls who aspired to a life of holy virginity, based to some extent upon the behavior expected of any respectable young Roman woman. They should remain with their mothers until they were professed, he said, and not frequent public places (including crowded churches) or walk with mincing steps, or exchange nods and winks with young men. Their dress should be unremarkable, neither too neat nor too careless. But they should also shun popular music and affected speech, should not seek vainglory either in almsgiving or devotional fervor, and should be cheerful when fasting. Nor should they associate with married women, but seek the company of women "whose faces are pale from fasting."

Bathing was also discouraged, a proscription strange to the modern mind. But bathing was then a largely public activity; nearly all cities had warm "baths" somewhat like swimming pools, where nude men and women of all ages customarily bathed together. Judging by Christian denunciations, however, some of these may have sadly degenerated. They are described as being decorated with licentious paintings and lewd graffiti, and as being a major source of town gossip. Then, too, bathing was seen as a pleasurable activity, and therefore another opportunity for sacrifice. To go bathless became virtuous, a perception that was extended to clothing as

The saintly hermit Mary of Egypt, after forty-seven years alone in the desert, receives the Eucharist just before her death. The icon is from Holy Transfiguration Monastery in Brookline, Massachusetts.

though the barbarian German tribes that constantly threatened the northern frontier were becoming Arian as well, having been converted by a very brave Arian missionary. (See earlier volume in this series, *By This Sign*, chapter 10.) Arianism, in other words, was more than a mere hypocrisy, a cloak of religiosity that one donned to ingratiate oneself with those in authority. However opportunistic the Arianism of the court, there were sincere Arians too, who rejected the Nicene Creed as fervently as Athanasius embraced it.

Moreover, not all the east was Arian. Some eastern bishops firmly accepted the Nicene formula and suffered growing official disfavor from Constantinople for doing so. Others agreed with the Arians in rejecting Nicea, because they did not believe that God the Son and God the Father shared the same quality or

well. "Dirty clothes," observed Jerome, "betoken a clean mind."

Meanwhile, the exhortations of the Council of Gangra notwithstanding, exaltation of virginity and of celibacy reached fever pitch. Some women became lone ascetics on their own property, often when very young. For example, a Roman girl named Aselia moved at the age of twelve into a cell on her family's estate, venturing out thereafter only to attend church. A devout Gallic Christian called Monegund lived as a solitary on her family's estate at Chartres, baking bread and growing vegetables to feed the poor.

Other Christians of wealth and aristocratic lineage founded monasteries. Olympias, a prominent widow at the court of Emperor Theodosius I, sold her entire estate to provide alms for the poor and to endow several monastic communities. A well-to-do couple named Paulinus and Theraisa, after the death of their child at eight days old, renounced further sexual intercourse. They founded a double monastery for men and women at Nola, near Naples.

Sometimes older couples, agreeing to part, would join separate monasteries. Such was the decision of Athanasia of Antioch and her husband, although their story had a different and curious ending. Twelve years later, meeting again on a pilgrimage to Jerusalem, they were reunited. Thereafter, they shared a cave, but adopted a strict rule of silence.

Monasteries centered on a single family became known as "domestic monasteries," and those with both men and women as "dual." Both proved to be somewhat dubious ventures. In the domestic institutions, family demands competed with communal demands. In the dual ones, sexual temptations led to frequent scandal, although examples of mixed communities with carefully separated quarters would continue, sometimes successfully, through medieval times.

Some women, possibly believing that men's monasteries observed more stringent rules, adopted male disguise to join them. Much cherished is the story of Marina of Lebanon, a covert female monk who was accused of fathering a child, and consequently expelled. Marina quietly kept her secret, raised the child, and then rejoined the monastery; not until her death was her gender discovered. A woman called Anastasia, a member of the emperor Justinian's court, founded a monastery at Alexandria. However, when Justinian's wife died and the emperor decided Anastasia must be her successor, the lady fled to the desert and lived there for twenty-eight years disguised as a male hermit.

Both female solitaries and female convents, like any human enterprise, exhibited weakness and sin as well as piety and austerity. Bishops and other spiritual leaders often castigated them—chiefly where much wealth was involved—for laxity and self-indulgence. Holy Cross Convent, for example, founded near Poitiers in 557 by Radegund, a queen of Frankish Gaul, is said to have resembled a large and luxurious villa. Here the saintly Radegund herself was noted for her devoted personal charities and rigorous austerities, but solicitously discouraged her many followers from excessive self-abnegation.

At Holy Cross, the talented poet and musician Venantius Fortunatus found a congenial home, while two hundred or so Gallo-Roman and Frankish ladies were pleasantly occupied with embroidery, studying and copying manuscripts. But Merovingian kings made a habit of consigning unwanted female relatives, involuntarily, to convents. After Radegund's death in 587, conditions at Holy Cross deteriorated, culminating in a riot led by two rebellious royal princesses.

Nevertheless, the women's monastic movement was destined to thrive. Right into the twenty-first century, its dedicated virgins would valiantly serve their Lord and Savior in every possible way. They would be ascetics offering prayer on behalf of all the faithful, educators of the young, nurses of the sick, and helpers of the helpless and the poor. What began in the Egyptian desert, in short, was the vital Christian vocation of the nun. ■

essence or substance of Divinity. But they rejected the Arian thesis as well, because they did not believe that Jesus was a mere creature of the Father. After all, they said, in the opening verse of his Gospel, John had declared Jesus both "God" and "with God." The west, meanwhile, remained almost solidly and immovably Nicene, scornful of Constantinople for intellectual arrogance and scorned by Constantinople as intellectual simpletons.

As in most theological controversies, human passions and pride soon fed the flames. The issue often seemed lost in the midst of all the strategies, schemes,

A ninth-century illustration from a book of canon law depicts the burning, under orders from Constantine the Great, of works by "damned Arian heretics." Such measures, however, notably failed to put a quick end to the theological ideas expressed in those books.

plots, ploys and manipulations of ecclesiastical politics. But to Athanasius, the issue remained clear. He saw the Nicene Creed as defining the central tenets of Christianity for the ages to come. Preserving that creed, therefore, meant preserving the faith that Jesus of Nazareth had bequeathed to the world. Whatever might happen, this was his task, a task that was usually bitter. For most of the next thirty years, nearly all the news was bad, and the first of it came just before Athanasius set sail for Rome.

Constantine II, his chief advocate in the imperial circle, had died under circumstances that challenged belief. Possessed with the conviction that he hadn't been given a fair share of the territories seized from his murdered cousins, he opened negotiations with his youngest brother Constans for a better arrangement, lost his temper during the discussions and in a fit of fury, ordered an invasion of Constans's holdings in Illyricum.[5] Though still only seventeen years old, Constans had better generals than Constantine II. Feigning retreat, they lured the older brother and a small body of his troops into a trap, cut him down and dumped his body in a creek. He was later buried with full imperial honors, but young Constans now held the larger part of the empire. He too would become a staunch supporter of Athanasius, but he had only ten years left to live.

At Rome, Athanasius found himself in the company of two other prominent deportees from the east—Bishop Paul, banished by Eusebius from the see of Constantinople, and Marcellus, ousted by Eusebius as bishop of Ancyra (the

5. Constantine's invasion of his brother's territory is deplored as ludicrous by the acid Edward Gibbon in his classic *History of the Decline and Fall of the Roman Empire*. Gibbon cherishes an unconcealed contempt for all three brothers. "After the partition of the empire," he writes, "three years had scarcely elapsed before the sons of Constantine seemed impatient to convince mankind that they were incapable of contenting themselves with the dominions which they were unqualified to govern."

future capital of Turkey). All three took their case before Julius, bishop of Rome and here they found a sympathetic ear.[6] Julius had already disposed of the case of Pistus, who had first been advanced as Athanasius's replacement. Eusebius had sent Pistus's credentials to Julius by special envoy. But Athanasius's refuting evidence, demonstrating Pistus to be an undoubted heretic, was so conclusive that after hearing it, the envoy left in the middle of the night and went home without even saying goodbye.

Julius then assembled a council of western bishops at Rome that deemed Athanasius innocent, cleared him of the charges made against him at Tyre and declared that he should be restored forthwith as bishop of Alexandria. Marcellus was similarly ordered restored at Ancyra. (Bishop Paul's case was apparently not dealt with.) The noted twentieth-century British church historian W. H. C. Frend discerns a major precedent here. "Julius took up Athanasius's cause," he writes, "with a self-assertion and confidence suggesting a see which was used to having its orders obeyed. . . . Moreover, though nominally reporting a decision of a Roman council, Julius speaks from his own episcopal position. He took no serious account of the findings of the Council of Tyre. Thus, while the rest of Christendom was accepting a council of bishops, judicial or otherwise, as the voice of the Holy Spirit, the papacy was staking its claim to speak to colleagues on the authority of Peter and nothing else."

Julius's accompanying letter, preserved by Athanasius, made his emphasis clearer still: "Why was nothing written to us," he demanded, "concerning the church of the Alexandrians? Are you ignorant that the custom has been for word to be written first to us [i.e., to the bishop of Rome], and then for a just sentence to be passed from this place? . . . What I write is for the common good. What we have received from the blessed apostle Peter, that I signify to you."

This communication reduced the eastern bishops to a state of apoplexy. Rarely had the see of Rome invoked such authority over the eastern church. It was now August of 341 and since they were assembling anyway for the formal dedication of the Church of the Golden Dome at Antioch, which had been started by Constantine the Great, they used the occasion to hold a counter-council. This Council of Antioch told Julius that it was "novel and unheard of" for eastern bishops to be judged by westerners. In the past, the east had respected disci-plinary and doctrinal decisions

6. The term "pope" or father, had not yet come into exclusive usage for the bishop of Rome. In the fourth century, other bishops were addressed with this title, and the bishop of Alexandria, head of the Egyptian Coptic Church, carries it to this day. Not until 1073 was the title formally restricted in the west to the bishop of Rome.

Bishop Julius tried to defend Athanasius on the basis that the anti-Athanasian faction had failed to consult Rome, but this only complicated matters and escalated the hostilities. A mosaic of Julius (left) in the Church of Santa Maria Trastevere in Rome, dates from the twelfth century. The first church on the site was commissioned by Julius himself in the fourth.

7. Dr. Eugene Teselle, professor emeritus of Church History and Theology at Vanderbilt University, Nashville, Tennessee, and an academic consultant to this series, offers an explanation for this irony, in which the west championed the creed that the east created and now opposed. "The tradition of the easterners," he points out, "emphasized the 'threeness' of God which the Nicene Creed did not, while the western tradition emphasized God's 'oneness,' without saying clearly how God is three." Moreover, "the east did not dare condemn or replace the Creed of Nicea, which remained the standard. Rather, they 'augmented' it with four creeds that seemed to express their doctrine in a more adequate way."

made in the west, such as the condemnation of the heresies of Novatian (see earlier volume in this series, *By This Sign*, pages 48 and 49), while the west had respected similar decisions made in the east, such as the condemnation of Paul of Samosata. (See *By This Sign*, pages 217 and 218.) If peace were to return between east and west, they said, Julius must reverse himself and condemn those bishops the east had expelled, meaning Athanasius and Marcellus.

Moreover, the eastern bishops announced, they were further refining the Christian faith and appending the first of four new creeds they would develop over the next few years. Though repudiating Arianism, all four failed to uphold Nicea. Finally, they sent Julius a letter, which, he announced, was too abusive to be read in public.

The emperor Constantius, who himself had presided over the Antioch council, eagerly took up the cause of the eastern bishops and endorsed a further crackdown on Athanasius's supporters at Alexandria. Bishop Potamon was ordered lashed, and later died of the wounds. Bishop Sarapammon was banished. Both had vociferously backed Athanasius. Laymen who endorsed Athanasius were deprived of their property and jailed.

By now, the Arian controversy had escalated gravely. Not only had it become poisonously personal between Eusebius and Athanasius, but it concerned a central belief of Christianity and it was threatening to split the eastern church from the western. In this, there was a certain irony. The Council of Nicea, which adopted the Nicene Creed, had been attended by some 310 eastern bishops, and only about eight from the west (though one of the eight, Hosius of Cordoba, was a leading participant). The bishop of Rome had not attended at all; he was represented by two priests. Yet by 340, only fifteen years later, the west, led by the bishop of Rome, had become the champion of the creed, while the east found itself championing the creed's revision, if not its rejection.[7]

Meanwhile, Athanasius plunged into the challenges posed by Rome— learning Latin, charming the emperor's household and rapidly winning the respect of the Italian bishops. He brought with him two desert monks, a species of Christian that the faithful in the old capital knew little about, and what they did know they didn't like. Though the concept of self-imposed disciplines for spiritual benefit was far from unknown to the

ATHANASIUS ON FAILED VIRTUE

Departure from virtue gives place for the entrance of the unclean spirit.

Roman senatorial class, the notion of isolation in the wilderness, living in a state of semi-starvation, refusing even to wash, did not strike them as the sort of life Jesus had in mind for his disciples. Yet the tranquil demeanor of the two monks and the benevolent light they seemed to exude, enraptured the Roman Christians. One of the two, Isidore of Alexandria, endeared himself to many senators and their wives. His companion, Ammonius, showed no interest whatever in all the great buildings of Rome, save one that he called the Church of Saints Peter and Paul.[8]

The monks made a larger impression on the city than anyone could have imagined at the time. Spurred by their example and by Athanasius's biography of

'Calumnies, murder, conspiracies, stripping of virgins, banishments, burnings,' these were the charges (and above all the raising of the ill-famed Arian heresy).

their mentor Anthony, the idea of monasticism would take hold all over Europe in the coming centuries and would provide a central Christian practice for the entire Middle Ages.

At the same time, Athanasius renewed his acquaintance with the Spaniard Hosius of Cordoba, the activist at Nicea. Now in his late eighties, Hosius eagerly took up Athanasius's cause in the west. More crucial still, Athanasius fortified another connection. In 343, he returned to his old place of exile, beautiful Trier, and there met again with Constans. The young emperor had been a baptized Christian since infancy, whereas his brother Constantius in the east, like his father, was putting off baptism until his last hours.[9]

Soon afterwards, Athanasius received a mysterious summons from the emperor Constans to appear before him in Milan. He left immediately for the northern Italian city, which, far more than Rome, was the administrative capital of the western empire. There, Constans gave him the news. He had written to his brother, proposing a major church council at Serdica (now Sofia, capital of Bulgaria), on the border between the eastern and western empires. His brother had agreed; the eastern bishops were coming and at last Athanasius could gain a fair hearing on the charges that had been made against him.

In July of 343, about eighty eastern bishops arrived at Serdica, moved into the Sofia Palace that had been reserved for them and heard something they considered outrageous. Athanasius and Marcellus were both to attend the council, they learned. Moreover, Athanasius had brought to Serdica several specimen victims, maimed for life by the attentions of Gregory and Philagrius at Alexandria, who would testify before the council about the treatment accorded anti-Arian Christians in the east. In his *Defense Against the Arians*, Athanasius sums up these complaints: "Calumnies, imprisonments, murders, wounds, conspiracies by means of false letters, outrages, stripping of virgins, banishments, destruction of the churches, burnings . . . and above all the raising of the

8. The fifth-century historian Socrates quotes the monk Ammonius's admiration for a "Church of St. Peter and Paul." There is no record of such a church, though Constantine built a basilica over the tomb of Peter on Vatican Hill and a church to Paul on the Appian Way. Ammonius was no doubt recalling one or the other, or perhaps both.

9. *The Oxford Dictionary of the Christian Church* notes that it was common in the first four Christian centuries to defer baptism until death was believed imminent, for fear of the responsibilities incurred by it. In such cases, baptism was conferred without ceremonies, and was considered inferior to regular baptism. People so baptized who continued to live were called *clinici* and were barred from ordination to the priesthood. The practice rapidly disappeared as infant baptism became more common.

ill-famed Arian heresy by these means against the orthodox faith."

The easterners exploded. How could two men, who (in their view) were no longer bishops, possibly attend a council of bishops? The very presence of the two in effect decided the case in advance, they contended. After a lengthy and acrimonious exchange, nearly all the easterners declared they would not attend the meeting unless the two were removed. But how could the two make their case, came the reply, if they weren't allowed to be there? At that, the eastern bishops denounced the whole council, declared that they were needed to celebrate Constantius's victory on the Persian front, packed their bags and headed for home. Serdica had failed.

But they didn't quite go home. They stopped at Philippopolis (now Plovdiv, Bulgaria) on the Constantinople road, where they drew up what the nineteenth-century Oxford historian Archibald Robertson calls "a long and extremely wild and angry statement," deposing all the western bishops active at Serdica from Julius down, affirming the deposition of Athanasius and declaring Marcellus a heretic. The next stop on their return journey was Adrianople (now Edirne in Turkey), 140 miles west of Constantinople, apparently a hotbed of anti-Arian sentiment. Hearing that they had boycotted the Serdica council, the bishop there, Lucius, refused them communion. They complained to Constantius. In consequence, reports Athanasius in his *History of the Arians*, six laymen were beheaded, two priests and three deacons banished and Bishop Lucius, with iron chains on his neck and hands, was sent into exile where he would soon die.

In response, the ninety-odd western bishops continued meeting at Serdica, affirmed Athanasius and Marcellus as bishops of Alexandria and Ancyra and excommunicated Eusebius of Nicomedia for heresy, along with ten of his closest supporters.

The east-west split now seemed irreconcilable,[10] but that was not quite so. The first break in the deadlock began insignificantly. It concerned Athanasius's fellow exile Marcellus, whose popularity was as universal in Ancyra as was Athanasius's in Alexandria. Though Marcellus vigorously supported Athanasius's opposition to Arianism, his theology went much farther than did Athanasius's, or that of the Nicene Creed. Marcellus taught, says the authoritative *Oxford Dictionary of the Christian Church*, that "in the Unity of the Godhead, the Son and the Spirit only emerged as independent entities for the purposes of Creation and Redemption. After the redemptive work is achieved, they would be resumed into the Divine Unity and God will be all in all." This meant that the kingdom of the Trinitarian God was transitory, and would one day come to an end. A clause declaring "whose kingdom shall have no end" was later inserted into the Nicene Creed, specifically to combat Marcellus's teaching.

Since Marcellus had been removed for this teaching, Julius had implicitly affirmed it when he directed that Marcellus be restored to his see. This alienated a great many eastern bishops, who, while opposing Arianism, were not prepared to rush into the opposite heresy either, particularly Marcellus's formulation, which viewed all three persons of the Trinity as mere "modes" of the same

10. Eerdman's *Handbook to the History of Christianity* describes the deadlock that followed the Council of Serdica as "a virtual schism of east and west from which they never fully recovered."

At the council of bishops gathered in 343 at Serdica (modern Sofia, Bulgaria), the presence of Athanasius and another bishop caused a mass walkout of the eastern delegates. Those two have been deposed and are not bishops at all, they said.

CONNOR

Person. At a little-publicized meeting of a few eastern and western bishops at Milan two years after Serdica, the westerners agreed that Marcellus's teaching was flawed. When word of that concession reached the east, the basis of a reconciliation was laid, but it would take nearly forty more years to be concluded.

All this ecclesiastical strife soon spurred political strife. Angered that his efforts as Christian peacemaker had so lamentably failed, the young emperor Constans now took matters a step farther. He warned his brother that unless Athanasius were restored to his see at Alexandria, Constans would send him there himself, along with enough soldiers to make sure he stayed.

This would surely have alarmed Constantius, distracted as he was with an endless Persian war. But three other developments also encouraged him to put an end to the controversy. For one, Eusebius of Constantinople, the main push behind the Arian cause for the last twenty years, had died in 341, leaving the Arians leaderless unless Constantius himself took on the job. Then, in 345, he received the news that Gregory, the man who was sent to resolve all the problems in Alexandria, had died after a lengthy illness, so that now Athanasius could be restored without ousting Gregory. Finally, and very upsetting to Constantius, was a scandal most embarrassing to the Arian cause, which had developed in Antioch.

Still keen for the restoration of Athanasius and Marcellus, the western bishops, with Constans's support, sent a three-man delegation to Constantius, asking him to reconsider the eastern position. The delegates, two bishops and an army officer, arrived at Antioch, and immediately became targets of a plot instigated by Stephanus, the Arian bishop of Antioch.

In order to wholly discredit the delegation, two of Stephanus's priests hired a prostitute, led her to the apartment where one of the two bishops was staying, had her undress and instructed her to go in and seduce the man she would find lying in bed there. She was expecting, she said, a young man. When she found an old one sound asleep and the apparel of a bishop beside the bed, she realized what was taking place and began to howl and yell that she was being made party to a plot. This created a public scene and a resulting inquiry, at which the girl's master testified that he had been approached by several clergymen who wanted to use the girl for an assignation. In the outcome, Stephanus was ousted, and another, less venturesome Arian bishop named in his place.

Thus, in 344, Constantius wrote three successive letters to Athanasius, asking him to return to his see, and vowing full imperial support for him there. Instantly suspicious, Athanasius refused to go—until, that is, Constans prevailed upon him to do so. In the spring of 346 he appeared before Constantius at Antioch

ATHANASIUS ON PUTTING ON LIFE IN CHRIST

We are clothed with him [Jesus] when we exercise ourselves in temperance and mortify lasciviousness, when we honor sufficiency, when we do not forget the poor, but open our doors to all men, when we assist humble-mindedness, but hate pride.

and was received joyously. Would the emperor now allow him to confront his enemies over the accusations they made against him? asked Athanasius. "No," Athanasius quotes the emperor as replying. "But God knows I will never again credit such accusations, and all records of past charges will be erased." Would Athanasius permit the Arians to use one church in Alexandria, asked the emperor? Certainly, replied Athanasius, provided the Arians allowed the orthodox to use one church in Antioch. The Arian clergy said that would be impossible, so the deal fell through.

Thereupon, Athanasius returned to his city. Crowds traveled as many as a hundred miles up the road to greet him, and the faithful, cheering and weeping, welcomed the beginning of what became known as his "Golden Decade." However, much of it certainly wasn't golden. For three years, at most, he lived in relative peace, writing a careful refutation of Arianism, an explanation of Nicene theology, numerous pastoral letters—one on Christian duty to a monk named Draconius, who had fled in horror after hearing he had been elected a bishop— and finally a defense of the orthodoxy of his third-century predecessor, Dionysius (see previous volume, *By This Sign*, page 30), who was being cited by the Arians as theologically on their side. Very satisfactory to him also was the fevered

To discredit the delegation, two priests hired a prostitute, led her to where a bishop was staying, and told her to seduce him. Suspecting a plot, she began to yell.

enthusiasm his return engendered for the monastic life. Monastic communities of men and of women were springing up in the Nile Valley and the surrounding desert, all of their members passionate supporters of the Nicene cause.

Finally, old foes were recanting their Arian allegiance, declaring their support for Nicea and formally begging Athanasius's forgiveness. Two of these no doubt startled him, notably Valens and Ursacius. They had been raised as Arians from youth, and had risen to become bishops in Illyricum. They had helped make the first case against Athanasius at the Council of Tyre, and had had a leading role in the Arian cause ever since. Now they recanted their Arianism before bishop Julius of Rome. They admitted that the evidence against Athanasius at the Council of Tyre had been faked. Since Valens and Ursacius were the only two Arian bishops in the territories controlled by Athanasius's firm ally Constans, their recantation, however sincere, was also politic.

But Athanasius was not destined to remain long in imperial favor. Once again, officialdom suddenly and radically changed. The pagan historian Zosimus tells the story. Constans, while a devoutly orthodox Christian, was also a sexual deviate. He "bought, or had as hostages around him, handsome barbarians," writes Zosimus. "He permitted them to do anything they liked to his subjects, provided they allowed him to corrupt their young people. Thus all his dominions were reduced to extreme misery." Finally, Magnentius, the commander of the

Would a visitor to a church built in the fourth or fifth century have been able to tell whether it belonged in the Arian or Nicene camp? In Ravenna, Italy, where the two faiths lived side by side, each constructed a baptistery, and the mosaics of the Baptism of Jesus in their domes appear remarkably similar. But they are exactly opposite in orientation. The mosaic in the "Orthodox Baptistery" (top) is so oriented that the figure of Christ is the primary focus. The icon in the Arian dome is so designed that it has as its focal point an empty throne (at the bottom of the figure).

Joviani and Herculiani Legions, aided by one Marcellinus, the imperial treasurer (not to be confused with the accused heretic Marcellus), plotted Constans's downfall. Zosimus continues:

Marcellinus declared he would celebrate his son's birthday and invited to the feast many prominent officers. When the banquet lasted until midnight, Magnentius rose from the table, as if from necessity, and leaving the guests for a short time, reappeared clothed in imperial garb as if in a play. All the guests acclaimed him emperor, and likewise all the inhabitants of Augustodunum [now Autun in southeastern France] where this happened. When the report of this went around the country, people flocked into the city, and some Illyrian cavalry, dispatched to reinforce the legions in Gaul, joined the conspirators.

To tell the truth, when the officers of the army met together and heard the leaders of the conspiracy shout out, they scarcely knew what was happening, but everyone cried out and saluted Magnentius as augustus. When he learned of this, Constans tried to flee to a small town called Helena, situated near the Pyrenees, but he was taken by Gaiso, who was sent for this purpose with some picked men. Without anyone to assist him, Constans was killed.

The implications for Athanasius of Constans's murder were obvious. His chief advocate in the imperial circle was now gone. Of the religious leanings of the usurper Magnentius, he probably knew nothing. If Constantius remained loyal to the undertaking he had made, he and the Nicene Creed were safe. If the Arians who still surrounded him could bend Constantius's ear, both were at risk. However, so long as the usurper prevailed in the west, Constantius was unlikely to launch a new persecution of the orthodox believers, because he would need all the friends he could get. So Athanasius ordered his churches to offer prayers for the emperor Constantius, rejected overtures from the would-be augustus in the west, Magnentius, and waited on events.

He didn't have long to wait. Constantius moved the legions west into Illyricum. When they confronted the army of Magnentius near Mursa (now Osijek in Croatia) on September 28, 351, Constantius stood by at the home of the local bishop for news of the outcome. And who was the local bishop? It was none other than Valens, the former zealous Arian, lately recanted. He had seen angels, said Valens. They told him that Constantius had decisively triumphed, and Magnentius had fled from the field alone. What Valens had actually seen, Athanasius later wrote, was a message from a courier he had posted behind the lines to bring first news of the outcome.[11]

But to Constantius, any man who saw angels had the power of God behind him. Then Valens suddenly had another revelation. Arianism had been right after all. He had repudiated it only because he was terrified of Constans. So he forthwith recanted his recantation and became leader of the Arian cause in the west. "Like dogs," sneered Athanasius, "they return to their own vomit." The fleeing Magnentius was tracked down at Lyon in Gaul, where he committed suicide. Constantius was now sole emperor. The time had come at last, he decided, to put an end to the antiquated Nicene Creed, and to the pestilent Athanasius of Alexandria as well. The year was 351. The "Golden Decade" was over. It had lasted five years.

The fate of both the empire, and in his own view anyway, the Christian church, now fell into the hands of the sole surviving son of Constantine the Great. In the opinion of most modern historians, Constantius was the brightest and best of the three. Still, according to A. H. M. Jones (*The Later Roman Empire*, Oxford, 1964 and *The Decline of the Ancient World*, London, 1966), he was "a well-meaning and conscientious man, but weak, timid and suspicious" who merely followed the lead of his father in attempting to direct the church, but was unfortunate enough to have advisers (i.e., Arians) whose views were not destined to prevail. Oxford historian B. J. Kidd is marginally more generous. "He was pure in life, sober in habits, a good soldier, by no means wanting in statecraft. . . . But he was essentially a little man. Small in stature, with short and crooked legs, his mental capacity was small, too. Vacillating as a reed, he swallowed flattery wholesale, was timorous and therefore cruel, and adept at plotting, but himself the prey of scheming and unworthy favorites." To Athanasius in his *History of the Arians*, Constantius was a pitiable creature: "In the name of freedom, he is the slave of those who drag him on to gratify their own impious pleasures."

Many of Constantius's advisers and aides, so offensive to his critics both ancient and modern, shared a single curious quality. They were eunuchs, a phenomenon almost unknown to the courts of the early empire, and particularly odious to the vituperative eighteenth-century historian Edward Gibbon. Constantius allowed power "to gravitate into the hands of eunuchs, a species of creature Constantinople gradually adopted from the east. . . . The eunuchs, the women and the bishops governed the feeble mind of the emperor."[12] The "women" in this case were led by the emperor's wife, a passionate Arian whose influence over her husband was great and whose female attendants strongly influenced the imperial guards. The bishops had been headed, of course, by Eusebius until his death and thereafter by Bishop Valens of Mursa and Bishop Acacius of Caesarea, who led the extreme Arian wing known as the Homoeans.

But these two bishops were not the leaders of what rapidly became the Arian ascendancy. That role was fulfilled by the emperor himself. With empire-wide

11. The losses of both sides at Mursa, totaling about fifty-four thousand, many of them first-class Roman troops, were blamed by some contemporary observers for the impending collapse of the empire in the west, as described in later chapters of this volume.

12. Eunuchs were common in the public affairs of China, India and Persia. Among Christians, voluntary castration to ensure religious celibacy emerged in the third century, but was never officially endorsed by the church and was ultimately condemned. However, Constantinople introduced the practice of employing eunuchs in government, and it persisted well into the Middle Ages. In the west, the use of *castrati*, as they became known, was much less common, though they sang in the papal choir until the beginning of the nineteenth century.

13. The name Lucifer translates as "light-bearer," and appears in Isaiah (14:12) as an epithet for the king of Babylon. Jerome, writing the name in the early fifth century, used it as the name for the devil, a usage that has continued. However, the early fathers saw it as referring to the state from which Satan fell, rather than to Satan himself.

appointments, banishments, imprisonments and even executions, Constantius launched a personal campaign to unite the church and empire under an Arian creed. He conceived himself as a competent theologian and enjoyed debate over "theological minutiae," wrote the contemporary pagan historian Ammianus Marcellinus. In other words, he took his religious responsibilities very seriously.

For Athanasius, once again at the top of the emperor's black list, this opened a second quarrel between them. Not only was the emperor an Arian, but he had now asserted the final authority

Although despised by many, eunuchs ("beardless ones") were privy to the secrets and the scheming of all the imperial bedchambers and meeting rooms. For centuries, such men as the courtier depicted in a Ravenna mosaic (above) were the major power brokers of the Byzantine Empire.

of the state over that of the church. "Where is there a canon [i. e., a church law] that a bishop should be appointed from the [royal] court?" demanded Athanasius. "Where is there a canon that permits soldiers to invade churches? What tradition is there allowing counts and ignorant eunuchs to exercise authority in ecclesiastical matters?"

His hand now free of his inhibiting younger brother, Constantius moved swiftly. He called a council at Arles in Gaul, then another at Milan in 355. Bishops from all over the western empire were summoned, confronted with a resolution to depose Athanasius at Alexandria, and told they would be deposed themselves if they didn't sign. Nearly all did, though there were holdouts—like Dionysius of Milan, Eusebius of Vercelli, Hilary of Poitiers, Paulinus of Trier, Maximus of Naples and Lucifer of Cagliari.[13] Old Hosius of Cordoba, now ninety-nine years of age, accompanied his refusal with a declaration that Athanasius would preserve for posterity. He told the emperor:

> Cease these proceedings, I beseech you, and remember you are a mortal man. Be afraid of the Day of Judgment, and keep yourself pure thereunto. Intrude not yourself into ecclesiastical matters, neither give commands unto us concerning them; but learn from us. God has put into your hands the kingdom; to us he has entrusted the affairs of his church; and he who would steal the empire from you would resist the ordinance of God, so likewise fear on your part lest by taking upon yourself the government of the Church, you become guilty of a great offense. It is written, "Render unto Caesar the things that are Caesar's, and unto God the things that are God's." Neither therefore is it permitted unto us to exercise an earthly rule, nor have you, Sire, any authority to burn incense [i.e., act as a cleric].

This pronouncement, writes Frend, made by a man fewer than twelve months short of his one hundredth birthday, enunciated what became known as the

Doctrine of the Two Swords. Upon it, western teaching on church-state relations would be based for the next twelve hundred years.

In a rage, Constantius brandished his sword, then sent the holdouts into exile. The next victim was equally significant. Liberius, who had been chosen bishop of Rome upon the death of Julius in 352, likewise defied Constantius in a fiery showdown before the Milan council. Three hundred western bishops were in attendance ("dragged there," according to Athanasius), along with a vast crowd of onlookers. When the emperor's letter demanding the deposition of Athanasius was read, such a clamor broke out that the meeting had to be adjourned to the imperial palace. There, Constantius himself stood up. "I myself am the accuser of Athanasius," declared the emperor. That was enough to cow most of the bishops, but not Liberius, who walked out and returned to Rome.

Constantius angrily brandished a sword and exiled the holdouts. The next victim was Pope Liberius, who likewise defied the emperor in a fiery showdown before the Council of Milan.

There, he was arrested by imperial officers and hauled back to Milan.

"I give you three days," said the emperor, "to make up your mind. Unless within that time you comply, you must be prepared to go where I may send you."

"Three days or three months will make no difference with me," replied Liberius. "So send me where you please."

He was dispatched to Beroea, in Thrace,[14] spirited out of the city under guard at night, says the historian Ammianus, because in daylight the crowds would have mobbed the soldiers. Constantius, ever generous, sent him a purse containing five hundred pieces of gold. Liberius sent them back. "Tell him to give it to his flatterers and players," he said. "They're always in want because of their insatiable cupidity."

Contemporary accounts say that Constantius then chose a deacon named Felix as bishop of Rome. When the Roman crowds wouldn't let Felix into any church to be consecrated bishop, Constantius moved the ceremony to the palace, where three acquiescent bishops performed the rite and three eunuchs stood in for the people.

However, Liberius's resolve seems to have flagged two years later. Under continuing pressure from the emperor, he appears to have relented and was returned to his see. The case becomes historically significant because of three letters in which he agrees to accept a heretical creed. This would make Liberius one of the few bishops of Rome ever to have ascribed to a heresy. And though a strong case can be made that the letters were forgeries, Athanasius accepts Liberius's lapse as a fact and forgives him. He yielded under threat, says Athanasius. In an effort at compromise, Constantius made Liberius and Felix joint bishops of Rome. However, such an arrangement soon became so absurd as to be untenable and Liberius once more reigned alone.

14. There were at least three Beroeas in the Roman world. The one to which Pope Liberius was exiled is in Thrace. This is not the Beroea in Macedonia from which, about 310 years earlier, Paul, Silas and Timothy had to flee on short notice because persecutors intent on doing them in were hard on their heels. (See earlier volume, *The Veil Is Torn*, page 130.) Nor is it the Syrian city of Aleppo, also known as Beroea.

Even the venerable Hosius briefly relented. In a third council, this one held in 357 at Sirmium (now Mitrovica in Serbia), the old man was persuaded to sign the creed that Constantius was advancing for acceptance by the whole church. This Creed of Sirmium, the one that Liberius was also accused of accepting, was termed the "Blasphemy of Sirmium" by the orthodox. It represented the extreme Arian position, omitting any reference to the "essence" or "substance" of the Godhead, and therefore leaving the relationship of Father and Son to whatever anybody wanted to make it. Ancient Hosius put his name to this, though he still stubbornly refused to acquiesce in the denunciation of Athanasius.

He relented on the creed, notes Athanasius, after intense pressure, denunciation from the Arian bishops around him, and the free use of the lash. Athanasius writes:

> For although for a little while, through fear of the threats of Constantius, he seemed to resist them, yet the great violence and tyrannical power exercised by Constantius, and the many insults and stripes [i.e., strokes of the lash] proved that it was not because he gave up my cause, but through the weakness of old age, being unable to bear the stripes, that he yielded to them for a season.

It was a short season. The old man, now in his one hundred and third year, returned to his Spanish diocese, and with his dying breaths urged all faithful

'Suddenly,' said the report, 'Duke Syrianus attacked the church with many legions of soldiers. While we were praying, they broke down the doors. Virgins were slain; men perished.'

Christians to stand by the Nicene Creed. However, because of his concession at Sirmium, Hosius of Cordoba was never made a saint.

With the western church thrashed into line and the eastern church already dominated by Arianism, the time had come to finally put an end to Athanasius, the emperor's arch foe at Alexandria. There was, of course, the incidental pledge of the emperor not to oppose him again. Obviously, some new grounds for disciplinary action must be found.

It was then discovered that Alexandria's bishop had used an unconsecrated building for an Easter service, because the existing Cathedral of St. Mark was dangerously overcrowded. The chosen substitute site had once been the pagan Temple of Hadrian, and had been rebuilt as a church, though it had not yet been consecrated. This was a distinct violation of church protocol, said the Arian authorities, a breach of "ecclesiastical discipline" and the "royal prerogative." Moreover, they said, Athanasius had conspired to turn the late emperor Constans against Constantius and had communicated with the usurper Magnentius.

Athanasius vehemently defended the use of the unconsecrated church, given the situation at the cathedral. He flatly denied he had urged the emperor's brother against him, and was particularly offended at the suggestion he had conspired with the usurper Magnentius. "Could I have said," he asked, "'You have done well to murder the man who honored me'? Or 'I approve of your conduct in destroying our Christian friends'? Or 'I approve of your proceedings in butchering those who so kindly entertained me at Rome'?"

On May 19, 353, a delegation representing Athanasius left Alexandria to see the emperor, currently in Milan, presumably to provide the bishop's response to these charges. Four days after the delegates sailed, another ship arrived bearing one Montanus, an imperial emissary with a message from the emperor. Since Athanasius had requested an audience, he would be pleased to see him. But Athanasius, who had sought no such audience, became instantly suspicious and said he would come immediately—if he received an imperial summons. He later discovered it was indeed a plot to get him away from Alexandria so that he could be arrested without incident. Since it didn't work, Montanus departed for home.

Then the imperial authorities ordered that the distribution of free grain, previously administered by orthodox clergy, would henceforth be handled by Arian clergy. Moreover, the Arians were given formal authority to publicly criticize the bishop of Alexandria. In August of 355 came another visitor, this time an imperial notary named Diogenes, who, with threats of violence, ordered Athanasius to Milan. Diogenes was thwarted, however, by the local magistrates and the common people, who prevented their bishop's arrest. Athanasius showed him letters from the emperor that had been written when Constantius had vowed his support for him. Did Diogenes have the emperor's written order that he come? No, Diogenes did not. So he, too, sailed for home without success.

However, Athanasius now knew it was only a matter of time until the real crackdown came. It arrived on January 6, 356, in the person of a military commander, the duke Syrianus, who began summoning into the city units of all the legions stationed in Egypt and Libya, until they numbered five thousand. But when he attempted an arrest on January 18, he too was initially foiled by the imperial letters that Athanasius held. He would have to wait, Syrianus said, until an arrest order arrived from the emperor.

He waited exactly twenty-one days. On the night of February 8, Athanasius was presiding at a vigil, again in St. Theonas Church. Outside, the worshipers heard troops assembling around the building. Athanasius ordered the deacon to chant the 136th Psalm, the worshipers making the reply to each verse, "And his mercy endureth forever."[15] In the midst of the psalm, the doors were suddenly smashed down and troops poured in at every entrance. They beat and slashed the congregation, wounding some fatally. A letter, which Athanasius attributes to "the people of Alexandria," describes the scene:

ATHANASIUS ON THE GRACE OF FEASTS

We duly proceed from feasts to feasts, from prayers to prayers, from fasts to fasts, and join holy days to holy days. For the grace of the feast is not limited to one time, nor does its splendid brilliancy decline; but it is always near, enlightening the minds of those who earnestly desire it.

15. The 136th Psalm, sung by the congregation of St. Theonas Church as the imperial troops smashed down the doors to arrest Athanasius, was a regular part of the Christian vigil service. The psalm has ancient liturgical roots. It holds a central place in the Jewish Passover ritual when the door to the home is opened to invite in the prophet Elijah, while the family recites the *Hallel ha-Gadol* Psalm 136, with its twenty-six-fold repetition of the refrain "His steadfast love is eternal," translated in the King James Bible as "His mercy endureth forever."

Suddenly about midnight, the most illustrious Duke Syrianus attacked us and the Church with many legions of soldiers armed with naked swords and javelins and other warlike instruments and wearing helmets on their heads; and actually while we were praying and while the lessons were being read, they broke down the doors. And when the doors were burst open by the violence of the multitude, he gave command and some of them were . . . shouting, their arms rattling and their swords flashing in the light of the lamps.

Forthwith virgins were being slain, many men trampled down and falling over one another as the soldiers came upon them, and several were pierced with arrows and perished. Some of the soldiers also were betaking themselves to plunder, and were stripping the virgins, who were more afraid of being even touched by them than they were of death.

The Bishop continued sitting upon his throne and exhorted all to pray. The Duke led on the attack. . . . The Bishop was seized and barely escaped being torn to pieces; and having fallen into a state of insensibility and appearing as one dead, he disappeared from among them. . . . They were eager to kill him. And when they saw that many had perished, they gave orders to the soldiers to remove out of sight the bodies of the dead.

But the most holy virgins who were left behind were buried in the tombs, having attained the glory of martyrdom in the times of the most religious Constantius. Deacons also were beaten with stripes even in the Lord's house and were shut up there.

In another account, Athanasius says he did not want to leave the building until most of the people were out. Then, in the midst of the bedlam, monks and other clergy were able to spirit him away. But he regards his escape as miraculous: "Truth is my witness, while some of the soldiers stood about the sanctuary and others were going round the church, we passed through under the Lord's guidance and with his protection withdrew without observation."

Athanasius headed immediately for the desert and one of the great manhunts of the ancient world began. ■

CHAPTER 2

Victim becomes victor in the ancient world's biggest-ever manhunt

The whole world groaned to discover itself Arian, Jerome laments—but in their hour of triumph Nicea's foes are foiled by doctrinal feuds

The year was 356. Christianity could now be considered Arian. The emperor, Constantius II, was Arian, and he ran the church. The bishop of Rome had been compelled under duress to sign an Arian creed, or so the jubilant Arians contended. Nearly all the other bishops in the west had been thrashed into line. Any who refused had been banished to the wilderness, and more intellectually sophisticated clergy named in their place. Most of the bishops in the east were in line already. Only the Egyptian hierarchs were still holding out, and once they were converted or removed, Christians would no longer believe that Jesus Christ, the man whom John's Gospel called "the Word made flesh," was actually of the same "substance" or "essence" as God.

Beyond its pragmatic and political advantages, Arianism had something else in its favor, less tangible, but more potent. It accorded with the spirit of the age. It was trendy—what twentieth-century Americans would call the "in thing." Fashionable people in Constantinople were Arian Christians; the senior imperial bureaucracy was Arian, as were the most distinguished preachers and the educated elite—in short, the inner circle of both government and church. Arianism, writes the twentieth-century Christian apologist C. S. Lewis, "was one of those 'sensible synthetic' religions which are so strongly recommended today and which, then as now, included among their devotees many highly cultivated clergymen."

These attributes lent it a quality of inevitability. It was going to happen anyway, so what was the point of resisting? "An atmosphere of resignation and heavy defeatism reigned over the entire western church," writes the historian Victor de Clercq in his biography of Hosius of Cordoba, "and communicated itself even to those few courageous men who had chosen exile above dishonor."

Bringing the recalcitrant Egyptian Christians into line, however, did entail one last task: capturing and silencing their patriarch, the bishop of Alexandria, the troublesome Athanasius. He had somehow escaped the massive military raid on St. Theonas Church, and would no doubt be trying to get out of the city. However, Duke Syrianus had five thousand men under his immediate command, and every road was blocked, every wagon searched, every departing vessel ransacked. Athanasius's leading supporters were rounded up, beaten and

Arianism, says C. S. Lewis, was one of those 'sensible, synthetic' religions, so popular today, which then as now attract 'many highly cultivated clergymen.'

ferociously questioned. Yet nobody seemed to know where he was.

He was in fact hiding, as one might have expected, in the desert monasteries. But which one? By now, in no small measure due to his ministry, there were scores of monasteries. The monks revered him. He was a particular favorite of the sainted Anthony, who now lay near death. Athanasius knew the monks would never betray him. Among them, he demonstrated that he could live as frugally as they, as much at home in their self-imposed poverty as he was in the courts of kings.

Moreover, in the desert he had time to write, and this was bad news for his pursuers. Every communication from him represented a triumph in itself, signifying that officialdom had not silenced him, and his letters and treatises were copied and copied again. They circulated everywhere, clandestinely passing from Christian to Christian. The magnificence of his prose stirred the hearts of the faithful, while his lethal logic cast doubt on both the learning of the ostensibly learned and the authority of the ostensibly authoritative.

People wondered: Were these exalted imperial pronouncements, these enunciations from what Lewis would call "highly cultivated clergymen," as sound as they made themselves out to be? To the unlettered laity, they seemed unnecessary. Was it all that preposterous to believe in a God who suffered and died? And if the Word was God, as the Gospels had said, would he not share the "substance" or "essence" of God, as the Creed of Nicea declared?

Athanasius's first letter in this, his third exile, was to the emperor himself. Constantius, he was sure, would never have authorized the outrages being perpetrated by Syrianus in Alexandria. After all, Constantius had pledged his support for Athanasius, and the emperor was assuredly an honorable man. "I know your long-suffering goodness," Athanasius wrote. "These men earnestly wish that I should suffer death. . . . You will be astonished, Augustus, most beloved of God, when you hear it."

But the emperor was not astonished, as Athanasius soon learned, for the sole and simple reason that he had authorized the persecution. A letter from the augustus to the citizens of Alexandria disabused Athanasius of all confidence in—and respect for—Constantius. Not only did the letter command his arrest and declare all who continued to support him "enemies of the emperor," it also pronounced him dethroned as bishop—and named his successor.

More blows kept falling. The Arians said that the bishop of Rome had gone over to them. Even ancient Hosius, one of the central architects of the Nicene Creed, and champion of Athanasius's cause since the beginning, had at one point briefly capitulated. Apart from a few loyal bishops, all in exile, and his huge flock in Alexandria and the Nile Delta, Athanasius seemed to be standing largely alone. It was *Athanasius contra mundum*—"Athanasius against the world"—a saying that would live on for untold centuries, inspiring countless crusaders for any number of causes to defy supposedly authoritative opposition in defense of what they believed to be true.

Meanwhile, the search for him raged across the desert. Monastery after monastery was ransacked by the troops, the monks beaten to make them talk. Their meager food supplies were confiscated, their buildings were destroyed, some were burned alive. They spirited him from place to place; not a single monk betrayed him. He lived in caves, tracked the desert by night, and hid with the hermits. "I endured everything," he later wrote. "I even dwelt among wild beasts." That he was more than sixty years old at the time, he did not mention.

His successor arrived in Alexandria on February 24, 357, with an army detachment assigned to reinforce ecclesiastical orders. This man, known as George the Cappadocian, had somewhat unusual qualifications for the leadership of the second biggest pastorate in Christendom. He had never been a priest or

To this day, monasteries large and small dot the bleak landscape of the Nitrian Desert west of the Nile Delta, as here at Wadi al-Natrun. At the time of Athanasius their number and their isolation would have made them logical hideouts for the fugitive.

Numerous contenders sought control of the episcopal see of Alexandria in the third and fourth centuries, and occupancy of its marble throne of St. Mark was often short. A sixth-century version of the Alexandrian bishop's throne (right) is now in St. Mark's Basilica, Venice. First taken from Alexandria to Constantinople, it was transported from there to Venice by pillaging crusaders.

deacon, but he had a well-established reputation (or so his many adversaries later attested) for greed, dishonesty, cruelty and brutality. He had been, in fact, a Constantinople meat broker with a contract to supply pork to the army, and he possessed a notorious temper. But he was a zealous Arian, and had been sent to Alexandria for one purpose only: to bash the stubborn Alexandrians into conformity.

Bishop George's first act was to turn all the churches over to Arian clergy, and forbid the faithful to meet anywhere else. Protests followed immediately, particularly from St. Theonas Church, scene of two attempts to arrest Athanasius. For the task of terrorizing St. Theonas, the new bishop recruited a gang of pagan youths, and turned them loose on the congregation. The gang arrived after most of the worshipers had departed, only a few women and older men remaining behind. Athanasius writes in his *History of the Arians*:

> A piteous spectacle ensued. The women had just risen from prayer and had sat down, and the youths, stripped naked, suddenly came upon them with stones and clubs. The godless wretches stoned some of them to death. They lashed the holy virgins, tore off their veils and exposed their heads. When they resisted this insult, the cowards kicked them with their feet.
>
> This was dreadful, exceeding dreadful, but what ensued was worse, more intolerable than any outrage. Knowing the holy character of the virgins, and that their ears were unaccustomed to any pollution, and that they were better able to bear stones and swords than any obscenity, they assailed them with such language. This, the Arians had suggested to the young men, and laughed at all they said and did; while the holy virgins and other godly women fled from such words as they would from the bite of snakes.
>
> After this, that they might fully execute the orders they had received, they seized upon the seats and throne and the table that was of wood, and the curtains of the church, and carried them out and burnt them before the doors in the great street, and cast frankincense upon the flame.

One young pillager, Athanasius notes with undisguised satisfaction, suffered God's vengeance on the spot. After seating himself on the bishop's throne and singing obscene songs, he tried to pull the throne out to the fire. It toppled over and killed him.

Soon afterwards, another group of holy women, denied access to their churches, met for worship in a cemetery. A large contingent of soldiers under a commander named Sebastian, known for his fierce temperament, descended upon them and demanded that they forthwith embrace Arianism. When they refused, he had them stripped and beaten so severely that some died, and then denied them a Christian burial.

A new governor, Cataphronius, then appeared, and sixteen bishops were sent into exile in the desert, the hope being, says Athanasius, that many would be unable to survive the conditions and would perish, as some no doubt did. This was followed by the banishment of thirty more bishops and the arrest and impoverishment of any leading laity suspected of supporting Athanasius. From his hideout, Athanasius poured scorn on the crackdown. He wrote:

> Where is there a house that they did not ravage? Where is there a family they did not plunder on pretense of searching for their opponents? Where is there a garden they did not trample under foot? What tomb did they not open, pretending they were seeking for Athanasius? How many men's houses were sealed up? The contents of how many persons' lodgings did they give away to the soldiers who assisted them?

All this and more was laid to the ministrations of Bishop George, whom contemporary historians denounced with fervor. Epiphanius, for example, describes him as steeped in vice, scrupling at nothing violent or disgraceful, robbing people of their inheritance and endowing himself with monopoly

The search raged across the desert. Monasteries were ransacked by troops, the monks beaten and burned alive, but none would talk. They spirited him from one hiding place to another.

control over the sale of papyrus (the antecedent of paper), fertilizer and salt. Most galling of all, George ordered that all burials be made in high-priced coffins of his own manufacture.

People bitterly recalled the letter from the emperor Constantius that had commended this man to them. He had placed them "under the guidance of the most venerable George," the emperor had written, "than whom no man is more perfectly instructed." Under George "you will continue to have good expectations, respecting the future life, and will pass your time in this present world in rest and quietness."

Constantius was to be disillusioned. Soldiers or no soldiers, eighteen months after George arrived he was mobbed by an infuriated crowd and rescued only "with difficulty." He soon departed from the diocese on an extended leave. Immediately, the faithful reclaimed their churches. But the return of Sebastian with the main body of troops, after a fruitless search for Athanasius in the desert, quickly restored the churches to Arian control.

The same process was going on all over the empire. At Milan, the Arian Auxentius of Cappadocia was arbitrarily appointed, and the Nicene bishop Dionysius exiled. At Nicomedia, the Arian Cecropius was made bishop. At Sirmium, Arles and Lisbon, the story was the same. At Trier, Toulouse, Vercelli and Cordoba, bishops were deported and their sees left vacant. An Arian bishop was dispatched even to distant Ethiopia. At Alexandria, laments Athanasius, "profligate heathen youths" were being made bishops to supplant those banished to the desert.

In 357, when Leontius, the bishop of Antioch died, the fervent Arian Eudoxius was installed in his place, putting Antioch firmly into Arian hands. Three years later, when Eudoxius became bishop of Constantinople, his successor at Antioch, Ananias, displayed theological ideas dangerously close to the Niceans. He was promptly banished in favor of someone more reliably Arian. When this man likewise proved to be too orthodox, he also was deposed, and the Arian Euzoius brought in. Euzoius's Arianism proved sufficiently dependable to keep him in office for the next seventeen years. At

In Athanasius's new perspective, Constantius is worse than Saul, Ahab or Pilate. He is a man who slays his kin, who breaks his oaths, who sends old bishops to perish in the wild.

Constantinople, says the historian Socrates, people who refused to take communion from Arian clergy were persuaded otherwise by propping their mouths open with pieces of wood and forcing it down their throats.

Unable to find Athanasius, the authorities decided to discredit him by declaring him a coward. How, they asked, could he justify abandoning his flock to the horrors they were enduring on his account? Why would he not come forward like an honorable man and surrender? He delivered his answer in another historic missive, *Defense of His Flight*, and it, too, spread everywhere.

Jesus himself had at one point escaped his persecutors (John 8:59), Athanasius writes, as had both Peter (Acts 12:7–10) and Paul (Acts 21:35–40). In each instance, no good purpose would have been served by their surrender, and this was true of his own case. When the time came, Jesus faced death and endured it, as did the apostles. He must do the same, if and when the time came. He made two other points: The real reason his pursuers sought his voluntary surrender was their humiliation over failing to find him. Moreover, if flight from persecution is cowardice, then what of the conducting of persecution? That would be diabolical, he writes, but his foes were doing it all over the empire.

Gone by now is all condescension to the emperor. In Athanasius's new perspective, Constantius is worse than Saul, Ahab or Pilate. He is a man who slays his uncles and cousins, who breaks his oaths, who sends old bishops to perish in the wilderness, who has no sympathy even for his own suffering kinsmen. After two military victories, Constantius had formally declared himself "eternal," sneers Athanasius, and adds, "Those who refuse to allow eternity to the Son (of God) have the boldness to declare it for the emperor."

It was now the year 358, and soon Constantius would have ruled as sole emperor for ten years. Like heads of state both before and after him, he leaned toward government by anniversary. How magnificent it would be if he could mark the decennial by announcing that he had persuaded the bishops of the

Christian church to cease their interminable wrangling over the identity of Jesus Christ and finally to come together in unity. He, Constantius, would have achieved what his legendary father had notably failed to do.

Apart from the Athanasius problem, however, another was rapidly emerging, though Constantius was slow to recognize it. It arose out of one of the sad certainties of human experience, namely that the negative case is easier to make than the positive one. It is always easier to attack a belief than to defend one, and consensus among the opposition survives only until the enemy falls and the rebels themselves get to take charge. Then they disintegrate.

As long as the central task was to attack the Nicene Creed, agreement among Arians was relatively easy. But when it came to proposing an alternative creed, cracks began appearing—cracks which developed first into crevasses and then into canyons. Over the next six years, the Arians would produce some eighteen new creeds, or variations of creeds, not one of which could even begin to gain sincere and wide acceptance.

The first such attempt had been the Creed of Sirmium, described in the last chapter. Far from producing unity, however, the "Blasphemous Creed," as even the moderate opponents of Nicea termed it, inflamed the eastern bishops into opposition. Most grouped themselves around the brilliant and acerbic Basil of Ancyra. They became known as the "semi-Arians," and adopted the term *homoiousion*, declaring the Second Person to be "of like substance" with the Father, rather than *homoousion*, "of the same substance," as declared in the Nicene Creed. The letter "i" (in Greek *iota*) in the middle of the word made a difference, enunciating their belief that the Word, whom John's Gospel said "was God," was a "like thing" to God, but not the "same" thing.

Swiftly from the desert came the message that Athanasius regarded these as "brothers in the faith." He described them as "those who accept everything else that was defined at Nicea and doubt only about *homoousion*." These "must not be treated as enemies," he said. "Nor do we attack them as 'Ariomaniacs,' nor as opponents of the Father, but we discuss the matter with them as brother with brothers, who mean what we mean, and dispute only about the word."[1]

The semi-Arians had signed the creed at Nicea, but only reluctantly, because they considered the *homoousion* clause suggestive

ATHANASIUS ON THE SEA OF LIFE

For the world is like the sea to us, my brethren. . . . We float on this sea, as with the wind, through our own free will, for everyone directs his course according to his will, and either, under the pilotage of the Word, enters into rest, or enticed by pleasure, he suffers shipwreck.

1. For an explanation of the terms homoiousion and homoousion, see the earlier volume, *By This Sign*, page 243, and chapters 8 and 9 on the development of the Arian heresy and the subsequent Council of Nicea. The readiness of Athanasius to accept those of the homoiousian school (with the letter "i," the iota, in the middle of the word) was at odds with the attitude of some of the creed's defenders back at the Nicene council. When three Arian bishops at Nicea saved themselves from deposition by surreptitiously inserting the iota, the historian Philostorgius branded them "hypocrites." Now, Athanasius was calling them "brothers." If nothing else, it showed he could not be described as uncompromising.

Artist's challenge: the face of Christ

Just as theologians struggled for centuries to define the nature of Jesus, artists struggle age after age to reflect the two aspects of his nature

From ancient catacomb frescoes to contemporary movies, the face of Jesus has always been an intriguing subject for artists, both Christian and non-Christian. That this is true is inevitable, writes the twentieth-century English author Dorothy L. Sayers: "To forbid the making of pictures about God would be to forbid thinking about God at all, for man is so made that he has no way to think except in pictures."

In the catacombs, the earliest frescoes paid little attention to detail, but by the fourth century, artists were beginning to decorate churches with more than simple, sketchy representations of biblical scenes. Even in the stylized art that would later be called Byzantine, Christian craftsmen were asking, "How should he appear? How ought he to be presented?"

The length and color of Jesus' hair became standardized, with appropriate postures worked out. The primary concern was not the "historical accuracy" of the face—after all, there were no historic descriptions to serve as models. He was generally represented as Semitic or at least Mediterranean. But of growing significance to artists was how his face could show his divinity or humanity, his compassion as Savior or his dispassion as Judge.

In the sixth century, the artist who painted the Sinai Christ (right) tried to resolve the paradox of Christ's nature by portraying him as loving and caring on one side of his face, stern on the other. Something of the search for the "soul" of Jesus can be found in virtually every depiction since, to the extent that even his race and ethnicity became optional.

After the late nineteenth century, some artists would attempt to depict a historically "probable" Christ, while others put him in modern forms. Sallman's *Head of Christ* (below right), was a Sunday School favorite in the mid-twentieth century, forerunner of a number of views of Jesus in various modern guises including laughing youth, Cuban revolutionary, enlightened guru or Rasta-man.

The advent of movies brought new visions of Jesus: moving, talking, suffering and dying on screen. But the essential problem remained for filmmakers as well: Who is Jesus, and what would a glimpse of his face reveal? ■

The Pantocrator (All-Sovereign Ruler) from the Daphni Monastery, Greece (ninth century).

The Pantocrator, twelfth century, Hagia Sophia Church, Istanbul.

Detail, Sacred Heart of Jesus, Anonymous, nineteenth century, private collection.

Face of Christ, Jean Auguste Ingres, nineteenth century, Museu de Arte, Sao Paulo, Brazil.

Detail, Head of Christ, Rembrandt, ca.1648, Metropolitan Museum of Art, N.Y.

Head of Christ, Warner Sallman, 1941, Wilson Galleries, Anderson University.

Hollywood's Jesus

From De Mille to Scorsese, the movie-Christ sometimes parted from the biblical portrayal

Director Cecil B. De Mille treated Jesus reverentially in his 1927 silent movie "King of Kings," setting the standard for a rash of cinema "spectacles" that followed, including a 1961 "King of Kings" remake with Jeffrey Hunter (2). Though respectful portrayals would continue in such movies as Franco Zeffirelli's 1977 "Jesus of Nazareth" (1), some overcautious filmmakers depicted Jesus as meek, mild and even effeminate—a woefully inaccurate rendering of his powerful New Testament personality. Perhaps in reaction, the end of the century brought iconoclastic tales of Jesus to the big screen and to television. Martin Scorsese's "The Last Temptation of Christ" 1988 (3), sparked worldwide protests with its scene of Christ living out visions of a "normal," which is to say sexual, life with a tattooed Mary Magdalene. In 2003, actor/director Mel Gibson's "The Passion" drew charges of anti-Semitism for its account of some Jewish leaders' involvement in the Crucifixion. ∎

The Sinai Christ, sixth century, St. Catherine's Monastery, Sinai.

2. Sabellianism, sometimes called Modalism, was the belief that the One God appeared in successive "modes" or operations, first as Father, then as Son, then Holy Spirit, but actually was always the same One God. The theory was rejected, because it failed to adequately distinguish between the "Persons" in God, all three of whom were deemed to be eternal.

3. The word Anomoeans, used to identify the radical Arians, derives from a Greek word, *anomoios*, which means "not like." It signified that the substance or essence of Jesus, the Divine Word, was "not like" that of the Father.

of the Sabellian heresy.[2] When the rebellion against Nicea broke out, they had joined it, though they were far more anti-Sabellian than they were pro-Arian. The historian B. J. Kidd in *A History of the Church* (Oxford, 1922) describes them as "a party of high motives and conscientious scruples, very nearly orthodox." The nineteenth-century British scholar Archibald Robertson, who remained for the entire twentieth century the most widely read translator of Athanasius, was less generous. They shared "the empirical conservatism of men whose own principles are vague and ill-assorted and who fail to follow the keener sight which distinguishes the higher conservatism from the lower," he writes. However, they had the numbers. Vague they might be, but they represented the views of most eastern bishops.

At the opposite end of the spectrum stood the extreme Arians, like the notorious George of Cappadocia, Athanasius's arbitrarily appointed replacement. Whatever the Bible called him, they held, Jesus was in the end a mere creature and nothing more. In other words, God did not die on a cross. Theologically, these people were known as the Anomoeans.[3] Their leader in the west was Bishop Valens of Mursa, a pupil of Arius himself, and who from Nicea onward had been the archenemy of Athanasius. His reputation was that of the complete ecclesiastical politician, entirely capable of repudiating today a position that he had taken yesterday, if it furthered his ultimate goal—which was the destruction of both Athanasius and the Nicene Creed.

By far the most formidable Anomoean spokesman was of a very different stripe, however. Aetius was not by profession a clergyman; he was a philosopher, an authority on Aristotle. Nor was he what a much later generation would call "smooth." Self-made and self-confident, he did not equivocate, and under the future emperor Julian, he would be made a bishop. "His loud voice and clear-cut logic," writes Robertson, "lost none of their effect by fear of offending the religious sensibilities of others." This inclination served Athanasius well, if only because Aetius's brash assertions horrified the moderate semi-Arians, to whom he was simply "godless."

Between these two groups stood what Robertson calls "the political Arians." Their leader was Acacius, bishop of Caesarea. Their party was named for him, the Acacians. "In the main," writes Robertson, "he had a rooted dislike of principle of any kind," though he was sure of one thing, namely "the union of all parties of the church in subservience to the state." The Acacian objective was to hold together the rapidly fragmenting Arian movement long enough for Constantius to proclaim at his decennial that the Christian church was at last united. To accomplish this, they must somehow gain universal approval for a creed whose language was so unspecific that it would adroitly avoid all the issues, while resolving none of them.

This was certainly not the Creed of Sirmium, which had caused the uproar that in turn produced the whole semi-Arian phenomenon. The Acacian leader, Basil of Ancyra, therefore boldly approached the emperor with a better idea. Why not have another council, another Nicea, which would correct the short-comings of the original creed? To Basil's astonishment, Constantius heartily agreed. Basil found himself suddenly basking in the imperial favor, which he swiftly exploited by securing the ouster of several Anomoean bishops.

These developments quickly activated the political Arians, along with the devious Valens. In one huge council, they feared, an accord could develop between Basil's semi-Arians and those still tacitly in favor of the Nicene Creed, resulting in the, to them, ghastly possibility of Nicea's reaffirmation. To divorce Constantius from his infatuation with Basil's ideas, they proposed instead that there be two councils, one in the east and one in the west. The western would be held at Rimini in Italy (then known as Ariminum) on the Adriatic, east of Rome and twenty miles south of Ravenna.

The eastern meeting proved more problematic. Hold it at Nicea, some suggested. No, that would tend to confuse the old creed with the projected new one. Better to choose Nicomedia, capital of Bithynia, at the eastern end of the Sea of Marmara, seventy-five miles from Constantinople: Invitations were sent out,

It became obvious—to the horror of the emperor—that despite all his efforts at 'cleansing,' only about 80 of the 400 bishops who assembled were Arian. Real disaster was to follow.

the eastern bishops embarked, and then nature intervened. Nicomedia was wrecked by an earthquake.[4] The site finally settled on was Seleucia (modern Silifke, Turkey), a mountain fortress with a reassuring concentration of troops, in case the bishops got out of hand.

But first, the new creed must be prepared. Drawn up with fastidious care, it was presented first to the Council of Rimini, where more than four hundred western bishops assembled in the summer of 359.[5] It not only eliminated the word *homoousion* (of the same substance) but also denounced it as "something the fathers used in their simplicity," and which "has become a cause of scandal." Instead, it proclaimed the Son to be "like the Father." But how like him? Everything was like him to a degree, some argued, since everything was made by him. The wording had to be more specific. Some wanted "like him in all respects." Others objected that this merely affirmed Nicea.

The proposed preamble also made many uneasy, since it suggested the emperor must authorize the creed of the church. It read: "The Catholic Faith has been set forth in presence of our master, the most pious and triumphant Emperor Constantius Augustus, eternal and venerable." Accompanying it was the emperor's order to the bishops to sign the creed, which became known as the "Dated Creed" because it was on this date that the Christians, under orders from the emperor, finally declared what they believed. Or so it was supposed.

Events shortly proved otherwise. Like most compromises intended to please everybody, observes the historian J. R. Palanque in *The Church in the Christian Roman Empire* (Paris, 1949) the Dated Creed pleased nobody. Worse still, it soon became obvious—to the horror of Valens and the emperor—that despite all their efforts at "cleansing" the episcopate, only about eighty of the four hundred assembled bishops were fully Arian. Real disaster, from their point of view, then followed. This episcopal majority, still harboring a loyalty to Nicea, took over

4. The historian Sozomen preserves an anecdote about the Nicomedian earthquake. A Persian zookeeper named Arcasius, he writes, was converted to Christianity at Nicomedia, and thereafter lived within the city as a hermit, reputedly able to cure the insane. Foreseeing the earthquake in a vision, he warned an assembly of clergy to get their people out of town. When they scoffed at him, he returned to his dwelling, prostrated himself before God, and there perished in the quake and ensuing fire that leveled most of Nicomedia, as he had foreseen. "He preferred death," his friends explained, "to beholding the destruction of a city in which he had first known Christ."

5. Although four hundred western bishops were at the Council of Rimini, the bishop of Rome was not one of them, probably because the council occurred during the time of the two bishops, Felix and Liberius, a confusion that neither side wanted to visit upon the council. (See previous chapter.)

The emperor Constantius II assembled councils in the east and the west to render the Nicene Creed more palatable to Arians. Neither of the sites he chose, however, was meant to put attending bishops at ease. Seleucia (right—now Silifke in Turkey, on the Goksu River), was a military outpost in desolate mountain terrain. Rimini, on Italy's Adriatic coast (above), although a sometime imperial resort, was infamous for heat and humidity.

the council, excommunicated Valens and other Anomoean extremists, and sent a delegation to Constantius to inform him of what they had done. Valens immediately followed, at the head of an opposing delegation of Arians.

Constantius refused to see the former, but warmly welcomed the latter and ordered them to talk the rival delegation around. Meanwhile, the remaining three hundred and more bishops awaited word at hot and humid Rimini, while the living conditions grew intolerable and the food began running out. Under pressure of argument and threat, the delegates finally surrendered to Valens's wishes and signed. Constantius then informed the main body back at Rimini that they must remain there until they, too, acquiesced. With the food supply by now very low indeed, they finally gave in, and thus did the Dated Creed become the creed of the western church. The Acacians, the political Arians, had triumphed.

They did not triumph at Seleucia, however. Here 150 eastern bishops met under the watchful eyes of a representative of the emperor. It immediately became plain that about 90 percent of those present were semi-Arians, firmly opposed to the Dated Creed and the emperor's plans. On the first day, they proposed adoption of the old creed formulated twenty years before at Antioch, which they saw as best representing their viewpoint. One hundred and five bishops promptly signed it, in effect resolving the debate before it got started.

Acacius and eighteen of his fellow political Arians walked out, returning two days later with another creed, similar to the one soon to be forced on the western bishops at Rimini. The defiant semi-Arians refused even to discuss it. "If the strengthening of the faith consists in allowing everyone to put forward a particular opinion every day," declared their new leader, Sophronius of Pompeiopolis, "there can be no more certainty as to the truth."

At that, the political Arians, accompanied by the emperor's representative, hastened to Constantinople to confer with Constantius. The remaining bishops, carrying on with the meeting, excommunicated and deposed eight radical Arian bishops, George of Alexandria among them. They also consecrated a new bishop for Antioch (who was seized by the army and banished before he could take office). Finally, they appointed a ten-man delegation to report *their* decisions to the emperor.

The situation had now reversed. The western bishops, the supposed champions of Nicea, had been browbeaten and starved into signing a creed repulsive to them. The eastern bishops, the supposed opponents of Nicea, had brazenly defied the imperial authority in its favor. This was too much for the outspoken Hilary of Poitiers, Athanasius's firm supporter in the west, who in a ringing indictment denounced his fellow western bishops for disloyalty:

> A slave—not even a particularly good slave, but an ordinary one—will not support an injury to his master. He avenges it, if he can do so. A soldier defends his king, even at the peril of his life, and even making a rampart of his own body. A dog barks at the slightest alarm, and leaps forward at the slightest suspicion. But you hear it said that the Christ, the true Son of God, is not God, yet you remain silent. Your silence is an adhesion to this blasphemy. In fact you even protest against those who do cry out, and join in with those who try to stifle them.

Even the easterners, however, finally caved in—or anyhow, their ten-man delegation did. These unfortunates were put under every form of pressure—promises, threats, intrigue—in a race against the deadline of December 31, 359,

Officers crossed the eastern empire with the same ultimatum for every bishop: Sign or be banished. Since most signed, Constantius declared that the church was united at last.

the eve of the year of Constantius's decennial. The tenth signature was wrested from the final reluctant signatory in the middle of the last night.

It was still necessary, however, for something resembling a new eastern council to ratify what its delegates had accepted on its behalf. This was arranged for the following week at Constantinople, and consisted of a gathering of bishops from nearby Thrace and Bithynia who were considered reliable. Its business moved briskly. The Dated Creed, adopted at Rimini, was ratified as a replacement for the Nicene. Various bishops were deposed, particularly the semi-Arians who had proved so hostile at Seleucia. The radical Arians known as the Anomoeans were likewise deposed as troublemakers, and the fiery Aetius deposed from the diaconate and told to quit writing books and articles. George of Alexandria was reprimanded, but recalled to office.

Imperial officers then spread out across the eastern empire to secure the signature of every bishop, always with the same ultimatum: Sign or be banished.

Most eventually did sign, although some few stubbornly refused and accepted exile. With that, Constantius declared the church united, the Nicene Creed supplanted, and the new faith established. "The world groaned to find itself Arian," Jerome would later write. Still, one very significant bishop had emphatically *not* become Arian, and had not been caught either: Athanasius remained at large. His powerfully reasoned denunciation of the imperially ordained creed soon appeared, to be clandestinely spread far and wide by sympathizers.

By now, it was April of the fateful year 360, and once again overwhelming political and military events suddenly dictated the affairs of the Christian church. Two young nephews of Constantine the Great had survived the bloodbath of the year 337. Gallus, the elder, had been about eleven years old when the soldiers arrived to execute his father and elder brother. Gallus may have been spared because he was a sickly child, expected to die shortly anyway; his younger half brother Julian was only six. Julian's mother had died soon after her son's birth. The two boys were raised thereafter in highly guarded isolation, lest they be seized by some ambitious military usurper and used to figurehead a revolt.

Each responded differently to these traumatic events. They left Gallus depraved, ferocious and utterly unstable. They left Julian with a rooted hatred of everything associated with his cousin Constantius, whom he regarded as the murderer of his family. He despised the man, and also the eunuchs and sycophant bishops who surrounded him. But most of all, he distrusted Constantius's religion, Christianity, whether Arian, Nicene or any other variety.

Constantius II was determined that the Rimini decisions would write the final chapter on Athanasian opposition to Arianism. He sent soldiers to every bishop in the eastern empire with orders to secure, under threat if necessary, the signature of each. Bishops were forced to sign wherever they were found, even if that meant being rousted from bed.

CONNOR

This eventually led him back to paganism, a fact he long kept secret. Constantius, either unaware of these facts about his cousins, or compelled to disregard them, would vest each in turn with enormous responsibilities, and he also gave one of his sisters to each of them as a wife.[6]

Constantius's civil war against the usurper Magnentius, with its toll of fifty-four thousand Roman troops killed, had dangerously weakened the whole Rhine-Danube frontier. The barbarians, largely inactive since their "pacification" by Constantine the Great, resumed their raids across the Rhine and Danube with greater success than ever. Constantius, up to then preoccupied with the Persian front, had to turn his attention westward. But who could replace him in the east? It was time to see what his cousin Gallus was made of. On March 15, 351, Constantius named him caesar of the east.

Gallus's new wife, Constantina, who was Constantius's sister, was the widow of another cousin, Hannibalian, who was also a victim of the bloodbath of 337. She was a "fury in human shape," writes the historian Ammianus, and she

Constantina was a 'fury in human shape' and exacerbated Gallus's worst tendencies. The consequence was a regime of brutality conducted from a palace known as a 'house of horrors.'

exacerbated Gallus's worst tendencies. The consequence was a regime of brutality conducted from their palace at Antioch, a place British historian Edward Gibbon describes as a "house of horrors." "Judicial procedure was disregarded and informers honored. Men were condemned to death without trial, and members of the city council imprisoned," writes Norman H. Baynes in the *Cambridge Medieval History*. Both husband and wife exhibited "a brutal lust for a naked display of unrestrained authority."

When the praetorian prefect sent word of all this to Constantius, Gallus had the prefect imprisoned and set the mob against him. They broke into the prison and tore him to pieces. Exasperated at last, Constantius summoned his caesar-cousin to appear before him in Milan. En route west, Gallus's wife Constantina was seized and murdered. Constantius, that is, must have ordered his own sister put to death. Gallus became the prisoner of his guards, and as the journey continued, was stripped of the imperial purple robes. In Italy, he was presented before a commission headed by Eusebius, the emperor's chief eunuch and administrator, who formally examined his record in imperial office and pronounced the death penalty. Gallus was beheaded in the Italian town of Polo, a place of ill memory in the Constantinian family. It was here that Crispus, eldest son of Constantine the Great, had been executed on his father's orders twenty-eight years earlier.

By now, the situation on the Rhine-Danube front had grown much worse, with one barbarian horde after another wreaking ruin on the Roman towns. In the north, the Salian Franks had taken full possession of a vast tract of Gaul.

6. Marriage between cousins was legal in Rome, as it later would be in the civil law of many American states, in Canada and in all European countries. It is forbidden by the canon law of the Orthodox and Roman Catholic churches, although there is a process of dispensation. Most Protestant churches simply follow the laws of the state in which they are located.

The Alamanni had overrun much of central Gaul, and captured Strasbourg, Worms and Mainz. The Franks had captured Cologne. Some forty-five Roman towns in the Rhine Valley had been pillaged and burned, and barbarians had formed settlements as much as fifty miles west of the river. Meanwhile, soldiers who had supported the usurper Magnentius had formed themselves into gangs and ravaged far and wide.

Constantius faced a dilemma. If a victorious general were assigned to subdue the tribes, and succeeded, he might become another Magnentius, and once again create civil war. Yet Constantius could not personally direct the defense of all three fronts—the Rhine, the Danube and the Euphrates. He was driven therefore to turn to the last surviving nephew of Constantine: Julian, now thirty years old. This, too, was dangerous, of course, since a triumphant Julian could also proclaim himself a rival augustus. But this seemed unlikely; the young man had become a philosopher, buried in his books.

Whatever the risk, Constantius had no alternative. On November 6, 355, he proclaimed his cousin caesar in the west, gave his sister Helena to him in

The unfortunate George chose that month to return to Alexandria. The faithful executed him, paraded his body through the streets on a camel, and dragged his enforcer behind in the dirt.

marriage, and assigned him to the Rhine frontier. Julian, although dreading the job, surrendered to the will of the gods. He secretly had himself inducted into Mithraism, the pagan religion of the Roman army, served briefly under another general, and then launched a military career that within the next five years would rival that of his renowned grandfather, the great Constantine.

Julian's victories followed one upon the other in quick succession. A brilliant defense of the fortress of Sens won him the loyalty of his troops. Then Cologne was recovered. Next, the Franks were smashed in a stunning series of defeats at and around Strasbourg, and their king was sent as a prisoner to Constantius. After a further drubbing the following spring, they too made peace, which put the whole lower Rhine back in Roman hands.

In the following summer, Julian completed the reconquest of the upper Rhine, and used his barbarian prisoners to rebuild the Roman forts there. He reopened the supply of British grain to Roman towns, and forced the barbarians to yield up twenty thousand prisoners and slaves they had taken while they had free rein in Gaul. He restored the civil administration, refused military pressure to raise taxes, fired crooked tax collectors and replaced them with his own men, and reduced special tax breaks for the wealthy.

Constantius had meanwhile subdued the tribes on the Danube, but on the Euphrates had met with failure. Sapor II, the Persian king, aware of Rome's problems in the west, suddenly required that the Romans vacate all of Mesopotamia and turn Christian Armenia over to Zoroastrian Persia. It was an outrageous demand, which Constantius rejected outright. Sapor's invasion promptly followed, thwarted initially by a heroic seventy-three-day Roman defense of Amida in Mesopotamia. When the town finally surrendered, Sapor murdered or enslaved the entire population, but he had lost thirty thousand men in the siege, and had to withdraw and regroup for a second attack the next year.

Constantius knew he could not hold the Persian front without reinforcements from the legions on the Rhine. He sent his own general to lead them to the east, rather than entrust the task to Julian, but the troops balked. Fearing that their departure would set the barbarians on the warpath again, thus endangering their own families, they rose in rebellion and proclaimed Julian as augustus. Julian, knowing that if he refused they would probably kill him and choose another, donned the purple robes and prepared to march on Constantinople and have it out with his cousin. But fate intervened. Constantius was disheartened, desperate and so stricken with fever that he accepted baptism from an Arian bishop at Mopsuestia (now Misis in Turkey) and died the next day, November 3, 361.

The unfortunate George, as it happened, had chosen that very month to return to his duties as bishop of Alexandria. Scarcely had he arrived when the faithful heard of Constantius's death. They clapped Bishop George smartly into irons and conducted him to prison. One morning, about three weeks later, they dragged him out again, executed him and paraded his body through the streets on the back of a camel, with the corpse of his latest military enforcer dragging through the dirt behind him. That afternoon, they burned both bodies.

ATHANASIUS ON JESUS AS MAN

When the Word became man, he did not cease to be God; nor because he is God does he avoid what is human. Far from it. Rather, the all-holy Word of God bore our ignorance so that he might bestow on us the knowledge of his Father.

Julian, meanwhile, issued orders that all banished bishops were to be returned to their cities. Athanasius, as if out of nowhere, appeared unannounced at an evening service in one of his churches, causing a sensation. Where had he been? How could he have returned so soon from the desert? The explanation then came out. He had been for some time under the care of a very devout virgin, a woman so beautiful (writes the Christian historian Sozomen) "that men of gravity and reflection kept aloof from her, for fear of giving rise to slander, or of exciting disadvantageous reports." That a bishop should live in her home seemed so preposterous, not only to the Christians but the Roman authorities as well, that in perfect safety she was able to provide him with shelter, food and writing materials.

Restored to office for the third time, Athanasius acted quickly. He called a council of his bishops at Alexandria, and set forth one simple basis for the restoration of church unity: acceptance of the Nicene Creed. Those who had departed from it, or signed other creeds, the council decided, must be instantly forgiven—once they had made that acceptance. When his old friends, the monks, attacked the semi-Arians, he told them to show charity and they did. When his longtime supporter, Lucifer of Calaris, created a new schism at

Antioch by taking a harder line, Athanasius repudiated him. Long regarded as the chief troublemaker, Athanasius became the chief pacifier overnight.

Far and wide, east and west, Christians answered his call. Arianism, so recently perceived as inescapable, had suddenly become very escapable indeed. Apparently, it could prevail only so long as it had something to attack. Having gained the ascendancy, it fatally fragmented. The battle was not over, for much of the imperial circle and high-ranking clergy remained Arian, but Christians everywhere, both lay and clerical, were uniting behind Nicea. The struggle came to resemble the old conflict of imperial officialdom against the Christians, especially in view of a new factor.

Julian, who now succeeded Constantius, made his paganism public as soon as he knew he was in charge. Neither Arian nor Nicene, he was opposed to them all. When he learned what the tireless Athanasius, now about sixty-five years old, was doing at Alexandria, he wrote in wrath to the prefect of Egypt:

> Even though you do not write to me on other matters, you ought at least to have written about that enemy of the gods, Athanasius, especially since, for a long time past, you have known my just decrees. I swear by mighty Serapis that, if Athanasius the enemy of the gods does not depart from that city [Alexandria], or rather from all Egypt, before the December kalends, I shall fine the cohort which you command a hundred pounds of gold. And you know that, though I am slow to condemn, I am even much slower to remit when I have once condemned.
>
> [*The remainder is added in the emperor's own hand.*] It vexes me greatly that my orders are neglected. By all the gods, there is nothing I should be so glad to see, or rather hear reported as achieved by you, as that Athanasius has been expelled beyond the frontiers of Egypt. Infamous man! He has the audacity to baptize Greek women of rank during my reign! Let him be driven forth!

The emperor Julian hoped to restore the empire's virility by eradicating Christianity and returning Roman citizens to their pagan roots. His personal renunciation of the Christian faith earned him forever the title "Julian the Apostate." This striking fourth-century statue of Julian is now in the Louvre, Paris.

He then wrote to the people of Alexandria, calling Athanasius "a meddlesome man, unfit by nature to be a leader of the people," and warning them that he wanted Athanasius out of the city. So their bishop was banished again. His sojourn in Alexandria this time had lasted eight months, but that was enough to set the restoration of Nicea in motion. "Be of good cheer," he told his weeping flock, as he prepared to leave the city. "This is a cloud that will very soon blow away." His prophecy was to prove altogether correct.

At that, Athanasius vanished from the city for the fourth time, as usual narrowly dodging plans to arrest him, but on this occasion, with comic consequences. For a change, he headed up the Nile by boat; when warned that imperial authorities were following him in another vessel, he came about and sailed back downstream. Soon his pursuers came in sight, and hailed his crew with an urgent question: Had they seen Athanasius? Indeed they had, the bishop's men shouted back, "and he's not far from here." At that, the authorities redoubled their upstream efforts. After they returned without him, Athanasius secretly ascended the Nile once again, and spent the next eighteen months visiting the ancient cities of the Pharaohs and the monasteries that were appearing all around the lower valley.

One scene on that voyage particularly moved him. As his vessel tracked along the bank by night near Hermopolis, about midway between Thebes and Memphis, he came upon an assembly of hundreds of monks, clergy and bishops, standing under torchlight to greet him. He came ashore, mounted a donkey and made his way among them. "Who are these," he intoned, echoing Isaiah (60:8) "that fly like a cloud, and as doves to their windows?" Then he answered the question. It was not the bishops like him, but these men of prayer, humility and obedience, who carry the cross in their own being. These, he said, are the real "fathers of the church."

Something else happened to him on that journey. He became obsessed with what he foresaw as his own impending martyrdom, and found himself dreading it. The monks again took him into hiding, but could do nothing to allay his horror. Finally, the abbot Theodore came to him and said he had no cause for fear. But the emperor was clearly determined to execute him, Athanasius argued. Not so, said Theodore, because the emperor, Julian I, had been killed in battle on the Persian front. Quietly back to Alexandria came its weary bishop, now about sixty-seven and restored to his see for the fourth time.

But the death of Julian in 363 ended the era of the Constantinian family. Since no kindred claimant remained, the army searched its own senior officer corps for a successor. One candidate turned down the job, pleading that he was

Long regarded as the chief troublemaker, Athanasius became the chief pacifier overnight. Far and wide, Christians answered his call. Arianism had suddenly become very escapable indeed.

too old. Attention then focused on a certain Jovian, the thirty-two-year-old commander of Julian's bodyguard. The son and son-in-law of two accomplished officers, he himself had done nothing of note except advance on the merits of his family connections. He was, however, Christian.

Jovian had immediate and urgent problems. Julian's death had left the Roman army trapped on the eastern frontier, in imminent danger of total destruction by Persian forces. Sapor offered crushing terms to free them. Rome must abandon the five provinces east of the Tigris that it had gained under Diocletian, and must give up three frontier fortresses, and half of Armenia as well. Jovian had to agree, so that the bedraggled legions, the Christian symbol now back on their shields, could begin the grueling trek back to Antioch.

Meanwhile, Athanasius and rival bishops representing the various Christian parties hastened thence to meet the new emperor. "The highways of the east were crowded with Homoousion and Arian, and semi-Arian and Anomoean bishops," sneers the skeptic Gibbon. These all "struggled to outstrip each other in the holy race; the apartments of the palace resounded with their clamors, and the ears of the prince were assaulted, and perhaps astonished, by the singular mixture of metaphysical argument and passionate invective." However, Athanasius had come at the specific invitation of the emperor, and the rest were soon informed of Jovian's position. His Christianity was defined by the Nicene Creed, he said. Athanasius returned triumphant to Alexandria, bishop once again.

But not for long. Jovian made speed for the capital where he knew his reign was in imminent danger, if only because of the catastrophic treaty with the Persians. At a little-known town called Dadastana, however, on the boundary between the provinces of Bithynia and Galatia, he was found dead in his bed one morning. He had been poisoned either by fumes from newly laid plaster, or possibly by eating mushrooms, or by overeating and drinking the night before. Murder was, of course, rumored, although no strong case for it was ever made. His reign had lasted eight months.

The popular choice of the army now fell on another officer, Valentinian, age forty-three, an accomplished general of commanding presence who had distinguished himself in the service of both Julian and Jovian. He, in turn, named his brother Valens, seven years his junior, as augustus for the east. Valens had in no way distinguished himself, however, and could speak no

The fugitive Athanasius, pursued up the Nile by imperial soldiery, has ordered his crew to turn back downstream, toward Alexandria. With his head covered against the blistering sun, and detection, they pass the pursuing vessel still upbound. An officer shouts a request for information as to the bishop's whereabouts. Cunningly—and truthfully—the captain of Athanasius's ship shouts back, "He is not far." The pursuers redoubled their efforts to ascend the river.

CONNOR

Greek, the language of the empire he was to govern.

Both brothers rapidly established a reputation for brutal authoritarianism, enforced by the swift beheading, burning or clubbing to death of any suspected conspirator or malefactor. Some few, it was said, were torn to pieces by bears caged in Valentinian's bedroom, to amuse him as he fell asleep. In his more refined moments, however, inspired by his Christian moral principles, he introduced a remarkable social program. This provided child medical care, prohibited the killing of unwanted infants by abandoning them to the elements, and laid the foundations of a public school system. In addition, Valentinian restored Constantine the Great's policy of toleration for all non-Christian religions except those involving criminal practices, and the Nicene Creed was soon well-re-established in the western churches.

Things were otherwise in the east, however, where younger brother Valens was chronically fearful for his own safety, both spiritual and physical, and especially of the horrors of continuing warfare against the barbarians. He therefore had himself instructed and baptized by the bishop of Constantinople, who persuaded him to become a committed and determined Arian. Thereafter, Arian bishops continued to gain the major eastern sees, often through rigged elections.

This conflict frequently became violent, even homicidal. When some forty-eight Nicene clergy (one historian puts the number at ninety) sought an audience with Valens, he provided them with transport by sea. No sooner was the vessel well off shore than fire engulfed it. The crew all reportedly escaped, which suggests the blaze was deliberately set, quite likely on the emperor's orders. The clergy all perished.

At Alexandria, political fortune once again turned against the aging Athanasius. In 365, Valens ordered all the clergy who had been banished under Constantius to be banished again. For the fifth and final time, Athanasius was

The trio who came to the rescue

The Cappadocians carry the Nicene Creed to its final victory, while one of them lays down the rules for a monastic life and service to the helpless

For the aging Athanasius, battling for years against emperors, bishops, bureaucrats, the military and the mob to preserve the Nicene Creed, the reports emerging from the east in the mid-360s must have come as the pale promise of dawn. Three men, he was told, all fearless, all magnificent preachers, all in their mid-thirties, had taken up his cause against the religion of Arius. Ironically, they came from Cappadocia, home of the notorious George, who had imposed Arianism on Alexandria with bludgeon and sword.

Two of the three were brothers, the third their close friend. The foremost was Basil, who would become bishop of Caesarea in Cappadocia. His brother Gregory, renowned for his lucid presentation of Trinitarian theology, would be bishop of nearby Nyssa. Their friend, another Gregory, this one from another Cappadocian town, Nazianzus, a persuasive preacher in the Nicene cause, would serve briefly as bishop of Constantinople. Both Gregorys would play key roles at the Council of Constantinople in 381, which decisively upheld the Nicene Creed.

The three are known to Christian history as "the Cappadocians." Basil is remembered by Christians as "Basil the Great," the man who laid down the structure and ethos of eastern monasticism, making prayer, holiness and the care of the sick and helpless the central work.

He and his brother would exemplify another phenomenon that would recurrently appear in Christian history, that of the Christian family, serving Christ for generation after generation. Their maternal grandfather had been executed as a Christian under Maximian. Both paternal grandparents had been forced to hide for seven years in the wilderness.

Their father, a lawyer and devout Christian, had ten children—five boys, three of whom became bishops, and five girls. Macrina, eldest of the ten, was so beautiful, wrote her brother and biographer Gregory, that "a great swarm of suitors crowded round her parents." To end the clamor, they betrothed her at age twelve. Following the premature death of her fiancé, she announced that she considered herself married, already and always. After caring for her siblings and the extensive family estate, she joined her widowed mother in establishing a monastery.

Basil was sent to law school at Athens. Precocious, prissy and acutely aware of his superior intellect, he presented a tempting target for student hazing. But he met Gregory at the university, son of the bishop of Nazianzus, who protected him, and the two formed a famous friendship. But an unequal one, writes John McGuckin in his *St. Gregory of Nazianzus* (New York, 2001). Gregory "suffered the unfortunate disability of loving his friend more than his friend loved him."

While Gregory reveled in the university life, Basil found the place frivolous. He returned from university insufferable, writes his brother, "puffed up beyond measure with the pride of oratory, and excelling—in ordered out, occasioning the usual hairbreadth escape. The imperial prefect assured him that the deportation order would be appealed and he should wait and see, but Athanasius did not believe him. He immediately departed. Next day, the prefect and troops ransacked his church in vain.

However, this time the faithful had had enough. The fifth eviction of their bishop set off a riot in the city. Valens, just then confronted with a usurpation attempt and also with major problems on the Danube, had no stomach for another rebellion in Alexandria. He relented, and four months after Athanasius's disappearance, a written order arrived from the emperor, restoring him to his see. This time, though, Athanasius had not even left town. He had hidden himself in the family crypt in a suburb of Alexandria.

He had seven years left to live, and they were rewarding ones. Notwithstanding continued loyalty to Arianism in high places, it was becoming

his own estimation—all the leading men in town." It was Macrina who brought him to his senses. He could take no credit for his intellect, she said. God had given that to him, and it should be employed in the service of God. In short, he should consider the monastic life.

Her words, Basil would later recall, awakened him as from a deep sleep. He began visiting religious communities in Egypt, Syria and Mesopotamia, and on the basis of what he saw, he founded his own. His brother joined him. So, briefly, did Gregory his friend, by now disillusioned with Athens, but he found the ascetic life too difficult, and returned to Nazianzus to assist his father, the bishop.

Basil refined his approach to the monastic life in the 360s, preaching it throughout Asia Minor and codifying it in what came to be called "The Long Rules." His monks began their day at midnight, with prayer. There was but one meal. However, the outstanding feature of Basil's monasticism from the outset was its emphasis on good works, bestowed especially on the poor and afflicted.

Basil and friend Gregory collaborated on a major academic work intended to claim for the Nicene cause the concurrence of the great theologian Origen, who himself had once taken refuge at Cappadocian Caesarea. This established them as theologians. Both were soon fully involved in the Nicene controversy as staunch allies of Athanasius.

It was not a comfortable role. With the emperor Valens fervently, often violently, advancing the Arian cause, Basil took refuge in his monastery, sleeping on the ground in a hair shirt, possessing just a single cloak and a single tunic, eating only bread, drinking only water, his heat the sun alone, and dogged by the ill health that attended him all his life. He was "without a wife, without property, without flesh and almost without blood," wrote his brother. But it was there in his monastery that he composed one of the great works on the Nicene controversy, *Against Eunomius*, re-arguing the debate from the Nicene viewpoint.

In 362, he helped elect an orthodox layman named Eusebius as bishop of Caesarea and became his adviser, tirelessly promoting clergy who supported the creed to senior church offices. He also became the dependable friend of the unfortunate. When famine struck, he fed the poor of Caesarea out of his personal wealth.

Eusebius died in 370, and a struggle developed over the succession. Caesarea was a provincial capital, its prelate a

Now considered "fathers of the church," the three Cappadocian bishops (left to right) Basil the Great, his brother Gregory of Nyssa, and Gregory of Nazianzus, did not always see eye-to-eye on matters of ecclesiastical administration.

apparent that even in the east the Arian cause was in sharp decline. In 365, the semi-Arians agreed to sign the Nicene Creed, thereby uniting with Athanasius. The following year, Acacius died, and the "political Arians" began to fragment and dissolve. In 369, a council at Alexandria confirmed the decision of another council at Rome to excommunicate the bishops Valens and Ursacius, who headed the Arian cause in the west. Aetius, leader of the radical Arians known as Anomoeans, died in or about 370, leaving no effective successor.

However, the greatest encouragement for Athanasius came from Cappadocia, the same region that had produced the deplorable George. Basil, a relatively young man, became bishop of Cappadocian Caesarea, and rapidly established

Tourists nowadays explore cells and churches carved from the sandstone formations of Cappadocia in eastern Turkey, first by Christians fleeing persecution, and later by monks as well. The artwork in some of these chapels (above) is remarkably well-preserved.

metropolitan, holding authority over some seventy bishops. Prior to Eusebius, it had been an Arian stronghold. Would the new bishop support the creed or the Arian emperor? Basil wanted the job himself, but it was unseemly to campaign for it. So he pretended illness and appealed urgently to his old friend Gregory to come to his bedside. There followed one of the frequent spats that characterized the trio, though never seriously divided them.

Gregory, by now a monk himself, left Nazianzus immediately to aid his stricken friend. On the road, however, he discovered (a) that his friend was not sick, (b) that his friend wanted to become bishop, and (c) that he wanted Gregory to run his campaign. In disgust, Gregory turned back and told his father what had happened. The father, a keen supporter of Athanasius and the creed, rebuked his son and wrote an appeal to the people of Caesarea, convincing enough to win the election for Basil.

Basil's ministry in Caesarea would produce a bountiful legacy. He developed there a whole complex

of buildings known as the Basileiad. It included a hospital, a home for the elderly, an orphanage, a school to train the unskilled, plus chapels and churches, becoming a monastic model that would be imitated across both eastern and western Europe.

To the see of Nyssa, a ramshackle little town not far from Caesarea, he appointed his brother, occasioning another altercation. His brother loved solitude and was highly reluctant to become a bishop anywhere, let alone in dreary Nyssa. Under protest, he took the post anyway. In a similar circumstance, Gregory of Nazianzus was far less acquiescent. When Basil made the miserable little village of Sasima into a diocese (to gain an extra vote for the Nicene side) and coerced Gregory into becoming its bishop, an angry exchange of letters followed, and Gregory never once visited the place.

A year after Basil's election, the emperor Valens, more determined in his Arianism than ever, began a brutal procession through Asia Minor, and a systematic persecution of the creed's supporters. Recalcitrant bishops were ousted from their sees, one of them Gregory of Nyssa, who went into exile.

Basil met the emperor's mission defiantly. He refused communion to the emperor's advance party. When Demosthenes appeared, once the emperor's himself as the new and extremely effective champion of the Nicene Creed. Basil's defense of it was rooted in the principles that Athanasius had battled to preserve, and Basil could pursue them with the vigor of youth.

To Basil, the old man became, even while still living, a "father of the church," and Basil urged him to continue working, in whatever time he had left, to restore the church's shattered unity. "The more the disorders of the church increase, the more do we turn toward your perfection," Basil wrote to Athanasius, describing his advice as "safer from error, both by virtue of your age and experience in affairs, and also because you have the guidance of the Spirit beyond other men."

Athanasius had indeed become a champion of unity, steadfastly insisting that anyone who could now ascribe to the Nicene Creed, whatever his previous errors, must be welcomed back as fully Christian. There must be no penalties for

cook, now his spokesman and strong-arm enforcer, Basil told him to go back to his pots and pans. Next came the prefect Modestus, threatening confiscation, torture and death. Basil replied tartly: "How can I suffer torture since I barely have a body left?" Modestus, astonished, said he'd never before met such defiance. "Perhaps," retorted Basil, "that's because you've never before met a true bishop."

Finally, the emperor Valens himself arrived. Brother Gregory describes the scene. With his courtiers, Valens crashed his way into Basil's cathedral. High drama followed in full costume, the emperor in his robes of state, the bishop in those of a metropolitan. Flanked by their seconds, the two faced one another across the sacred altar, the haunting tones of the Liturgy echoing through the church.

The emperor, suddenly awestruck, fell to his knees, holding out the accustomed imperial offering to the church. Basil refused it. Abashed, the emperor departed. He returned the next day as a penitent. He knelt. Basil threw his stole across the imperial head, and pronounced absolution in the name of Jesus Christ.

The two men began quietly discussing the Nicene issue. It seemed serious. The imperial aides became alarmed. Demosthenes sought, with an ungrammatical interjection, to halt the discussion. "Behold," quipped Basil, "we have a Demosthenes who can't speak Greek." The emperor roared laughing. Basil had won. His defiance was overlooked. Valens later cut Cappadocia in two, halving Basil's territory, but unquestionably Basil had captured the emperor's respect.

As the influence of the three grew, so did the force raised against them. Brother Gregory was accused of misappropriating church funds, Basil of extorting money from a rich widow. Both charges were so absurd that when the prefect Modestus came to take Basil into custody, all Caesarea rose to defend him, and prevented the arrest. Then Basil was attacked theologically, accused of diminishing the role of the Holy Spirit in the Trinity. His treatise in response

asserting the equality of the Three Persons became a classic.

In 378, when Valens fell in battle and was succeeded by the committed Nicene Theodosius I, radical change began. Basil died in 379, mourned by Christians, Jews and pagans alike, but his friend Gregory was invited to Constantinople by Theodosius to champion the Nicene cause in the Arian heartland. He was escorted into the city by an armed guard and took up residence in a small house. There he wrote the sermons that played a major role in turning opinion.

But not without sharp resistance. He was mocked by his foes for his rural accent and his ascetic's rags. He was stoned in the streets, even in his own cathedral. Nevertheless, five of his orations stand as landmarks of Trinitarian doctrine, listing and countering each Arian argument in turn, and earning him the title "the Theologian." There was another curious incident. A would-be assassin penetrated his little house at night. Encountering his intended victim, he suddenly felt conscience-stricken, fell to his knees and asked Gregory's forgiveness. Gregory acceded, and his would-be assassin became his supporter.

Both Gregorys would preach at the Council of Constantinople in 381, where the Nicene Creed triumphed. Gregory of Nazianzus was made bishop of Constantinople. But the connivance and fury over the appointment of a bishop for Antioch so dismayed him that he resigned within a month and retired to his monastery. There he died in 389. Gregory of Nyssa preached and wrote theological treatises until his death in 395.

A fitting eulogy for all the Cappadocians could be taken from Gregory of Nazianzus's so-called *Last Farewell*: "This was my field," he wrote. "It was small and poor, unworthy not only of God, who has been and is cultivating the whole world . . . but not deserving to be called a field at all." Even so, the harvest was "great and well-eared and fat in the eyes of him who beholdeth hidden things."

One fact, of course, Gregory did not know. That field, meager as it was, would be harvested century after century through all the ages of Christian monasticism. ■

past mistakes. Consequently, people were returning to the Nicene fold in ever-greater numbers. Athanasius's life came to a tranquil end in 373, at his little house in Alexandria, nearly half a century after Nicea, probably on May 2. He "ended his life in a holy old age," writes Gregory of Nazianzus, "and went to keep company with his fathers, the patriarchs, prophets, apostles and martyrs, who had fought valiantly for the truth, as he had done."

Not everyone viewed Athanasius so fondly, of course, then or later. In some respects, he would remain almost as controversial in the view of future generations as he was in his own. For example, Paul Johnson's *History of Christianity* (New York, 1976) cites against him assorted charges of violence, with no effort to refute them. One document that came to light in 1922 would certainly support Johnson's charge. A letter from a Meletian Christian, the schismatic group that broke away from the Alexandrian church in the previous century, charges Athanasius with either conducting, or at least countenancing, a crackdown in which some were beaten up and others imprisoned. If so, he was clearly capable of violence himself.

University of Toronto historian Timothy D. Barnes, in his *Athanasius and Constantius* (Cambridge Massachusetts, 1993), goes farther. He accuses Athanasius of being such "a subtle and skillful liar" that for generations he held historians in thrall. On the other hand, Barnes notes, the skeptical Edward Gibbon in his classic anti-Christian polemic, *The History of the Decline and Fall of the Roman Empire*, unaccountably presents a virtual panegyric on Athanasius. But Athanasius, says Barnes, "could not have cut such an impressive figure had he not been conspicuously lacking in the Christian virtues of meekness and humility." However, the same could be said, and was said, of Jesus himself.

Critics of Athanasius find less to deplore in what he did than in how he did it. He was deeply convinced that in the Arian controversy, the central message of Christianity was under attack. In its defense, he was brazen, fearless, confident, and unimpressed by established authority, and very possibly did not on occasion shrink from violence either.

Such unshakable certainty evokes disgust in some people but admiration in others, which explains why the fault line on Athanasius does not lie along the Catholic-Protestant divide. He is a hero to both Protestants and Catholics, writes his biographer R. Wheeler Bush—although he should have said to *some* Protestants and *some* Catholics. Johnson, who is critical in almost every reference, is Roman Catholic; Bush himself, whose attitude is close to adulation, was an Anglican clergyman. Perhaps the most perceptive summation of Athanasius's accomplishment comes from Mark Noll, professor of history at Wheaton College, Illinois:

> Athanasius did not consider Arius's arguments as philosophical curiosities. Rather, he viewed them as daggers aimed at the very heart of the Christian message. His memorable treatise, *On the Incarnation . . .* summarized the case he would continue to make for the rest of his life: If Christ were not truly God, he could not bestow life on the repentant, and free them from sin and death. Yet this work of salvation is at the heart of the biblical picture of Christ, and it has anchored the church's life since the beginning. What Athanasius saw clearly was

This massive statue of Valentinian I, now in Barletta, Italy, is thought to have been lost in a storm while en route from Byzantium. At some time in the Middle Ages, it was discovered on a beach, minus its legs, which have since been restored.

that unless Christ was truly God, humanity would lose the hope that Paul expressed in 2 Corinthians 5:21, "that in Christ we might become the righteousness of God." (From: *Turning Points: Decisive Moments in the History of Christianity*, Grand Rapids, 1997.)

But whatever his virtues and faults, few would deny that Athanasius was the chief barrier to the Arian heresy. When Catholic, Orthodox, Anglican, Lutheran and many other Christians recite the Nicene Creed, they can properly thank God for the stubborn, cantankerous and heroic bishop of Alexandria, and his astute realization that the alternative to the Nicene Creed was a downward slide in the content of the Christian faith, with each concession calculated to widen its intellectual appeal, eventually to the point where there remained scarcely anything to believe at all.

Athanasius could die satisfied that Arianism would soon die, too—which it did, though not gently. In fact, his death set off a new round of persecution, first in Alexandria, then elsewhere in the east. To assure the continuity of the Nicene cause in Egypt, he had nominated his longtime supporter Peter to succeed him. But the Arians had already chosen a candidate for the see, and before Peter could be consecrated, they once again invaded St. Theonas Church, with a gang of pagan ruffians who offered the usual displays of obscenity.

The historian Theodoret preserves Peter's account of what followed. The holy women were "insulted, assassinated, violated and led naked through the town." A young man, painted and dressed as a woman, danced on the altar, while another, stark naked, delivered crudities as a homily from the bishop's chair. In the midst of these festivities, says Theodoret, the Arian candidate was led into the venerable old church to be proclaimed bishop. Executions and banishments of Nicene supporters followed, along with confiscation of their property. Peter sought refuge in Rome, just as Athanasius had done thirty-four years earlier.

The source of this latest anti-Nicene fury was never in doubt. The emperor Valens, who early in his reign had survived one usurpation attempt, remained ever alert to the dangers of another. He saw those Christians loyal to Nicea as one of two likely sources. His other and even more acute fear was any whiff of the magic and divination aspect of paganism. Discovering that some pagans at Antioch had concluded from a mystical Delphic rite that the name of the next emperor would begin with *Theo*, and that others by a different magical formula had come to the same conclusion, he unleashed a slaughter of every conceivably eligible candidate unfortunate enough to possess such a name. Ammianus says the purge was conducted "with the utmost ferocity," and the tortures and executions resembled the

ATHANASIUS ON OUR DESTINY

[God] was made man that we might be made God.

What a creed is—and what it is not

'Creeds are not set forth as the conditions for membership in some club,'
says a noted Christian dramatist, 'but as statements of fact that are either true or false'

Dorothy L. Sayers, the twentieth-century British detective story writer, classics scholar and Christian dramatist, in an examination of the creeds of the Christian church, describes a misunderstanding of their nature and function, which remains as common today as it was when she wrote this sixty years ago. The essay is taken from her book on the triune nature of human creativity.

Volumes of angry controversy have been poured out about the Christian creeds, under the impression that they represent, not statements of fact, but arbitrary edicts. The conditions of salvation, for instance, are discussed as though they were conditions for membership in some fantastic club like the Red-Headed League. They do not purport to be anything of the kind. Rightly or wrongly, they purport to be necessary conditions based on the facts of human nature.

We are accustomed to find conditions attached to human undertakings, some of which are arbitrary and some not. A regulation that allowed a cook to make omelettes only on condition of first putting on a top hat might conceivably be given the force of law, and penalties might be inflicted for disobedience; but the condition would remain arbitrary and irrational. The law that omelettes can be made only on condition that there shall be a preliminary breaking of eggs is one with which we are sadly familiar. The efforts of idealists to make omelettes without observing this condition are foredoomed to failure by the nature of things. The Christian creeds are too frequently assumed to be in the top hat category; this is an error; they belong to the category of egg-breaking.

The proper question to be asked of any creed is not, "Is it pleasant?" but "Is it true?" Christianity has compelled the mind of man, not because it is the most cheering view of man's existence, but because it is truest to the facts. It is unpleasant to be called sinners, and much nicer to think that we all have hearts of gold—but have we? It is agreeable to suppose that the more scientific knowledge we acquire the happier we shall be—but does it look like it? It is encouraging to feel that progress is making us automatically every day and in every way better, and better, and better—but does history support that view? "We hold these truths to be self-evident: that all men were created equal"—but does the external evidence support this *a priori* assertion? Or does experience rather suggest that man is "very far gone from original righteousness and is of his own nature inclined to evil?"

A creed put forward by authority deserves respect in the measure that we respect the authority's claim to be a judge of truth. If the creed and the authority alike are conceived as being arbitrary, capricious and irrational, we shall continue in a state of terror and bewilderment, since we shall never know from one minute to the next what we are supposed to be doing, or why, or what we have to expect. But a creed that can be shown to have its basis in fact inclines us to trust the judgment of the authority; if in this case and in that it turns out to be correct, we may be disposed to think that it is, on the whole, probable that it is correct about everything.

The necessary condition for assessing the value of creeds is that we should fully understand that they claim to be, not idealistic fancies, not arbitrary codes, not abstractions irrelevant to human life and thought, but statements of fact about the universe as we know it. Any witness—however small—to the rationality of a creed assists us to an intelligent apprehension of what it is intended to mean, and enables us to decide whether it is, or is not, as it sets out to be, a witness of universal truth. ∎

From *The Mind of the Maker*, by Dorothy L. Sayers, Harper Brace, New York, 1941. Reprinted by permission of the Estate of Dorothy L. Sayers and the Watkins/Loomis Agency.

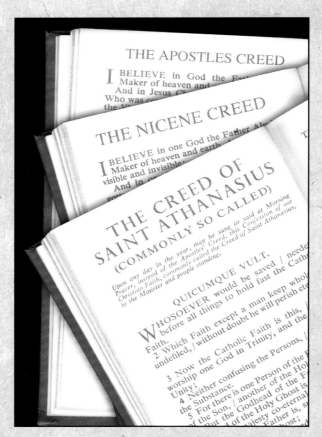

slaughter of animals. Valens himself so enjoyed these spectacles, Ammianus adds, that he became a connoisseur of torture, and would be visibly saddened when the victim escaped it by dying.

His brother Valentinian had another failing, an uncontrollable temper. On November 17, 375, he became so enraged at what he considered the cocky arrogance of a delegation of barbarians admitted to his presence, that he collapsed in a fit of apoplexy and died before doctors could calm him down. His heirs in the west were two juveniles: his sons Gratian, sixteen, and Valentinian II, four. The effect was to bolster the power of Valens as senior augustus, and the confidence of the phalanx of Arian bishops he had installed throughout the east.

But this power was soon to prove a facade. Led by the skillful Basil and two Cappadocian colleagues (see sidebar, page 60), the rank and file of the Christian church, along with almost all its younger clergy, saw Arianism only as an unworkable attempt to avoid the unavoidable. Either Jesus the Word was substantially and essentially God, or as Augustine was about to declare, he was "not a good man." Arianism and all the other "in-between" expedients could not be rationally, historically or theologically sustained. Valens's successor, whose name incidentally would indeed begin with *Theo*, would before very long call the church into formal council and declare Arianism dead. Only among the barbarian nations would it long survive, and even there it would gradually perish over the next two hundred years.

As for Valens, he too was about to perish, in a battle that many historians view as the greatest catastrophe ever suffered by the army of the Roman Empire. ■

Athanasius was very much an Alexandrian, fiercely dedicated to his flock in that city, as well as to the things he held to be true. In his stained glass window at St. Athanasius Episcopal Church, Brunswick, Georgia, artist Jon Erickson encapsulates the saint's life. Athanasius stands on a Nile riverboat, recalling the many times he fled along that river. The triangular sail is a figure of the doctrine of the Trinity he so tenaciously upheld. The dove on his stole symbolizes the Holy Spirit, who inspired his teaching.

Mass exodus to the wilderness

Stories of Anthony's recurrent battles with the devil draw men to follow him, first as hermits, then in communities, and the monastic ideal spreads far

It was not easy to surprise, astonish or even mildly impress the citizenry of Alexandria; their appetite for thrill was distinctly jaded. Riots were commonplace there, big fires were a constant problem, hideous plague was not infrequent, public torture and death by crucifixion were regular spectacles. Alexandria had seen it all, again and again. Yet on this day, probably in the year 311, it was to see something definitely novel.

A crowd, mostly Christians, had assembled at the docks along the harbor known as the Kibotos. A river vessel from up the Nile, fitted with sails but now under oar, threaded its way among the triremes, galleys and feluccas riding at anchor, then eased gently toward the jetty. Standing serenely among the grain bags piled high upon it was a curious assembly of about a dozen men, skeletal but sinewy, skin burnt black, barefoot, dressed in ragged woolen cloaks. Keen-eyed and cheerful, they were chanting the words of a song:

> Behold how good and joyful a thing it is
> For brothers to dwell together in unity. . . .

Although few of the onlookers had seen them before, they recognized them as the strange individuals who had abandoned ordinary life for a solitary existence in that least hospitable of all habitats, the desert. There, they were said to live alone in barren caves, tombs, ancient ruins and hovels, subsisting on dates, dry bread and practically undrinkable water. They had no physical comforts, they never even washed themselves, and all the while they wrestled against demons that attacked them from within and without. Not everyone who tried it could endure this life; many a hopeful ascetic gave up and went home. As for those who triumphed, they were rarely seen again; they lived and died in the wilderness.

Very occasionally they left their hermitages, however, and came together to sing praises to God. "Behold how good and joyful" was their favorite chant, and if any of the Christians on the dock spoke Coptic, the language of backcountry Egypt, they would have recognized the opening verse of Psalm 133. Today, these eccentrics had broken their self-imposed exile and come to the great city for a very special reason. The worst persecution in the history of Christianity was under way, and they were here, they said, to comfort those who would suffer martyrdom, and if they should be so favored, to suffer martyrdom themselves.

The onlookers were particularly eager to greet one man, whose reputation had preceded him. "Anthony!

Anthony! Anthony!" they shouted when the vessel neared the dock, and one of the travelers raised his hand as though in a blessing. Anthony of the Desert, he was called. He was said to have lived ten years in an empty tomb, and twenty more walled in one room of an ancient fort. Thence he had emerged some five years ago to instruct and strengthen those who kept coming to the desert seeking to follow his example. And now he was here in Alexandria for all to see.

What the enthusiasts on the dock could scarcely realize, however, was that this man was developing a religious vocation, which over the next twelve hundred years, would be central to the worldwide propagation of Christianity. For Anthony of the Desert goes down in history as the first Christian monk, and the men with him were among his earliest followers. He was not the first to adopt a desert life of contemplation; others preceded him there. But it was he who first came to public attention, who enthralled the Christians of Alexandria, and who was to inspire their patriarch, Athanasius, to write the biography of Anthony.

Almost everything known about Anthony is based on Athanasius's vivid, but spare, *Life of Anthony*. Yet for untold generations, his story would inspire young people throughout the Christian world. It has captivated artists like Hieronymus Bosch, writers like Gustav Flaubert, and later biographers like Catholic academic and essayist Henri Queffélec, recipient of the French Academy's 1958 Grand Prize in Literature. In the introduction to his *Saint Anthony of the Desert*

(New York, 1954), Queffélec explains his aim: to write as accurate a book as possible, and where necessary, to offer his speculations as such.

Some of the vivid details of Anthony's momentous visit to Alexandria, for instance, although not the basic facts, fall into the latter category. The monks disembarked that day, and were soon confronted by the city's belligerent downtown hoodlums, who jeeringly surrounded them, and threatened to beat them to death. Could this, they wondered, be the martyrdom they coveted? It certainly seemed possible. Go ahead, cried the monks, by all means go ahead—they would truly be grateful! So the

In a scene substantially unchanged in two thousand years, a monk in search of a solitary place for prayer and contemplation climbs a hill in the parched desert of modern Jordan.

hoodlums abandoned them as crazies.

But the crowd was enraptured. The monks then marched to the jails in search of Christians imprisoned in the current Galerian persecution, in order to bow before them. Encouraging them to hold fast to the faith, even to death and the glory that lies beyond, the monks accompanied them to their executions. Afterwards, the monks gathered up their bodies like treasure and conducted their funerals in awestruck reverence, as befits the entry into paradise of great saints.

Anthony and his monks then proceeded to launch an evangelical mission in the city, attracting hundreds of admirers. They went everywhere—to the beauty parlors, the philosophic salons, the homes of high officials, the brothels. Although at first people were appalled by them, many came to recognize the spiritual emptiness of their own lives in contrast to the material poverty and spiritual wealth of these confidently joyous men. Officialdom, dismissing them at first as absurd, began to regard them as dangerous to the public peace. The crowds were growing too large, and there was talk of other young men, and even women, following these fellows back into the desert. So the order came down: They must leave the city.

Instead, writes Queffélec, Anthony did something he had never done before. He washed his woolen cloak, which turned it brilliant

The Monastery of St. Bishoi in Egypt enshrines this Coptic icon of Anthony the Great. A disciple of Macarius of Egypt, another pioneer of communal monasticism, Bishoi (or Paisius) also greatly admired Anthony. He took to the desert with his followers late in Anthony's life.

white. Then he stood calmly on one of Alexandria's main streets, surrounded by a hushed crowd, and waited for the prefect and guard to pass. That official, ordering his litter bearers to pause, stared at this white-cloaked man with the beatifically tranquil face, and apparently decided that no purpose would be served by arresting and executing him. It might even set off yet another riot. So he went on his way. Soon afterward, so did the monks, back to the desert—but they were drawn to it, not driven. There they knew they would always find God, and there was home.

The story of Anthony, as many Alexandrians knew, had begun some thirty years earlier, in the village church at Heracleopolis. One Sunday, he was powerfully affected by the appointed Scripture reading, Jesus' injunction to the rich young ruler in the nineteenth chapter of Matthew's Gospel: "If you want to be perfect, go, sell what you have and give to the poor, and you will have treasure in heaven; and come, follow me." Pondering deeply on this, Anthony concluded that he must take it literally.

By the standards of the grain-growing farmers of the Nile Delta, Anthony himself was rich, young, and the ruler of a sizable property. He was in his early twenties. His parents, both Christian, were dead, and he had inherited the estate they spent a lifetime creating, along with responsibility for their only other child, his younger sister. His father, typical of the rural Coptic Christians, distrusted the Greek culture of Alexandria, and had therefore safeguarded his son against book learning. Hence, Anthony could neither read nor write, but he had memorized vast passages of the Bible.

Persuaded that Jesus' words were directed squarely at him, he sold the farm, the house and the furniture, and placed his sister in the care of some holy women, friends of his family. Thus far, he was satisfied; he had obeyed the Lord's command. But now what? What should he do next? He recalled that an aged recluse, a holy man, lived nearby in the borderland between the Nile Delta and the desert. This individual, according to Athanasius's biography, agreed to take him on, and his instruction was explicit. In order to become one of Jesus' spiritual "athletes," Anthony must closely watch and imitate him, the holy hermit, as his mentor.

The recluse earned a meager living by weaving baskets and carpets, so Anthony did, too. When the old man sang psalms, Anthony sang along. Sometimes his mentor would set a time for their meal of bread and dates and then ignore it, or he would precede a meal with a seemingly endless prayer, or eat only half the meal. Anthony never protested, and always did likewise. The old man would wake up at intervals in the night to chant a psalm eight or nine times over; Anthony accompanied him. Each time, it seemed, he passed a sort of test. Finally, his master pronounced him an "athlete," and they parted. Anthony would use the same syllabus on those who followed him in the years to come.

For a time, he lived in a small hut he built in the garden of his former home, later moving to a more distant location. He did not beg. He made his mats and baskets, leaving his hut from time to time to sell them, to buy a supply of bread, and to give anything left over to the poor. Visiting the other ascetics in the vicinity of his village, he discovered they all had individual specialties. One labored long to achieve, and overcome, exhaustion. Another specialized in charity, another sought to be endlessly joyful, still another studied long into the night.

Anthony found himself trying to outdo them all, each in his individual pursuit, until he realized he was acting out of envy, and also falling into pride, the worst of sins. Then he began to hear voices, urging him to abandon his strange quest and return to his village, to serve Christ in more practical ways. As soon as he fought off these temptations, the attack shifted. Was he in fact refusing to go home because he was too proud to admit defeat? Would not capitulation represent true humility? These suggestions he also rejected.

Then his imagination took fire, and lust assailed him. He saw himself as a young soldier: brawling, drunken, abandoned to sensual pleasure. By fasting, prayer and meditation, he was able to defeat these attacks as well, bringing his imagination under control, but not before there appeared to him in his hut a little black boy, who described himself as the spirit of fornication. Recounting in seductive detail his past conquests, the boy wanted to

> He sold his house and farm and placed his sister in the care of holy women.

know whether Anthony realized what delights he was missing, but when Anthony laughed at him, the creature departed. After that, he was beset by wanderlust, tempting him out of his hut. No, he decided, the place for a hermit is his hermitage, and one more temptation was defeated.

Finally came the worst assault of all. Other recluses had warned him about this, describing it with horror, as a dread assault on the very citadel of the soul. In English it is called "acedia," from a Greek word meaning negligence or indifference. But the

hermits, and the monks who would follow them through the Middle Ages, understood acedia as a far more insidious thing than mere laziness. They experienced it as a dreary, restless, debilitating moodiness—an aimless spiritual torpor in which they could focus their minds neither on prayer nor on anything else.

Scores of medieval essays and manuals would be written on acedia, often linking it with the "midday demon" of Psalm 91:6. Later still, ranging far outside monasteries, it would be romantically featured in English novels of the eighteenth and nineteenth centuries as "melancholy." And in the twentieth, pernicious as ever, some would say it would acquire new credentials as a psychological condition or chemical imbalance, and would afflict millions under the name "depression."

The ancient Christians who regarded acedia as temptation and sin,

however, also realized it had physical as well as spiritual aspects, and prescribed physical as well as spiritual remedies. In the *Sayings of the Desert Fathers*, (a collection of anecdotes and aphorisms attributed to the monks and hermits of Egypt), the recommended antidotes include drinking more water, eating more bread, and taking long walks. And at worst, the fathers acknowledged, the sufferer might have to give up the ascetic life altogether, rather than permanently succumb to loss of faith in prayer and in God.

Anthony was not spared this experience either, of course, and he emerged with a profound conviction that the power of evil is not a blind force. On the contrary, he concluded, it is an intelligent entity, possessed of purposes and objectives—in fact, the being the Bible refers to as the devil. To contend against this entity was an integral part of his vocation as an

ascetic, so now he must seek out the devil and confront him.

Not far from his village a high ridge of hills separates the fertile Nile valley from the desert beyond. For thousands of years, back into the days of the pharaohs, the Egyptians had tunneled tombs in the side of such hills. Each was in effect a room, some tiny and others up to sixty or more feet square, depending on the wealth of the occupant. Tombs of the affluent often featured depictions of the gods: strange creatures with the bodies of men and the heads of dogs, serpents, bulls and jackals.

Somewhere within each lay the remains of its long-dead owner, reduced to dust or mummified and wrapped.[1] In the midst of the hills and among these tombs, Christians said, dwelt the devil and his legions. Anthony selected one for his abode, noting the remains of its ancient owner at the far end. He arranged to have bread delivered

1. The desert hermits were not discernibly disturbed by the macabre features of their habitations. A biography of Anthony by Henri Quefféléc recounts how a subsequent disciple, following Anthony's example and occupying another tomb, used the skull of its original occupant as a pillow.

periodically in exchange for his woven rugs and baskets. Then he settled in, praying, meditating and awaiting his adversary.

Eventually there came a night, he told Athanasius, when the devil arrived, accompanied by a troop of demons, who beat him savagely and left him for dead. The man bringing his bread, who happened to arrive next day, found him in a coma, loaded him on his donkey and brought him to the village. Believing him dead, the villagers kept vigil around him (his sister likely among them), but that night he awoke from the coma, and instantly besought his rescuer to return him to his tomb.

Despite the dark and his fears, the man reluctantly did so, while hyenas eerily cried and huge bats flew overhead. He deposited Anthony in his tomb, shut the door on him, and fled the forbidding place. Left alone, Anthony would recount to Athanasius, he cried, "Here I am! Here is Anthony! Come nearer, if thou art the devil!"

Then the ground outside began to tremble, he said. The door burst open, and ravening beasts swarmed into the room: leopards, scorpions, bears, lions and wolves. Bulls bellowed, snakes hissed, jaws snapped. The cacophony seemed to fill the world. Were they

trying to scare him away, to make him flee his tomb? Anthony stood his ground and made an astonishing discovery. Not one of the creatures touched him. He suffered terrible pains internally, but his skin was not so much as scratched. It was as though they were leashed and could not reach him. He gained courage. He began taunting them, inviting them to tear him to pieces, which seemed to enrage them to a further pitch of fury.

At last, the noise abruptly stopped. All was silent. The creatures vanished. The tomb seemed to open up, and a light more brilliant than the sun shone into it. Anthony realized that he was now in the presence of Jesus Christ. Why, he wondered, had his Lord not

come sooner? "I was there, Anthony," a voice seemed to say. "I was waiting to see your struggles. I saw them, and I will always be there to help you, and I will make your fame known to everyone." And so it was to be.

Precisely how long Anthony had lived in that tomb is not recorded, but it seems to have been at least ten years. Now he took the appearance of Jesus as a signal to move on. Crossing the Nile, he ascended the high hills on its right bank, traveled eastward, and entered the Arabian desert, where he found an abandoned Roman fort. He made his usual arrangements to have bread brought from time to time, says the account, and settled in one of the larger rooms, while a colony of snakes or some other desert reptiles moved out. Nearby, he found water. Compared to the tomb, it was a palace, and here he remained for the next twenty years.

However, he was never alone. Demons were still his constant assailants, Athanasius writes. They would shake the fort's disintegrating walls, wailing dolefully and yelling at him to get out. The desert, they said, belonged to them. He would laugh at them, singing hymns and psalms to taunt them, and there he stubbornly remained, weaving his mats and baskets, praying and communing with God, who protected him.

Increasingly, he had other visitors as well, human ones: the curious, the

devout, and those seeking to follow him. One such party, spending the night outside his cave and hearing hideous cries within, climbed a ladder to peer in through an opening. They saw only Anthony, sitting at rest. The noise, he assured them, was just the demons, which were indeed a great nuisance. But his guests need only bless themselves with the sign of the cross, and they would be safe. They did, and they were.

On another occasion, visitors heard Anthony chanting the words of Psalm 68 at the demons in the darkness of his cave: "Let God arise. Let his enemies be scattered. Let them that hate him flee before his face. As smoke vanishes, so let them vanish. As wax melts before the face of the fire, so let the sinners perish before the face of God." (This same chant, accompanied by the lighting of candles one to another throughout the congregation, ushers in Pascha [Easter] in the ancient Liturgy of the Orthodox Church.)

As the years passed, human visitors became ever more numerous. Many opted for the ascetic life and settled in the vicinity, consulting with Anthony whenever they could, and at length there came a day when he actually emerged from his refuge. For years, he had rarely been seen except through the openings in the walls, and people expected an emaciated form, shriveled, hollow-eyed and spectral. Instead, they beheld a vigorous man in his mid-fifties, lithe, muscular, fully alert, and persuaded that Christ now wanted him to counsel and befriend these crowds

of newcomers to the ascetic life.

He took to walking from one little lodging to another, and periodically traveled to the nearby Nile valley to heal the sick, and in particular to cleanse those believed to be devil-possessed. On one such visit, he met his sister, now a grown woman and a holy virgin, following in the footsteps of the elder brother she revered as a model servant of Christ. But periodically, he returned to his lodging in the fort, to regain in solitude the grace he could always find there.

As his fame and that of his fellow ascetics spread, Anthony was perceived as the champion of both the rural Copts and the urban Alexandrians. He became Egypt's mystic hero, the rich young ruler who (unlike his biblical counterpart) actually had sold everything and had given it to the poor, who had lived alone with God for thirty years, who had wrestled with demons and won.

Meanwhile, catastrophic events were occurring in Alexandria. The Diocletian persecution had burst upon the city, followed by the even more brutal regimes of Galerius, Daia and Licinius, whose predations against Christians had spread far up the Nile. (See earlier volume, *By This Sign*, chapter 4.) At some time during this ordeal, the message came to Anthony of the Desert: Go to Alexandria and help your suffering brethren. It was this appeal that brought him and the other "athletes of Jesus" into the city, riding atop the grain bags. A little later, with the death of Daia, the persecution

He was never alone. Wailing demons constantly assailed him and his fort.

in Alexandria abated.

By then, Anthony had established himself at his final abode. He had hitched a ride with an Arab caravan heading east into the true desert, carrying enough bread to stay alive for several months. Three days' journey from the nearest human settlement, the caravan left him at the foot of Mount Qolzum, within sight of the Red Sea. Nearby, he found to his delight an oasis with a cool, clear spring, and built there a hut of stones with a palm-leaf roof, but even here he also sought a hideaway. He scaled the mountain and found, high up on its slope, a crevice through the rock, two feet wide and ten high, leading into a spacious cave.

Sure enough, within months, his neighbors from his previous abode near the fort arrived, insisting that without him they felt bereft of spiritual sustenance. They too built huts, and began growing grain for their bread. Then came visitors, and Queffélec speculates that one of these was a young man named Athanasius, a youth with many earnest questions about God and the ascetic life to which he aspired. Instead, Athanasius would become both patriarch of Alexandria and defender before all the world of the Nicene Creed. But he and Anthony would form a powerful partnership, as the hermits and monks of the desert became Athanasius's unswerving friends and supporters. Meanwhile, Queffélec writes, he left Anthony a gift, a sheepskin cloak, which the hermit accepted and wore.

After Anthony's notable visit to Alexandria, the numbers of his emulators grew still greater. By scores, hundreds and finally thousands, men and women flocked to the wilderness to find God. At first, they sought him alone, as Anthony had, and later in desert communities up the Nile valley and into the bordering desert, whose members became known as monks. But Anthony, although he has been called the father of the monks, was not the father of the monasteries.

That distinction belongs to a contemporary, one Pachomius, who was born in the upper Nile district of Egypt. Drafted into the Roman army about the year 312, he probably served in the campaign of Licinius against Maximus. The generosity and care shown by Christians to Roman soldiers led to his

Living atop a column, Simeon Stylites attracted thousands to the base of his sixty-foot aerie. Some came to gawk, but many to gain from his wisdom or ask for his prayers—and others, as in the fifth-century relief (below) to honor him with incense. Eventually Simeon descended and founded a monastery (bottom), now in ruins in the Syrian wilderness. The base of his pillar can be seen between the arches.

conversion, and after his discharge, he resolved to pursue the life of a hermit, submitting himself to the guidance of an old man named Palaemon, with whom he worked and prayed night and day near the banks of the Nile.

Many others were doing the same in that vicinity, and Pachomius observed how they cherished solitude, but sometimes liked to come together for common meals or discussion of the pleasures and pains of their chosen life. He perceived that God was calling him to build a large dwelling where men could live in community, but where each would have a "cell" and could be alone with God. Thus was born the concept of monasticism.

> Throughout the Middle East, some monks became known for vicious violence.

In numbers that were positively alarming, the hermits poured into Pachomius's monastery at the deserted village of Tabennisi in the Thebaid, the upper Nile region whose capital is Thebes. Another factor, too, may have raised alarming possibilities. These hermits, by definition, were dedicated extremists, and extreme behavior can become deplorable as well as exemplary. For example, at Alexandria in particular, but throughout the Middle East, monks would shortly become almost as noted for vicious violence as pious prayer. (See chapter 7.)

Ex-soldier that he was, Pachomius realized that he must fashion a disciplined "rule of life" for his community. This he did, specifying lines of authority, hours for prayer and work and sleep, times when members could converse and times when they must keep silent, how conflicts between brothers were to be resolved, and so on. He decreed for them simple garb: a tunic and leather belt, with a short cloak and cowl for cold weather. (Later, in the west, distinctive robes would identify, by color and sometimes by cut, the house to which a monk belonged.) Eventually some members were ordained priest, to provide the brethren with the sacraments.

Not every eastern ascetic hastened to a monastery, of course. Many still preferred a strict solitary life, which could take curious (and extreme) forms. Such were the stylites, of whom the first and best known is Simeon Stylites (390–459). Simeon left a Syrian monastery to live atop successively higher pillars, reportedly beginning quite low and reaching sixty feet by the time he died. There he spent his hours in adoration of God, prayerful intercession, theological correspondence, and discourse with the many pilgrims down below, who were attracted by this novel austerity. Simeon became, says *The Oxford Dictionary of the Christian Church*, a notably effective evangelist and defender of Chalcedonian orthodoxy. He also inspired imitators.

But monasticism was the way of the future, and the "Rule of Pachomius" became the basis for regulations governing monasteries in both east and west. Meanwhile, so rapidly did the Tabennisi membership grow, that Pachomius had to start a second community and then a third. Before he died in 346, according to contemporary

accounts, he had opened ten, and two more for women, with a total of some seven thousand members.[2] Scores of similar institutions appeared throughout the Nile valley and adjoining drylands, and the movement spread to the Syrian desert as well. They operated farms to feed their members, manufactured wares for public sale, and some monks continued in the monastery the trades they had learned before they had joined. "How good and joyful a thing it is," they sang, "for brothers to dwell together in unity."

If the monastic phenomenon is virtually incomprehensible to the twenty-first-century mind, this is partly because of the greatly differing conditions of that time. It grew and spread during the decline of the imperial economy, when high taxes and extreme poverty had reduced many people to misery. Significantly, the word "anchorite," a synonym for hermit, originally meant simply "a person living apart," a situation that increasingly included peasants fleeing their homes to escape taxes. More

significant yet, when state persecution of Christians ended, the ascetic life was eagerly embraced by people who craved deep commitment to Jesus Christ as a substitute for martyrdom.

Meanwhile, Anthony's renown spread all the way to Constantinople. Even the emperor Constantine the Great had written him to seek spiritual advice, and thousands of ascetics regarded him as their spiritual father. When his death approached, monks from all over the desert came to wish him farewell. His last act, Queffélec writes, was to send Athanasius the sheepskin cloak, now in tatters— returning it, he explained, to its original owner. He asked the two monks who cared for him in his last years to hide his body, lest any seek to preserve it in the old Egyptian fashion. He died in 356 at Mount Qolzum, where the Coptic Monastery of St. Anthony stands to this day. Most historians agree he was 105 years old. ∎

Anthony inspired a host of others to follow him into the desert or its equivalent, be it located in Russia, Greece, Ireland, France or, as above, in the Judean wilderness. The monastery of St. George in Israel, built in crusader times, was located to benefit from the same qualities Anthony sought: harshness, quiet, solitude.

2. The word "monk" probably derives from the Greek *monachos* (a solitary) and the related word *monos* (alone, single). It generally signifies men living under vows of poverty, chastity and obedience in enclosed religious communities, who do not take up active outside ministries. Comparable women ascetics were referred to as "holy virgins" in Anthony's day; the later term "nun" derives from a Latin word meaning an elder.

In flight from the Huns pressing into their territory, the Visigoth chief Fritigern and his warriors cross the Danube to take refuge inside the frontier of imperial Rome. Two years later, the emperor Valens would pay—with his life—for granting them entrance. (Illustration from The History of France *by Francois Guizot, late-nineteenth century.)*

CHAPTER 3

A disaster foreshadows the last man to govern both east and west

With Valens's huge army demolished at Adrianople a desperate empire turns to the devout Theodosius, who affirms the creed and sustains the frontier

P ut that man in chains!" shouted Valens Augustus, emperor of the east. "And keep him there! I'll see he's properly punished when I return." Immediately, the soldiers seized the old monk where he stood, hurling his prophecy at the Arian emperor. "Give back the churches you grabbed from those who maintain the Nicene doctrines," he had cried, "and victory will be yours!"

A chill silence had fallen upon the crowd, writes the historian Sozomen, and people stared anxiously at Isaac the monk, a man known for great virtue and fearless holiness. The legion columns had halted. The drums had fallen silent. All had waited uneasily. Would Isaac now issue the other half, the dire corollary, of that prophecy? Would he dare say what would happen if the emperor *refused* to give back the churches? He would indeed. "Unless you restore the churches," came his ringing voice, "you will not be returning at all." The soldiers hustled the monk away, and the legions moved on, Valens at their head, drummers pounding the march.

Valens didn't need such an omen, delivered with prophetic authority in full view of the very people he sought so earnestly to impress. He didn't need it at all. It was the summer of 378. Nine years earlier, he had been an acclaimed hero.

The monk Isaac, fearless in his conviction, warns the emperor Valens that he will die in the coming battle "unless you restore the churches." The emperor, spurning this irritating prophet, orders the man dragged off and kept in chains.

He had thrashed the Visigoths, terrors of the frontier, to their knees. But led by their crafty chieftain Fritigern, they had risen again, spreading havoc for a full year across the northern provinces, and raiding right to the gate of Constantinople itself.

So Valens was no longer a hero. The brazen mobs of Constantinople had taken to jeering him in the streets as a spineless coward. But at last, he had decided, his army was sufficiently large and experienced to repeat the victory of 369. Cohort after cohort, it was marching through the capital city. He, Valens, was about to bring peace to his provinces, and incidentally show his cocky young nephew, the western emperor Gratian, what a really seasoned commander could do.

His troops did not have far to travel. Fritigern's Visigoths and some of their barbarian allies were about a week's march away, ranging near the city of Adrianople in Thrace, 140 miles to the west on the old highway, the Via Egnatia. At Adrianople, Valens's troops met up with a small force commanded by the experienced German general Richomer, sent by Gratian, who, much to Valens's disgust, was the senior emperor. Gratian himself was said to be on his way to join them with a substantial army. While Valens's men set up a fortified camp outside the walls of Adrianople, he pondered his options. Should he attack right away, or wait for Gratian?

His scouts reported that Fritigern's host was eight miles from the city. It was relatively small, probably no more than ten thousand fighting men, with the usual barbarian entourage of women, children, household baggage, captured slaves and loot. Valens had every reason for confidence. His army probably numbered thirty thousand. Why share the victory with Gratian? Richomer demurred. He wanted to wait for the western legions. But Valens's own chief general, Sebastianus, an old campaigner with a distinguished career, advised prompt action. That did it. On August 9, Valens resolved to attack immediately.

Then came the unexpected, a deputation from the enemy, headed by a minor Christian cleric. They had a proposition. If the emperor would give the Visigoths most of Thrace as a homeland, Fritigern would guarantee (with perhaps the aid of an occasional show of Roman might) to keep his countrymen law-abiding. It may have been a *bona fide* offer, notes the fourth-century historian Ammianus Marcellinus, but more probably Fritigern was buying time so that his scattered and various allies could assemble, something they were in fact doing.

Valens, suspicious and determined to fight anyway, refused to give an answer. The deputation departed, and the emperor marched his army to the point where they could see the Goth wagons drawn up in their customary *carrago*, their circular defense formation. In mid-morning, there again came emissaries from Fritigern, seeking a truce. Wavering the other way this time, Valens parleyed. He agreed to send the Goths a high-ranking hostage. Richomer volunteered to go.

Meanwhile, the Roman legions, having marched eight miles in full armor, were sweltering under the blazing August sun and choking on the smoke from burning crops, which the Goths had deliberately set afire.

Then, suddenly, there erupted shouts and a clash of arms near the front ranks. As Ammianus describes events, some Roman light cavalry skirted too close to a contingent of Goths, and fighting unexpectedly broke out. In the confusion, Valens's infantry charged without orders. Assuming the attack underway, half his cavalry drove forward as well, broke through the Goth lines, and then, to their horror, discovered themselves cut off.

At the same time, Fritigern's reinforcements began arriving, and plunged immediately into the fray. Contingents of Ostrogoths (or East Goths, ethnic cousins of the Visigoths, or West Goths), along with bands of allied Alan horsemen, charged down upon the Roman flanks. Fritigern's main force rushed in with a frontal attack.

"Our left wing had advanced actually up to the wagons," Ammianus recounts, "with the intent to push on still further if they were properly supported; but they

No coward, Valens tries to rally his troops against the Visigoths—in vain. That day, the emperor of the east would fall—and disappear forever—amidst the pain, smoke, dust and blood of the Battle of Adrianople: and with him would perish two-thirds of the eastern army. An illustration from Guizot's nineteenth-century History of France.

were deserted by the rest of the cavalry, and so pressed upon by the superior numbers of the enemy that they were overwhelmed and beaten down." Finally, amid thick clouds of dust and hideous cries, with the enemy pushing so hard against them that they could scarcely move, the infantrymen "at last began to despise death, and again took to their swords and slew all they encountered . . . then might you see the barbarian, his right hand cut off sword and all, or his side transfixed, and still, in the last gasp of life, casting round him defiant glances."

For hours, the two armies fought on, but exhaustion and confusion eventually began to tell on the Roman ranks. Their infantry first fell back, the barbarians hard upon them. Then the Romans appeared to panic. Some began to flee the scene. At last, the whole bulk of the Roman infantry broke and ran.

About then, Ammianus writes, the emperor Valens was seen riding frantically over heaps of corpses, seemingly abandoned even by his bodyguard. One of his

Valens rode frantically over heaps of corpses, abandoned even by his bodyguard. Somewhere in that melee, he vanished. Neither body nor imperial accoutrements were found.

generals, Trajanus, may have died in an attempt to save him. Another commander, Victor, tried to rally the reserve auxiliary units about the emperor, but failed. At length, "a dark and moonless night put an end to the irremediable disaster that cost the Roman state so dear." The Thracian plain was soaked in blood and covered with the dead and wounded, the roads choked by corpses of men and horses.

Somewhere in that horrific melee, Valens Augustus vanished. Some participants suggested that late in the day, he had been mortally wounded by an arrow and died on the spot, but neither body nor imperial accoutrements were ever found. Others claimed that a picked body of soldiers carried the wounded emperor to refuge in a small tower nearby, where they all perished when the barbarians set fire to it.

1. At the Battle of Cannae in 216 b.c., during the Second Punic War, the Romans faced their implacable enemy, the Carthaginian general Hannibal, near the village of Cannae (modern Monte di Canne) on the Aveidus River. The Battle of Adrianople would bear several similarities. First, the numbers of combatants involved were comparable. Second, in both encounters the enemy cavalry outflanked the Roman infantry, and the enemy foot soldiers consequently pressed so hard upon the foot soldiers that the Romans could scarcely wield their weapons. Third, a Roman army was virtually annihilated in both.

However that might be, with him there also perished that day two-thirds of the army of the eastern empire—some twenty thousand soldiers, and many of their best commanders. It was disaster indeed. To find a Roman defeat of comparable magnitude Ammianus had to reach back to Cannae, in 216 b.c., when the Carthaginians wiped out the last Roman army in Italy.[1]

Next morning the Visigoths launched a determined attack on Adrianople, where they correctly believed the imperial regalia and war chest had been stored. After great slaughter, they gave up, conclusively demonstrating that the barbarians could not take a walled city. "I do not fight stone walls," Fritigern bitterly concluded. Unconvinced, dissident bands of Goths proceeded to attempt an assault on the capital itself, and failed. Nevertheless, the eastern empire now lay leaderless, prostrate before the Visigoths—or any other invader.

Hearing the calamitous news, Gratian drew back to Sirmium, the fate of the whole empire now in his hands. He was only nineteen, but no neophyte.

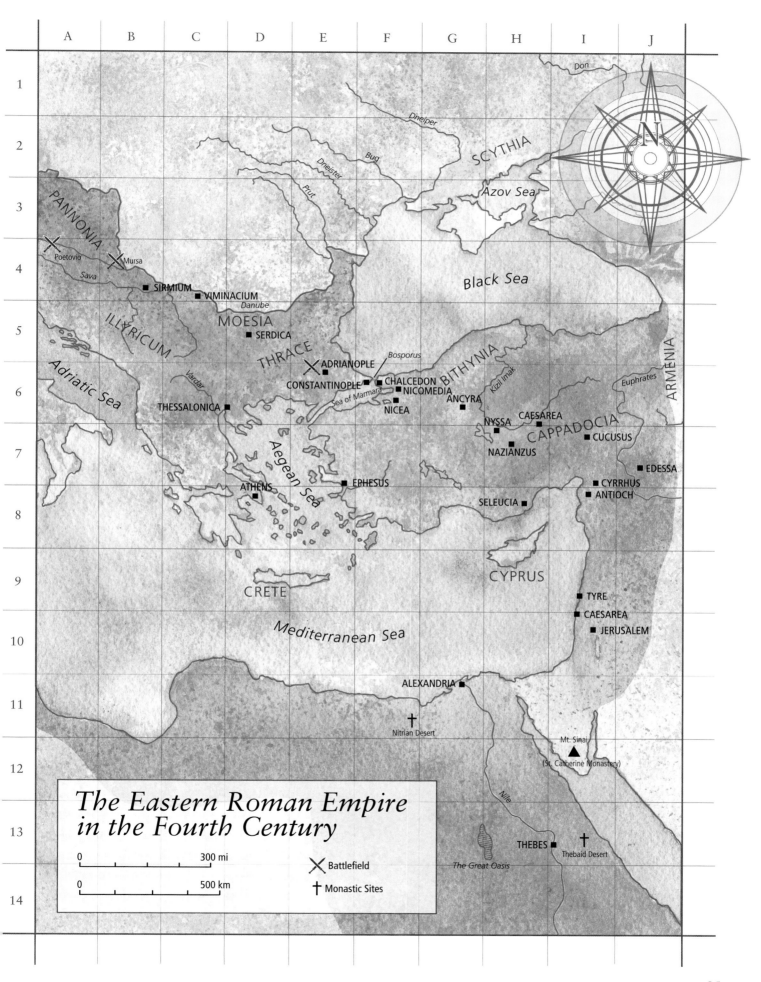

The Eastern Roman Empire in the Fourth Century

0		300 mi	✗ Battlefield
0		500 km	✝ Monastic Sites

His knapsack on his back, an infantryman of the eastern empire goes off to battle in this fifth-century mosaic at the imperial palace at Constantinople.

Since the age of eight, he had accompanied his father Valentinian I on campaign; in his mid-teens, he had commanded legions. Like much of the empire, he had watched uneasily ever since that April day two years before when Valens had, in effect, opened the dikes to the barbarian horde (as described in the closing pages of a previous volume in this series, *By This Sign*, chapter 10).

It was then that Fritigern's Visigoths, fleeing in their thousands from fearsome Hun invaders, reached the Danube frontier and pleaded for permission from the Roman guards to cross the river. Their panic was understandable. While the Goths were themselves ferocious enough, they paled beside the Hunnic horsemen who swept out of the Asian Steppes in the early 370s, demolished the considerable empire the Ostrogoths had established in Scythia (modern Ukraine), and were now at the backs of the Visigoths.

The Huns were not human, their terrorized victims said. They were thick, squat, crooked creatures without necks, who seemed to live on horseback, gnawing on herbs and raw meat, and who rode shrieking into battles they never lost. Some of the Visigoths had been driven into the Transylvanian Mountains, but most had followed Fritigern to the Danube River.

Valens, not knowing the fate awaiting him two years hence, had had good reason to allow them to enter. Otherwise, refugee Ostrogoths might combine with the Visigoths and actually invade, and he could divert no troops from his imperiled Persian front to meet a major Danube threat. Besides, barbarian groups had been admitted into the empire before, although on a smaller scale, and under careful military supervision. Now these Visigoths poured across the river like lava from a volcano. Ammianus describes the scene:

> They crossed the stream day and night, embarking in troops on board ships and rafts, and canoes made of the hollow trunks of trees, in which enterprise, as the Danube is the most difficult of rivers to navigate, and was at that time swollen with continual rains, a great many were drowned, who because they were too numerous for the vessels, tried to swim across, and in spite of all their exertions, were swept away by the stream.

Estimates vary, but some one hundred thousand Visigoths, far more than Valens probably expected, are thought to have crossed the Danube that day. Worse still, at least a fifth of them must have been warriors, most of whom retained their weapons. This was a crucial violation of the agreed-upon conditions which Lupicinus, the Roman *comes* (or count) of Thrace, was under orders to enforce. He had also been told to help the Visigoths cross the river, to immediately provision them from state supplies, and to allot them land. Instead, writes the fifth-century Greek historian Zosimus, Lupicinus's officials merely crossed the river to the Visigoth camps, "selected good-looking women, pursued mature boys for disgraceful purposes and seized slaves and farmers."

Ammianus portrays Lupicinus as corrupt to the core. He delayed moving the Visigoths to the promised settlements, and issued them such meager rations they came close to starvation. Then he allowed his minions to charge them exorbitant prices for almost inedible food, such as dog meat obtained by killing every hound for miles around.

The enraged warriors, reduced to selling their children as slaves to maintain bare existence, wanted to fight then and there, but Fritigern counseled patience. He had dealt with Rome before; it was not yet time to attack. The time came in the summer of 377, after Lupicinus finally decided to escort the Goths to their settlements. In a stop at Marcianople, fighting broke out with the escorting

He allowed his minions to charge exorbitant prices for almost inedible food. The enraged warriors, reduced to selling their children as slaves, wanted war there and then.

troops, while Lupicinus was entertaining the Visigothic leaders at a banquet (preparatory, Ammianus suspects, to having them murdered).

When Lupicinus, possibly drunk by then, was informed of the rebellion, he ordered his barbarian guests killed. Kill us, Fritigern warned him, and things will get a lot worse. Either credulous or cowed, Lupicinus let them go. Fritigern returned to his men and gave the signal for battle. Joyfully they slaughtered the hated Roman guards and began a rampage through the provinces, soon reinforced by the Ostrogoths, wandering Germans, and a few Hun tribes as well. Lupicinus fled the battle, and vanished from history, too. The Visigoths were hungry no more, and when they trounced Valens the following year at Adrianople, the whole Roman world seemed theirs for the taking.

Of all this, Gratian was painfully aware. He knew also that while he could manage the west, the death of Valens had left a huge void in the east. Who could fill it? He knew of only one possible candidate, a gifted officer named Flavius Theodosius, who had served under Gratian's father and had retired, still in his thirties, to his family estate in Spain. The imperial couriers dashed across Gaul and over the Pyrenees with Gratian's offer: supreme military command in the east, and by implication the imperial purple. Thus does Theodosius I enter history where he will be known as the last Roman emperor to rule both east and west.

Theodosius's acceptance of the offer was not a foregone conclusion. His father had served Valentinian I loyally and with distinction, but then had fallen victim to court intrigue and been executed. That was why the son retired early to their provincial estate, where he married Aelia Flacilla, daughter of a noble Spanish family; already they had produced two children, a daughter Pulcheria, and a son Arcadius.[2] He was apparently well-enough informed of court politics, however, to

2. Immediately following the death of Valentinian I, Count Flavius Theodosius, father of the future emperor, was executed on a trumped-up charge of treason—seemingly on imperial orders. Whether his cunning enemies used the imprimatur of Valens or Gratian or Valentinian II is not clear, write historians Stephen Williams and Gerard Friell in *Theodosius: The Empire at Bay*. Whatever the details, his son may have feared a similar fate for himself. Nor did his father's fate bode well for his own army advancement. The prudent course was to retire to his Spanish estates, which curiously enough had not been confiscated, as was usually the case when a high official fell into disgrace or disfavor.

conclude that his father's enemies were now either dead or departed. So he accepted, and beat back an invasion of Sarmatians on the Danube with such celerity that Gratian knew he had the right man. He made Theodosius augustus in the east.

Events swiftly vindicated the decision. With the whole lower Danube region now wide open to the barbarians, and communication cut off between Constantinople and Italy, Theodosius set up a temporary capital at Thessalonica on the Aegean, that could be easily supplied by sea. Then he started creating a new army out of the survivors of Adrianople, plus whatever barbarians he could recruit and whatever Roman citizens he could draft. Since he could not yet defend the countryside, he garrisoned the walled towns instead and used them as refugee centers, confident that Fritigern still would not "fight stone walls." As soon as his troops were ready for battle, he began harrying the Gothic marauders, conducting raids, as it were, on the raiders, so that their supplies began running short.

However, in 380, there came a frightening setback. Theodosius fell gravely ill, and was thought to be dying. Bishop Acholius of Thessalonica was summoned to baptize him, thus purging him of sin and preparing him for death. But in a few months the emperor recovered, thoroughly convinced that he had been saved by the grace of baptism, the prayers of his people and the favor of God. Furthermore, by fall, he had sufficient military control of the east to make a grand ceremonial entry into his true capital of Constantinople.

A major opportunity followed in January 381. Fritigern, an Arian Christian, had an old rival for the Visigothic leadership: Athanaric, the venerable high chief who had insisted on standing by his pagan gods and on fighting the Huns.[3] Aging and ill, Athanaric now led his weary and dwindling followers back out of Transylvania and besought Theodosius to accommodate them too, within the empire.

It was a chance for the kind of magnanimous gesture for which Theodosius would become noted, and his response must have pleased the old Goth not a little. The emperor rode out to greet him and conduct him as an honored guest into Constantinople, to gratifying effect. Athanaric was dazzled by its magnificent buildings, splendidly accoutred ceremonial troops, thronging populace and crowded harbor. "Truly the emperor of Rome is a god on earth," the old man declared, "and whoever lifts a hand against him is asking for death!" Scarcely ten days later he died (of natural causes, historians agree), and Theodosius gave him a full-scale royal funeral, inviting as many Visigoths as he could, and heading the procession himself.

Athanaric's warriors proved happy to fight for the Roman army rather than against it, and were especially helpful on the frontier, where in 381, another Hun

3. The rift in the Visigoth nation pre-dated the Hun menace, and Christianity seems to have been a definite factor. Athanaric, head chief until 376, was a militant pagan, who despised what he saw as an effete religion that would destroy his people by making them soft. Nor would he willingly have any dealings with Rome after the punishing treaty Valens imposed on the Visigoths in 369. The sub-chief Fritigern, on the other hand, almost certainly participated in several negotiations with Constantinople, and may have come early under the influence of Bishop Ulfila, the Apostle to the Visigoths. (See earlier volume, *By This Sign*, chapter 10.)

The story of Athanaric and Fritigern, incidentally, was carried for centuries in oral tradition, as far afield as Iceland.

Rallying his forces after the devastating loss at Adrianople, the new emperor Theodosius (center) established a temporary capital at Thessalonica. He fortified the city with massive walls (above), which still remain, and commissioned public buildings befitting a seat of imperial government. Near the public baths he constructed the massive Church of St. Demetrios. This church was rebuilt in 1917, but the crypt of Theodosius's basilica survives, together with remnants of the baths (far left).

onslaught had to be defeated. Meanwhile, Fritigern was still spreading havoc. The city of Nicopolis (near modern Pleven, Bulgaria) had fallen to him in 380, when its citizens simply gave up. Even some garrisoned towns were paying him "protection" money. Still, Fritigern was not leading an army but a people, numbering in the tens of thousands. To keep them consistently supplied through raiding was a daunting task, and Theodosius obviously knew this.

Probably, therefore, he was not surprised in the fall of 382 that Fritigern, hard-pressed, was ready to negotiate. He and Theodosius agreed that his Visigoths would occupy much of lower Moesia (modern Bulgaria), almost entirely under their own governance, creating in effect a sovereign Visigothic nation within the empire. They were to receive subsidies, and to fight for Rome when required, as separate units under their own leaders.

But no sooner was the east settled than calamity struck in the west, where Gratian had ruled for eight years in seemingly exemplary fashion. In 383, the legions in Britain conferred the title augustus upon their extremely popular general, Magnus Maximus. When Maximus confronted Gratian in Gaul, the bulk of Gratian's army deserted to the usurper. Fleeing south with just one cavalry detachment, Gratian was intercepted at Lyon by agents of Maximus, and was killed there on August 25, 383. He was twenty-four.

Maximus established his court at Trier, as Gratian had, and sent a brusque message to the guardians of Valentinian II at Milan (which had now superseded the city of Rome as administrative center for the empire of the west and location of the imperial court). Twelve-year-old Valentinian, Gratian's half brother and legitimate heir, Maximus instructed them, must be sent north right away to be under his personal tutelage.

Maximus's message to the eastern emperor was equally peremptory. Was it to be peace, or war? Neither one appealed to Theodosius. His eastern army was not yet ready for a major war, but neither was he willing to make peace with the usurper, nor grant official recognition to the killer of his co-emperor. So he dismissed Maximus's emissaries without an answer.

Meanwhile, Bishop Ambrose of Milan, guardian of the young Valentinian, did likewise. The bishop traveled to Trier to explain why the boy could not possibly make such a journey in winter, while troops loyal to Valentinian blocked Maximus's entry to Italy. Thus, for the next several years, an uneasy

The time had come, he decided, to make Nicene Christianity the state religion. Before he left Thessalonica, Theodosius issued the first of eighteen penal laws against heresy.

three-way truce was obtained. Maximus was effectively, if not officially, ruler of Britain and the Gallic provinces. Young Valentinian remained nominal ruler of Italy, the western Danube region and Africa. Theodosius continued to consolidate his control of the east.

Theodosius used this interval to formally terminate the Arian heresy within the empire. By now, Nicene Christianity predominated as far east as Macedonia. The time had come, he decided, to make it the state religion, despite the fact that Arians installed by Valens held most senior ecclesiastical offices in the east. Even before he left Thessalonica, Theodosius issued the first of eighteen penal laws against heresy. All his subjects, he ordered, were to embrace forthwith the Nicene Christian definition of the Holy Trinity, "the religion followed by Bishop Damasus [of Rome] and by Peter, bishop of Alexandria, a man of apostolic sanctity."

Arriving in Constantinople, the emperor informed the city's Arian bishop, Demophilus, that he must accept the Creed of Nicea. Demophilus declined, and peacefully departed. His flock, mostly Arian, was not so acquiescent, and Nicene clergy had to be installed in the capital's churches under armed guard. To succeed Demophilus, Theodosius chose Gregory of Nazianzus and personally accompanied him in solemn procession to the Church of the Apostles—along with a military guard to hold off the shouting, weeping mobs. Gregory, a gentle soul with little stomach for internal ecclesiastical conflict, ruefully described these proceedings, with himself shuffling along among

During the rebellion led by Magnus Maximus, London produced its last Roman coins. On the obverse was the likeness of the rebel leader himself, while the reverse depicts two emperors (east and west) jointly holding a globe—symbol of the empire, and thus of the civilized world.

the emperor and his soldiers, as more like the entry of a hostile army into a defeated city than any Christian ceremony.[4]

By the following spring, Christian bishops were still seriously at odds, however. The emperor, therefore, summoned them to a council in Constantinople (in May 381), to confront and resolve these persistent problems, and thus to complete the work of the Council of Nicea. Theodosius saw very clearly that if Christianity was to function as Rome's new state religion, its warring components must—by favor

4. Gregory became *de facto* archbishop of Constantinople when the emperor escorted him to his church, but could not assume the title until his appointment was later ratified by the Council of Constantinople—and then he resigned within a month. He was a brave man, however, if a pacific one. In the days of Arian ascendancy, writes Sozomen, the firmly anti-Arian Gregory of Nazianzus "presided over those who maintain the consubstantiality of the Holy Trinity" in Constantinople. They had to assemble for worship in a converted dwelling house, but "the power of God was there manifested by dreams, by visions and by miraculous cures of diverse diseases." This church was given the name Anastasia (Greek for "resurrection"), Sozomen adds, because "the Nicene doctrines which were, so to speak, buried beneath the heterodoxy at Constantinople, were here brought to light and maintained by Gregory."

In a detail from the silver missorium of Theodosius the Great, wrought in celebration of the tenth anniversary of his accession in 379, the emperor's son, Arcadius, sits enthroned and guarded by Germanic soldiers. (See page 106 for a full view of this artifact.)

or by force—be reconciled. Thus occurred what became known to Christian history as the Second Ecumenical Council.

Unlike the first, Nicea, or those that would follow, it was a relatively uncontroversial assemblage, attended by one hundred and fifty bishops committed to uphold Nicea, and thirty-six opposed to it. To such diminished numbers had Arianism dwindled.

In the sphere of church government, Theodosius's efforts proved similarly effective. As the emperor's Spanish co-religionists and other Nicene Christians were appointed to important secular positions, Arianism began to fade in

AMBROSIVS

Bishop Ambrose still gazes down on worshipers entering his basilica in Milan. This mosaic was created in the early fifth century, shortly after the death of the illustrious saint.

government circles and in the upper levels of Constantinople society. Among the populace, meanwhile, it was notably discouraged both by social disapproval and by a continuing barrage of anti-heresy laws. Before very long, Arianism would linger chiefly among the Germanic tribes and in the heavily Germanic army.

Some contemporary sources claim that Theodosius would have preferred persuasion to coercion, but that state necessity required him to use stern measures. He is also said to have disapproved of the mob action that constantly erupted against both heretical Christian sects and other religions. However, one undoubted effect of his legislation was to embolden zealots for Nicene Christianity to commit acts of extreme violence against their opponents in religion, frequently with ecclesiastical approval—and whether or not Theodosius approved, he hardly ever condemned them.

Against paganism, he proceeded much more gently at first. The Roman pantheon of gods and goddesses, revered as guarantors of the glory of the illustrious empire, was still too close to the hearts of the old Roman families for brutal extermination. Maintaining the city's various cults was an honor and responsibility they deeply cherished. These rituals were still the focus of Roman patriotism, and pagan mythology was practically inextricable from Greek and Latin culture. That pagan scholars should be excluded from the education of the young, for example, was in court circles unthinkable. The eloquent, classical, pagan philosopher Themistius, for example, was tutor to the emperor's elder son, Arcadius, and such arrangements would long continue.

Perhaps Theodosius hoped that Christianity would gradually and gently eclipse the Olympian gods. In any case, he seemed not to see them as a threat to the true faith. Their temple buildings, he suggested, should be put to other civic purposes, and their statues admired as works of art.

Before long, however, he began to legislate against paganism as well. Christian bishops emphatically disapproved the gentle approach; they generally wanted the old gods eradicated root and branch, both spiritually and physically. Anti-pagan laws were also popular among the common people, writes the historian W. H. C. Frend in *The Rise of Christianity* (Philadelphia, 1984) either on account of their fervent Christian faith, or because they "provided a pretext to pay off old scores against the former pagan ruling classes."

In the east, the great temples at Edessa and Apamea were totally demolished, the latter by troops under the command of the local governor, and quite possibly on the orders of Maternus Cynegius, praetorian prefect of the east and one of the Spanish Christians appointed by Theodosius. Many lesser temples were also destroyed by troops of fanatic monks and spontaneous mob action.

In the west, such tendencies were less pronounced, although they had one especially powerful advocate. No one was more determined to destroy paganism than Ambrose, bishop of Milan, a major influence upon both Gratian and Valentinian II. (See sidebar page 94.) In 381, almost certainly in obedience to Ambrose, Gratian had removed from the Senate in Rome the Altar of Victory with its winged statue, installed there by Augustus after the crucial Battle of Actium. Before it, since time out of mind, the senators had taken oaths and regularly offered libations and incense.[5]

Gratian further repudiated paganism by refusing to assume as emperor the title and sacramental role of *Pontifex Maximus*, high priest of the state cult, and by ending state grants for the vestal virgins and other pagan foundations. After Gratian's death, the greatly respected Quintus Aurelius Symmachus, prefect of Rome, eloquently petitioned Valentinian II to restore the Altar of Victory at least. How could mere humans, was his reasonable and dignified argument, completely comprehend the infinite truth of divinity? Surely all men need not come to that truth by the same road. The gods of the Romans had for centuries served them well. In a climactic finale, Symmachus spoke eloquently in the *persona* of Roma herself, the tutelary spirit of the city:

> Excellent princes, fathers of your country, respect my years to which these rites have brought me. Let me use the ancestral ceremonies, for I do not repent of them. Let me live after my own fashion, for I am free. This worship subdued the world to my laws. These sacred rites repelled Hannibal from the walls, and the Gauls from the Capitol. Have I survived so long that in my old age I should be blamed? . . . May there be a return to the religious policy that preserved the empire for your highness's divine parent, and furnished that blessed prince with lawful heirs!

Ambrose countered by warning Valentinian that any such action would bring excommunication upon him. He also composed a detailed and equally impassioned rebuttal, dealing point by point with Symmachus's arguments, for the boy emperor to deliver. This was accompanied by a powerful exhortation to that young person himself.

"Ambrose, bishop, to the most blessed prince and most Christian emperor Valentinian," he wrote. "Just as all men who live under Roman rule serve in the armies under you, the emperors and princes of the world, so too do you serve as soldiers of almighty God and of our holy faith. For there is no sureness of salvation unless everyone worships in truth the true God, that is, the God of the Christians, under whose sway are all things. For he alone is the true God, who is to be worshiped from the bottom of the heart, 'for the gods of the heathen,' as Scripture says, 'are devils.'"

Such hostile treatment of the old religion predisposed Symmachus and other Roman aristocrats toward the claims of Maximus, the usurper at Trier. When, after three years of *de facto* truce, Maximus made his first move, the result was dramatic. He proclaimed his infant son Victor as augustus, left the child at Trier, and forced open the mountain passes into Italy, perhaps with the help of some treachery. All resistance from the forces of Valentinian II collapsed instantly, and the emperor and his court fled to Thessalonica via Aquileia.

5. At the Battle of Actium in northern Greece in 31 B.C., Octavian, the future Augustus Caesar, completely routed the forces of his rival, Marc Anthony, and Anthony's ally, Cleopatra. This made Octavian undisputed master of the Roman world, and in thanksgiving he installed the winged statue and altar of the goddess of Victory in the Senate. There it stood in honor for almost four centuries, while Rome, as organized by Augustus Caesar, its first emperor, mightily prospered. Well might the pagan senator Symmachus plead before Gratian—although in vain—that the well-being of the empire depended upon the rites performed at Victory's altar.

The Basilica of Santa Maria del Piliero in Syracuse, Italy, built two centuries after the emperor Theodosius ordered that pagan temples be converted to churches, incorporated the classic columns of the fifth-century B.C. Temple of Athena.

By now, however, Theodosius's army was ready for Maximus. Augmented by the Hun and Alan cavalry, and supported by a fleet on the Adriatic, he moved west. It was a short war.[6] At a stubborn and bloody battle at Poetovio, in northwestern Illyricum, the forces of Maximus were badly beaten. He retreated to Aquileia, hoping to make a stand, but his army had disintegrated. On August 28, 388—five years and three days after the execution of Gratian—Maximus was beheaded. Theodosius also sent a small force to kill his son, Victor. He himself headed for Milan to exercise his talent for magnanimity and conciliation. He was resolved to remain for some time at Milan with his co-augustus, Valentinian II, now seventeen and still noted for weak character and inexperience.

Residence in Italy put Theodosius into close contact with Ambrose, who, with

The man who ruled the ruler

Whether Ambrose, the senator-bureaucrat-turned-bishop, was Theodosius's mentor or his autocrat, the emperor heeded him—as did most of the fourth-century church

On that momentous fall day in the year 374, the cathedral of the imperial city of Milan was packed with excited and determined Christians, there to elect a new bishop. Auxentius, the clever and influential Arian who had ruled the diocese for two decades, had died. A successor had to be chosen, and other bishops of the region, both orthodox Christian and Arian, were seated at the front of the church. Both parties were also well represented among the increasingly restive townspeople crowding into its nave, and both were determined to replace Auxentius with one of their own.

The debate soon turned ugly, and rioting seemed imminent until a stocky, black-bearded man with an authoritative manner pushed his way forward. He was Aurelius Ambrosius, governor of Aemilia-Liguria, whose headquarters were in Milan, and who had anticipated just such a disturbance. Ambrose was orthodox Christian, but well respected by Arians as well, and his words began to calm the mob. Just then, so the story goes, the shrill voice of a child cut through the tumult. "Ambrose bishop!" it cried, whereupon the entire crowd began chanting, "Let Ambrose be bishop," and would not be silenced.

Thus it was that Ambrose, a member of a senatorial family and a career bureaucrat, became a kind of instant bishop, to his own astonishment and chagrin. Not quite instant, of course. The other bishops had to formally acquiesce in this popular decision, and they did. Courtesy and prudence also dictated that Emperor Valentinian I be informed as well, and he, too, approved. In fact, writes the historian Rufinus of Aquileia, the emperor practically ordered Ambrose to accept.

The only disapproval seemingly came from the bishop-elect himself. "How I objected to my ordination!" he later wrote. Paulinus, another aristocratic Roman who became his longtime secretary and first biographer, says Ambrose made extraordinary attempts to evade it. Returning to his regular court, he uncharacteristically ordered witnesses tortured, hoping to disillusion his admirers. Undeterred, they just kept shouting: "Your sin be upon us." Inviting prostitutes to his house also failed to upset them. And when he tried to flee town by night, he somehow lost his way in the dark and found himself back at the city gate, whereupon his followers imprisoned him in his residence until the emperor's approval arrived.[1]

Twentieth-century detractors doubted Ambrose's fabled reluctance, and impugned his motives in finally accepting. But the job of a bishop in the contentious fourth century was no sinecure, not nearly as attractive as the government post Ambrose already held, and would also require him to remain single. In any case, his exemplary subsequent life favors the most obvious explanation for his change of heart: He sincerely believed that, like it or not, he was called by God.

His childhood tutor, Simplicianus, a scholar and presbyter and later a bishop himself, put him through a hasty preparation for baptism and consecration. (Many upper-class men in the fourth century remained catechumens because baptism carried with it so many obligations.) He was baptized on Sunday, November 30, 374, and consecrated bishop a week later. After that, writes the Italian historian Angelo Paredi in *Saint Ambrose: His Life and Times* (Notre Dame, Ind., 1964), one of his first official acts was to turn over most of his personal fortune to the church, to benefit the poor.

the backing of his large and vociferous Milan congregation, was accustomed to act as God's premier spokesman on earth to anyone, including emperors. As things turned out, the redoubtable bishop had no difficulty whipping Theodosius into line, tough campaigner though he was. The bishop had powerful weapons, chief among them the emperor's sensitive Christian conscience and his lively fear of eternal damnation.

Their first clash occurred when a disorderly band of monks (the holy men of the monasteries were accumulating an unholy reputation for such activity) robbed and burned down a Jewish synagogue at Callinicum on the Euphrates River. This was illegal, since Jews were specifically exempted from anti-heresy laws. The emperor

It was probably a substantial fortune. The Ambrosii were a minor but well-connected senatorial family. His father, who died when Ambrose was a boy, was administrator of the Praeterian Prefecture of the Gauls.[2] His widowed mother moved the family from Trier to Rome, where Ambrose and his older brother, Satyrus, received a typical Roman education in the masterpieces of Greek and Latin literature, as well as dialectic, rhetoric, and jurisprudence. It was a devout family, too. A great-aunt had been martyred under Diocletian, and Ambrose's sister Marcellina had been consecrated a virgin by Pope Liberius in 353.

He had been appointed governor about 370, an excellent apprenticeship for administering a diocese that covered most of northern Italy. As bishop, he used the church's accumulating wealth to alleviate need in a society where other succor was signally lacking. He made good use of ecclesiastical prerogatives to rescue individuals enmeshed in the legal system. And once, to ransom captives, he even proposed melting down church vessels.

He energetically promoted monasticism as well. So eloquently did he preach on the ideals of asceticism and virginity, it was said, that Milan's patrician families were reluctant to let their marriageable daughters listen to him. He also encouraged the finding and honoring of the bones of Christian martyrs, and on occasion he performed miracles. For example, Paulinus writes, when the graves of St. Nazarius and St. Celsus were found, Bishop Ambrose cured several people possessed by devils.[3]

Above all, however, Bishop Ambrose emerges from the pages of history as a devoted pastor of souls, whether the soul belonged to a fugitive or an emperor. His writings attest that this required much prayer, fasting and scriptural study. At first, he had to study especially hard to bring his Christian learning up to the level of his Latin classics. In this he succeeded so well as to be enshrined as a doctor (i.e., a preeminent teacher) of the church. So effective were his sermons that their fame drew to him, in 384, even that restless intellectual

This gilt statue of St. Ambrose, a man numbered among the highly revered "doctors" (theological fathers) of the western church along with Augustine, Jerome and Gregory the Great, stands beside the great throne of St. Peter's Basilica, Rome.

ordered the monks punished, and ordered the local bishop (who had urged them on) to pay for restoration of any stolen property and rebuilding the synagogue. But Ambrose severely admonished Theodosius. If he persisted in protecting Jews like this, God would no longer grant him victory, but would smite his armies just as the Jews had been smitten throughout their history.

The emperor had already decided to make the town, not the bishop, financially responsible, but Ambrose was not mollified. He regarded Jews as enemies of Christ, undeserving of legal protection, and in his view, their synagogue should not be replaced at all. Getting no satisfaction from Theodosius, the bishop took to his pulpit and stirred up his congregation. Finally, with Theodosius still stubborn,

The remains of Bishop Ambrose (above), director and nemesis of an emperor, were preserved in the Milan basilica that bears his name (right). Although the present church is largely of tenth-century construction, building began in the saint's lifetime, and parts of it date to his era.

Augustine, who three years later would accept baptism at Ambrose's hands. (See chapter 5 in this volume.)

Equally impressive were his dealings with the three emperors who followed Valentinian I. For the youthful Gratian, he was a spiritual father and an earthly inspiration. "The military eagles and the flight of birds no longer guide your armies," he told Gratian, "they march in the name of your Lord, Jesus Christ, and in the name of your loyalty to him!" When Gratian asked to be baptized, Ambrose wrote for his instruction a work he titled *On the Holy Spirit.* For Gratian's half brother, Valentinian II, the renowned bishop was a familiar childhood figure, a sometime protector and diplomatic courier, and a potent influence despite the antipathy of the boy's mother, who favored the Arian cause.

But Ambrose's most significant relationship was unquestionably with the emperor Theodosius, where he alternated between ecclesiastical autocrat and spiritual father as the situation demanded. They were well-matched: the despotic emperor contending with

his sensitive conscience; and the bishop contending, no doubt, with demons of his own. Then too, both were skillful negotiators when conciliation was called for, and both were implacable adversaries when they believed it was not.

As allies in the fight against Arianism, they pursued the eradication, in the west, of that persistent heresy. Nor did it expire gently, thanks in no small measure to Justina, second wife of Valentinian I, a forceful Sicilian of strong Arian convictions. After her husband's death, Justina filled the court at Milan with Arians and Arian sympathizers and vigorously promoted their cause. Her campaign to acquire Milan's Portian Basilica for Arian worship, for example, went on for almost a year.

In April 385, imperial tribunes demanded that Ambrose turn the basilica over to the emperor, since he owned everything anyhow. "Sacred things," replied the bishop, "are not subject to the power of the emperor." Later on, soldiers actually infiltrated a service at his church. On that occasion, as he later wrote to his sister, he decided to preach on the misfortunes of Job, blaming them largely on Job's wife. "Each man," he declaimed, clearly with Justina in mind, "is persecuted by some woman or other in proportion. As my merits

Ambrose announced that he would not again celebrate the holy Eucharist, the Lord's Supper, until the Callinicum reparation order was canceled. At that point, to the astonishment of his court, the emperor gave in.

Nevertheless, Theodosius's authority and popularity easily survived this public humiliation. On his triumphal entry to Rome in June 389, both plebeians and patricians were captivated by his courtesy, dignity, urbanity and generosity. He provided lavish public games. He paid personal visits to individual aristocrats. He presented to the assembled senators as future ruler his younger son, five-year-old Flavius Honorius. (Arcadius, his elder son, who already held the title augustus, remained at home in Constantinople.) He honored and promoted

are far less, the trials are heavier."

Paulinus records a less amicable exchange between Ambrose and Calligonus, the eunuch who held the important position of Provost of the Sacred Bedchamber to the young emperor. "You despise Valentinian while I am alive?" roared Calligonus, "I'll have your head!" Replied Ambrose: "God grant you do so—then I will suffer as befits a bishop, and you will act as befits a eunuch."

At length came a final confrontation on Palm Sunday in 386. This was an imperial ultimatum to Ambrose: Relinquish the basilica or leave Milan. When he refused to do either, soldiers blockaded him all night in the church, together with a large and agitated congregation. He reportedly reassured them by having them sing psalms and hymns, perhaps Christianity's first historically recorded extemporaneous hymn-sing.[4] In the end, the troops were inexplicably withdrawn, and no more was heard about expelling Bishop Ambrose.

The fighting bishop must equally be credited with furthering the demise of Roman paganism. He seems uniquely qualified for that job, embodying as he did the best of classic Roman morality, then in sad decline, and the fervor and faith of Christianity. His opposition to pagan ritual was absolutely uncompromising, perhaps because he so thoroughly understood its implications (and this although the leader of the pagan party, Symmachus, was actually a distant kinsman). But Ambrose maintained a clear distinction between pagan worship and Greek and Latin philosophy, whose truths he helped incorporate into the new Christian world.

All this he accomplished in an episcopate of just twenty-three years. Historian W. H. C. Frend, in *The Rise of Christianity* (Philadelphia, 1984), calls him "incomparably the most influential cleric in the west." As he lay ill in the spring of 397, the powerful general Stilicho, fearing that without Ambrose Italy was doomed, begged him to pray for longer life. "I have not lived among you in such a way that I would be ashamed to live longer," Ambrose replied, "but

neither do I fear to die, since we have a good Lord." He died that Good Friday, two years after his friend and adversary Theodosius, and was buried beneath the altar of his basilica.

Within fifty years, his city, and much of his country, would be demolished by barbarian invasion, but his church in the wider sense would survive, in large part due to his life and work. Bishop Ambrose, concludes Henri Daniel-Rops, in *The Church of Apostles and Martyrs* (London, 1960), embodied fourth-century Christianity in all its aspects. This enabled him to be "a man of transition, linked to the past, but whose action was creating the future." ■

1. The well-known account of Ambrose's election and consecration may seem far-fetched, but it was not unique. The laity still played a major role in episcopal elections in the west, especially disputed ones. Nor was it unusual for reluctant men to be forced into holy orders. A gang of admirers allegedly dragged Augustine weeping to his priestly ordination. Jerome's brother Paulinian had to be gagged to be ordained, and Cyprian of Carthage crawled through a lattice to escape from friends determined to make him a bishop.

2. Only one extraordinary manifestation is recorded of the infant Ambrose. As he slept outside in his cradle, writes Paulinus, a swarm of bees alighted on him, crawled in and out of his mouth, and finally took flight again. "If this child lives," predicted the governor of the Gauls, "he will surely be a great man."

3. A homelier miracle attributed to Ambrose involved a member of his congregation called Nicetius, who suffered from gout. As Nicetius approached the chalice one day, Ambrose inadvertently trod on his gouty foot, causing severe pain. Ambrose not only apologized to Nicetius, he cured the gout.

4. Bishop Ambrose made Milan a center of hymnody and antiphonal singing. An accomplished poet and composer, he is credited with many hymns, of which four are still included in the Roman office in the twenty-first century. The best-loved are probably *Aeterne rerum Conditor* (O Everlasting Architect) and *Splendor Paternae Gloriae* (O Thou the Father's Image Blest).

many prominent Roman pagans, whether or not they had flirted with Maximus.

Theodosius even forgave the apprehensive Symmachus, who had rashly delivered a public panegyric to the usurper. Furthermore, in the Senate ceremonies Theodosius so complacently accepted a markedly pagan endorsement, that Symmachus was emboldened to ask once again for reinstatement of the Altar of Victory. But the emperor would not go quite that far.

However, as emissary of the new religion, he appears to have achieved a monumental evangelistic success. The fourth-century Latin poet and hymn writer Aurelius Clemens Prudentius records that hundreds of members of Roman patrician families—the Probi, the Anicii, the Paulini, the Bassi and the Gracchi—sought baptism at the time of Theodosius's visit to the old capital. In *A History of the Church to A.D. 461*, historian B. J. Kidd attributes this to admiration for the emperor (and possibly also to "the recent influence of St. Jerome with the great ladies of the capital").

Nevertheless, in 390, there came an incident that imperiled the emperor's prestige and put him incontrovertibly into the power of Bishop Ambrose. In Thessalonica, where enthusiasm for the chariot races in the city's huge Hippodrome bordered on

More terrible still was Theodosius's infuriated reaction. Amid the usual throng assembled at the races, soldiers embarked on indiscriminate slaughter. The toll was put at 7,000.

hysteria, a particularly popular charioteer was imprisoned for a sexual crime, possibly homosexual rape. The historian Sozomen says the charioteer had "made a declaration of obscene passion" to the Germanic commander of Thessalonica's barbarian garrison. Other sources say the charioteer was enamored of one of the commander's more attractive slaves.

In any event, the citizenry demanded the release of their star. The commander, doubtless sharing the common barbarian contempt for what they called "the Greek vice," refused. A riot ensued, the rioters rampaging through the city, killing the commander and several other officers, and dragging their mutilated corpses through the streets. The citizenry, without doubt, had no great fondness for the barbarians, the same folk who not many years before had inflicted such terrible suffering upon the Roman towns.

More terrible still, however, was Theodosius's infuriated reaction. With neither investigation nor trial, he reportedly dispatched a new Gothic garrison to Thessalonica, with shocking instructions. When the usual throng assembled for the races, the soldiers at a given signal barred the gate and embarked on indiscriminate slaughter. Sozomen puts the death toll at seven thousand. In Theodosius's defense, it was said that he soon cooled off and countermanded his fatal order, but was too late to stop it. Moreover, it was so uncharacteristically ferocious, and its execution so speedy, that some saw in it the hand of Rufinus, the emperor's devious and unscrupulous master of offices.[7]

7. The notorious Rufinus, serving Theodosius as *Magister Officiorum*, would certainly have had a hand in dispatching Theodosius's countermanding clemency order to Thessalonica. Apologists for Theodosius's claim that Rufinus, who is described by Zosimus as notably lacking in scruple, deliberately delayed it. Rufinus was assassinated in 395, after the death of Theodosius.

A great fan of the races in the Hippodrome, Theodosius is shown ready to bestow the laurel wreath on the victor. This relief carving is from the base of a column that still stands on the site of what was the central "spine" of the racecourse at Constantinople.

Theodosius's defenders point to another incident three years earlier, when mobs in Antioch, protesting brutally heavy taxation, threatened to kill the governor. Further, they burned down the home of a leading citizen, and—most heinous of all—dragged through the streets the ceremonial bronze images of the imperial family. The enraged Theodosius ordered the mob leaders executed, and the city (third biggest in the empire) deprived of its civic status and rank and of its corn subsidy. Theaters, the circus, and baths were to be closed. But Antioch's venerable Bishop Flavian begged for mercy, and Theodosius relented. The imperial pardon was read on Palm Sunday. Jubilant citizens held banquets in the streets. Moreover, historian Kidd notes, here as in Rome the emperor's clemency was followed by many conversions to Christianity.

The Thessalonica massacre had quite the reverse effect. It shocked everyone, Christian and otherwise. Bishop Ambrose's response, while calmer than in the synagogue affair, since this was not a direct challenge to the church, was actually more devastating. He did not publicly challenge the emperor. Instead, he composed a private letter, not dictated to a secretary but written in his own hand, expressing his sorrow that a monarch so renowned for piety and mercy should have sinned so grievously. His violent temper had terribly betrayed him, Ambrose wrote, but there must be expiation. Like the biblical King David, Theodosius must truly and publicly repent before the Lord God—as an example to his horrified subjects and for the sake of his own soul.

Ambrose knew his man. Theodosius must have been suffering agonies of

Theodosius the Great spent many months doing penance on the cold marble floors of Milan's cathedral in contrition for ordering the massacre of thousands of his subjects at Thessalonica. The emperor's abject expressions of penitence finally earned his release when Bishop Ambrose ordered him to rise, restored him to communion with his fellow Christians, and allowed him once more to receive the Eucharist.

moral guilt and fear. That summer, he promulgated a law establishing a thirty-day lapse between any death sentence and its execution. If he meant this as expiation, however, it was not enough. Consulting Ambrose, he was no doubt reminded that the church regularly imposed public penance upon Christians guilty of adultery, idolatry or homicide.

And thus it happened that Flavius Theodosius Augustus, his imperial regalia cast aside and exchanged for the garb of a humble penitent, was for several months to be seen prostrate on the floor of the Milan cathedral, weeping over the massacre at Thessalonica and reciting Psalm 119:25: "My soul clings to the dust." At Christmas, the bishop finally readmitted him to the Eucharist.

The spectacle of the all-powerful emperor abasing himself before God Almighty must have been deeply edifying for Christians—but what pious pagans saw was their all-powerful emperor abasing himself before a bishop. It is also noteworthy, as Williams and Friell observe (*Theodosius: The Empire at Bay*, London, 1994), that Ambrose in his momentous letter never once mentioned such traditional Roman virtues as clemency, humanity, justice and prudence, or

even the bedrock principle that a ruler must be bound by his own laws. His admonition was phrased entirely in Judeo-Christian terms. What brought Theodosius to his knees was fear of the Lord God Almighty and hope in the compassion of Jesus Christ. Just how far, thoughtful Romans wondered, would the emperor take his unswerving conviction to his religion?

Very far, they soon discovered. Within six months, the pagan state ceremonies in the Senate at Rome were for the first time forbidden by law. So were the rites observed at Alexandria since time immemorial to ensure the annual rising of the Nile, and the consequent fertilization of the land. Nor must anyone approach a shrine, reverence the statue of a god, or enter a temple, said this law of 391. Apostasy from Christianity was to be punished by loss of testamentary rights, the civic right to bequeath or inherit property, or testify as a witness. This law, contends N. Q. King in *The Emperor Theodosius and the Establishment of Christianity* (London, 1960), clearly demonstrates that Theodosius, by then regarded Christianity and Roman citizenship as one and the same. Of course, it may also owe something to Bishop Ambrose's new and powerful hold over Theodosius. The timing seems significant.

Further attacks on temples naturally followed, and although many such buildings survived even this period, many did not. Among the casualties was the magnificent and many-columned Temple of Serapis in Alexandria, which housed the mammoth statue of this Graeco-Egyptian god, and also the Nile Cubit, the measure of the river's yearly rise. The destruction began with Christian versus pagan riots, as chronicled by the fourth-century Christian historian Rufinus of Aquileia (not to be confused with Rufinus, Theodosius's ill-reputed master of offices). The pagans ended up besieged inside the temple and holding Christian hostages, some of whom they killed. At that stage, says Rufinus, the emperor was consulted, and responded with a puzzling, oracular-style pronouncement. First, the slaughtered Christians were holy martyrs. Second, there should be no reprisal against the killers. Third, the cause of the trouble must be eliminated.

The Christians, perhaps taking this last as imperial approval to demolish the temple and its pagan images, set about doing so. Even with help from civic and military authorities, the massive temple resisted their best efforts. They fared better with the great statue, although at first they were afraid to attack it. When their bishop, Theophilus, bravely struck the first blow and suffered no untoward consequences, however, his flock finished the job. (Another version claims that a soldier struck the first blow.) They also looted or destroyed whatever precious objects they could find, and probably the books in the adjoining library as well. But the Nile reportedly rose as usual that year, presumably to the gratification of

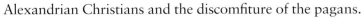

Alexandrian Christians and the discomfiture of the pagans.

Like the Christians before them, beleaguered pagans had by now resorted to meeting in their homes to propitiate the divinities of their ancestral faith, and in 392 Theodosius promulgated laws still more oppressive. These ordered the death penalty for any sort of divination or sacrifice, and confiscation of any house in which a pagan symbol—from an altar or a lamp to a votive wreath or garland—was found. Informers were encouraged. Such bans on private observation can hardly have been strictly enforced, it is thought, but they must have bitterly disappointed the group of Roman aristocrats still hopefully promoting a pagan revival.

The emperor, meanwhile, was much preoccupied with the balancing of power, loyalty and dynastic ambition in the governance of his sprawling empire. Valentinian II, at nineteen, was bitterly unhappy as puppet emperor at Milan. In Constantinople, fourteen-year-old Arcadius was at odds with his youthful stepmother, Galla, who had just borne Theodosius a baby daughter, Galla Placidia. Theodosius reached a solution that must have seemed reasonable enough at the time.

He dispatched Valentinian II to the north, to establish his own court at Trier and rule the Gallic provinces from there. Theodosius's accomplished and loyal Frankish general Arbogast, as Magister Militum for Valentinian, could be counted on to defend the Rhine frontier, besides essentially functioning as regent. The trusted pagan senator Nicomachus Flavianus was made responsible for Italy, Illyricum and Africa, as prefect of all three and directly responsible to Theodosius.

The eastern emperor thereupon ended his three-year sojourn in Italy and set out for Constantinople. In some respects, his plan for the west proved workable. Arbogast performed brilliantly in holding the northern frontier against the Franks, his own people, and efficiently governed the realm assigned to Valentinian II. But the general's dealings with the young augustus were much less satisfactory.

Perhaps his job as *de facto* regent was an impossible one. Valentinian, now twenty-one years old, moved his court from Trier to Vienne on the Rhone River, but became more and more discontented over his lack of real authority. He sorrowfully complained to Ambrose in Milan and to Theodosius in Constantinople that he felt like a prisoner. Exactly what happened next has been much disputed. In *Saint Ambrose, His Life and Times* (Oxford, 1935) however, historian Angelo Paredi suggests that matters came to a head in the spring of 392, because Arbogast killed a friend of the young emperor, causing Valentinian to publicly fire him. Arbogast tore up the dismissal, retorting that he took his orders from Theodosius.

Responding to the crisis, Bishop Ambrose hastened to Vienne to mediate

After a Christian mob tore down the Temple of Serapis at Alexandria, pagans feared the offended god (above) would prevent the Nile from rising in the annual flood that fertilized the fields. They watched in astonishment and some chagrin, as the Nilometer (top) depicted in a sixth-century mosaic, registered as usual, the rise of the waters.

between Valentinian and Arbogast. Before he arrived, on May 15, 392, the nominal emperor of the west was found hanged in his imperial apartments. Arbogast announced the death as suicide, proclaimed his own grief and his loyalty to the house of Theodosius, and sent the body to Milan for a state funeral. Was it indeed suicide? Some contemporaries suspected that Arbogast had had Valentinian murdered. The most telling argument against this theory, however, is that Valentinian's death was more a problem than an advantage to Arbogast, who as a barbarian could not himself aspire to the purple.[8]

Response from Constantinople was curiously slow in coming. Perhaps Theodosius was suspicious or uncertain. Perhaps, it has been alleged, he was

Just how far, the Romans wondered, would the emperor take his commitment to Christianity? They soon found out. Within six months, the Senate's pagan rites were for the first time banned.

simply so indolent about routine administration that he preferred to leave everything to the dubious Rufinus, then at the peak of his power in Constantinople.

For three months, Arbogast tried to carry on as usual, issuing coinage inscribed to Theodosius and Arcadius, but his position became increasingly precarious. In late August, he had Flavius Eugenius, a teacher of rhetoric and formerly chief secretary to Valentinian II, proclaimed emperor of the west. Eugenius was not an impressive choice, but as a Roman and a moderate Christian he was not unsuitable. He sent embassies to Constantinople; Theodosius dismissed them with ambiguous replies, and in January 393 proclaimed his younger son Honorius, then eight, augustus for the west.

With this act, Theodosius openly repudiated Eugenius as western emperor, yet seemingly took no further action either to avoid or prepare for the costly civil war that would surely follow. In April 394, Arbogast and Eugenius marched into Italy. The senators, smarting from Theodosius's last and toughest anti-pagan laws, welcomed Eugenius and petitioned him to reinstate the Altar of Victory. After a brief hesitation, he agreed.

When Eugenius also confirmed the appointment of the pagan Nicomachus Flavianus as prefect of Italy, pagan joy and optimism knew no bounds. Under the direction of Flavianus and his namesake son, the senatorial party sponsored the reopening and rededication of temples, along with restoration of ceremonies and festivals of every kind. The elder Flavianus himself drove the chariot, drawn by two lions, which carried Cybele's sacred effigy triumphantly through Rome. This time, Symmachus remained quietly in the background. He was delighted to marry his daughter to Nicomachus the younger, however, in a splendid ceremony invoking Jupiter and Cybele, the *Magna Mater* (Great Mother).

War was now inevitable, and a holy war at that. Theodosius readied his army, significantly bulked up by the Visigoth *federates*, who were now led by a new chief, Alaric. With fasting, prayer and processions, the churches made

8. The death of Valentinian II remains one of history's classic unsolved mysteries. Zosimus presents a rather implausible scenario whereby Arbogast decided to replace Valentinian with his friend Eugenius ("because of his great learning and dignity"), and then killed the young emperor in full public view. Other ancient historians theorized that Arbogast killed him, or had him killed, by strangulation or suffocation, then faked a suicide. Still others reserved judgment. Bishop Ambrose made no accusations, though in his funeral oration he speculated that word of his own trip north might have hastened Valentinian's death. But Ambrose also revealed that the young man had urgently asked to be baptized. This could indicate that he expected death, and in final despair over a futile and thwarted life, might have been contemplating suicide.

supplication to God for a timely victory. Theodosius consulted a holy hermit, John of Lycopolis, who told him his army would be victorious after much slaughter, but he himself would die in Italy. More daunting yet, on the eve of his departure, his beloved Galla died in childbirth along with their baby. The emperor allowed himself just one day to mourn. Then he prayed at the church that he had erected to St. John the Baptist, and set out with his army under the Christian banner.

Meanwhile, in Italy, the senators were invoking the gods of Rome with all due ceremony. Flavianus, consulting the sacred entrails, announced that the auguries were favorable. Moreover, 394 marked the beginning of another "Great Year" and a new epoch in human destiny.[9] Victory for Eugenius and Arbogast was certain, Flavianus proclaimed, as their army marched forth under the standards of Jupiter and Hercules Invictus. On his return, he vowed, he would draft monks as soldiers and turn churches into stables.

Theodosius soon had good cause to fear just such an outcome. When he reached the mountain passes west of Aquileia, he found Arbogast strongly entrenched near the river Frigidus, with his flanks adroitly protected, and

The next day, the outlook remained grim. But suddenly a mighty wind blew straight at the faces and shields of Arbogast's soldiers. Both the physical and psychological effects were devastating.

commanding the pass. On September 5, Theodosius launched a frontal attack and fought all day long to no advantage, while several thousand of the Goths who formed his vanguard were slain. That night, Arbogast's troops rested, confident of imminent victory. Theodosius is said to have spent it in fervent prayer, and to have been vouchsafed a heavenly visit (by two white-clad heavenly riders, thought to be St. John and St. Philip), the historian Theodoret says.

But next day the outlook remained grim as the stalemate continued—until suddenly there arose a mighty wind that blew straight against the faces and shields of Arbogast's soldiers, deflecting their javelin blows, forcing them backwards, throwing their enemies down upon them. The physical effects were devastating, the psychological effects worse still. The army of Eugenius and Arbogast broke. Eugenius was captured, executed, and his head impaled on a spear. Flavianus killed himself in the classic Roman fashion, falling on his sword. Arbogast, who initially escaped into the mountains, followed suit a few days later.

But what of this miraculous wind? There was, and is, a well-known phenomenon of the Adriatic region of Italy, called the Bora (from *boreas*, Greek for the north wind). It blows from the northeast when cold air crosses the mountains from the east and descends on the coast too rapidly to warm up; the change in barometric pressure produces gales as high as sixty miles per hour, sufficiently powerful to overturn a heavy vehicle. It is also true the Bora usually occurs in winter. However, whether or not its appearance on September 6, 394, was indeed miraculous, it could

9. The Roman concept of the Great Year came in part from their predecessors the Etruscans, explains Italian historian Marta Sordi in *Christians in the Roman Empire.* The concept was later modified by Pythagorean philosophy. Every nation was thought to have a fixed life span, which was divided into cycles (*saecula*). Each period, known as a Great Year, consisted of 365 ordinary years. The conclusion of a Great Year inaugurated the beginning of a new cycle, marked by signs and portents, which might be more blessed by the gods.

not fail to be seen as such by both sides. The Christian God had on that fateful day clearly defeated the heathen army and discredited their idols.

Soberly and thankfully, the emperor Theodosius again entered Italy. The usually implacable Ambrose met him at Aquileia, to kneel before him and ask clemency for the vanquished and for their sympathizers. The emperor raised the bishop to his feet and knelt in his turn, acknowledging the efficacy of Ambrose's prayers in the victory of the Frigidus River.

Another precedent occurred in storied Rome. The victory was celebrated with a Christian liturgy of solemn celebration, not the traditional procession through the triumphal arch. There, too, Theodosius proceeded to mete out amnesty all around. At the behest of Symmachus, he even exempted from penalty the old pagan's son-in-law, Nicomachus Flavianus the younger. The full range of anti-pagan laws was

As pagans in Rome prepare to meet the army of Theodosius, a priestess makes offering to Bacchus and Jupiter (right). Commissioned by the prominent pagan senator Symmachus for a family wedding, this marble panel is now in the Victoria and Alberta Museum, London. And while her augury assured the rebels victory, the Bora winds that still pound areas of Croatia (left) gave the victory instead to the imperial troops.

promptly reinstated, however, and demolition or conversion of temples resumed.

Paganism was in effect finished, although among the Italian aristocracy, pagan belief and tradition discreetly and stubbornly continued for some time. This was evidenced in such practices as posthumously erecting statues to notable pagan officials. Years after the Frigidus, the Christian court at Milan, letting bygones be very much bygone, even commissioned a statue honoring the stalwart Nicomachus Flavianus the elder.

In Gaul, Spain and the eastern empire, the upper classes were already for the most part Christian, and Italy eventually came around, especially after the church allowed mixed marriages in noble families. Devout Christian wives often converted stubbornly pagan husbands. "After three generations of opposition to their husbands' religion, the Roman *matronae* had their way," writes historian Frend. Pagan traditions became mere ghosts of the past, nostalgic wisps. That day at the Frigidus, when the Bora blew away the proud Olympian standards of Arbogast's army, it also blew away the last faint hope of a pagan revival.

Two notable commissions of Theodosius diverge greatly in scale: the massive Golden Gate in the walls of Constantinople (left); and the thirty-inch silver platter known as the "Missorium of Theodosius" (right). The forty-foot high Gate flanked by two glistening marble towers above the Sea of Marmara, used for the ceremonial entry of esteemed state visitors and victorious generals, got its name from the heavy gold plating that adorned it until the collapse and looting of the empire. The missorium, fashioned for the tenth anniversary of Theodosius's rise to power, is a curious mix of Christian and pagan themes, considering that it was intended for church use. The emperor, with a halo indicating his exalted office, is flanked by the co-emperors Valentinian II and Arcadius. All have eyes cast heavenward, while below them, the goddess of fertility cavorts with her attendants. The missorium is in the Royal Academy of History, Madrid.

To the victorious emperor Theodosius, the future must have looked quite satisfactory. Having eliminated the latest imperial challenger, he was again sole ruler of the entire empire. His viceroy in the east was the prefect Rufinus, his longtime colleague. Rufinus had by now become preoccupied with acquiring holy relics and building a monastery, complete with imported Egyptian monks, but he certainly had not lost his talent for politics and power.

In the west, Theodosius could count on his supreme military commander, Flavius Stilicho. Ten years earlier, he had allowed Stilicho to marry his beloved niece (and adopted daughter) Serena, thus incorporating the half-Vandal, half-Roman general into the imperial family. He had also taken thought for the succession, entrusting to Stilicho the guardianship of both his young heirs (or so it would later be averred), confident that the respected general would honor this trust, literally to the death.

But that necessity, Theodosius must have thought, was still in the future. He himself, after all, was not yet fifty. He may have hoped to use this relatively peaceful period to stabilize his immense domain. Perhaps he might even have turned his attention to the alarming state of taxation and trade in the west, and to the pitiable poverty of most of his western subjects. It is quite possible, of course, that Theodosius actually had no real notion how bad things were. A late fourth-century Roman emperor, writes British historian F. Homes Dudden in *The Life and Times of St. Ambrose* (Oxford, 1935) was so divorced from anything resembling the life of ordinary people as to be completely dependent for information on the swarm of ministers and courtiers who made up his extensive court.

Whatever the emperor's intentions, he was to have no opportunity to fulfill them. Ailing for some time, he was stricken that winter with vascular disease. Anxious courtiers summoned Honorius from Constantinople. Theodosius was well enough to preside only briefly at the customary games held to celebrate their meeting; then his son had to take his place. The man who would be known to history as Theodosius the Great died on January 17, 395.

As the body lay in state at the cathedral in Milan, Bishop Ambrose delivered the funeral oration. He dwelt little on the emperor's military triumphs, impressive though they were, and much on his lifelong service to Jesus Christ. Even the great victory over Eugenius at the Frigidus, he proclaimed, demonstrated that it is faith, far more than military might, which brings victory. The pious emperor had prayed, and God sent the wind to scatter his enemies.

"He is victorious who hopes for the Grace of God, not he who presumes on his own strength," declared Ambrose, who would himself follow the emperor in

The church hasn't seen fit to canonize Theodosius, who never evinced pretensions to sainthood anyway. But his endeavors on behalf of the Christian faith would prove lasting indeed.

death two years later. "Theodosius is now in heaven with the crown of saintliness, and he is now a true king in the company of our Lord Jesus Christ."

The church has never seen fit to canonize Theodosius, who never did evince pretensions to sainthood. But he did honestly seem to try to act on his faith, and often succeeded, and occasionally suffered for it. Ambrose's funeral oration would turn out to be right about his wayward disciple and sometime antagonist. The lasting legacy of Theodosius lay not so much in his efforts to safeguard the empire, for half the empire was already at the point of death. His endeavors for the Christian faith, however, would prove lasting indeed.

Unlike his predecessors from Constantine onward, Theodosius never did try to bend the church to his own will (except to unite it). Rather, he tried to serve both church and state to their mutual benefit. Nor was he a Diocletian in reverse. Apart from the catastrophe at Thessalonica, he shed relatively little blood, either heretical or pagan. By the standards of his time, his use of force was unusually minimal. Theodosian legislation, observes historian King, was generally more ferocious than its enforcement, and even in enforcement the seeming intent was to intimidate people into conversion, or at least thwart them in what he saw as their errors, rather than kill them.

Finally, for better or for worse, Theodosius founded the orthodox Christian nation by effectively integrating Christian church and Roman state. "Give unto Caesar the things that are Caesar's," Jesus had said, "and unto God the things that are God's." Theodosius sought to give Caesar himself unto God. To what degree he succeeded, history would soon begin to disclose. Meanwhile, other events superseded the ecclesiastical. The unimaginable was about to occur. ■

The Golden Mouth is silenced

Greatest preacher of the early church, John Chrysostom was a clear choice for archbishop, until he defied officialdom and was hounded to death

The invitation seemed innocent enough. Would he, the man called John Chrysostom, meet a certain Count Asterius at a martyr's shrine outside the walls of Antioch? John knew, of course, that the imperial government must appoint a new patriarch of Constantinople. He knew, too, that his reputation as a writer and preacher made him a candidate for the job. But who was this Asterius? He could not connect that name with the search for a new patriarch.

So he met the count and accepted an invitation into his carriage. Suddenly, the doors were closed and the carriage lurched toward Constantinople. He had been kidnapped. His orders were, said the count, that he bring John to the capital, where the emperor had arranged his consecration as patriarch of Constantinople, successor to Nectarius, who had died in office.

John Chrysostom took his eventful carriage ride in the spring of 398. In the ensuing nine years, the most renowned preacher in the Christian world would fiercely collide with an imperial empress and her irresolute husband, and die miserably as he was being dragged, sick, staggering and exhausted, into a wilderness exile.

Chrysostom was no stranger to theological controversy. Martyrs' shrines ringed his native city of Antioch, and the Arian controversy had raged there, as it had all over the empire, from the Council of Nicea in 325 to Arianism's decisive defeat at the Council of Constantinople in 381. This was the troubled world in which he had grown up. His mother, a staunchly Trinitarian Christian, widowed at age twenty, had raised her children in Nicene Christianity and sent John to Antioch's best secular schools. There, Libanius, the era's greatest pagan philosopher, taught him to write eloquently and schooled him in classical thought.

However, his mother's influence prevailed over that of his schoolmaster, and John seems never to have even contemplated a secular career. "God, what women these Christians have," lamented the disappointed Libanius. John studied law and rhetoric as a curriculum requirement, but only, says one biographer, "for the service of the Word of God." Similarly, he read pagan literature, but only in order to fashion a model for a Christian philosophy. At about eighteen, he met the revered Meletius, patriarch of Antioch, a man so holy that even before he died, parents named their children for him. An instant rapport developed between the two, and they fell spontaneously into the roles of teacher and disciple.

In his mid-twenties, John was baptized, and soon thereafter joined one of Antioch's many monasteries. Then he retired to a cave near the city where he attempted the life of a hermit. When severe stomach problems forced him to abandon that plan, he returned to Antioch and became a deacon. Five years later, in 386, the patriarch Flavian, Meletius's successor, ordained him a priest, and he established the daily routine of prayer, worship and ministry to the sick and helpless that he would observe for the rest of his life.

But he was chiefly distinguished as a preacher. So powerful were his sermons that people would laugh, weep or applaud. When published, they gained a vast circulation, and the more than sixteen centuries since they were written have not diminished their readability. Significantly, however, they broach none of the great doctrinal debates of his age. Chrysostom refuted no heresies, brokered no deals among rival theologians. He wrote as he believed, putting the case for Christ with such clarity and emotive power that even hardened skeptics sometimes found them irresistible.

Wherever possible, he took the Bible at face value. In his view, what God said was what God meant, and what the church said was what the church meant. He talked directly to his audience, asking them questions, reminding them of unfulfilled past promises, congratulating them on current achievements, urging them to resist temptations, to get back on their feet after stumbling, and to remember that Christ loves as well as judges them.

The sermons are not essays; they are outpourings of his spirit, unstructured but translucent, poetry in the form of prose. His contemporaries called him *Khrisostom* or "Golden Mouth," a tribute to his enduring eloquence, borne witness to in the prayer books and devotional literature of Christians through the ages. More of his works have survived than those of any other early Christian author.

Because of his importance as a preacher and liturgist, icons of John Chrysostom, such as this fifteenth-century Russian example, were frequently placed on the sanctuary doors of Orthodox churches.

Small wonder therefore, that he was sought as the next patriarch of Constantinople. Officialdom knew that Antioch would not lightly part with him; hence his furtive removal to the capital. At first, all went well there. He quickly preached his way into the affections of his new flock. The empress Eudoxia, daughter of a barbarian general and manipulator of her unresisting husband, the emperor Arcadius, became an early enthusiast. Even Theophilus, the patriarch of Alexandria, who had advanced another candidate for the patriarchate in the capital, signaled his support by consecrating the new prelate before hurrying back to Egypt. Finally, Eutropius, the emperor's first minister, had not only persuaded Arcadius to promote Chrysostom, but had organized the kidnapping.

This acceptance in high places, however, was short-lived. His predecessor, Nectarius, had been

pleasant, easygoing, always careful to say the right things, and appreciated the value of good cheer. Chrysostom was different. Prevented only by a weak stomach from a lifetime commitment to asceticism, he introduced deep cuts in the episcopal entertainment budget, stopped throwing banquets, dined alone on a spartan diet, and sold off all unnecessary palace furnishings, using the money to finance a hospital.

This did not meet with universal enthusiasm. His popularity waned among Nectarius's old dining companions and also among the clergy, particularly when he condemned their predilection for avarice and luxury. Moreover, he ended a practice that allowed priests to take in consecrated virgins as housekeepers. Then, adding injury to insult, he defrocked two deacons, one for murder, the other for adultery. He ordered the monks to stop wandering the streets and return to their monasteries. He attacked the problem of scandalously living widows by requiring them either to remarry or observe appropriate standards of chastity and decorum.

In short, notes his biographer Palladius, he began "by sweeping the stairs from the top." At the top was the empress Eudoxia. She and her female courtiers took offense at his constant harping on the sinfulness of obsessive interest in dress and adornment. And after Eudoxia had allegedly used questionable means to acquire for herself a choice vineyard, Chrysostom saw fit to remind the faithful how Elijah had rebuked Jezebel for contriving the murder of Naboth, simply because Naboth refused to sell *his* vineyard to her husband, King Ahab (1 Kings 21).

CHRYSOSTOM ON FORTITUDE

Many are the waves and severe is the storm, but we do not fear drowning, for we stand upon a rock. Let the waves rise up! Let the sea rage! Tell me, what do we fear? I do not fear poverty, I desire not riches, I am not afraid of death, and I do not seek to live but for your advantage.

The bishop's defenders, far more numerous among the people than in the court, no doubt pointed out that admonishing sinners is a spiritual work of mercy, which all Christians are obliged to perform. After all, the bishop was a pastor whose job it was to oversee the moral and spiritual lives of his flock. Those he criticized, however, saw him as merely arrogant, tactless and self-righteous.

In 399, an ironic event pitted Chrysostom against the palace. Eutropius, the emperor's erstwhile chief minister, who had once vigorously opposed the right of the church to provide sanctuary against the state, had fallen sharply from imperial favor, probably through gambling debt. He himself took sanctuary in Chrysostom's cathedral, the Church of the Holy Wisdom, known as the "Great Church" of the capital. "And so," declaimed the preacher, a cringing Eutropius pressed to a pillar behind him, "the Hippodrome having exhausted your wealth has whetted the sword against you. But the church, which has experienced your untimely wrath, is hurrying in every direction to pluck you out of the net." In the end, Eutropius broke sanctuary himself, was arrested, exiled and murdered. Chrysostom meanwhile, was accused of rendering unto God the things that were caesar's.

Thus far, Chrysostom's foes had been confined to the imperial circle. In 401, he made a move that created a lethal ecclesiastical enemy. Exercising an authority conferred by the First Council of Constantinople in 381, that put all the eastern bishops under the patriarchate of Constantinople, Chrysostom appointed a new bishop for Ephesus. He also deposed, for taking bribes, six bishops from around that city. Alexandria took instant umbrage. As second city of the empire, it was keenly resentful of the powers being acquired by (as they saw it) upstart Constantinople. Theophilus, its patriarch, perceived the Ephesus episode as a warning. If Constantinople could unilaterally hire and fire at Ephesus, then Alexandria might be next. So Theophilus set out to destroy Chrysostom. It didn't take him long.

> In 401, a lethal ecclesiastical enemy joined his many imperial foes.

He had another grievance. Many Egyptian monks had developed an avid devotion to Origen, the third-century Alexandrian theologian. (See earlier volume, *A Pinch of Incense*, chapters 7 and 8.) They singled out, in particular, what they took to be Origen's teaching that Jesus Christ had no genuinely human existence, and that Jesus must therefore be regarded as a kind of ghost. When this was challenged, four monks acting as spokesmen for the "Origenists," and known from their height as "the Tall Brothers," took their case to their patriarch, Theophilus. He denounced them as heretics, so the four took their cause to Constantinople. Chrysostom refused to rule on it and referred the case back to Theophilus, meanwhile providing shelter and food for the four. To Theophilus, this amounted to interference by Constantinople in

Alexandria's affairs. Chrysostom was harboring heretics, he said.

Theophilus, along with supporting bishops from Egypt and others he had recruited along the way, descended upon Constantinople in 403, where they planned a synod that would depose Chrysostom. He soon won over the empress, still smarting from Chrysostom's sermonizing and further angered at Chrysostom's invective against three of her friends, all widows, and therefore all targets of his remarriage-or-celibacy dictum.

Theophilus assembled his supporters at a villa outside Constantinople called The Oak, in fact the home of a friend of the empress. There they drew up a list of twenty-nine accusations against Chrysostom. Some of the charges seem absurd: He assaulted people physically. He deposed bishops and appointed them without proper inquiry. He wasted ecclesiastical property. He ate lozenges in church after taking Holy Communion. He dined alone and gorged "like a cyclops."

The synod summoned Chrysostom to answer these in person. Not wishing to be judged by his enemies, he sent messengers bearing word that he refused to recognize the Synod of the Oak. The bishops took the rebuff out on the messengers: one was beaten, one had his clothes torn off, one was heaped with the chains they had planned to

heap on Chrysostom. Nevertheless, the emperor Arcadius ordered Chrysostom to appear. When he still refused, the synod condemned him, not on the schedule of charges, but for defying the synod's authority. They also charged him with treason (i.e., criticizing the empress) but referred this to the emperor as a civil offense. Arcadius ordered him deposed and exiled.

When crowds assembled to prevent his arrest, Chrysostom calmed them, urged them to not resist, gave himself up, and was quietly removed from the city aboard a vessel by night. Theophilus attempted a triumphal entry into the city the following day. He was chased out of town by a mob, which then clashed with his Egyptian sailors. Meanwhile in the palace, some unknown but serious mishap occurred. It is usually assumed that the superstitious Eudoxia miscarried. She pleaded with her husband to bring Chrysostom back. An imperial courier promptly tracked him down with a message from the empress. "Your Holiness must not suppose I was privy to what was done," she said. "I am innocent of your blood. This conspiracy is the work of depraved and wicked men. I remember that my children were baptized by you. God, whom I serve, is witness of my tears."

So Chrysostom sailed home. As he approached the city, he found the harbor and the Bosporus ablaze with the lights of welcoming vessels, the shore lined with the torches of people cheering his return. But he did not return to his church. Instead he went to a home that the empress had provided. He knew that a synod at Antioch, actually an Arian synod, had some time ago passed a rule that no

CHRYSOSTOM ON CHRISTIAN CHARITY

Nothing is colder than a Christian who does not work for the salvation of others. Do you wish to honor the body of Christ? Do not neglect him when he is naked. Do not honor him here inside with silken robes, but neglect him outside as he is perishing of cold and nakedness. God has no need of golden chalices but of golden souls.

deposed bishop could return to his church unless another synod authorized him to do so. None had. Crowd approval, even imperial approval, did not count.

But to the crowd such ecclesiastical niceties meant nothing. They seized their beloved bishop, carried him bodily into the Great Church and deposited him on the episcopal throne. As events would soon prove, however, they had done him no favor. Meanwhile, the Constantinople crowd clashed in the streets with Theophilus's supporters, threatening to throw Theophilus and company into the Bosporus. They hurriedly left for home.

Peace prevailed for two months. Then, in October 403, another incident terminated it. The Great Church stood beside a big square near the center of the city, across from the Senate House. In the midst of the square was a rostrum, used for public speaking. Here the empress Eudoxia had the city erect a large column, topped by a silver statue of herself. As was customary, festivities accompanied the unveiling of the statue. The cheering interfered with a service in the church. A sermon attributed to John, one that some historians think spurious, describes the consequence. Alluding to the biblical story of the execution of John the Baptist (Mark 6:21–26), the bishop declared from the pulpit: "Again, Herodias storms and runs wild. Again she dances. Again she asks for John's head on a platter." Whether he said it or he did not, the story got back to the empress and the war was on again.

Spurred by Eudoxia, bishops opposed to Chrysostom began demanding a new synod to try him on a new charge, namely that he had occupied his church without first being cleared by another synod. Again the emperor vacillated. Two attempts on Chrysostom's life failed. Then, at Christmas 404, came the first certain sign that the emperor was turning decisively against him. Arcadius pointedly neglected to attend the Christmas Liturgy at the Great Church. How could he be present, he asked, when the archbishop had not been cleared of the charges made against him? At the end of Lent 405, the emperor finally acted, forbidding Chrysostom to officiate at the Easter services. Chrysostom defied him. "I have received this church from God," he said. "I am responsible for the salvation of my flock, and am not free to desert it. The city is yours and you can turn me out by force, if you like. It will be on your head that I leave my post."

On Easter Eve, the emperor responded. The Great Church was crowded for the vigil service and the baptism of catechumens. Suddenly, soldiers burst in through the doors. They surrounded the altar. Baptism was then by total immersion, and many women were half-dressed in preparation for it. They fled screaming. Some were wounded and thrown outside. The waters of the great font ran red with blood. Most of the churches of Constantinople were empty that Easter, people

CHRYSOSTOM ON SPREADING THE WORD

Witnessing to others is part of the very nature of being a Christian. It would be easier for the sun to cease to shine or give forth heat than for a Christian not to send forth light; easier for the light to be darkness than for this to be so.

being too terrified to attend.

Chrysostom retired to his house, vigilantly guarded by the faithful. Five days after Pentecost, Arcadius signed an order expelling him from the city. To prevent a riot, John quietly surrendered to a military guard, and a vessel rapidly removed him from the city he would never see again. Meanwhile, a pandemonium of protest broke out in which the Great Church was set afire. It spread to the Senate House.

Several nights before the bishop's forced departure, a hailstorm had burst upon the city, terrifying the empress. Throughout the summer, she seemed to suffer from some undisclosed illness. She died in childbirth on October 6.

The place of exile chosen for Chrysostom was Cucusus in the

Austere and fierce in life and manner, John Chrysostom nevertheless composed many of the beautiful prayers in the Divine Liturgy that bears his name, and is still the common Sunday service in Eastern Orthodox churches from the Aleutian shores to the hills of Lebanon. This well-worn Liturgy book is open at the first prayers of the "Anaphora," the Offering section of the Eucharist. (The icon is fourteenth-century Russian.)

Taurus Mountains of Lesser Armenia, a town constantly under attack by the wild Isaurian barbarians. In the sweltering August heat, he was trekked across the uplands of Asia Minor, living on hard, moldy bread and rank water. At Caesarea, capital of Cappadocia, conditions briefly eased. But then the Isaurians sacked the town, and the local monks blamed the presence of Chrysostom for such bad luck and late one night drove him away.

Sick and unable to walk, he was carried into the mountains on a litter borne by a mule. The animal slipped and fell, almost killing him. He dragged himself to his feet and trudged on, over the rocky ground in pitch dark. Finally, early in September, they reached Cucusus. He was treated kindly there. Someone gave him a town house. But two successive winters gradually destroyed his health entirely. He was suffering from vomiting, headaches and sleeplessness. He could not eat.

Then came word from the capital. He was to be moved to Pityas, a tiny port at the eastern end of the Black Sea, with not even a road to connect it to civilization. Accompanied by two praetorian guardsmen,

---

THE ANAPHORA

DEACON: Let us stand aright! Let us stand with fear! Let us attend, that we may offer the Holy Oblation in peace.

CHOIR: A mercy of peace! A sacrifice of praise!

The deacon returns to the sanctuary. The priest blesses the faithful:

PRIEST: The grace of our Lord Jesus Christ, the love of God the Father, and the communion of the Holy Spirit be with all of you.

CHOIR: And with your spirit.

PRIEST: Let us lift up our hearts.

CHOIR: We lift them up unto the Lord.

PRIEST: Let us give thanks unto the Lord.

CHOIR: It is meet and right to worship the Father, and the Son, and the Holy Spirit; the Trinity, one in essence, and undivided.

PRIEST: It is meet and right to hymn Thee, to bless Thee, to praise Thee, to give thanks to Thee, and to worship Thee in every place of Thy dominion: for Thou (127) art God ineffable, inconceivable, invisible, incomprehensible, ever-existing and eternally the same, Thou and Thine

62

only-begotten Son and Thy Holy Spirit. Thou it was who brought us from non-existence into being, and when we had fallen away didst raise us up again, and didst not cease to do all things until Thou hadst brought us up to heaven, and hadst endowed us with Thy Kingdom which is to come. For all these things we give thanks to Thee, and to Thy only-begotten Son, and to Thy Holy Spirit; for all things of which we know and of which we know not, whether manifest or unseen; and we thank Thee for this Liturgy which Thou hast deigned to accept at our hands, though there stand by Thee thousands of archangels and hosts of angels, the Cherubim and the Seraphim, six-winged, many-eyed, who soar aloft, borne on their pinions

Singing the triumphant hymn, shouting, proclaiming and saying:

As the priest chants the above, the deacon touches the paten with each of the points of the star (making the sign of the Cross); then kisses it and lays it aside; he goes to the right side of the altar.

CHOIR: Holy! Holy! Holy! Lord of Sabaoth! Heaven and earth are full of Thy glory! Hosanna in the highest! Blessed is He that comes in the name of the Lord! Hosanna in the highest!

63

he began the trek. After four hundred miles, they came to a little village, and a chapel dedicated to the martyr Basiliscus. That night, said Chrysostom, Basiliscus himself came to him in a dream and said: "Cheer up, brother. Tomorrow, we'll be together." The following day, September 14, 407, he found he could no longer keep walking. They brought him back to the chapel, where the local clergy dressed him in clean white clothing and put him to bed. In about two hours, he turned to them and said:

> The Liturgy ascribed to him is still sung on most Sundays in Eastern churches.

"Glory be to God in all things." Then he died. He was buried in the tomb of St. Basiliscus.

Meanwhile, at Constantinople, those bishops and laypeople who supported him were ruthlessly persecuted with fines, imprisonment, torture and exile. Laymen who refused Communion from his successors, the patriarchs Arsacius and Atticus, lost their jobs. Soldiers were demoted. In the midst of his trials, Chrysostom had appealed to Pope Innocent I, who sent a nine-man delegation—five western bishops and four eastern—to Constantinople, urging Chrysostom's reinstatement. The four eastern bishops were imprisoned, the western bishops jailed, then sent home on a leaky ship that was expected to sink. It didn't. Innocent cut off communion with the patriarch of Constantinople until John's name could be cleared and restored to the dignities of the church.

After the death of Arcadius a year after Chrysostom, this process of rehabilitation went slowly forward.

Finally, in 438, his relics were moved to Constantinople, where the emperor, Theodosius II, bowed to kiss the reliquary and beg God's forgiveness for his parents, Eudoxia and Arcadius. The relics were then buried beside the tomb of Eudoxia in the Church of the Apostles.

John Chrysostom became one of the Three Holy Hierarchs of the Eastern Churches (with Basil the Great and Gregory of Nazianzus), and the Liturgy ascribed to him is sung in all Eastern churches most Sundays of the year. From that Liturgy, the Anglican Church for more than four hundred years preserved in its *Book of Common Prayer* what it called "The Prayer of Saint Chrysostom." It reads:

> Almighty God, who hast given us grace at this time with one accord to make our common supplications unto thee; and dost promise that when two or three are gathered together in thy Name thou wilt grant their requests: Fulfill now, O Lord, the desires and petitions of thy servants, as may be most expedient for them; granting us in this world knowledge of thy truth, and in the world to come life everlasting. Amen.

Perhaps more closely related to Chrysostom's own life than to his theology is the "Gradual," sung between the epistle and gospel in the old Roman Catholic Mass for the Feast of St. John Chrysostom, January 27: "Blessed is the man who suffers trials, for when he has been proved, he shall receive the crown of life. Alleluia!" ■

They came in marauding bands and in great swarms, speaking tongues that grated on Roman and Greek ears. They were seemingly indifferent to the human pain and cultural carnage they inflicted, and intent only on destruction. They represented a range of many distinct tribes, those depicted above being early Franks who attacked Gaul from the north. But the effect of their depredations was similar, and the people of the empire called them all "barbarians" (aliens) and saw them as inferior. They were certainly not inferior in battle. (From an engraving in François Guizot's History of France, late-nineteenth century.)

CHAPTER 4

Civilization crumbles as a barbarian tide rolls over the west

Alaric's sack of Rome is only the beginning. Soon scores of cities are destroyed, while roads and farms revert to wilderness as the world seems to be coming to an end

Theodosius the Great was dead. The wealth, grandeur and plenty that six or seven centuries of civilization had created in the "eternal" empire now lay within tantalizing reach of the barbarians. At the empire's heart gleamed the greatest jewel of all, the city of Rome, with its priceless artworks, its dazzling furnishings, its stockpiles of gold—and of course, its beautiful women.

In the coming two centuries, most of this grandeur was destined for destruction, not only at Rome, but throughout the western empire. Countless towns, even whole cities, would be looted and burned, their populations slaughtered or driven into the countryside to starve. Great buildings, temples, monuments, amphitheaters, baths and luxurious homes would be stripped of everything of conceivable value. Vast tracts of what had once been lush farmland would lapse back into wilderness. Aqueducts would be demolished and the water supply cut off.

Bridges would collapse and roads fall into disrepair, hampering the distribution of food. Famine would spread, and with it disease. Schools would close, libraries disappear. Illiteracy would become the rule, making both the recording of current events and communication at a distance extremely difficult. Finally, the great city of Rome itself would be three times sacked and five times taken by assault. Eventually, it would become a sort of ghost town, its population

1. The *Song of God's Providence* is something of a historical enigma. The poem is attributed traditionally to Prosper of Aquitaine, a contemporary of Augustine. Scholars now question whether Prosper wrote it however, and regard the author as unknown. But beyond doubt it is one of the few surviving eyewitness accounts of the Dark Ages.

reduced from the one million of Theodosius's time to about thirty thousand inhabitants sharing with foxes, wild dogs, rats and wolves what was left of its magnificent buildings.

"For hundreds of years," wrote the twentieth-century statesman and historian Winston Churchill (*History of the English-Speaking Peoples*, London, 1956), "there had been order and law, respect for property and a widening culture. All had vanished. The buildings, such as they were, were of wood, not stone. . . . Barbarism ruled in its rags, without even the stern military principles that had animated and preserved the Germanic tribes. The confusion and conflict of petty ruffians sometimes called kings racked the land. We wake from an awful, and it might have seemed, endless nightmare to a scene of utter prostration."

"If the entire ocean had poured over the fields of Gaul," reports one account of this prostration, the *Song of God's Providence*, "more people would have survived the vast waters. For the flocks are gone, the seeds of the fruits are gone, and there is no place for vines or olive trees. Destructive fire and rain have even taken away the buildings on the farms, while it is still more saddening that some of them stand empty."[1]

"In village, villa, crossroads, district, field, down every roadway and at every turning," runs a sixth-century account in verse, "death, grief, destruction and arson are revealed. In one great conflagration, Gaul is burning. Why tell the death roll of a falling world? Why count how many unto death are hurled when you may see your own day hurrying near?"

"Brigands fell upon travelers and merchants on the edge of the woods and at the fords across rivers," writes the French historian Prosper Boissonnade (*Life and Work in Medieval Europe*, translated by Eileen Powers, New York, 1927). "Armed bands prowled about the country, and journeys became perilous expeditions undertaken only with caravans and armed escorts. The ports declined, the seas

were so infested with pirates that maritime trade became as uncertain as land commerce. The great transport companies had for the most part broken up, and the shipbuilders were ruined."

"The human pain which accompanied and followed the fall of the western Roman Empire is beyond even the figures of astronomy to calculate," comments the historian Stewart Irvin Oost (*Galla Placidia Augusta*, Chicago, 1968). "Every kind of suffering that man is capable of inflicting on his fellows, from wounded pride to loss of livelihood, to witnessing the tortured death agonies of those one loves, became a relatively common experience of life."

In letter after letter, Jerome bewailed the fate of the commonwealth. "I shudder when I think of the catastrophes," he laments. "How many of God's matrons and virgins, virtuous and noble ladies, have been the sport of these brutes. . . . The Roman world is falling. . . . The whole country between the Alps and the Pyrenees, between the Rhine and the ocean, has been laid waste by the hordes." What struck him hardest, however, was the unthinkable ultimate: the fall of the city of Rome itself. "The bright light of all the world was put out . . . the Roman Empire was decapitated . . . the whole world perished in one city. . . . As the common saying goes, I forgot my own name."

This event, the first fall of Rome, was in fact more terrible as a precedent than as an occurrence, for the subsequent sacks of the city were infinitely worse. Moreover, it was perhaps rendered less fearful because it was accomplished by a man trained by the Romans themselves. He was known as Alaric, though this was probably not his actual name, but a title derived from the Germanic *alla reikus*, meaning "everyone's ruler."

As he looked toward the city in that fateful year 410, Alaric knew that between his barbarian horde and that coveted goal stood only two obstacles. One was inconsequential: the emperor Honorius, just sixteen years old, an

The invading barbarians, including the Gothic tribes (1), seemed uninterested in the engineering advances, economy and culture that were the pride of the Roman Empire, and were certainly unable to maintain them. Thus, bridges like the one at Casares, Spain (2), fell into disrepair. A villa in what is now Gloucestershire, England (3), must have been of little interest to a people accustomed to reed huts. Paved roads became overgrown and virtually impassable, as witness this access to the once prosperous town of Dougga, Tunisia (4)—soon weed-infested and broken, as it remains to this day.

easy target for a quick kill. But the other was formidable indeed: the senior general of the Roman army, Stilicho, Vandal on his father's side and Roman on his mother's. Honorius, installed as augustus of the west in 395 following upon his father's death, was fated like other hapless juvenile emperors to be a mere puppet whose strings were pulled by bureaucrats and ambitious military strongmen at Rome, Milan and Ravenna. To the barbarians, he seemed little more than an annoyance.

But Flavius Stilicho was another matter. A resolute believer in the Roman Empire and Roman virtue, Stilicho would fight brilliantly and valiantly to save the boy whose guardian he had been appointed by Theodosius. He had risen quickly and fiercely in the Roman army, defeating Radagaisus, king of the Goths, on an Italian battlefield in 405, but the cost of that victory was great. To defend Italy, Stilicho had had to strip Gaul of Roman troops, which opened the way in the following year for a ravening barbarian horde to pour through Rome's most prosperous western provinces, leaving smoldering ruin in its wake. Britain, likewise undefended, had fallen prey to the ferocious Saxons, and an avalanche

When an imperial emissary assured Stilicho he would be spared he surrendered, and was thereupon beheaded. So Alaric didn't need to defeat Rome's defender; Rome had done it for him.

of frantic British refugees had streamed across the channel to Armorica. So many were they that Armorica would become known as Brittany, and for centuries to come would speak a British tongue.

Alaric, the man destined to live in history for seizing and despoiling the greatest city in the ancient world, unconquered for precisely eight hundred years,[2] was, curiously enough, a friend and devoted admirer of Stilicho. He had even followed Stilicho's career path, volunteering for the officer cadre of the Roman army. Born about 370 into a noble family of Visigoths (western Goths), Alaric was probably Arian in religion, and began his military career as a member of the Gothic *federates*, tribesmen whom the Roman Empire tried to keep peaceful with grants of territory and payments of tribute money. Hot-tempered but quick and capable, he became a tribal chieftain at twenty-four, then underwent training at a Constantinople military academy set up by Theodosius to teach promising Goth leaders how to be Romans. However, where Stilicho subscribed unreservedly to the Roman ideal, Alaric came to quite different conclusions. He observed that, whatever its pomp and grandeur, the empire had become flabby and vulnerable, its leaders largely focused on fulfilling their personal ambitions.

Nevertheless, Alaric at first aspired to advancement in the service of Rome. Tireless and ambitious, he served as a commander under Theodosius at the Battle of the River Frigidus (see Chapter 3), where his immediate superior was the redoubtable Stilicho himself. Theodosius's battle plan there required the sacrifice

2. In 390 B.C. Gallic Celts sacked and burned Rome. Only the strongly fortified settlement on the city's Capitoline Hill was able to withstand the invaders. One of the city's many legends tells of the sacred geese that, by their agitated honking, alerted the hilltop fortress and thwarted an attempted night attack by the Celts. The attackers stayed for seven months, leaving only after they demanded and received a large ransom in gold.

of some of his best Gothic troops, a sacrifice he did not adequately acknowledge. Alaric did not forget this omission.

But a worse disillusionment was still to come for this Visigoth officer. The River Frigidus was Theodosius's last battle. Now the boy Honorius took over the west, and his older brother Arcadius, eighteen, reigned in the east. Scholarly opinion of them is hardly flattering. Historian Henri Daniel-Rops (*The Church of the Apostles and Martyrs*, Garden City, N.Y., 1962) not atypically describes Honorius as "a little booby of only eleven," and Arcadius as "a puny adolescent of halting speech and dull wits." In conferring office and honors, the young emperors and their bureaucratic managers casually bypassed Alaric, an oversight upon which history would now turn. His notorious temper aflame, Alaric resolved to move things forward on his own. If the Romans would not recognize him, others would. He would rebel.

Many of the federates were more than ready to join him. They too had grievances. The empire was becoming increasingly delinquent, for example, in its promised subsidy payments. Alaric drew these men together. History does not record his challenge to them, but it can be easily imagined. The empire was no longer what it had once been, but much of its wealth and luxuries, some of the greatest riches of humanity, remained—theirs for the taking. The Romans were soft and decadent, but they, the German peoples, the so-called barbarians, were strong. They could fight, and by fighting they could win. What was their alternative? To die miserably in Rome-imposed destitution? His hearers would have cheered and loudly renounced all remaining allegiance to the emperor. Now they had a king of their own, a king named Alaric. It was 395. Rome had fifteen years left to remain unconquered.

The first assault of Alaric's men was on the eastern capital Constantinople, where the city's newly built walls proved too much for them. But then, why bother with Constantinople? Why not head west? Why not loot, burn and lay waste the whole countryside, then move on to Rome? Only the boy Honorius, the "booby," and of course, Stilicho, stood in their way. So they regrouped and moved through Greece, spreading devastation as they went.

When they encountered Stilicho's legions from Italy, which stopped them cold, they fled north along the Adriatic into Illyricum, long the breeding ground of Rome's best soldiers. The Illyrians too now denounced the empire and declared for King Alaric of the Visigoths. But Stilicho was following Alaric, cornered him in Illyricum, and was about to wipe out his army when an order to desist arrived from Arcadius (the teenager of the "dull wits") in Constantinople. Stilicho had intruded upon eastern territory, Arcadius declared, and must immediately withdraw. The veteran general reluctantly obeyed, and Alaric escaped.

The two sons of Theodosius the Great, Honorius (above) and Arcadius (left), presided over the dismembering of the empire their father had left them. Self-absorption and stupidity delivered Rome to Alaric and his Gothic troops.

Next year, Alaric struck south again. Athens bought him off with a large bribe, but Corinth, Sparta and a host of other cities were left in ruins, the populace butchered or enslaved. Again Stilicho arrived from Italy, surrounded Alaric's force, and prepared to move in for the kill. Again the orders came from Constantinople, presumably from Arcadius: Get out of the east. Again Stilicho obeyed, and again Alaric escaped. He moved back into the eastern empire, safe from his old friend and nemesis. There he diligently worked to convert his mob into something of an army, brokering his support between Honorius and Arcadius, playing the imperial brothers against each other, so that each rewarded him with generous gifts of Roman arms, and his arsenal grew. In effect, write historians Stephen Williams and Gerald Friell (*Theodosius: The Empire at Bay*, London, 1994), Alaric had become a "third power" within the empire, whose loyalty and services must be bid for.

By 408, he was ready to move against Rome itself, and so his invigorated forces invaded Italy and cut a swath through the north, stealing or destroying everything in their path. Arriving at the gates of Rome, however, Alaric stopped short and did not attack, knowing that a direct frontal assault was risky. Instead, he established a blockade that cut off the flow of food and goods to the city. He knew that Stilicho must still be confronted.

That canny general had been very hard at work. Brilliant strategist that he was, he had blocked another barbarian invasion on the Rhine, contained a revolt in Britain, then sped to North Africa and quashed a rebellion there. Then, before going to the relief of Rome, he reported to Honorius at Ravenna, 235 miles northeast on the Adriatic coast, where the young western emperor maintained his court. Now occurred one of those astounding events that from time to time, incomprehensibly, punctuate history and pivotally determine its course. Stilicho found himself facing an arrest order from Honorius, who had been persuaded by his courtiers that his general was planning an insurrection.

The charge, however ill based, was not without plausible explanation. Although Stilicho's loyalty to Theodosius's family had been unfailing, notes historian John M. Flynn (*Generalissimos of the Western Roman Empire*, Edmonton, 1983), he nevertheless had shunned imperial titles, preferring to remain close to his power base, his troops. This independence made him an object of suspicion, seemingly untrustworthy. The general now took refuge in a church, claiming sanctuary, which the imperial troops respected. But when an imperial emissary assured Stilicho his life would be spared, he left the church and surrendered—whereupon this official had him beheaded with an ax. At Rome, his adversary Alaric could now inform his wildly cheering army that they need not defeat Stilicho. Rome had done it for them.

To call Alaric's troops an "army" is misleading, however. The historian Oost describes his Germanic hordes as "ill-disciplined barbarian bands, which with wives and children, bag and baggage, were whole tribes on the move rather than armies." Such an assemblage now squatted patiently outside Rome. Alaric had, in the words of the historian Edward Gibbon, "encompassed the walls, commanded the twelve principal gates, intercepted all communication with the adjacent country, and vigilantly guarded the navigation on the Tiber, from which the Romans derived the surest and most plentiful supply of provisions."

Sheltered for years against the grim realities of life in the vulnerable frontier provinces, the comfortable Roman gentry had acquired the lofty confidence that is born of ignorance. Inside the now isolated city, the Romans were at first shocked, then indignant. A clot of crude barbarians, threatening the most important city in the world, the very capital of civilization? Surely there was some mistake. The stinking rabble milling outside would soon wander off and return to their filthy huts or caves or wherever it might be they had come from.

The consul Stilicho (left) and his wife Serena (right, with an unnamed child) were rewarded for their loyalty to Theodosius and his sons with death sentences from the emperor Honorius and the Roman Senate respectively.

But as the days wore on, the citizens became increasingly alarmed. And hungry. The stinking rabble did not wander off. How could this be happening? And then a seeming answer to that question swept through the city's rumor mills. Obviously, thought conspiratorially minded Romans, this must be the evil work of Serena, widow of Stilicho and niece of the emperor Theodosius. Had not her late husband, a barbarian himself, made various alliances with this same Alaric over the years? Even now, it was whispered, Serena was in secret communication with this Goth, plotting to have the gates opened so that he and his vile companions could come in. It all seemed perfectly obvious. No unwashed barbarian could have established such a blockade by himself. Therefore he must have had inside help. The solution was equally obvious: Get Serena out of the picture and the plot would fail, and with it the siege.

The Senate listened with great interest to this paranoid tale, for which no evidence was offered either then or since. Unable to come up with any other course of action, however, the senators seized

Now in the Museo Civico, Belluno, Italy, a fifth-century Gothic bronze sword sheath shows the attention that the invaders lavished on their weapons. Other facets of life came a remote second.

the opportunity of doing at least something. Without holding a trial or seeking any substantiation for the wild claims against her, they ordered Serena executed by strangulation.

If Roman citizens then breathed a sigh of relief, the respite was brief. To their consternation, the murder of the innocent Serena had no effect whatever on Alaric's barbarians; the blockade continued. The daily allotment of food for each citizen was cut in half, then reduced to a third. With poor nutrition, and ultimately starvation, came illness. Soon an alarming number of deaths was being reported. Because no one could go outside the walls to bury the dead, the bodies began piling up. They rotted and stank. Disease spread. As hunger grew more acute, there were even reports of cannibalism, of mothers devouring their deceased children. At last two city officials were appointed to attempt negotiations with the barbarian enemy. Arrangements were carefully made and the two men walked out, no doubt apprehensively, to parley with this barbarian commander.

Although their kinsmen were starving and dying, the envoys were supremely aware of the fact that they were Romans, and this unwashed Alaric was not. The Roman people, they confidently assured Alaric, were fully prepared to engage in warfare if they had to, and if they did, they would certainly succeed. They had excellent weapons, extensive experience and superior knowledge. Despite these obvious advantages, however, they were willing to overlook all the recent unpleasantness in order to avoid unnecessary bloodshed, and would therefore reluctantly agree to "moderate" terms for peace.

At this, Alaric laughed out loud. "Thick grass is easier mowed than thin," said he, repeating a proverb he had learned as a child at work in the fields. Terms? They wanted terms? "Deliver to me all the gold that your city contains, all the silver, all the moveable property that I may find there; and moreover all your slaves of barbarian origin. Otherwise the siege goes on."

The two Roman negotiators were shocked. "But if you take all these things, what do you leave to the citizens?" they asked. Alaric, in full command of the situation, replied firmly: "Your lives."

Back through the gates went the chagrined ambassadors to report Alaric's impossible demands to the senators, who, reeling at the thought of Rome being subject to these sorts of indignities by such people, cast around desperately for some alternative. This time, the pagan historian Zosimus records, another explanation for their terrible predicament was mooted. They suddenly "perceived how they were now abandoned . . . in consequence of having deserted the religion of their forefathers."

Yes indeed, they agreed, it was undeniable that Rome had for centuries been immune from this kind of trouble—until, that is, it abandoned its faithful gods and took up with the Christian one. This being the case, a return to the old religion was called for. The ancient rites so foolishly discarded should be dusted off and performed again. Rejected gods could be placated.

According to pagan chroniclers, the prefect of the city sought the advice of Innocent I, bishop of Rome, who in distress and perplexity agreed that under the circumstances they could employ the old incantations, but only if they did so in secret. However, historian Oost finds implausible the suggestion that the Christian leader would agree to any such thing. "If the fourth century was not an age of freethinkers, the fifth was even less so; the cynical Rome of the Renaissance papacy was many centuries in the future. That the bishop of Rome should thus risk damning his own soul to hell forever in accordance with the strict injunctions of his religion, not to mention the souls of the participants in such sacrifices, is absolutely beyond belief."

In any case, ceremonies performed in secret did not satisfy the pagan priests. They declared that the result they sought—fire and lightning boiling down from heaven and consuming the barbarians outside the gates—could be

Despite Rome's 'obvious advantages,' said the city's envoy, they would agree to 'moderate' terms to avoid unnecessary death. In response to this offer, Alaric laughed out loud.

achieved only if the rites were performed in full view of the senators and the populace, with due ceremony and spectacle. But then they discovered they could not round up enough Romans who were willing to turn away from Christian worship. The proposed reversion to public paganism had to be abandoned, and a new delegation limped dispiritedly out through the gates to reach some agreement—almost any agreement—with Alaric.

This time, the Roman envoys were humbler, and protracted negotiation persuaded Alaric to moderate his demand a little. He would free the city, he said, if it delivered to him five thousand pounds of gold, thirty thousand pounds of silver, four thousand silken tunics, three thousand hides dyed with scarlet and three thousand pounds of pepper. It was "a strange catalogue of the things which were objects of desire to a nation emerging from barbarism," observes an amused Gibbon. "The pepper suggests the conjecture that the Gothic appetite had already lost some of its original keenness in the fervent southern lands; and the numbers of the special articles of luxury prompt the guess (it is nothing more) that the nobles and officers of this great nation-army may have been about three thousand, the extra one thousand silken garments perhaps representing the wives and daughters who accompanied some of the great chiefs."

The Romans quickly began gathering the required tribute, collecting property from the citizenry and a portion of the recorded wealth of each senator.

When even that was not enough, they scavenged jewels and precious metals from such idols and images as still stood within the city, and even melted down some statues of the deities. Zosimus was appalled at these indignities to the pagan gods. "This was in fact nothing less than to deprive of life and energy, by diminishing the honor done to them, those statues which had been erected in the midst of solemn religious rites," he laments.

After calling off the blockade, Alaric entered negotiations about his future role in the empire. The Senate was ready to grant him a favorable military alliance, but the inexperienced emperor Honorius, safely distant at Ravenna and typically possessed of a less than realistic estimate of his own judgment, flatly refused, even after the Senate dispatched delegates to explain the gravity of the situation.

For one thing, they informed the emperor, many slaves had escaped from Rome during the confusion, and together with an even larger number of barbarians were throwing up barricades along the roads to Rome, seizing for

Honorius, who spent his time raising fancy poultry, refused to deal with a petty chieftain. Negotiations with Alaric would cease, he declared. So Alaric tightened the screws again.

themselves the emergency supplies sent to resupply the city. Actually, when Alaric learned of this, he dealt forcefully with the interlopers and ended their robbery. Barbarian he might be, but his own honor was at stake, after all, in the matter of his deal with the city of Rome.

Honorius, who was devoting more and more of his royal time to raising fancy poultry as pets, refused to be bothered anymore about the activities of some petty barbarian chieftain. There would be no further negotiations with Alaric, he ordered. So Alaric tightened the screws again by reimposing his blockade. More ambassadors went back and forth; more tentative deals were struck. Alaric said he would withdraw in exchange for a yearly payment of gold and provisions, and the grant of a broad swath of territory in the provinces of Noricum, Istria, Venetia and Dalmatia, where his men and their families could live independently, as allies of Rome.

Honorius had now come under the influence of one Jovius, his chief counselor, a conniver clearly intent upon his own interests. Although Alaric seemingly never demanded a command position in the Roman army as part of any alliance, Jovius told Honorius that he had, and the emperor responded to Jovius in writing: "Military command is mine alone to bestow, and I hold it unfitting that such offices as you name should ever be held by Alaric or any of his race." For whatever reason, the maneuvering Jovius took the letter and read it to Alaric, who angrily broke off talks and vowed revenge.

After further posturing and saber rattling on both sides, Alaric, although he clearly held the upper hand, moved once again to negotiate peace. He sent an

Modern-day visitors to the Roman Forum (below) are likely to conclude that Alaric and his army were responsible for the ruins they observe, and understandably so, based upon depictions like the unidentified engraving (left). In fact, Alaric's Goths wrecked and torched only a small section of the capital, preferring to expend their energies plundering its portable treasures.

envoy to the emperor saying that he would settle for Noricum alone, and would not insist on the other provinces. He even dropped his demand for gold, saying that he sought only reasonable supplies for his soldiers.

Jovius, apparently seeing some advantage for himself in Alaric's concessions, persuaded Honorius to reject even this, and once more the exasperated Alaric laid siege to Rome. This time, the desperate Romans, no longer willing to defer to their emperor's whimsical decisions, decided they must act on their own. Renouncing all ties to Honorius, they named a new augustus, Priscus Attalus, onetime prefect of Rome, who also had the endorsement (and followed the orders) of Alaric.

The perpetually scheming Jovius, however, contrived somehow to drive a wedge between the new emperor and Alaric. His patience at an end, the Visigoth leader thereupon publicly demoted his puppet Attalus. He stripped him of crown and purple robe, and dispatched these symbolic items to Honorius—a gesture the obtuse young ruler misinterpreted as full recognition of his own imperial authority. Again he refused to negotiate.

Alaric therefore amassed his forces for a full assault on the city. At midnight on August 24, 410, he sent his warriors forward to smash down the Salarian Gate—or in the version of events recorded by Procopius, to walk through the gate unimpeded after it was opened from within by conspirators. The terrible breach of the venerable city's sanctity was then announced to the inhabitants by a fearsome trumpet blast.

"Eleven hundred and sixty-three years after the foundation of Rome," Gibbon writes, "the imperial city, which had subdued and civilized so considerable a part of the world, was delivered to the licentious fury of the tribes of Germany and Scythia."

The sack of the city lasted at least three days, and according to some accounts as many as twelve, but it was not uncontrolled. While Alaric's men eagerly began grabbing everything of value, their leader ordered them not to kill except in self-defense, not to pillage the churches, and not to rape the women. At his command, the basilicas of Saints Peter and Paul were recognized as places of refuge for any harried Romans who managed to get inside. Visigoths, after all, were by way of being Christians themselves.

The fifth-century Christian historian Paulus Orosius (*History Against the Pagans*, New York, 1936) tells the story of an elderly woman whose door was forced open by a Gothic captain, and of the delight that spread across the barbarian's face when he spied the gleaming silver and golden vessels arrayed inside, all cleaned up and ready for the taking. The woman, however, was an altar server, and she lectured him sternly: "These are the consecrated vessels belonging to St. Peter; if you presume to touch them, the sacrilegious deed will remain on your conscience."

By the standards of future assaults on Rome by other barbarians, that of the Visigoth Alaric was downright civilized. He warned his men to kill only in self-defense, he prohibited rape, and he declared the churches off-limits. Still, his troops left happy, their wagons and sacks piled full of the city's accumulated treasure.

When Alaric was informed of the treasure trove, he ordered the sacred objects to be returned to the church. Orosius describes what happened next: "A numerous detachment of Goths, marching in order of battle through the principal streets, protected with glittering arms the long train of their devout companions, who bore aloft on their heads the sacred vessels of gold

and silver, and the martial shouts of the barbarians were mingled with the sound of religious psalmody. From all the adjacent houses, a crowd of Christians hastened to join this edifying procession. . . ."

War being what it is, however, some women reportedly were raped despite Alaric's orders, and some such victims killed themselves in shame. Residents who fought back were killed forthwith, and others were slaughtered even though they did not resist. One senator was slain, but apparently just one. Some of the killing, according to current accounts, was done by slaves, gratefully seizing their chance to turn against hated masters. One way and another, bodies of men, women and children lay unburied on the streets.

The triumphant Goths also burned a palace and a number of other buildings, especially in the area around the Salarian Gate where they had entered. They lined up captives in the streets, demanding ransom from their families, and hauling off into slavery those who could not pay—and some who did. But so little food remained within the walls of the long-besieged city that the victors did not stay long. They filled their sacks and wagons with gold, silver, silk, and precious gems, along with any vases and artwork that they had not trampled or smashed. Then they headed south.[3]

When the self-absorbed emperor Honorius received word of Rome's fate, it is said, he became distressed only because at first he misunderstood the message. As

3. Included in the booty pillaged from Rome by the Visigoths may have been certain sacred objects taken from the Temple in Jerusalem in A.D. 70 by the Romans. Early in the sixth century the Visigoths, under attack by the Franks, moved all their loot to their stronghold at Carcassonne. Thereafter, this treasure disappears from history. Speculation has offered one possible resting place for it: the fortress of Rheddae, more commonly known as Rennes-le-Château, a sleepy little village in the backwoods of the Languedoc region of France on the Mediterranean coast. However, the fabled trove has yet to be found.

CONNOR

the probably fictitious story goes, Honorius at first thought the couriers were trying to tell him that some evil had befallen one of his prize roosters, a bird he called Roma, and was relieved to hear that the news concerned only a catastrophe to the city of that name.

Though Alaric had conquered and pillaged the greatest city in the ancient world, he did not have long to enjoy this celebrity. His apparent plan was to move his forces south to take Sicily, and then to carry the campaign into North Africa, with its rich stores of grain. His ultimate goal was never in doubt, observes historian H. V. Livermore (*The Origins of Spain and Portugal*, London, 1971). He wanted to rule the empire, but God, fate, happenstance or plain bad luck had another plan for Alaric.

Soon after his final victory at Rome, he was stricken by fever, and died after a brief illness. The sixth-century Gothic historian Jordanes (*History of the Goths*) recounts the probably fanciful story of his burial. Roman slaves were put to work diverting the course of the little river Busentinus, says Jordanes, and building a royal sepulchre upon the exposed riverbed. Carefully arranged inside, with Alaric's body, were many of the treasures looted from Rome. Then the river was restored to its former course, and the secret location of the king's tomb concealed forever by drowning every slave who worked on it.

Still standing in the eighteenth century when this engraving was made, the Salarian Gate had been the point at which Alaric entered and exited Rome. As if to erase the entire event, nothing remains of the infamous portal, and the spot is now a collection of apartments and shops.

But Alaric's effect upon history was not confined to the physical conquest and sack of Rome. Far more devastating was his destruction of a myth. "The psychological blow to the empire was enormous," says *Eerdman's Handbook*. To the people of that day, writes historian Peter Brown in *Augustine of Hippo* (London, 1967), the fall of the city was "inconceivable." For twenty or more generations, Rome had stood immovable, imperishable, unassailable and unconquerable, in every mind whether civilized or barbarian. Her fall was akin in the general assumptions of the western peoples to the fall of the sun or moon. The inconceivable had occurred. The only certainty was that there were no more certainties.

In the ensuing years, all across the western empire, catastrophe followed catastrophe in the form of barbarian victories. The towns and cities were hit first because they promised the most loot and slaves. The fifth-century account of the priest and scholar Salvian (*A Treatise on the Government of God*, translated by Eva Sanford, New York, 1930) describes the appalling fate of beautiful Trier, where Athanasius had first been exiled (see chapter 1), and which Salvian calls "the greatest city of Gaul, three times destroyed by successive captures." He writes:

Those who escaped death in the capture did not survive the ruin that followed. Some died lingering deaths from deep wounds. Others were burned by the enemy's fires, and suffered tortures after the flames were extinguished. Some perished of hunger, others of nakedness, some wasting away, others paralyzed with cold, and so all alike, by diverse deaths, hastened to the common goal. Worse than this, other cities suffered from the destruction of this single town. There lay about the torn and naked bodies of both sexes, a sight that I myself endured. These were a pollution to the eyes of the city as they lay there, lacerated by birds and dogs. The stench of the dead brought pestilence on the living; death breathed out death. Thus, even those who had escaped the destruction of the city suffered the evils that sprang from the fate of the rest.

Priscus, a civil servant and historian, provided a vivid description of the fate of Nis, Yugoslavia: "We found the city deserted, as though it had been sacked; only a few sick persons lay in the churches. We halted a short distance from the river, in an open space, for all the ground adjacent to the bank was full of the

Those who escaped capture in Trier perished amidst its ruins. Some died of wounds, some of hunger, some of nakedness; some were burned and others simply wasted away.

bones of men slain in the war." St. Jerome writes: "The once noble city of Mogumtiacum [Mainz, Germany] has been captured and destroyed. In its church, many thousands have been massacred. The people of Vangium [Worms, Germany], after standing a long siege, have been extirpated. . . . Tournai, Spires and Strasbourg have fallen to Germany, while the provinces of Aquitaine, of the Nine Nations, of Lyon and Narbonne are with the exception of a few cities one universal scene of desolation."

Historian Prosper Boissonnade lists nineteen abandoned cities in the Danube provinces. Some (like Bude of the future Budapest, Vindobona, which would become Vienna, and Juvavum, which would become Salzburg) would subsequently be reoccupied and resume life. Some would never recover. He says the Huns alone destroyed seventy towns and cities in Illyricum. To this list he adds Cologne, Utrecht, Mainz, Worms, and Aix-la-Chapelle in the Rhine Valley. In Britain, London, York, Colchester, Norwich and Bath were "transformed into heaps of ruins" by the Saxon hordes. In Sicily, the Vandals wrought so much damage to Palermo, Syracuse and Catania that they remained desolate even by the end of the sixth century.

Identifying thirteen cities in northern Italy that were left a "total or partial ruin," Boissonnade concludes: "Within the crumbling walls of these ghostly towns, and in their half-deserted streets, a few artisans still vegetated, all that was left of the flourishing crafts of the past. Ploughed fields and gardens occupied the greater part of the open spaces, destitute of houses and inhabitants. . . . The west fell back again into the elementary economic life of primitive peoples."

Viewing the devastation in Britain, the monk Gildas observes that while the great buildings and massive fortifications of the Roman era were still standing,

In some former Roman cities on the edges of the empire, it would take centuries to either restore the remnants of empire in their midst, or invent other uses for them. In the late twentieth century, Strasbourg would turn a ruined aqueduct into a fountain.

"there is no living creature inside them except the wild beasts and the birds that have made their lairs there." Life in the cities, he notes, "is no longer possible." Many cities, observes historian Edith Ennen (*The Medieval Town*, Amsterdam, 1979), "shrank to the level of walled military encampments, which were now cut off from their surrounding territories."

Population plunged in both country and city. Boissonnade estimates that the Gallic lands, which probably numbered thirty million in the second century, were now down to about a third of that number. In the year 536 alone, famine claimed fifty thousand peasants in Italy, and plague wiped out one third to one half of the population of Wales and Ireland. In Auvergne, in the year 571, three hundred persons died of plague in one church, on one Sunday. At Rome, one pope recorded, he had seen eighty people lying on a street in the throes of death. Some took refuge in drink, and writes Salvian, died in drunken debauchery. In the city of Mainz, "all the people reveled together. . . . Men too feeble to live proved mighty in their cups. Too weak to walk, they were strong in drinking, stumbling along like nimble dancers."

Throughout most of western Europe, and in North Africa, food production shriveled. The barbarians, writes Boissonnade, "set fire to the harvest, cut down the fruit trees, tore up the vines, pillaged barns and cellars, drove away before

Populations plunged. Gallic lands lost two-thirds of their people. Plague wiped out a third of Wales and Ireland. One Sunday 300 perished of plague in one church.

them troops of captives and domestic animals, and sowed desolation and death all round them," leaving few people to work the land. Thus dikes and drainage systems were not maintained, productive land returned to swamp, and once-rich districts became wilderness.

The devastation, being indiscriminate, did entirely miss some few districts. Sir Samuel Dill, classics scholar and pro-chancellor of Queen's University in Belfast, uses the letters of Sidonius, bishop of Auvergne, to show that the invasions scarcely affected Sidonius or his neighbors. Similarly, Boissonnade notes that some local officials who escaped the onslaught set themselves up as "chiefs"— Churchill's "petty ruffians"—who oppressed the local population, heaped up fruits of their rapine, filled their harems with girls, their stables with horses, their kennels with hounds, divided their leisure between banqueting and the chase, dog fights and violent exercise.

As the western empire crumbled, the death throes of its expiring court became increasingly bizarre. Central roles, for example, would be played by two women of royal birth: one who fell deeply in love with a Visigoth chieftain, and one who offered herself as one of the many brides of the dreaded Attila the Hun.

Among the captives carried off by Alaric's men after the sacking of Rome was a twenty-two-year-old woman of imperial parentage. It is unlikely she was

The powerful Galla Placidia (the figure on the right) commissioned this nearly photographic portrait of herself and her children Valentinian and Honoria, as the center of a fabulous, jewel-encrusted, gold cross. It is now in the Museo Cristiano, Brescia, Italy.

treated as an ordinary prisoner, of course, but few could have predicted the extraordinary fate that awaited her. From the status of royal captive, she would rise to rule the expiring western empire—and do it better than any of the men who succeeded one another in and out of power during her time.

Galla Placidia, the only daughter of the emperor Theodosius I to survive infancy, and the half sister of rooster-raiser Honorius, was born in 388, raised in privilege, and instructed in Christianity. Her mother, the empress Galla, died when Placidia was a child; her father soon followed. At the age of seven, the orphan was sent off to Rome to be raised by Serena—the same Serena, Stilicho's wife, who was to be murdered by the Senate (with Placidia assenting, for reasons that remain unclear) in its vain attempt to forestall Alaric's advance on the city.

Among those attracted to Placidia as she was carried away from Rome was Alaric's brother-in-law, Athaulf, who would assume command of the Goths after Alaric's death. A man as decisive and ambitious as his brother-in-law, he decided to marry her. Placidia and Athaulf were wed in a splendid ceremony in Gaul in 414. Athaulf, hoping to reach an alliance with Rome, may have arranged the marriage largely for political reasons. Nevertheless, Placidia reportedly gave every appearance of true love for her Visigoth chief, and he appears to have returned her affection, despite the circumstances of their meeting and the disparities in their backgrounds.

Theirs was indeed a storybook romance, though a brief one. The pampered Roman princess seems to have enjoyed her new life among the wandering Goths, and to have made good-natured attempts to Romanize Athaulf—perhaps even to win him over from Arianism to orthodox Christianity. "There seems little doubt," writes Oost, "that it was she who led the way, convinced of a union of Visigoth and Roman, of civilization and barbarism, as a key to the future welfare of both people." And so it would be, although "long centuries . . . were to elapse before the union of two cultures which the royal pair had dimly envisioned was to become a reality."

Athaulf and Placidia had a baby boy, naming him Theodosius in honor of

Placidia's father, but the child died in infancy. Then, before the marriage was two years old, Athaulf was mortally wounded by a disgruntled servant while inspecting horses in his stable. With her husband dead, Placidia's fairy-tale life came to an abrupt end. She found herself once again an outsider and a captive, and her husband's successor enjoyed letting her know it. This was Singeric, a bitter foe of Athaulf, who forced Placidia to walk on foot in front of his horse with the common prisoners. But Singeric's vindictiveness was not confined to Placidia; it extended to everyone around him. After a reign of seven days, he was murdered by an irritated warrior named Wallia, who proceeded to sell Placidia to her brother Honorius for six hundred thousand measures of grain. Thus she wound up back in Rome.

In 417, under pressure from Honorius, Placidia reluctantly married Constantius, a Roman general whom she considered both ugly and more uncouth than any Visigoth. She knew her own future depended upon the ascent of her new husband, however, and therefore persuaded Honorius to proclaim Constantius as

Among the captives carried off from Rome was a young woman of imperial parentage. She was not being treated as an ordinary prisoner, and the fate awaiting her would prove astonishing.

emperor of the west in 421. Placidia was clearly the force behind him, administering the empire through him. Co-emperor Constantius III was doomed to a short reign in any event, dying of pleurisy after seven months on the throne, but by then, Placidia had borne him two children. Her son would in due course become Valentinian III. Her daughter, Honoria, would embroil herself in scandal, face charges of treason, and help provoke one of the most famous battles in history.

Early on, Placidia got along well enough with her brother Honorius. Perhaps too well—they were seen kissing each other on the lips, causing gossip about incest. But eventually they had a falling out, and Honorius accused Placidia of treason. Fearing for her life, in 423 she fled with her children and took refuge in Constantinople with the new emperor of the east. This was Theodosius II, son of the lamentable Arcadius (he of the "dull wits"), who had died in 408, at the age of thirty-one (an early demise caused by a kick from a horse in some accounts, an illness in others).

Placidia, having survived the sack of Rome, captivity, marriage to a barbarian, ransom and accusations of treason, was now to experience a new adventure: shipwreck, or near shipwreck. En route to Constantinople, her vessel was enveloped by a raging storm, so fierce that all aboard feared for their lives. Placidia prayed for deliverance to St. John the Evangelist, the New Testament apostle, believed to have died as an old man on the very coasts her ship would have skirted. (See earlier volume, *A Pinch of Incense*, pages 19, 25 and 45.) Within a short time, the wind slacked and the sea calmed. Placidia vowed to erect a church in honor of St. John, and would later do so. The Church of St. John the

Divine in Ravenna was one of a number of ecclesiastical and other public buildings she would construct during her forthcoming reign.

She arrived in Constantinople as an exile from the west, and not a happy one. She chafed at her status, which ranked below that of her niece, Pulcheria, granddaughter of Theodosius I through Arcadius, and also below that of Eudocia, wife of Theodosius II. So she waited upon events. Her brother Honorius seemed promisingly insecure; if he were not assassinated, he might at least be deposed. In the event he was neither, but to equivalent effect died in 423, of dropsy.

But who was to succeed him? No descendant of Theodosius I was on hand in the west, and the general Castinus, whose enmity toward Placidia was well established and fierce, decided he had just the man. He advanced the case for Honorius's former secretary, Johannes—intelligent, unassuming, moderate and not too likely to disrupt the established order. And certainly there was a need for a western authority, someone on the scene, not distracted by the far-off concerns of the east. It took weeks to get even a message to Constantinople and back. Moreover, Johannes had another backer, the Roman general Aetius, who in his boyhood had been a hostage in the camps of both the Goths and Huns, and had friends among their leaders. The choice was obvious. Johannes was named Augustus of the west and emissaries were sent east to Constantinople to obtain the eastern emperor's blessing.

However, the choice of Johannes was seen in Constantinople as something

Still impressive as ruins, the walls constructed at the order of Theodosius II ran more than four miles across the peninsula of Constantinople. The emperor lived long enough to see his original construction reduced to rubble by the earthquake of 447, and to oversee its rebuilding before the next wave of barbarian raiders reached the city.

less than obvious. There it was viewed as a blatant power grab, and Theodosius II swung into action. Granted there must be a western emperor, but he must be of imperial pedigree, not some upstart clerk. When Johannes's envoys arrived, a few were sent home and the rest were jailed. Then the childless Theodosius named his closest male relative to the rank of caesar, second in rank only to himself. This was Placidia's son, Valentinian, aged six. Valentinian had the right blood; he also had a remarkably determined mother.

So Johannes knew he faced a fight, and in that fight, who better to help him than the Huns? He would play the Aetius card. He sent Aetius off with a large amount of gold to confer with his old friends. Yes, they agreed, they would take his side in the looming war with Theodosius.

Events now moved swiftly. Theodosius mounted a massive expeditionary force by land and sea to depose Johannes. Placidia, accompanied by the child-emperor Valentinian (and also her daughter Honoria) met with the army at Thessalonica. At first, things went badly. The eastern fleet under general Ardaburius was caught up in a storm and wrecked; Ardaburius himself made it safely to the Italian shore and was immediately captured. Johannes treated him hospitably at Ravenna, however, and gave him the freedom of the town, hoping to keep everything as calm as possible while he waited for his allies, the Huns. But Ardaburius escaped and got out a message warning the eastern army of the

Swampland sanctuary

Fleeing Hun fury, refugees wade into a trackless marsh and establish one of the great wonders of the world

As the Huns raged along the north coast of the Adriatic, butchering nearly everyone in prosperous Aquileia, burning its magnificent buildings, and threatening towns like Concordia, Altino and Padua, the remaining citizenry fled in terror to the marshy bay at the sea's northwest corner. They waded out among the soggy islands, the inlets and lagoons, settling on what little dry land they could find, and establishing themselves as impoverished fisher folk.

The year was 452, and the Huns saw no point in following them. What loot could so many thousand acres of swamp possibly offer them? Succeeding waves of invaders reasoned the same way. Besides, whenever the barbarians did encounter them, the swamp dwellers proved particularly pugnacious.

As a result, the pauperized settlers of the Adriatic marshlands were left to themselves to drain the marshes, raising the ground level of some islands with earth dredged out of the lagoons between them.

The new settlers set up a government run by twelve tribunes representing each of the twelve occupied islands. Though nominally part of the eastern empire, it was in fact independent, and in the seventh century would become a republic under an elected doge.

In time, the place would acquire a name: Venice. It would become one of the commercial capitals of the world. ■

The swamps that gave refuge to fugitives fleeing Attila and his Hunnish horde would eventually be transformed into the islands, lagoons and canals of cultured Venice, here depicted in a sixteenth-century panorama.

Huns' approach. The forces of the east then attacked Ravenna via a hidden route through the marshes, shown them by a cooperative shepherd, and Johannes was taken captive.

Placidia, acting on behalf of her son, showed none of the mercy toward Johannes that he had shown to Ardaburius. She ordered one of his hands cut off, had him tied backwards atop a mule and displayed in this humiliating fashion to jeering crowds at Aquileia, and then had him beheaded. Johannes had ruled slightly more than two years, from 423 to 425, during which time the record shows that he implemented a policy of tolerance for all Christian sects.

Three days after the execution, Aetius and the Huns belatedly arrived in Italy. After a few skirmishes, Placidia shrewdly sought out Aetius and offered terms. There is no doubt she would have preferred to execute Aetius as she had Johannes, but she needed him to make the indispensable pact with the Huns. Paid handsomely for their trouble, they departed. Aetius was made a

This man Attila, Honoria surmised, might be interested in a Roman princess—interested enough to come to her aid. At 31, she quietly offered herself as one of his wives.

count and given a military command in Gaul, a decision Placidia would live to rue. Before long, he would rise to be the chief military power in the west, and her chief rival. Meanwhile, Theodosius's victorious troops hailed her little son as Valentinian III, and in October 425, Theodosius made it official at a ceremony in Rome, attended by the Senate and other dignitaries.

On behalf of the trembling child, his mother became supreme authority in the west in everything but title. For the sake of form, her son signed imperial decrees, but Placidia wrote them and showed him where to scrawl his name. It was she who made all appointments to important offices. Observes Gibbon: "The mother of Valentinian . . . reigned twenty-five years in the name of her son, and the character of that unworthy emperor gradually countenanced the suspicion that Placidia had enervated his youth by a dissolute education and studiously diverted his attention from every manly and honorable pursuit." Other historians are less harsh. General Aetius took over once Valentinian became an adult, notes Oost. Even so, "we will be fairly safe in ascribing his acts before he was eighteen to his mother's will."

Whatever Placidia might have done or not done, however, she was ruling an empire in the throes of dissolution. Various barbarians were pressing hard upon it on all sides, its resources were shrinking, and a general malaise had spread through every level of a society top-heavy with bureaucrats who remorselessly heaped an increasing tax burden upon its citizens. Furthermore, Placidia soon discovered a pressing personal problem. Where her son had become an avenue into power, her daughter threatened to become an avenue out of it. Justa Grata Honoria was under orders from her brother Valentinian III (meaning, of course, mother Placidia) to remain unmarried—and celibate—but it did not escape Honoria's attention that since her brother had no male heirs, any son of hers would present long-term political possibilities.

When Honoria was sixteen, a scandal erupted in the imperial household. The supposedly chaste princess had been entertaining a visitor in her bedroom, and was said by some to be pregnant, although no birth was ever recorded. Her lover, Eugenius, an administrator of the family's properties, paid dearly for this dalliance. Having sexual relations with an unmarried princess was high treason, not just in the eyes of the angry family, but because it was spelled out clearly in Roman law. Eugenius was executed forthwith. Honoria was banished to a convent back east in Constantinople, where she languished in disgrace for the next fifteen years. For all those years she seethed, outraged and unrepentant.

Beyond the human suffering, the empire's fall exacted another cost, namely the setback to technology. Not for 1,400 years did travel times in Europe equal those of the Roman roads.

Some whispered that Honoria and Eugenius had been hatching a plot against Valentinian, a charge not entirely without evidence and not unlikely. Growing up as Placidia's daughter, she was steeped in practical politics, well aware that clever manipulation could turn events in desirable directions. In any case, she now began plotting in good earnest. These shirttail relatives of hers in Constantinople, she observed, seemed mightily impressed by the king of the Huns. He was known as Attila, and his name would come to ring down through history, but Honoria knew little about the man except that he was said to be a lusty beast with a well-populated harem.

This Attila, Honoria surmised, might very well be interested in a Roman princess—interested enough even to come to her assistance. At the age of thirty-one, she composed a letter to the Hun chieftain, and dispatched it by her eunuch, Hyacinthus. Along with the letter, which besought Attila's help in righting the wrongs inflicted upon her, she sent her ring and a sum of money.

Whether attracted by this bold woman or sensing political advantage, Attila let it be known that he intended to wed her. He had received from her a *bona fide* proposal of marriage, he announced, and by the way, he expected half the western empire as her dowry. When the account of Honoria's letter and Attila's outrageous response reached Theodosius at Constantinople, he threw up his hands. This impertinent woman was impossibly complicating his already strained relationship with the Huns. The situation was as ridiculous as it was dangerous. Honoria may not have known it, but Theodosius had been trying for some time to arrange for Attila to be assassinated.

He proceeded to get rid of Honoria by sending her, and her eunuch, back to Valentinian, along with a stern letter suggesting that Valentinian take up Attila's offer, and get the woman married off. Valentinian, naturally enough, did not see it that way.

Torn from his flock in the midst of a vigil entreating God's help against the barbaric raiders, an elderly bishop is led off to an uncertain fate. His captors may have seen him as a potential source of revenue from ransom. Most of his flock would have simply been slaughtered or enslaved.

CONNOR

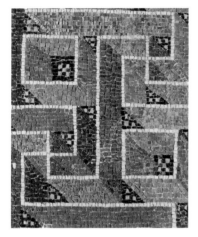

The wealth and influence of Galla Placidia is not immediately apparent from her mausoleum at Ravenna (top), but this sort of brick exterior was common to buildings in the once-powerful city. The interior however is covered with rich mosaics that eloquently attest to the fact that this was the final resting place of a great matron of the imperial court. The detail (above) of the decorative bands is actually about two feet wide.

4. Honoria's name vanishes from the official record in 455; whether or not she was eventually executed by her brother is not known. The "love story" of Attila and Honoria has been elaborated in at least three motion pictures: a silent epic in 1918, a 1954 "spectacular" with Sophia Loren as Honoria and Anthony Quinn as Attila, and a four-hour drama made for television in 2001 by the USA cable network.

Honoria's teenaged affair with the hired help had caused great embarrassment fifteen years earlier, and now this! He would get to the bottom of it. He ordered Hyacinthus interrogated under torture; when the poor wretch had told what he could tell, he was beheaded. Honoria must suffer the same fate, Valentinian decided; conspiring with the enemy was high treason, sister or no sister. But their mother, Placidia, intervened. To calm things down, Honoria was given in marriage to a thoroughly trustworthy senator named Flavius Herculanus Bassus.[4]

Meanwhile, however, Attila sent an envoy to Valentinian to press his claim for the hand of his princess. Told that she was already married, he persisted in repeating his demand, and finally, in 451, crossed the Rhine with a massive force and began an invasion of Gaul. He had been driven to this war, he claimed, by the denial of the dowry—half of Valentinian's kingdom—to which he was entitled. What followed was a military confrontation regarded by many historians as a crucial determinant in the future of western Europe. This was the Battle of Chalons, fought not far from Paris, in which Placidia's enemy Aetius decisively defeated the Huns.

With the turning back of the Huns, however, Aetius became expendable in the eyes of Valentinian III, Placidia's now-adult son. On September 21, 454, the emperor provoked a quarrel with his general, accusing him of imperial ambitions. Then Valentinian drew his sword, and with the help of a servant, killed Aetius on the spot. Within months, Valentinian in his turn was killed by a usurper, and thus died the last direct male descendent of the great Theodosius I.

As for Placidia, she had died in her sleep in Rome some four years earlier, on November 27, 450, at the age of sixty-two. Aside from her other influences, she left a distinctive physical mark on the empire, building or restoring such churches as the Basilica of St. Paul Outside the Walls in Rome, the Church of the Holy Cross in Jerusalem, and the Church of St. Stephen at Rimini. At Ravenna she built the Church of the Holy Cross and—as promised in that long-ago storm—the Church of St. John the Divine and a mausoleum which remains a major example of late Roman architecture.

Church building, however, could not relieve the cold doubt that continued to chill Christians, many of whom saw their empire's unfolding disasters as God's judgment on a sinful world, in which the faithful suffered along with the backslider and the pagan. "For ten years we have been cut down by the slaughtering swords of the Vandals and the Goths," writes Prosper of Aquitaine. "Perhaps men of more advanced years, whose wickedness was greater, have suffered what they deserved from an offended God. But what crime did innocent boys and girls commit? The honor of their dedicated virginity did not shield maidens nor did their zeal for religion protect widows. Priests were not spared the torments of their wretched flocks out of reverence for the Sacred Name. They, too, were lashed with rough whips; they were burned with fire, and they groaned with heavily fettered hands."

Beyond the toll in human suffering lay another cost, notably the setback to human technology. This showed very clearly in the field of transportation. Julius Caesar had once covered eight hundred miles in ten days; imperial couriers could travel 360 miles in sixty hours; Roman horse and mule carts averaged four to six miles an hour. Very early in the medieval period, says Boissonnade, "this Roman road system simply ceased to exist." Desultory efforts were made to restore it. The Frankish kingdom tried briefly to maintain some of the roads with forced labor, then gave up the attempt. The Visigoth kingdom passed regulations on minimum road widths, but these were abandoned. The Web site of the International Museum of the Horse notes it would take fourteen hundred years before humanity would equal travel time on the original Roman roads.

Harbor facilities likewise fell to pieces, partly because the formula for hydraulic cement, which sets underwater and allowed the Romans to build dock and moorage installations, was somehow lost to human capability. It is noteworthy, observes Paul J. Gans, professor of chemistry at New York University, "that the large-scale organization of society allows its inhabitants to do many things that cannot be done otherwise. It may not be the actual detailed knowledge that is lost, but the practice ceases anyway."

Amidst the chaos and decay, however, one reality gradually became discernible. "The Christians who were to prepare for the transformation of the world were those who never allowed themselves to be overwhelmed by the sense of inescapable doom," writes historian Daniel-Rops (*The Church in the Dark Ages*, Paris, 1950). This was particularly evident in their bishops, who came to provide the only stability and continuity there was. Not only did they preach the Word of God and direct their clergy, they often filled administrative roles abandoned by the imperial bureaucracy, organizing food provisions, road and bridge repairs, developing methods of intercity communications, restoring dikes and establishing water supplies. They became responsible for hospitals, schools and prisons. Beggars and orphans usually depended on the bishop's charity, often for their very survival.

"But their greatest service to the men of the fifth century," says Daniel-Rops "was to give a meaning to their drama, and not to abandon them, lonely and distraught, on the edge of an abyss beyond which they could see no further." For all were much aware that the supposedly indestructible empire was being destroyed before their eyes. What was not in ruins was in turmoil. And if Rome, the "Eternal City," could fall, and its empire with it, was anything eternal?

One bishop in particular had an answer to this question, and his answer would stand as the foundation of a new Christian world, which would rise in the ashes left behind by the barbarians. Yes, he said, there was an eternal city, but it was not the City of Man, whose works perpetually rise and fall. It was the City of God, the only lasting reality. The name of this bishop was Augustine. ■

A phoenix rises from ashes amidst a field of flowers in this fifth-century mosaic from Antioch. The mythical bird came to symbolize the hope, which would prove futile, that the empire would be restored. In particular, in some quarters and on some later coinage, the phoenix was used to represent the Eternal City, Rome itself.

The reputation for demonic ferocity that history has accorded the Huns is evident in this nineteenth-century illustration. Very possibly, the heads of slain enemies did adorn their horses, as shown, adding a gruesome element to the physical threat. Sketch from Guizot's nineteenth-century History of France.

Attacked by seeming half-humans

Squat, flat-nosed, arrogant, deadly and, so it appeared, indefatigable, the Huns were feared most of all, but after Attila died, they faded fast

His head was large, people said, and the ferocious glare of his deep-set little eyes terrified everyone within range. His nose was flat, his beard sparse, his skin dark, his body squat and powerful, his demeanor arrogant, and his energy inexhaustible. He was rumored to have dined upon two of his own sons. His name was Attila, and for two decades of the fifth century, no one in the world struck more acute terror into Roman hearts, nor did their empire more damage.

The people Attila led to so many stunning victories (the seventy-some cities they flattened during their savage campaigns through Europe included Cologne, Trier, Milan, Verona and Padua) were known as the Huns. Nomadic horsemen, they lived in rudimentary felt tents, subsisted mainly on milk and cheese, and dressed in skins and leather. Their ears were pierced and their heads shaved to a tuft on top and short braids behind their ears. They were uneducated, unwashed and brutal, a reputation they earned well before Attila's time.

They originated in central Asia, and for twelve hundred years, some sources say, their eastward raids kept China on edge, until the emperor Chin-Shi-Hwang-Ti built the Great Wall in the third century B.C., specifically to block the Huns. In the mid-fourth century A.D., they moved westward from the great Eurasian steppe, along the north coast of the Black Sea.

The Goths, first among the Germanic tribes to experience their fury, thought the Huns must be descendants of witches and demons, "a stunted, foul, and puny tribe, scarcely human, and having no language save one which bore but slight resemblance to human speech" (from *The Goths*, by the sixth-century Goth historian Jordanes). They were consummate horsemen, charging on their tough little mounts without stirrup or spur, as they discharged deadly arrows from bows which arguably were then the world's best.

Emerging from the valley of the lower Volga River, they plundered their way southward through Armenia and Cappadocia into Syria. Farther north, Ostrogoths, Visigoths, Alans, Suevi and Vandals fled westward before them as they crossed the Danube and slaughtered and burned their way through the Roman provinces and into northern Italy. In 434, when Attila became their leader, Rome ceded them the province of Pannonia outright.

By then, a Hunnic confederacy stretched from the Baltic Sea to the Caspian, with Attila and his older brother Bleda ruling jointly until 445, when Bleda was killed (probably by Attila). They ravaged the eastern empire to the very gates of Constantinople, and sent threatening embassies to the emperor Theodosius II.

The most complete description of Attila at home comes from a minor official of the eastern empire called Priscus of Panium, who in 449 accompanied a mission from Theodosius to Hun headquarters far

His Huns in disarray and about to experience decisive defeat, Attila was probably shocked at such an unaccustomed turn of events. A pragmatist, he chose a speedy retreat to central Europe, where his brutal legacy finally disintegrated in family feuding. From Ward Lock's nineteenth-century Illustrated History of the World.

north of the Danube. This was a vast tent village with one stone building, a public bath constructed by a captive Roman architect. There the Romans waited in frustration while Attila alternately rebuffed, entertained and berated them.

The explanation later emerged. Unbeknownst to Maximinus, head of the mission, or to its other members, the chief eunuch in Constantinople had conspired with the delegation's interpreter to offer one of Attila's aides fifty pounds of gold to assassinate his chief. (Only the interpreter could speak Hunnish.) The aide informed Attila instead. Amazingly, the Hun allowed all the Romans to get home safely.

Such diplomatic diversions aside, Attila's confederacy needed continual plunder to survive. He raided through Gaul right to Toulouse, and crossed the Rhine to attack Orleans in 451. There the Roman general Aetius decisively defeated him at the Battle of Chalons, although he failed to destroy the Hun army. The next year Attila headed into Italy, where the "Eternal City" itself lay vulnerable. But he did not reach Rome—for reasons never adequately explained.

Two hundred miles northward, he was met by a Roman delegation. Ignoring the rest, Attila demanded the name of the white-bearded old man who, although lost in prayer, seemed to be in charge. "I am Leo, the pope," said this man, moving forward. The unexpected upshot of their talk was that Attila meekly retired from Italy with only a modest tribute payment.

This astonishing withdrawal provoked wild surmise. One persistent legend claimed that Attila saw behind Leo a white-robed figure brandishing a sword—perhaps Paul or Peter. The pope would only say "Let us give thanks to God, for he has delivered us from great danger."

Or perhaps the Huns had simply reached the end of their strength and resources. Whatever the explanation, admiration for the intrepid pope grew mightily. As for Attila, he led his Huns back to the homeland they had established in Hungary, although he vowed to return if the empress Honoria's promised dowry remained unpaid. (See page 143.)

He also decided to marry again (he reputedly sired at least sixty children), with a beautiful young German girl, named Ildico, as his latest bride. At the wedding feast, he ate heartily and drank heavily, as usual, and next morning was found dead with Ildico weeping beside him, possibly having choked on his own blood when an artery burst in his throat. However, on the off chance that Ildico poisoned him, his warriors slew her on the spot.

Attila's death in 453 marked the end of the glory of the Huns. His sons fought bitterly; by 470, his confederation disintegrated, and the storied Huns laid down their bows. They had produced no epics, observes historian E. A. Thompson (*A History of Attila and the Huns*, Oxford, 1948), and left few archeological traces. They were absorbed among other barbarians in Scythia, and the Roman Empire feared them no more.

To this day, however, their name is preserved in that of Hungary, although most Hungarians are descendants of the Magyars, another fierce tribe from the Asian steppes. It moved into the area in the ninth century.

But despite the brevity of their appearance in history, Attila and his Huns had set off a world-altering chain of events. ■

After their victory at Chalons, Goths fighting in a coalition against Attila's Huns celebrate the heroism of their leader Thorismund. Sketch from Guizot's nineteenth-century History of France.

CHAPTER 5

Rome might be gone, but here was a city destined for eternity

As the world seemed to crumble all around them, Christians asked: Can anything be permanent? Then Augustine showed them the City of God

As the shocking accounts of Rome's fate at the hands of Alaric spread throughout the empire in the year 410, Christians asked themselves a new question. For nearly three hundred years they had suffered the awful power of Rome murderously intent on erasing their faith. Now, less than a century after Rome began offering support and comfort instead of torture, slavery and death, the very city they had converted was plundered by barbarians. Was Christianity somehow to blame?

The remaining pagans raised that very question. Wasn't it clear, they asked, that this calamity was entirely the Christians' fault? Hadn't those unrepentant worshipers of Jesus blasphemed the very gods, denouncing and often destroying the images of the ancient deities who kept Rome powerful and secure for so long? Was it mere coincidence that Rome had been conquered, for the first time in eight hundred years, at the very moment in its history when its emperors were giving themselves over to the insane beliefs of the Christians?

And did not the Christians themselves admit that their faith was centered, not on Rome or its ancient gods, but on something no one could really see or touch? Did not Christians teach their children and their converts to reject the world? That surely meant rejecting Rome. Could there be any doubt, the pagans asked,

Behind the ancient Christian quarter of Hippo in Algeria rises the ornate nineteenth-century basilica named in honor of its most famous citizen and bishop, Augustine. The great theologian (shown below in a mosaic at the Duomo in Cefalu, Sicily) would have walked these very stones avoiding, with other citizens, the huge drain in the center of the high street (right).

that such teachings had led inevitably to the decay and destruction that surrounded them?

One pagan insistently asking such questions was a young nobleman named Volusianus. Although his mother and other women in his family had taken up Christianity, he resolutely resisted it. Articulate and thoughtful, Volusianus put his questions not scornfully, but politely; he was deeply curious about these beliefs that were spreading so rapidly and with such consequence.

One whom Volusianus questioned was a Christian layman, Flavius Marcellinus. Could anyone doubt, Volusianus asked him, that the rejection of the pagan gods had brought about the fall of Rome and other calamities? Unable to assemble an argument that would satisfy the insistent Volusianus, Marcellinus spelled out the pagan case in a letter he sent in 412 to Hippo, a seaport in North Africa, asking for the bishop's help.

The bishop's name was Augustine. He had corresponded previously with both men about Christianity, and now he wrote another letter to Marcellinus, answering these new charges briefly, but with great conviction. The fall of Rome did not begin when it embraced Christianity, said Augustine. It began well before the coming of Christ, when the Roman historian Sallust (86–34 B.C.) had observed that "the army of the Roman people began to be wanton and drunken; to set a high value on statues, paintings and embossed vases, and to take these by violence both from individuals and the state, to rob temples and pollute everything, sacred and profane. . . .

The famous honor and safety of the [Roman] commonwealth began to decline."

Whatever his pessimism as regards Rome's fate, Augustine had nevertheless been deeply affected by the fall of the city. He hoped, writes historian Peter Brown (*Augustine of Hippo: A Biography*, London, 1967), that Marcellinus would circulate his letter in the literary circles frequented by pagan intellectuals. Marcellinus, however, wrote back and asked the bishop to provide something deeper and more far-reaching, because nothing less than a full and complete discourse, a "splendid solution," would refute Christianity's opponents.

"Fired with a zeal for God's house, I determined to write against their blasphemies and errors," Augustine later explained. The book he composed over the next fourteen years would become more than simply a Christian classic. It would act as a light to guide the faithful through the dark age now engulfing them. Fifth-century Christians in the thousands, trudging into slavery, sick and starving, loved ones forever vanished, homes burned, farms gone, villages, towns and whole cities in ruins, death and destruction everywhere around them, found themselves facing something akin to the end of the world. Where was God? It was to them that Augustine directed an unshakable answer.

The city of Rome, he said, like all cities at all times, would one day pass away. Christians must expect this. At heart, they did not really belong to Rome

Empires, societies, cultures and lifestyles would come and go, Augustine said, but the City of God stood immovable. That city, and nowhere else, is a Christian's true home.

or to its empire, or to any empire. Like Abraham, "they looked for a city which hath sure foundations, whose builder and maker is God" (Heb. 11:10). This provided the name for Augustine's book: *The City of God*. Empires, societies, cultures, lifestyles, fads, and fashions would come and go, he said, but the City of God would stand immovable, the city on the hill that Jesus had described (Matt. 5:14). That city, and nowhere else, is every Christian's true home.

Martin Luther's great hymn, written in German during another era of cataclysmic change eleven hundred years later, put the same message into verse. The fourth stanza of *Ein' Feste Burg* (a mighty fortress or fortified city) translates:

> God's Word, for all their craft and force,
> One moment shall not linger,
> But, spite of hell, shall have its course;
> 'Tis written by his finger.
> And though they take our life,
> Goods, honor, children, wife;
> Yet is their profit small;
> These things shall vanish all;
> The City of God remaineth.[1]

"The tone and ethos of *The City of God* is the ethos of the church and of the true Christian to this day," writes the Jesuit scholar Joseph Rickaby (*St. Augustine's*

[1]. This is the Scottish essayist and historian Thomas Carlyle's translation of the fourth verse of Luther's magnificent 1529 hymn, *A Mighty Fortress Is Our God*. Of the many hymns attributed to Luther, this is the best known and the noblest. Luther is also generally credited for the music to which the hymn is usually sung, although he may have adapted a previously existing tune for this purpose.

City of God, New York, 1925). "In that sense *The City of God* is an immortal work." To British historian Marthinus Versfeld (*A Guide to the City of God*, London, 1967), Augustine was "one of the great bridges between classical antiquity and the modern world," who "brought together what was living in the intellectual and spiritual life of his time in a synthesis which did an incalculable amount to shape the minds and institutions of the subsequent centuries."

Augustine was born in 354 in Tagaste, North Africa (now Souk-Ahras, Algeria)—far from the heart of the Roman Empire. He was the eldest of three children. Second came his brother Navigius; his sister Perpetua was the youngest. Their father, Patricius, was a pagan country squire whose landholdings were extremely modest; his mother, Monica, was a devoted Christian who attempted, with some initial success, to raise the bright and energetic Augustine in her faith. During a serious illness, the child asked to be baptized, but he recovered quickly, and the baptism was postponed, not to be accomplished until his profound conversion as an adult, years later.

His nimble wit and outgoing nature led Augustine's parents to arrange for his education at Madaura, an old Numidian town that was a Roman colony. Despite his broad studies of grammar, rhetoric and classical literature (including what we would now call history and a bit of philosophy), he flatly refused to learn Greek, finding word-by-word memorization, the approved method of the time, tedious and boring. His failure to learn Greek "was a momentous casualty of the late Roman educational system," historian Brown asserts, and the result was that Augustine became "the only Latin philosopher in antiquity to be virtually ignorant of Greek."

Augustine's early life would have included an idyllic period at his family's country villa, probably very similar to this one, depicted in a mosaic at the Bardo Museum in Tunis.

Still, as Patricius and Monica had expected, Augustine was a success as a scholar. His proud father decided to send him off to Carthage for advanced study. Clearly gifted, he won a prize at school for an oration and seemed well on his way to becoming a lawyer, as his family and a supportive patron wished. Getting the additional money together for higher education, however, took his parents the better part of a year, and Augustine spent that empty interval back at home in Tagaste, unchallenged, increasingly wallowing in idleness and pleasure-seeking. He was a small-town boy, barely seventeen in 371 when the money issue was finally settled and he set out for Carthage, the great city on the Bay of Tunis.

Its big-city fare—theaters, nightlife, women, intelligent conversation—utterly seduced him, adding to the erosion of his spirit that his wasted year had begun. Once settled at Carthage, he entered upon a career as a schoolmaster and professor.

"I came to Carthage," he later wrote, "where a cauldron of unholy loves was seething and bubbling all around me. . . . I was looking for something to love, for I was in love with loving, and I hated security and a smooth way, free from snares." Before long he had set up housekeeping with a young woman, and in 372, the unmarried couple had, unplanned, a son. They named the boy Adeodatus.

Augustine's relationship with the woman, whose name never appears in any of his writings and remains unknown, lasted fifteen years. Though they never married, their union was legal and respectable under Roman law; she was his concubine, and such arrangements were recognized at that time, even by the church. Moreover, Augustine writes that far from being promiscuous, he was completely faithful to her during their years together, although he describes their relationship as "the compact of a lustful love." His mother, Monica, had warned him of the difficulties he could get into with women, and later in life he writes that it would have been better for him if his parents had arranged an early marriage, to "blunt the thorns" of his sexual appetite.[2]

He was captivated by his reading of Cicero, Rome's greatest orator; it sent him on the search for wisdom. "I was inflamed to love, to seek, to obtain, to hold, and to embrace, not this or that sect, but wisdom itself, wherever it might be." But, he would write later, his early exposure to Christianity put a distance between him and his pagan studies. "The name of Christ was not in it. . . . And whatsoever was lacking that name, no matter how erudite, polished, and truthful, did not quite take complete hold of me." He continued to attend vigils and other services of the church.

Still, when he tried to dig deeper into Christianity, he was put off by the crude Latin translations of the Christian Scriptures then available. He also found the Old Testament disturbing, with its emphasis on obedience to the Divine Law and with its stories that were, at face value anyway, of puzzling morality. "Are those patriarchs to be esteemed righteous who had many wives at one time, and who killed men and who sacrificed living creatures?" he asked.

This seemed a reasonable line of questioning when he heard it posed by a man who was a missionary for what appeared to be a new Christianity. It was called Manichaeanism, and there were a number of its missionaries in Carthage, engaging in public debates and delivering well-ordered discourses. "And so it was," Augustine later wrote, "that I was subtly persuaded to agree with these foolish deceivers when they put their questions to me: 'Whence comes evil?' and, 'Is God limited by a bodily shape, and has he hairs and nails?'" The Scriptures

AUGUSTINE ON THE USE OF GOD'S GIFTS

The good things that you love are all from God, but they are good and sweet only as long as they are used to do his will. They will rightly turn bitter if God is spurned and the things that come from him are wrongly loved.

2. Twentieth-century psychiatrists, heavily influenced by Freud, took to "explaining" Augustine from such sexual references as they can glean from his writings. To some he was a homosexual, to others incestuous. From his reference to a time his father saw him nude in a public bath that made the old man "happy to realize his son would give him grandchildren," they contrived a virtual anthology of sordid speculations, which, notes the historian Garry Wills, tell us more about the predilections of the psychiatrists than those of Augustine.

The Latin Bible's testy translator

He was cherished by his admirers and denounced by his critics, but none could deny that crusty old Jerome, who worked in a cave, knew his stuff

He was irascible, argumentative, sarcastic and disdainful of all who disagreed with him. In the heat of debate, he and his opponents would spit in each other's faces, and he actually prayed for more of these confrontations with doctrinal foes. Of one of his enemies he said: "If he will only conceal his nose and keep his tongue still, he may be taken to be both handsome and learned." Embroiled in the Pelagian controversy (see sidebar page 160), he referred to Pelagius as a "dolt weighed down with Scots porridge."

Yet Jerome was also one of the fourth century's greatest Christian scholars, and for this and other positive attributes would be declared a saint. As a linguist, the rapier-tongued academic shone with particular brilliance. Notably testifying to his expertise is his Latin translation of the Bible, the Vulgate, which stood as the standard Roman Catholic version until 1979, and even then was merely revised, not retranslated. Both this and his extensive scriptural commentary reflect a remarkable mind—and the man whose mind it was did much of his work in a cave.

Eusebius Hieronymus Sophronius ("Hieronymus" became "Jerome" in English) was born about 340 at Stridonius in what is now Croatia. His Christian parents, probably prosperous Greek settlers, dispatched him to Rome to study. Although he enthusiastically embraced the classical pagan writers, he was baptized there, and is said to have spent Sundays deciphering grave inscriptions in the catacombs.

Jerome's travels ranged from France to the eastern Mediterranean, where for five years he lived as a hermit in the Syrian Desert. He did not enjoy the experience. "My hideous emaciated limbs were covered with sackcloth," he later wrote; "my skin was parched dry and black, and my flesh was almost wasted away. The days I passed in tears and groans, and when sleep overpowered me against my will, I cast my wearied bones, which hardly hung together, upon the bare ground, not so properly to give them rest, as to torture myself."

Even in these extremities, however, he forced

himself to study Hebrew, which he called a language of "hissing and broken-winded words," compared to his beloved Greek and Latin classics. He records a dream of Christ's final judgment that testifies to the importance he attached to literature. The Just Judge inquires as to his spiritual condition. "A Christian," he asserts. The Judge responds: "You lie. You are a Ciceronian, not a Christian. Where your treasure is, there is your heart." (Cicero was the greatest orator of the Roman republic.)

When a three-way struggle broke out over who should occupy the see of Antioch, Jerome aggressively argued that such decisions were the prerogative of the bishop of Rome, as successor to Peter. Also at Antioch, he was ordained priest by the pro-Roman bishop. Then he moved on to Constantinople, where he studied theology under Gregory of Nazianzus, and became the friend of Gregory of Nyssa. (See sidebar, page 60.)

At about age forty, he returned to Rome, where Pope Damasus assigned him the daunting task of providing a complete and official Latin Bible. Books of the New and Old Testaments were circulating by then in a variety of unofficial Latin translations, and this assortment, which modern scholars call the *Vetus Latina* (Old Latin Versions), was both confusing and varied widely in merit. Jerome began by revising the four Latin Gospels. For the Old Testament, however, he decided he must not simply retranslate the Greek Septuagint. He must go back to the original Hebrew, a revolutionary idea, and a controversial one as well, since this venerable text had come to be considered sacrosanct. Jerome's translation would finally win popular acclaim, however, through its sheer excellence.

In Rome, he also helped establish an upper-class Christian community of holy women. "I had the joy of seeing Rome transformed into another Jerusalem," he writes. "Monastic establishments for virgins became numerous, and there were countless numbers

An illumination in the ninth-century Bible of Charles the Bald shows Jerome distributing copies of his Scripture translations to monks, who in turn are depositing them in monastery libraries throughout the known world.

of hermits. In fact, so many were the servants of God that monasticism, which had before been a term of reproach, became subsequently one of honor."

A number of his ascetic female devotees would later be regarded as saints, among them Melania the Elder, Albina and her daughters, Marcella and Asella, and Paula and her daughters Blesilla and Julia Eustochium. Jerome's letters to them, the last three in particular, would greatly influence medieval convents. At the time, however, his numerous foes spread all sorts of malicious speculation about his relations with these ladies.

His eloquent castigation of women who caked themselves with cosmetics, wore wigs and so on, increased the number and indignation of his critics. So did the vitriol he poured upon pagans, heretics, and luxuriously clothed clergy. When his papal protector Damasus died in 384, Jerome prudently emigrated to the Holy Land, where he was joined by Paula. With her wealth, they established three convents for women.

The Renaissance artist Caravaggio (1573–1610) evinced a remarkable fondness for painting Jerome, founder of monasteries and translator of the Bible; he produced nearly a dozen moody portraits. The saint is invariably shown naked, except for the seemingly incongruous red cloak, which bespeaks high rank in the church. On Jerome's desk, the artist has set a skull, an item the saint was said to have kept in view to remind him of his death and judgment.

In a letter to his friend Pammachius back in Rome, Jerome reports: "I, for my part, am building in this province a monastery and a hospice [for pilgrims] close by, so that if Joseph and Mary chance to come to Bethlehem, they may not fail to find shelter and welcome. Indeed, the number of monks who flock here from all quarters of the world is so overwhelming that I can neither desist from my enterprise nor bear so great a burden." To further finance the relief work, his brother Paulinian returned to Italy and sold their family property.

Jerome himself never could be accused of lavish living. His workplace, for example, was in a cave near Bethlehem, where he is said to have secretly studied Hebrew under Bar Ananias, a famed Jewish scholar. He in turn taught the language to Paula, whose death in 404 came as a fearful blow to him. "All of a sudden, I have lost her who was my consolation," he lamented. (Paula too would be recognized as a saint.)

The sack of Rome by Alaric's Goths in 410 triggered a flood of refugees to Palestine. Jerome writes: "Who would have believed that the daughters of that mighty city would one day be wandering as servants and slaves on the shores of Egypt and Africa, or that Bethlehem would daily receive noble Romans, distinguished ladies, brought up in wealth and now reduced to beggary? I cannot help them all, but I grieve and weep with them. . . . For today we must translate the precepts of the Scriptures into deeds. Instead of speaking saintly words, we must act them."

Controversy was his natural habitat, however. "It seems," observes Butler's Lives of the Saints, "that sometimes he unwarrantably assumed that those who differed from himself were necessarily the church's enemies." Thus, during the Pelagian fight, a mob had forced him into hiding. In 393, he had attracted great hostility by attacking the belief that Mary had children other than Jesus, and by just as vigorously defending clerical celibacy and veneration of relics. Nor did sentiment subdue his zealous pursuit of heretics, as when he targeted Rufinus, a childhood friend who appeared to support Origen's controversial ideas. And when Augustine questioned his exegesis of the second chapter of Paul's Epistle to the Romans, Jerome blasted the sage of Hippo, too.

His scholarly production was prodigious, reportedly compiled at the remarkable rate of a thousand lines per day. Besides his momentous translation work, he wrote biblical commentaries, historical essays, spiritual advice and more. All this would win him the title "doctor of the church," awarded to the most exemplary interpreters of the divine word.

At his death in 420, Jerome was entombed beneath the Church of the Nativity in Bethlehem. His reputation for pugnacity in defense of his ideals and ideas would vividly survive the centuries. Sixtus V, a sixteenth-century pope, contemplating a painting of Jerome beating his breast with a stone, is said to have commented sardonically: "You do well thus to use that stone. Without it, you would never have been numbered among the saints." ■

were largely in error, said the Manichaeans, who taught that the problem of the existence of evil could be understood by seeing life as a primal conflict of two principles, light (or spirituality) and darkness.

The Manichaeans were named after Mani, a charismatic third-century Persian who had been executed by his government after receiving what he described as a divine revelation. Good and evil were separate realms, Mani said. When the realm of evil was attracted to the realm of good, a conflict ensued. The good God sacrificed some of his realm, letting it be absorbed by the evil world, and from this mixture came the world of material things, with Satan its champion. Human beings, material in composition, but also possessing a spiritual nature, were pulled from both sides.

All man's problems, according to the Manichaeans, resulted from the enlightened human spirit's enforced cohabitation with evil matter. However, man did not sin on his own. He could suffer misfortune, but he need not feel guilty about things over which he had no control. As for Jesus, he was important because he represented the ideal spirit of wisdom and illumination. He was not God, but he brought enlightenment to those who failed to realize that their souls

While he thought he was moving toward truth, Augustine was in fact retreating from it. He found himself preaching the absurd, that a tree's sap is its tears, for instance.

were divine, and he could sort out each person's personal share of the light. In the end, the Manichaeans declared, this dualism of light and dark would resolve itself, with each purged of any trace of the other.

Augustine decided he had found in the Manichaeans what he had been looking for: a solid, defensible doctrine, neatly knitting together the observable facts of science and the soaring tenets of philosophy. With his friend Honoratus he joined them, embracing their beliefs with his usual enthusiasm and devoting nine years of his life to the sect.

Historian Brown attributes this Manichaean venture to Augustine's deficiency in Greek, which left him "pathetically ill-equipped" to contend with the philosophical questions the Manichaeans posed. Augustine would later attempt his own explanation. "I was seeking after you," he confessed to God, "but not according to the understanding of the mind, only by the guidance of my physical senses."

While he thought he was moving toward truth, he was in fact retreating from it, he says, and he soon found himself believing and preaching the ridiculous—for instance, "that a fig tree wept when it was plucked, and that the sap of the mother tree was tears." If some Manichaean saint ate the figs, his sighs would send forth particles of God that would have otherwise remained bound in the fig. "Wretch that I was, I believed that God showed more mercy to the fruits of the earth than to men, for whom these fruits were created." In his zeal, he ignored such absurdities out of misplaced hope; he deeply wanted to have found the truth. He became a highly successful evangelist for the Manichaeans, winning numerous bright young men as converts, proselytizing many of his friends and the pupils to whom he was supposed to teach grammar.

Eventually, his Manichaeanism began to wear thin. Though the Manichaeans insisted they held the compelling, rational explanation for things, he found their leaders at Carthage unable to contend with his increasingly troublesome questions. Eagerly, he awaited the arrival of one Faustus of Mileve, a noted Manichaean bishop who was reputedly able to answer any and all questions about the sect's beliefs. But Faustus failed him. The bishop's reasoning and logic, Augustine quickly realized, were fundamentally flawed, and he offered none of the insights that had been promised by the Manichaeans. With that, Augustine rejected them.

Meanwhile, his widowed mother, Monica, clung to the promise she received in a dream, that Augustine would abandon his wanton ways and return to her faith. She prayed without ceasing for his salvation. Her son writes:

A thirteenth-century manuscript in Avranches, France, illustrates the debate between Augustine and the Manichaean bishop Faustus. The failure of the Manichaeans to provide convincing arguments turned Augustine away from that sect and put him on the road toward Jesus Christ.

> Nearly nine years passed in which I wallowed in the mud of that deep pit and in the darkness of falsehood, striving often to rise, but being all the more heavily dashed down. But all that time this chaste, pious, and sober widow—such as you [God] love—was now more buoyed up with hope, though no less zealous in her weeping and mourning; and she did not cease to bewail my case before you, in all the hours of her supplication. Her prayers entered your presence, and yet you allowed me still to tumble and toss around in that darkness.

In turmoil, Augustine set out in 383, at the age of twenty-nine, for Rome, where he spent a year made miserable by illness. After regaining his health, he opened a school, but his students repeatedly cheated him out of their tuition fees, and he gave up self-employment, accepting the position of professor of rhetoric for the city of Milan. A visit to Milan's bishop, Ambrose, greatly impressed him—the man was both intelligent and kindly, and Augustine was soon listening attentively whenever Ambrose preached. Conscious of his career and knowing that Milan's power structure was largely Christian, Augustine decided to become a catechumen of the church there.

It took him three more years to sort wheat from chaff, truth from fantasy. He spent some time with the "academics," who as a matter of principle withheld judgment on most matters; then with "neo-Platonists," whose books rekindled his hope that he could eventually find the truth. He wanted to dedicate his life to that search, abandoning everything else—not only wealth and recognition, but pleasure. He longed for celibacy, but was still buffeted by the one frailty that, he realized, prevented him from making a full commitment to God.

That factor was lust, but his real weakness lay in his inability, his lack of willpower, to overcome it. While his most influential book is *The City of God*, his most read book is his *Confessions*, a spiritual autobiography constructed as a prayer to God, relating his youthful errors, his dogged search for truth, and his dramatic conversion. In it appears a much-noted sentence, the prayer of his youth: "Give me chastity and continence, but not yet." As a "wretched young

Augustine longed for God, yet his commitment was buffeted by one frailty. That factor was lust. But his real weakness, he realized, was that he lacked the will to overcome it.

man," he writes, he had indeed feared that God would hear his prayer "and cure me too soon of my disease of lust, which I wanted satisfied, not extinguished."

Even so, notes Northwestern University journalist-historian Garry Wills in

This depiction of the young Augustine and his mother Monica, gazing beatifically into the heavens, may seem melodramatic. In view of the deep bond of affection and spiritual connectedness that eventually characterized their relationship, however, it may not be far off the mark. The work of nineteenth-century artist Ary Scheffer, it hangs in the Louvre, Paris.

his biography *Saint Augustine* (New York, 1999), the "very common view of Augustine [as] the great sinner, an ex-debauchee obsessed with sex," does not fit the facts. The point has been made by others, but it is well stated by Wills: "People feel . . . that Augustine was a libertine before his conversion, and was so obsessed with sex after his conversion that they place many unnamed sins to his account—though his actual sexual activity was not shocking by any standards but those of a saint."

Wills regards even the title "Confessions" as a misleading translation. It might better be rendered as "Testimony," he writes: "Augustine was not confessing like an Al Capone. . . . [Augustine's] favorite part of the Jewish Scriptures, the Psalms, says that man articulates the universal testimony to God. 'Confess' and 'testify' are used interchangeably (in the autobiography) for the witness that his believers must give the Lord."

However lustful Augustine had been, he seems in no sense to have been ready to shift the blame for his conduct, as did the Manichaeans, onto other people or to factors beyond his control. They had said he need feel no guilt. Christianity placed the guilt squarely upon himself. And, he reflected, it was this sense of guilt that had caused him to behold the magnificence of Christ, his Deliverer. It turned even his guilt into a triumph. "*O felix culpa,*" he cried, "*quae talem et tantum meruit redemptorem*" ("O happy guilt, that did require such and so great a Redeemer").[3]

It was in Milan that his ultimate confrontation with God took place. Monica, hoping to help him straighten out his life, went to him and urged him to marry. Yielding to his mother's insistence, he became betrothed to the young heiress of a wealthy and respectable family. He reluctantly sent his mistress back to Africa, where she took a vow never to know any other man, perhaps in the course of becoming a nun. "My mistress was torn from my side as an impediment to my marriage, and my heart which clung to her was torn and wounded till it bled," he writes. Because his intended bride was very young, he would have to wait two years for her. He found that idea impossible and quickly abandoned it, taking another mistress.

As Monica continued to pray for his salvation, he returned to reading the Bible. This time, he found that he understood what had seemed murky or arbitrary before. Ambrose's sermons helped, especially those that led Augustine to a solid understanding of immaterial, spiritual reality. Later, Ambrose's successor, the elderly priest Simplicianus, also helped shape Augustine's thinking.

Then one day in August 386, Augustine's life changed suddenly and completely. His account in his *Confessions* of what happened that day would become one of the best-known conversion stories in history.

As he chatted with a visitor to his home, his guest—a Christian named Ponticianus—noticed a copy of one of St. Paul's books on a table and smiled in delight. Startled, Augustine felt at that moment that God "turned me toward

AUGUSTINE ON HERETICS

For you are not to suppose, brethren, that heresies could be produced through any little souls. None but great men have been the authors of heresies.

3. Some historians ascribe the phrase "O felix culpa" to Augustine's mentor, Ambrose of Milan. The words were later incorporated into the Easter hymn of praise to Jesus Christ, sung at the Easter Vigil after nightfall on Holy Saturday to mark the onset of the Resurrection. The hymn rings out after the Paschal Candle lights the Easter procession into the darkened church. From the Paschal Candle, the candles held by the faithful are lit, thus gradually illuminating the whole church.

myself." For the first time, he saw clearly "how crooked and sordid, blotched and ulcerous" his life had become.

He fled from the house into the garden, "angry at myself with a turbulent indignation because I had not entered thy will and covenant, O my God," but his old sins tugged at him, whispering: "Are you going to part with us? . . . Will we never be with you any more?"

Then, from the neighboring house, he heard a child chanting "Pick it up, read it; pick it up, read it." He opened St. Paul's book, which he had brought with him into the garden, and read: ". . . put on the Lord Jesus Christ, and make no provision for the flesh, to fulfill its lusts." (Romans 13:14)

Instantly, he writes, "there was infused in my heart something like the light of full certainty and all the gloom of doubt vanished away. . . . Then we went in to my mother, and told her what happened . . . and she leaped for joy triumphant."

Augustine was only in his early thirties when he experienced his dramatic and joyful conversion, but his health was poor. The nature of his illness remains unknown, but he had developed a weakness in his chest and voice that, for the

After years of tearful prayer on the part of his mother, Monica, and of hovering at the edges of Christianity, Augustine concludes his long seeking and commits himself to Christ. Here, he receives baptism at the hands of Bishop Ambrose, his persistent mentor.

present, made teaching impossible. He resigned his professorship, and in the company of his mother, his son, and a handful of friends, he traveled to a country estate that had been lent to them by one Verecundus, at Cassiciacum, near Lake Como in the Alpine foothills.

He had no thought of relaxing, however. Instead, he plunged into writing, turning out numerous books and papers celebrating his new "philosophy" or faith. At the tranquil country villa, there were also literary readings, philosophical conferences, and daily discussions on such topics as truth, certainty, happiness, the problem of evil, the soul and God. He had, in Brown's phrase, "regained a sense of purpose."

On or about Easter Day in 387, Augustine finally received, from Ambrose at Milan, the baptism that had been postponed since his childhood. He spent that spring and summer in Milan, writing. He and his mother, who resolved their remaining differences as they grew closer spiritually during those months, were visiting Christians in Ostia, near Rome, when she contracted a fever. Nine days later she died. She was fifty-six.

"I closed her eyes," wrote Augustine, "and a great sadness flowed through my heart. . . ." At first he could not weep, but once he began, he could not stop. Adeodatus (her grandson) burst into tears as well. Then all fell silent. "For we did not consider it fitting to celebrate that death with tearful wails and groaning. . . . She neither died unhappy nor did she altogether die. For of this we were assured by the witness of her good life." Moreover, she had seen her son turn to God after years of prayer.

Try as he might, however, he could not stop weeping. "There came back to me," he tells God in the *Confessions*, "memories of your handmaid: her devout life toward you, her holy tenderness and attentiveness toward us, which had suddenly been taken away from me—and it was a solace for me to weep in your sight, for her and for myself, about her and about myself."[4]

Augustine returned home to Tagaste, sold all his goods, and gave the money to the poor. With a group of friends who became known as *servi Dei* or servants

Instantly, Augustine writes, 'there was infused in my heart the light of full certainty. At that, all the gloom of doubt vanished away.' His mother, hearing this, 'leaped for joy triumphant.'

(slaves) of God, he entered upon a life of poverty, prayer and religious study on his family's property. He had no intention of becoming a priest, and he reportedly beat a hasty exit from more than one city when a priest or bishop was needed, and the recruit was likely to be conscripted rather than to volunteer.

However, on a mission to the ancient seaport of Hippo (modern-day Annabah, in Algeria), where an acquaintance was in deep spiritual anguish, Augustine was, as he would later write, "grabbed" as he prayed in a local church. A friendly and cheering mob demanded that Valerius, the bishop of Hippo, admit Augustine to the priesthood. Valerius, who was aging and needed some help, was altogether agreeable. Augustine finally yielded after fervid protests, and in 391 he was ordained.

He established a monastery at Hippo on church property provided by Valerius, and for the next five years ministered as a priest. Valerius overlooked the African rule that only a bishop could preach, allowing Augustine to address his congregations, especially on the dangers of heresy—particularly the heresy of Manichaeanism. At one memorable gathering in a public bathhouse, he spent two days debating with Fortunatus, a well-regarded Manichaean priest who had been his friend. So effective was Augustine's argument that the devastated Fortunatus left town.

It was during this period that Augustine's son, Adeodatus, died. Augustine was deeply grieved at the passing of this intelligent young man, who could escape with ease from the rhetorical traps that ensnared others who debated with Augustine.

4. Monica was buried in Ostia. By the Middle Ages she had been elevated to sainthood in recognition of her years of faithful prayer for Augustine and the answer she finally received. She had also by then become the object of a growing cult, and her relics—the remains of her body—were moved to Rome, where they were eventually placed in a chapel within a church built to honor her son.

In 396, the aging bishop Valerius persuaded his superiors at Carthage to consecrate Augustine to serve alongside him as bishop of Hippo and to succeed Valerius upon his death. (The senior bishop of Numidia, Megalius of Calama, had previously refused to consecrate Augustine a bishop, accusing him of being a secret Manichaean and of sending a love potion to a married woman.) Valerius soon died, and Augustine, forty-two years old, would remain bishop of Hippo for thirty-four years. He now founded a second monastery, this time in the residence he shared with his clergy, all of whom took an oath of religious poverty. That house became a seedbed for bishops, with as many as ten of its residents promoted to the episcopacy during Augustine's time.

Meanwhile, Augustine conducted a sustained assault on current heresies. His public debate with Felix, one of the "elect" of the Manichaeans, left Felix so demolished that he renounced the sect and embraced Christianity.

In another struggle, Augustine pitted himself against the Donatists, who said that those who lapsed from the faith could never be fully readmitted, and that bishops and priests who yielded under persecution could never again administer the sacraments. (The Donatist controversy helped Augustine work out the idea that sacraments and their power do not depend upon the purity of a priest, but come from Christ, who acts in and through the priest. The church, he taught, inevitably contains both weeds and wheat; a weed such as a priest who is in a state of sin will be sorted out only at the Judgment.)

Augustine wrote and saw enacted tough governmental sanctions against the Donatists, then confronted their bishops in a conference at Carthage in 411, which proved to be a turning point in the Donatist movement. They were further overwhelmed in the Vandal attacks in northern Africa, and never regained their former strength.[5]

However, his next challenge proved far more formidable, remaining unresolved at his death. It began after the sack of Rome in 410, when a British monk named Pelagius, fleeing the barbarians, arrived in North Africa and began making his religious views known. Christians in the ensuing centuries would repeatedly condemn Pelagianism, beginning almost immediately with regional councils at Carthage in 412, 416 and 418. The Third Ecumenical Council of Ephesus 431 also condemned the sect. (See sidebar, page 160.)

In 412, the letter from the Christian layman Flavius Marcellinus arrived with its plea for a defense against the pagan charge that Christianity had brought on the fall of the empire. Augustine's response was *The City of God*. He "kindled the light of things eternal in human hearts no longer supported by temporal institutions which had seemed eternal but which were crashing on all

AUGUSTINE ON TRUE PEACE

Thou hast created us for thyself, and our heart knows no rest, until it may repose in thee.

5. When gangs of pro-Donatist thugs called "Circumcellions" raged out of control in North Africa, Augustine reluctantly concluded that the church could endorse the Romans' use of force against them—after all, they were brutalizing and murdering innocent people. In response, a group of Circumcellions laid a plot to kidnap and kill Augustine himself. Their plan went awry when a guide mistakenly led Augustine off the route where the assassins lay in wait. (For more on the Circumcellions, see earlier volume in this series, *By This Sign*, page 170.)

sides," writes historian Versfeld. "If we want to find the whole man in the widest scope of his interests and powers, we shall find him in *The City of God*. Here we find Augustine as theologian, as philosopher, as moralist, as political thinker, as interpreter of history, as literary and dramatic censor, as critic of his times, and as apologist."

Etienne Gilson, historian of medieval philosophy, observes in his foreword to an English edition of *The City of God* (New York, 1950) that the book is not addressed merely to the people of the collapsing Roman Empire. Augustine offers all people in all ages the radical claim "that the whole world, from its beginning until its final term, has as its unique end the constitution of a holy society." In preparation for this, everything has been made, even the universe itself. "Perhaps never in the history of human speculation," says Gilson, "has the notion of society undergone a change comparable in depth, or provoked such an enlarged perspective in view of the change."

The City of God consists of twenty-two books, the first three of which appeared in 413, just three years after Rome's capture by the Goths. By the time the work was finished in 426, Augustine had only four years left to live.

Five books deal with those who worshiped the gods for felicity on earth, five with those who worshiped them for eternal felicity; the other twelve elaborate on what biographer Brown calls Augustine's "great theme" of the Eternal City. Four deal with the origin of the two cities, one of God and the other of "the world,"

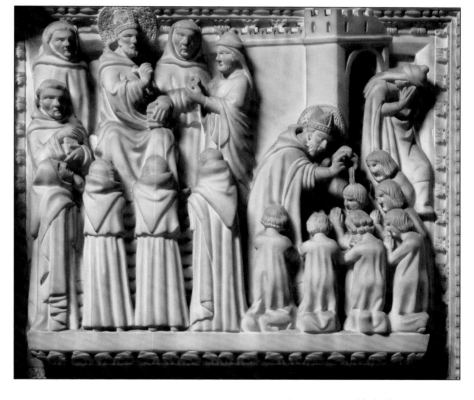

Augustine established a monastic tradition that has survived the centuries, with one particularly notable defector, namely the reformer Martin Luther, an Augustinian monk. This panel depicting the institution of the Augustinian fraternity, is on the tomb of the saint in Pavia, Italy.

four with their "unfolding course" in the past, and the remaining four with their ultimate destinies.

Augustine sees Rome as just one in a succession of earthly cities. Babylon, Nineveh, Jerusalem all had their days of glory, then fell. "The earthly city," he writes, "though it be mistress of the nations, is itself ruled by its lust for rule. . . . It works good in the world, and rejoices in it with such joy as such things can afford. . . . But this city is often divided against itself by litigations, wars, quarrels, and such victories which are either life-destroying or short-lived."

Such has always been the way of the world, Augustine concludes. However, "the things which the earthly city desires cannot justly be said to be evil. Its goal is good, for the city is in itself better than all other human good." It desires peace, but the wars it must wage to attain it deprive it of the satisfactions which peace can bring.

Can we be good if we try hard?

Pelagius, the man who said yes, set off a major theological dispute,
but in the end Christians agreed that goodness depends on God

God helps those who help themselves." This pronouncement has been repeated so often that many people believe it to be biblical. Not so. Its source is *Aesop's Fables*. A man whose wagon is stuck in the mud cries to Hercules to help him. Hercules tells him to put his shoulder to the wheel and push the wagon out. "Until you have done your best to help yourself, you will pray in vain," he says.

Even so, the popular proverb sums up the core belief of a fifth-century Christian named Pelagius. Like so many visionaries and rabble-rousers, he was an eloquent Celt, the first significant writer to emerge from the British Isles into the Roman world.

Swiss theologian Karl Barth remarked that "British" Christianity remained "incurably Pelagian" right down to the twentieth century. This trait persists in the Anglo-American ethos, despite the formidable fact—noted by American Reform theologian Michael Horton—that Pelagianism has been condemned "by more church councils than any other heresy in history" (*Pelagianism: The Religion of Natural Man*, www.modernreformation.org).

At the heart of the Pelagian controversy lies a theological riddle. Christians define God as perfect and infinitely powerful. Human nature is God's creation, made in his own image, although infinitely less, and subsequently corrupted by sin. Therefore, a man cannot achieve good solely through his own efforts. Even the desire to do good, as well as the strength to succeed, requires the might of the Creator.

On the other hand, if we humans are utterly incapable of achieving goodness, or even desiring it, why are the Scriptures filled with commands to do just that? No prophet exceeds Jesus himself in demanding that every human strive to behave rightly, even in his thoughts. Pelagius's attempt to resolve this riddle inaugurated an enduring controversy. It was exacerbated by his followers, who went on to deny the entire concept of original sin.

Little is known about this man despite his theological notoriety—or because of it. His teaching was condemned by councils at Rome, North Africa, and Palestine. The Roman state banned possession of his written work; such of it as survived did so chiefly by accident. Even so, a plausible portrait can be drawn from the taunts of his critics.

He was probably born after 350 in Britain or Ireland; some think his Celtic surname was Morcant (modern Morgan). About 380 he reached Rome,

where his austere lifestyle made people think him a monk. He must have been physically imposing. A Spanish adversary, Paulus Orosius, described him as "a most monstrous great Goliath of a man . . . confronts one head-on, with his great solid neck and his fatness."

Rome appalled him. The city's upper classes, avowedly Christian, waxed ever more opulently wealthy, while the lives of its workers grew more grindingly poor. Historian Peter Brown (*Augustine of Hippo*, London, 1967) observes that Roman aristocrats "were capable of discussing at the dinner table both the latest theological opinion, on which they prided themselves as experts, and the kind of judicial torture which they had just inflicted on some poor wretch."

Christians in this increasingly corrupt society tended to rely heavily on God's forgiveness to accommodate their misdeeds. One notable indicator was their long-standing habit of waiting for old age before being baptized, in the hope that the saving grace of the sacrament would not be canceled through sin before death. This seemingly languid reliance on grace rather than on decent behavior became Pelagius's chief concern.

He reportedly liked to stroll the streets, bareheaded, chatting earnestly with people of every rank. His message: God does not demand from man behavior which man cannot fulfill. True, fallen humanity could not reach heaven save through Jesus Christ. But the believer, once empowered through baptism, could achieve a good life by the faithful, loving exercise of his own redeemed will.

The most reliable expression of Pelagius's convictions is a letter he wrote to a fourteen-year-old girl, Demetrias, at the request of her mother. (The letter survived because it was mistakenly attributed to other authors.) "Because God created man in his image," Pelagius advised, "you ought to measure the good of human nature by reference to its Creator. The individual was not bound in sin by Adam's personal fall," he told the child. "Nor is there any reason why it is made difficult for us to do good other than that long habit of doing wrong, which has infected us from childhood and corrupted us little by little over many years, and ever after holds us in bondage and slavery to itself, so that it seems somehow to have acquired the force of nature."

This upbeat message sparked a large-scale movement in Rome and far beyond. The concept that the individual could rise above even the most evil circumstances had a particular appeal for Romans; it recalled their ancient pagan reliance on human virtue. Dozens of bishops embraced Pelagianism, as many highborn and influential women, and a far-flung network of Pelagian cell groups spread throughout the west.

From North Africa, Augustine warily monitored the Pelagian surge, which ran counter to his own teaching that man is completely captive to sin. An Augustinian maintains that only the light of Christ within can enable us to really see the utter sickness of our own souls. And even then we cannot heal ourselves; the awakening soul can only cry for help to God. Thereupon, he in his mercy will begin to sanctify it, and eventually restore its freedom to behave in concert with perfect goodness. In this view, freedom stems solely from the grace-giving presence of the Holy Spirit. Any efforts of our own contribute little if anything.

Pelagius fled Rome shortly before Alaric conquered the city in 410, taking refuge briefly in North Africa, and later Palestine. Opponents hounded him, triggering heresy-hunting councils throughout much of Christendom. The battle swung back and forth until 418, when Pope Zosimus declared Pelagianism heretical. In southern Italy, eighteen bishops lost their sees for refusing to renounce it. Pelagius himself disappears from history, and is thought to have died in some eastern Mediterranean land.

Some monasteries, however, continued to nurture belief in a divine-human partnership—not an equal partnership, to be sure, but a notably asymmetrical partnership, in which God is chief initiator and savior as well. John Cassian, who helped introduce the rules of eastern monasticism to the west, argued that the unredeemed soul can take of its own volition at least one small first step toward Jesus and salvation, and after that, God responds with grace to keep going.

This view, dubbed semi-Pelagianism, was officially condemned at the Council of Orange (Arausio, in Aquitaine), in 529. Canon 8 of its ruling reads: "If anyone maintains that some are able to come to the grace of baptism by mercy but others through free will, which has manifestly been corrupted in all those who have been born after the transgression of the first man, it is proof that he has no place in the true faith."

But the bishops assembled at Orange also rejected the concept of predestination by God to sin, or to hell. Whether this was Augustine's own teaching, or promulgated only by his more extreme followers, is a question on which theologians are vehemently divided. In any case, the doctrine seems to have been roundly condemned by the Council of Orange: "We not only do not believe that any are foreordained to evil by the power of God, but even state with utter abhorrence that if there are those who want to believe so evil a thing, they are anathema."

A man cannot in any degree save himself, the council concluded, but he does assent to his salvation. Even this cannot be achieved, however, until God alters the will of the man to the point where he can cooperate with the divine goodness. ■

Aesop, a Greek slave on the island of Samos ca. 500 B.C., to whom is attributed a collection of fables that have enchanted the world ever since, would have been spotted by Christians of Augustine's era as a Pelagian heretic. His tale of "Hercules and the Waggoner" is the source of the familiar proverb: "God helps those who help themselves," a succinctly popular expression of that persistent heresy. (The version below is from a copy of Baby's Own Aesop, *at the Seattle Public Library.)*

THE GODS HELP THOSE WHO HELP THEMSELVES

HERCULES & THE WAGGONER

WHEN the God saw the Waggoner kneel, Crying, "Hercules! Lift me my wheel,, From the mud, where 'tis stuck! He laughed—"No such luck; Set your shoulder yourself to the wheel."

Shortly after Augustine's death in 430, Hippo was abandoned to the Vandals and the remains of the great teacher were carried away by devout refugees. His final resting place was at Pavia in northern Italy in the church of St. Peter. There an ornate tomb, featuring scenes from Augustine's life, was eventually fashioned for his relics and placed prominently at the high altar.

"There are no more than two kinds of human society," Augustine writes. "The one consists of those who wish to live after the flesh, the other of those who wish to live after the spirit."

Thus, each person is pulled in two directions within his heart: upwards to light and life, downwards to darkness and death. Most people have one foot in both cities most of the time. The two cities have existed side by side throughout history, some humans struggling more to turn their faces toward the peace of God's eternal city, while others turn toward the ultimately fatal attractions of the earthly city.

Those who strive for the City of God find that it extends beyond the very limits of the earth or world; it includes the world and explains even the very existence of the world. "Everything, that is, except God himself is for the City and has no meaning apart from the City."

In describing the two cities, Augustine lays out an astonishingly diverse and non-racist view of humanity. In one remarkable passage, he raises the question of whether "certain monstrous races of men, spoken of in secular history, have sprung from Noah's sons" and are therefore part of mankind. Are these capable of dwelling in the City of God? His answer is yes. Mankind includes all rational beings, even such as those of whom "it is reported that some have one eye in the middle of the forehead; some, feet turned backwards from the heel; some, a double sex, the right breast like a man, the left like a woman. . . ." If there are such beings, he says, they are included, because God first created one man, and all others are his descendants.

Although one city is characterized by the love of God, the other by self-love, Augustine does not propose that all those within the City of God are

There will be bad Christians in the City of Man, writes Augustine, and in the City of God there will be good men who never heard of Christ.

Christians, or that there are no Christians in the City of Man. Instead, there will be bad Christians among the citizens of the City of Man, and within the City of God there will be good men who lived before Christ or who never heard of him. What's more, while he clearly views the City of God as superior, Augustine says its citizens should not force their beliefs or habits upon citizens of the City of Man.

"This was no transitory pamphlet for a simple audience," says Brown. "It was a book which men of leisure, learned men, must be prepared to read again and again to appreciate." In response to the pagan claims, Augustine compared the pressures of life after the sack of Rome to the working of an olive press, a process by which the whole of humanity was being disciplined—the punishment was for universal sin, not specifically that of the Romans. Addressing his arguments to pagan intellectuals, he said the Roman virtues they prized had been held only by an elite, and had no intrinsic virtue but reflected merely "an overweening love of praise."

Augustine's lifetime output as a writer was immense. Many place his great *On the Trinity* on a level with *The City of God* and the *Confessions* in significance. Besides these and his treatises against the Manichaeans, the Donatists, and the Pelagians, there were many other dissertations on Christian doctrine, along with commentaries on the Scriptures and countless letters.

He dictated, often into the early morning hours, to teams of stenographers. His stream of sermons (an estimated eight thousand), was taken down in shorthand,

A flock of sheep symbolizes faithful Christians gathered at the gates of the Heavenly Jerusalem, their true home, in this fifth-century mosaic at the Church of Santa Maria Maggiore, Rome.

then reproduced by copyists. In his *Retractations*, a catalogue of his own work, he says that he wrote ninety-three books, though others say the number is higher. Some four hundred of his sermons still survive, along with three hundred letters.

As he worked on *Retractations*, dictating and putting his works in order, he was stricken with illness. After three months of increasing weakness and fever, he died on August 28, 430, at the age of seventy-six. He had spent his final days alone in his cell, at his own request, reading and rereading copies of penitential Psalms that he had posted on his walls.

The city of Hippo, attacked by Vandals, endured an eighteen-month siege before being evacuated a year after Augustine's death. But the library of his works was preserved, and their influence on Christianity has continued, as they have been republished and studied century after century.

Before the fifth century ended, vast tracts of Europe would be reduced to ruin in succeeding waves of barbarian invasion. Then in the seventh, all of North Africa and much of the Middle East would fall to the armies of Islam and eventually cease to be Christian. In short, blow after blow was about to descend upon the faithful. But all of these reversals affected only the city of man. The Christian's ultimate confidence lay in another city, a city with sure foundations, whose builder and maker was God. ■

He wrote the rules that worked

The hermit Benedict resisted running monasteries, and some monks tried to kill him, but his formula became the basis of all western monasticism

Benedict of Nursia, like many a serious young Christian, wondered how he could best follow Jesus Christ. Around the year 500, in fact, this earnest seeker grew so weary of the immorality and laziness of his fellow students in Rome that he betook himself, at about the age of twenty, to a cave in the rugged hills east of the city.

There he lived alone, in near-secrecy, for three years, and out of this hermit experience emerged the basis for the *Rule of St. Benedict*, a discipline for monks that would revolutionize European education, agriculture and much more. Among the hundreds of thousands who would embrace the Benedictine rule would be twenty emperors and empresses, thirty kings and queens, and upwards of twenty clerics who would later become popes.

Benedict—the name means "blessed" in Latin—was probably born about 480 in Nursia, a small town some one hundred miles north-west of Rome. Little is known of his background and early life. Almost the sole source of information about him is a biographical sketch known as the *Dialogues* and traditionally attributed to Gregory I (the Great), who was pope from 590 to 604. Gregory cites the authority of abbots who had known the monastic master, and focuses primarily on his miracles.

Authorship of the *Dialogues* has been questioned, however, on grounds of style, theology and content. Some scholars contend that they may have been written in another time and place, and possibly by a different Gregory. In any event, most people agree that Benedict can be best understood through his Rule, a regimen that blends firmness, flexibility and the infusion of prayer into all aspects of daily life.

According to the *Dialogues*, the precocious student was sent by his well-to-do family to study at Rome, taking along his old nurse as servant. When his disillusionment with the decadence he encountered there caused him to abandon the academic path, the pair went to live in Enfide, a village about forty miles east of the city, probably today's Affile.

Here, Benedict formed some sort of association with "a company of virtuous men," and performed the first of many miracles ascribed to him. It was a modest, homely miracle. He simply restored to its original condition a borrowed earthenware grain sifter, which his servant had broken. This apparently was sufficient to attract unwelcome local fame, however, which prompted him to flee farther east, to a cliff overlooking an artificial lake. (Nero, the notorious Roman emperor, had owned a villa nearby.)

There he lived secretly in a cave ten feet deep for three years. His food was delivered by Romanus, a monk from a monastery perched higher on the same mountain, and some friendly shepherds helped as well. Lust ferociously afflicted the hermit Benedict, and he dealt with it by rolling naked in nettles and bramble bushes. But by using the sign of the cross, he was eventually able to banish temptation, writes biographer Gregory, when the tempter took the form of a blackbird and flew away from him.

Benedict later taught that the life of a hermit or anchorite can be adequately managed only by individuals of great spiritual maturity. He particularly disliked a species of holy hobos, called gyrovagues, who wandered about begging from others while practicing no real discipline. Even more detestable were Sarabaites, a species of monk who lived in groups of two or three, with neither experience nor a rule to guide them. Whatever these rudderless fellows liked, they called holy, he complained, and what they disliked, they forbade.

Benedict believed passionately in discipline. He thought that hard physical work under careful supervision should be required of every monk, an outlandish conviction for a man of high birth in a time when such labor was chiefly

equated with slavery and serfdom.

His convictions on the dangers of idleness may well have been drawn from his experience at Enfide. When their abbot died, residents of the nearby monastery pleaded with hermit Benedict to become their leader, and he eventually yielded. The venture degenerated into an emotional quagmire, probably because the monks found the discipline imposed by their new abbot too strict. Some of them tried to kill him, Gregory reports, but the cup of poisoned wine broke when Benedict blessed his meal with the sign of the cross. So he quietly returned to his cave.

But word spread of his character and his miracles, and other monks kept begging him for leadership. Over time, he established twelve monasteries in the vicinity of Enfide, each consisting of a dozen members headed by a superior. He himself headed another one. Five centuries earlier, of course, a far more illustrious teacher had chosen twelve as an optimum number for spiritual instruction.

A number of different models for the ascetic life developed between the fourth and ninth centuries. Anthony of Egypt (251–356) disposed of his wealth to live alone in the desert. Others grouped loosely to form communities. In this *eremitic* (hermit-like) style, members might meet for the Eucharist on Saturdays and Sundays, and some more often for prayer and discussion. But otherwise, each lived as he felt independently led by the Holy Spirit.

Pachomius (290–346) inaugurated in Egypt the first *cenobitic* (community) model, with members bound to each other and to an abbot and

One of the earliest extant images of Benedict, painted perhaps a century after his death, is found in the catacombs of St. Hermes in Rome. Already evident is the monastic garb of hood and scapular (long vest), which is typical to this day.

following a common daily schedule of worship and work. (Pachomius himself would reputedly have remained a hermit, had not a commanding vision delivered by an angel prompted him otherwise.) His degree of coordinated monastic administration would not emerge in western Europe for more than a century.

In the east, Pachomius influenced Basil the Great (ca.330–379), who established monastic communities in Cappadocia, and composed a rule to govern them. Basilian ideas and methods also influenced monasticism generally. Still other pioneers included Gregory of Nazianzus, Gregory of Nyssa, Martin of Tours, Ambrose, Jerome and Augustine. Benedict seems, in his researches, to have explored the writings of them all. He must also have known of a contemporary, Caesarius of Arles, who created a rule for nuns that still endures.

An overarching influence was the *Rule of the Master*, an anonymous guide produced several decades before Benedict wrote his own *Rule*. He clearly drew extensively upon this document, particularly in his prologue and the first seven of his seventy-three chapters. Still another model of primary importance was likely the work of John Cassian in southern Gaul.

John Cassian was born to a wealthy family in about 360, possibly near the Black Sea, and received a good classical education. Seeking spiritual wisdom, he journeyed in his youth to the Holy Land and settled in Bethlehem, where he shared a cell with an Egyptian monk named Pinufius. This old man enthralled Cassian and his boyhood friend Germanus with a tale about fleeing from his monastery in the Nile Delta to preserve his humility, and how fellow monks tracked him down and dragged him back to assume the position of abbot. Pinufius's stories filled Cassian and Germanus with a thirst for desert monasticism.

So Cassian spent a decade in Egypt, moving among its spiritual loners, when the eremitic form of asceticism was at its zenith. He was not so captivated by the popular accounts of monks as miracle workers, or otherworldly warriors in frequent combat with the powers of evil. The best of the desert fathers, he concluded, were wise and balanced models of holiness and piety. Self-denial should not be embraced for its own sake; rather, self-sacrificial offerings to God were rungs on the ladder leading to perfect charity—that is, to love.

Like Benedict later, Cassian endorsed the eremitic ideal but insisted that such a life was not for everyone: "If we go into the desert with our faults still hidden within us," he writes, "they no longer hurt others, but our love of them remains." Upon leaving Egypt, he migrated, via Constantinople and Rome, to the port of Marseilles in southern Gaul, where he was appalled by the attitude and practices he observed in local monasteries.

He was horrified by the spectacle of

> Benedict dealt with his lust by rolling naked in nettles and bramble bushes.

a young Gallic monk openly defying the commands of a superior. The conduct of the daily offices struck him as anarchic, and much of the monks' behavior as "sloppy and indecorous." Some lazy fellows, he noted, actually went back to bed after matins, the night office sung not long after midnight. And these people, who had supposedly renounced the world, often cherished lavish wardrobes and kept their jewelry under lock and key.

Therefore, Cassian himself founded two monasteries at Marseilles, for men and women respectively, and to guide them he wrote the two important works for which he is chiefly remembered: *Conferences* and *Institutes*. Orderliness was his watchword, as it would be with Benedict. By the time of his death in 435, Cassian had created a pilgrim's spiritual road map for the entire Latin-speaking world.

All these things Benedict eagerly absorbed. His own Rule was actually written at Montecassino, the monastery he established between Rome and Naples. Here he remained until his death, around 550. His beloved sister Scholastica, identified by some authorities as his twin, often visited him there, and nearby she founded a community of nuns. As for *Benedict's Rule*, it is not available in anything resembling an original edition, but many later copies were preserved. Passed down through medieval Latin into modern languages, its principles are more guideline than detailed regulation.

In general, the *Rule of St. Benedict* avoids the exceedingly strict asceticism of some eastern monasticism in favor of a *via media* (middle way). Although Benedict as reformer sanctioned what

now seem severe corrections for miscreants, his fundamental message is clearly couched in compassion. Its first challenge: "Listen carefully, my child, to my instructions, and attend to them with the ear of your heart. This is advice from one who loves you; welcome it and faithfully put it into practice."

The Benedictine vows were threefold—to stay in the monastery for life (*stabilitas*), to adapt to the way of life without grumbling (*conversatio morum*) and personal poverty. Remarkably to the twentieth-first-century view, he did not require a vow of chastity. It was assumed.

His recommended chastisements for misbehavior included reproof, shunning, scourging and expulsion. The abbot, elected by the members of the community, was to be chosen for his capacity to act as a loving father, and was to receive no special favors. Precedence otherwise depends solely on the length of time a monk has given himself to God.

Chapters 9 to 19 of the Rule deal in considerable detail with the regulation of communal prayer and praise. An ordinary day includes seven daily offices of communal worship, spaced through the twenty-four hours. One clause stipulates the Psalms to be sung during different days and seasons. Rule 20 states that prayer in common should be short enough to allow a Benedictine monk to perform at least five hours of work a day.

The Rule seems reasonable and

moderate even today, let alone by medieval standards. Much reading is required. Clothing must be plain and cheap but serviceable. Special arrangements are permitted for the elderly and ill, such as the right to eat meat when specifically required for physical health and strength. The quantities of food and wine permitted to the monks appear frugal (for instance, there are only two meals daily) but not punitive. The abbot has the right to make

achieving of sanctity, its author acknowledged, but he believed it to be an excellent start.

Besides actual monks, tens of thousands of laypeople also follow it. Called *oblates*, they are affiliated through a signed commitment with a particular monastery, and occasionally join the monks in their daily ritual of prayer. They are also committed to embodying Benedict's instructions to his followers: "Your way of acting

Montecassino, reduced to rubble in 1944 during the Second World War battle between the Axis and the Allied armies for the Italian peninsula (1), was completely rebuilt and again dominates its hill near Lazio, Italy (2). The monastery's imposing size is not unique; some Benedictine monasteries, particularly in Europe, rival or surpass it in physical extent. Still other Benedictines, like these brothers at the New Camaldoli Hermitage, Big Sur, California (3), pursue their monastic vocations in smaller communities, very reminiscent of their patron's early ascetic career.

changes when necessary.

Benedict repeatedly urged his monks to "work and pray" while constantly contemplating their death. Everything in their regime is meant to keep them pointed toward God, consumed with the divine presence, and wholly engaged in *Opus Dei*. Literally this translates as "the work of God," but for Benedict it had a special meaning. The *Opus Dei* was worship, specifically the eight daily offices and the Divine Liturgy itself. He wanted these to be at the center and everything else (work, reading, meals, sleep) to be structured so as to put liturgy first. Their Rule was not a full recipe for the

should be different from the world's way: the love of Christ must come before all else. You are not to act in anger or nurse a grudge. Rid your heart of all deceit, never give a hollow greeting of peace or turn away when someone needs your love."

He fondly repeated a story told of an ancient sage: "Once upon a time, a disciple asked the elder: 'Holy One, is there anything I can do to be enlightened?' The holy one answered: 'As little as you can do to make the sun rise in the morning.' 'Then of what use,' the surprised disciple asked, 'are the spiritual exercises you prescribe?' 'To make sure,' the elder said, 'that you are not asleep when the sun begins to rise.'"

Although Benedictines are enjoined as individuals to remain materially poor, their order energetically seeks the resources needed to be helpful in the world. Chapter 53 of the Rule instructs that guests are to be received "as Christ himself," and this constant hospitality and charity have become famous over fifteen centuries. And since prayer patterns deliberately permit members to perform most types of work, these men and women have exerted a profound impact within society.

The first three hundred years of Benedictine development are difficult to assess, in part because written records from the darkest ages are sparse, and also because many early houses blended several rules. By 650, however, most religious communities in England had adopted or adapted the *Rule of St. Benedict*. By the eighth century, Benedictine missionaries were spearheading the conversion of pagans in the German heartland. Meanwhile, they were also playing a crucial role in agricultural development.

Unlike most secular landholders, the monks were literate, and could carefully tabulate and record results. They furthermore had the manpower and resources to clear land, drain swamps, and so on. They made improvements, and other farmers followed. "We owe the agricultural restoration of a great part of Europe to the monks," asserts the nineteenth-century historian Henry Hallam in

History of Europe during the Middle Ages (New York, 1900). His French contemporary, Francois Guizot, agrees, in his six-volume *General History of Civilization in Europe* (New York, 1899): "The Benedictine monks were the agriculturists of Europe."

There were an estimated thirty-seven-thousand Benedictine monks by the thirteenth century. Nearly all European schooling was long in the hands of monks, primarily Benedictines, as was most aid for the poor. So influential did the order become in education, theology, art and mystical writing that the years 900 to 1200 are sometimes referred to as "the Benedictine centuries."

True to his principle of staying in one place, Benedict traveled little. In 543 the Ostrogoth king, Totila, visited Montecassino, thereby providing the only certain date in the life of his host. The monk reportedly rebuked the monarch for his wicked deeds: "For nine years you shall reign, and in the tenth you shall leave this mortal life," he predicted. Alarmed by this, Totila fell to his knees begging forgiveness. (A decade later he died in battle, and his kingdom dissolved.)

Gregory recounts how Benedict, in one vision, found himself admitted to the very presence of God. He also was said to have seen Scholastica's soul ascending to heaven as a dove, and later learned that she had indeed died at just that time (probably in 543). His own death came soon after, when, fever-racked, the old monk received the Eucharist in the monastery chapel. Then, with his brothers holding him upright, he lifted his arms in prayer, and his soul left him. ■

Benedict and his sister Scholastica had a strong and lifelong bond, and parallel callings. Fittingly, in death, they share the chapel of the Abbey of Montecassino. When Scholastica died, Benedict placed her body in his own prepared tomb.

CHAPTER 6

Church unity shatters as the bishops contest the person of Jesus

The fervid Nestorius attacks the empress Pulcheria and as their feud becomes doctrinal, Alexandria assails Antioch and a bitter schism follows

With the Council of Constantinople in the year 381, the question that had always beset Christians—Who was Jesus?—had finally been settled, or so it was supposed. He was the "Word," as described in St. John's Gospel (1:1). The Word was both "with God" and "was God" (1:1). The Word was "made flesh," fully human, as the man Jesus, who "dwelt among us" (1:14). Therefore, whatever "substance" or "essence" God consisted of, so too did the Word. This assertion and others had been embodied as the Nicene Creed in 325, and affirmed by the Council of Constantinople, so now there need be no more argument about it.

But there was more argument—far more. If Jesus were both God and man, how could these two be united or combined in one individual? Did God die on that cross or did just the human side of Jesus suffer death? Or was Jesus of Nazareth a schizoid, two persons, one doing those things only God could do, the other his human side? Or might it be that he was one person who uniquely unified the divine and human natures, and was thus in literal fact both God and man? How could Christians ignore these questions? The world would certainly raise them. So what were their answers?

Over such issues, for the next seventy years, there raged an embittered argument, so fierce as to occasion the calling of three church councils. One was later repudiated. It had dissolved into a brawl in which an aged bishop was so severely clubbed and kicked that he died on the road to exile. These controversies pitted powerful and deeply devout men against one another in a seeming death struggle. And behind the scene, for forty of those seventy years, often playing a pivotal role, was not a man but a woman, just as powerful, devout, and seemingly uninhibited by scruple. Her name was Aelia Pulcheria Augusta. She was empress of the New Rome, and she spent much of her life running it.

Pulcheria came from a family of determined women, and was the granddaughter of the emperor Theodosius the Great. Her mother Eudoxia had ousted the sainted John Chrysostom, making sure he died miserably in exile. Her aunt Galla Placidia ruled the west through her ineffectual son for twenty-nine years. Her cousin Justa Gratia Honoria tried to make a private marital contract with Attila

The palace took on the aspect of a convent. At age 14, Pulcheria formally dedicated her virginity to Christ; her body was to be consecrated like a martyr's.

the Hun, furnishing him with legal grounds to invade the western empire. But none of them would prove as lastingly influential as Pulcheria. As much as any bishop, she affected the foundational doctrines of the Christian faith.

She was raised in the splendor of the imperial palace where her father, the emperor Arcadius, unlike the soldierly frontline augusti of the Old Rome, ruled amidst unimaginable luxury. Her earliest memories were of palatial apartments, vast gardens, ornate galleries, and the resplendent icons in the Great Church called *Hagia Sophia* (pronounced *i-yah so-fee-yah*), the Church of the Holy Wisdom. As a little girl, she came to expect the crisp salute of the imperial guards as she frolicked past them, while not far away she could hear the shrieking mobs of sports fanatics in the Hippodrome.

Her mother died when she was five, and her father four years later, orphaning Pulcheria, her two sisters, and their brother, the boy-emperor Theodosius II. The eunuch Antiochus, undisputed ruler of the household, was named their guardian. American historian Kenneth G. Holum, in his fascinating biographies of the imperial women of the era (*Theodosian Empresses*, Berkeley, 1982), cites as at least partially credible an attempt on the life of the young emperor by a pagan army officer who confronted the child with his sword drawn, but fled when he beheld a terrifying vision of a gigantic, spectral woman, seemingly assigned to protect the boy.[1] Antiochus had all four children schooled in both Latin and Greek, but the star pupil was always the oldest sister (who became fluent in both languages).

In one significant respect, however, Pulcheria and her sisters acquired convictions far beyond the comprehension of their guardian, Antiochus. This may well have come from their grandmother Flacilla, second wife of Theodosius the Great.

1. Historian Kenneth G. Holum confers credibility on another report. Recorded over a century later, it recounts that the dying Arcadius placed his little son under the protection of Yazdgard I, king of Rome's ancient enemy Persia, who accepted the responsibility. The king formally warned the Senate in Constantinople that if anything happened to the child, Persia would take this as a declaration of war. Nothing did.

Flacilla had established such a reputation for sanctity that the great bishop Gregory of Nyssa eulogized her unreservedly as "the rudder of justice . . . pillar of the church . . . wealth of the needy . . . common haven of the heavy laden," words which clearly must have sunk deep into Pulcheria's heart. Yet virtuous as her grandmother had been, Pulcheria thought, she had withheld from Christ one gift. She had married and borne children. How much more noble, her grand-daughter decided, would be a lifetime of holy virginity.

Antiochus might disapprove, of course, but the year was 412; Pulcheria was thirteen and the emperor eleven. It was high time, in her view, that she and her siblings direct their own education (under her guidance, naturally). She persuaded her brother of this truth, as she would persuade him of many other such truths for the next thirty-nine years. He was an emperor, was he not? Then he should act like an emperor. Antiochus was thereupon fired and Pulcheria took charge, appointing the teachers who would school her brother in rhetoric, Christian and classical literature, deportment, proper dress, swordsmanship, and horsemanship. She herself taught him the disciplines of prayer, meditation and the reading of the Scriptures.

The imperial quarters took on the aspect of a convent, and at age fourteen, Pulcheria formally dedicated her virginity to God. Her sisters did the same. They would forgo the innumerable benefits of motherhood in an imperial house-hold. Like the Christian martyrs, as they saw it, they would consecrate their bodies to Christ. The sermon preached the following Christmas by Bishop Atticus must indeed have assured Pulcheria that she now shared in the experience of Jesus' mother herself. "You women," he declared, "have discarded every stain of sin and have shared in the blessing of the most holy Mary. You also may receive in the womb of faith the one who is born today of the Virgin. For even the Virgin Mary first responded to God through faith, and not until she had made her body worthy of the kingdom did she receive the king of the universe in her womb."

This phenomenon of "holy virgin women" went far back into Christian history. (See sidebar, page 20.) Reverence for virginity was accompanied by intensified devotion to the Virgin Mary, and by a new emphasis on the role she played in the Christian drama of salvation. Her exultation, the *Magnificat*, much like a psalm, and recorded in Luke's Gospel, was widely quoted: "For behold, henceforth all generations will call me blessed. For he who is mighty has done great things for me, . . ." (1:48–49).

As far back as the second century, some writers had described the Virgin as Theotokos (birth-giver of God). In particular, she was seen as redeeming womankind from the stigma of Eve, who was portrayed in the Book of Genesis

In the mid-fifth century, the link between the women of the imperial family and Mary, the mother of Jesus, was strong enough to blur the line between the two—at least in terms of the iconography of the period. The Virgin of Clemency *in the Church of Santa Maria in Trastavere provides a case in point, depicting Mary wearing the crown and jewels of a Byzantine empress.*

Though this icon of the Annunciation dates from the twelfth century, it expresses in graphic terms one of the mysteries that engaged fifth-century church councils in impassioned debate: What actually happened at the moment of the Annunciation? (See the icon detail, opposite).

2. The idea of a universe of infinite dimension, with the earth a mere speck somewhere within it, did not begin with Copernicus in the sixteenth century. Rather it goes back to Democritus, a Greek philosopher of the fifth century B.C., who postulated that space is infinite, that the Milky Way is a vast conglomeration of stars, and that everything in the universe is composed of "atoms," which are themselves microscopic and indestructible. Most Christian theologians in the fifth century would have been fully aware of a creation of infinite dimension. The Antiochenes recoiled from the idea that the creator of such a universe could have somehow dwelt within the body of one of his creatures.

as chiefly responsible for the fall of humanity. "Through Mary, all women are blessed," said Bishop Atticus. "The female can no longer be held accursed, for the rank of this sex surpasses even the angels in glory. Now Eve is healed." Other women of the Old Testament were similarly rehabilitated. The odious memories of Delilah and Jezebel may now be assigned to "oblivion," Atticus said. Rebekah is honored, as are Leah and Deborah.

Married women, too, became devoted to Mary, but for a different reason, and a subtle conflict developed. Should the virgin mother of Jesus be honored because she was a virgin or because she was a mother? Historian Kate Cooper, writing in the *Scottish Journal of Religious Studies*, cites letters from the period that equate the birth pains of childbearing with the birth pains of conversion to Christianity. Such reassurance was necessary, she writes, because some feared "the increasing emphasis on Mary's virginity would drive a wedge between the ascetic party and the married householders of the Christian congregations."

Pulcheria, of course, was both a holy virgin and an imperial princess. The former role, she contended, enhanced her status in the latter, making her a very special empress. Atticus agreed, as did his successor Sisinnius. They used her cloak as an altar cloth in the Great Church. They hung her picture above the altar as an icon of Mary. At Easter, she was allowed to receive communion with the priests and her brother in the sanctuary of the church, an area from which laymen and women were excluded. She was to dedicate three churches in Constantinople to Mary.

The Theotokos movement found powerful support in the theological tradition of Alexandria and among the desert monks. In Antioch, however, where theology had always stressed the humanity of Christ (without necessarily denying his divinity) the term Theotokos met with a very different response. To bishops like John of Antioch, or Ibas of Edessa, or in particular to a theologian like the brilliant Theodoret of Cyrrhus, the concept of God, maker of the universe, being carried in the womb of one of his creatures, on what was even then known to be a very tiny planet among millions upon millions of stars, was incomprehensible. It was also, they warned, a dangerous move back toward goddess worship and paganism.[2]

This dissension had become evident during the Arian crisis of the previous century, but in the general desire of Christians everywhere to restore the unity of the church, it had been carefully avoided. The tacit agreement to disagree came to an abrupt end, however, on account of one calamitous decision. In 428 the see of Constantinople was conferred upon a man particularly distinguished for tactlessness and insensitivity, a man uniquely capable of launching his opponents into paroxysms of rage. His name was Nestorius, and the central target of his vitriol soon became the empress Pulcheria.

"He was distinguished by his excellent voice and fluency of speech," notes the contemporary Christian historian Socrates, and he came highly recommended by John, bishop of Antioch, his close friend. Raised in Syria, Nestorius had been a pupil of the celebrated Antiochene scholar Theodore of Mopsuestia, whose every word he had embraced as literal truth. Before taking office, he visited Theodore on his deathbed. "I admire your zeal," his old tutor warned, "but I should be sorry if it brought you to a bad end."

It did. Bishop Nestorius perceived himself as God's instrument to correct the capital's laxities. In his inaugural sermon, he told the emperor: "Give me, my Prince, the earth purged of heretics, and I will give you heaven as recompense. Help me to harry the heretics, and I will help you to harry the Persians." Socrates comments: "He could not rest, but sought every means to harass those who did not share his views." Within his first few days in office, he seized an Arian church, causing the congregation to burn it down rather than let him have it. Next, he turned on the wayward amusements of the bawdy Hippodrome crowd, suppressing the circus, the theater, the games and the dances. To make his unpopularity almost universal, he next addressed himself to the monks. They must remain in their cloisters, he ordered, rather than hang about in the city.

This upset not only the monks, but also their chief ally, the emperor's sister. For Pulcheria, however, there was worse to come. Arriving as usual to take her Easter communion, she found herself denied entrance to the sanctuary by the bishop. The icon of herself had been painted over. Her cloak was gone from the altar. "Only priests may walk here," said the bishop.

"Why?" she replied, echoing Bishop Atticus, "Have I not given birth to God?" Nestorius answered: "You? You have given birth to Satan." The lines were drawn, and the war was on.

But over exactly what? That became clear when a further turn of

In an enlarged detail from the Annunciation icon on the previous page, the unborn Jesus is visible in the womb of Mary. One question the councils debated was: At what point in his physical, earthly life did the Lord become both fully God and fully man?

The empress Pulcheria had been accustomed to special treatment in the churches based on her claim that she, a virgin, ranked with Mary in prestige. She is therefore utterly shocked that the new bishop of Constantinople, Nestorius, would dare to angrily deny her entry into the sanctuary of the cathedral.

events vastly widened the conflict. Nestorius had appointed as his chaplain another outspoken advocate of Antiochene theology, a man named Anastasius. "No one," thundered Anastasius from the pulpit of the Great Church, "should call the Virgin Mary Theotokos. She is but a woman." There were loud protests and demands for his dismissal, but the bishop just as loudly refused. Indeed, he endorsed Anastasius's assertion, and set forth a series of sermons to "clarify" his position. Each made the situation worse.

If God had a mother, he argued, this meant that God could die. It was impossible that the divine nature could be accommodated in human nature. God "could not become a baby, two or three months old." This would be pagan, not Christian, treating Mary as a kind of goddess. And while he did not deny the divinity of Christ, he pictured the two natures existing in the one man as "a moral conjunction" or "a merging of wills." Mary should be called *Christotokos* (birth-giver of Christ), he said, not Theotokos, for Jesus was a man "clothed with the godhead as with a garment," and Mary could not therefore be called "the Mother of God."

Nestorius's views were in accord with those of his mentor, Theodore of Mopsuestia; he, too, had warned against making Mary into a pagan-style goddess. Moreover, adds the British historian B. J. Kidd (*History of the Church to A.D. 461*, Oxford, 1922), "Theodore felt that to accentuate the divine side of the Savior's being would end by removing him far away from any true sympathy with us, as well as from our power to imitate him. Theodore was anxious for a Savior with experiences really like our own, one who grew up from infant to child to boy to man, who was troubled by passions, both of soul and body, and knew well what the struggle with concupiscence was."

But others asked: Then what happened in Mary when Jesus was born? Who or what did she give birth to? God? Man? Or if Jesus were an unstable composite of both, was Mary then the mother of this composite but not of God?

Whatever the answers, the response to Nestorius's sermons was explosive. Midway through one sermon, a layman named Eusebius roared at him that he was a heretic. Pulcheria opened a separate church for the growing crowd who refused to attend Nestorius's services. As the monks assailed him with charges of heresy, Nestorius had them arrested and flogged. The priest Proclus, who had lost the Constantinople episcopal appointment to Nestorius, preached in the bishop's presence, defiantly describing Mary as "Mother of God." Nestorius invited Bishop Dorotheus of Moesia to the capital to refute Proclus and pronounce anathema upon him. Meanwhile, Nestorius's castigation of the empress grew more caustic and more specific. Her vaunted virginity, he declared, was a fraud. She had enjoyed adulterous relations with at least seven men.

That this should bring upon him Pulcheria's fury did not surprise him. What did genuinely shock him was the ferocious popular response to his theology. When he had said the same things at Antioch, no one objected. He did not understand the capital city, observes the twentieth-century church historian W. H. C. Frend ("Popular Religion and Christological Controversy in the Fifth Century," in *Studies in Church History*, Cambridge, 1972). Since the late fourth century, theology had become a subject of keen popular interest in Constantinople, as it had long been in Alexandria. Here the crowd mattered, and the crowd stood solidly against the bishop.[3]

But it was neither Pulcheria nor Nestorius who escalated the battle to encompass the whole eastern church. The monks of Constantinople alerted their friends, the monks of Egypt, who alerted their bishop, a man with the theological

3. "Throughout the city," wrote Gregory of Nyssa, when he visited Constantinople for the council of 381, "everything is taken up by theological discussion: the alleyways, the marketplace, the broad avenues and city streets; the hawkers of clothing, the money-changers, the food sellers. If you ask for change, they philosophize about the begotten and the unbegotten. If you ask the price of bread, you are told, 'the Father is greater and the Son inferior.' If you ask, 'Is the bath ready yet?' they say, 'The Son was created from nothing.'"

capability of an Origen and the social graces of a street hooligan. This formidable Christian figure, Cyril of Alexandria, now plunged rowdily into the fray. He was in his early fifties, having been born around 378, five years after the death of the mighty Athanasius to whose memory and theology he was devoted.

Cyril's uncle, a prominent if worldly clergyman, had sent the boy to the desert to be schooled by the monks. Since asceticism did not appeal to him, he returned to the city and was ordained a reader. He attended the Synod of the Oak, where uncle and nephew voted in favor of the deposition of Chrysostom (see sidebar, page 108), a deed of which Cyril was very slow to repent.[4] His uncle

The bishop was a man with the theological capability of an Origen and the social graces of a hooligan. The striking Cyril of Alexandria now plunged rowdily into the fray.

4. According to Cyril's biographer John McGuckin, the Alexandrian patriarch may never have fully endorsed the "rehabilitation" of John Chrysostom, there being "no standard practice at that period which would require him to do so." Nestorius actually accused Cyril of hypocrisy in this matter, writing to him, "I will pass over John in silence, whose relics you have now come to venerate, however unwillingly."

5. The Parabolani were an order of male nurses, operating under the bishop, and organized during the great plagues that assailed Alexandria in the fourth century. Their name derived from a Greek word that translates as "those who disregard their lives," and their number was set by imperial order in the range of five to six hundred. By the fifth century, their function appears to have been expanded, no doubt due to the repeated persecutions of Athanasius in the fourth (see chapters 1 and 2), and they have assumed the additional role of bodyguard to the bishop. Hence, by Cyril's time, they still disregard life—but often it is the lives of other people.

became a particularly powerful bishop of Alexandria and died in 405, bitterly ruing (reports Socrates) a misspent life. Cyril was elected to succeed him—over loud objections, some from Constantinople, where the phenomenon of a hereditary episcopacy was regarded with suspicion.

Once in office, Bishop Cyril embarked upon a career of oppression so vicious as to darken the reputation even of the Alexandrian church, renowned for mob violence ever since Constantine. His first victims were the heretical Novatianists, still active a hundred years after Novatian himself had died, whose churches he closed tight and whose property he seized. Then he took on the Jews, and a minor incident exploded into a city-wide pogrom. (See sidebar, page 194.)

An even more infamous tragedy soon followed. The beautiful Hypatia was the daughter of a highly respected pagan philosopher and was herself a scholar, eloquent and poised, who drew large crowds, Christians included, to her lectures. She had, however, links to Cyril's enemies, a fact that persuaded the fanatical Parabolani squad to drag her from her carriage, tear her limb from limb and publicly burn her remains.[5] Since the Parabolani worked under the direction of the bishop, Theodosius II blamed Cyril, and issued a rescript requiring the clergy to stay out of public affairs and curtailing the powers of the Parabolani. Even the British classicist John Mason Neale,[6] an admirer of nearly all things eastern, calls the murder of Hypatia "an audacious crime," which "deservedly threw a dark cloud over the reputation of Cyril."

But fifteen years had passed since the murder, and Bishop Cyril had regained the respect of the church at Rome and the emperor's sister, though the emperor himself still regarded him as a chronic troublemaker. As for Nestorius, Cyril already considered him an adversary because Nestorius had agreed to hear the appeal of several clergy he had ousted as heretical, thereby implying that the New Rome could sit in judgment on Alexandria. Receiving accounts of Nestorius's alleged heresies, therefore, Cyril forwarded them to Pope Celestine at the old Rome, recommending that Nestorius be deposed.

He also set forth his theological criticisms in a series of letters to Nestorius himself, repeatedly pointing out the fatal weakness in Nestorius's position. Taken to its only possible conclusion, he said, what Nestorius was in fact painting was not one Christ but two, one of them the son of Mary, the other the Son of God, with only a vague "moral agreement" uniting them. Nestorius had even cited as an illustration the marital union of a man and a woman who become, in the biblical phrase, "one flesh." Nevertheless, Cyril pointed out, they remain two persons—not one.

Against this, Nestorius could not easily contend, says historian Kidd. "Cyril was in the right. He had far greater gifts of theological penetration than Nestorius, and he was now convinced that teaching was being given which would render redemption through the Incarnate Word impossible." Pope Celestine was likewise convinced. So was Bishop John of Antioch, although he did not yet say so because Nestorius was his friend. Even Nestorius himself appeared to be yielding. "I have said many a time," he wrote, "that if any simple soul among you or anywhere else finds pleasure in the term Theotokos, I have no objection to it. Only do not let him make the Virgin into a goddess."

So a settlement was within reach, but by now events were running out of control. A council held at Rome condemned Bishop Nestorius's teaching. Pope Celestine communicated notice of this to Bishop Cyril, asking him to go to Constantinople and formally serve it on Nestorius. But what exactly was the pope's position? Celestine did not specify, so Cyril helpfully provided an answer. He called his own council, had it adopt twelve anathemas against the teaching of Nestorius, and dispatched them to Constantinople, giving that cleric ten days to recant or resign. The enraged Nestorius replied with twelve anathemas against Cyril and sent them to Rome with the recommendation that Cyril be forced out.

But Cyril was not finished. He wrote to the emperor refuting Nestorius and to the emperor's sisters reinforcing

6. John Mason Neale (1818–1866), an Anglican historian and hymn writer, worked diligently for the union of the Anglican and Eastern Orthodox churches during the mid-nineteenth century. He is best known as the translator, into graceful and stirring modern English, of scores of early Christian hymns, both eastern and western.

With Egyptian monks backing his violent attacks on Nestorius, the patriarch Cyril of Alexandria waded into the battle. A thirteenth-century Serbian fresco (top) illustrates the determined pursuit of perceived truth that inspired Cyril's ferocity. The group of monks (below right) is from a more recent fresco, at Mount Athos, Greece.

Ephesus, in the fifth century, had become a center of devotion to the Virgin Mary. One half of the great "Double Church," seen here looking from the baptistery to the sanctuary (1), was dedicated to her. The other half was dedicated to John the Evangelist. Ephesus also claimed to have preserved the house where Mary dwelt, and today this claim draws thousands of pilgrims annually to a simple square dwelling there (2 and 3).

his case. This proved a bad move, however. The emperor wrote back, angrily berating him for stirring up dissent in the imperial household. His miscalculation is easily explained: Cyril did not know the extent to which another woman was now influencing the emperor. The little brother had become a married man.

Despite his sister's undoubted warnings from his childhood onward of the dangers of ambitious women, Theodosius had found a wife. A charming "Cinderella" legend, circulated by the palace to enhance the imperial mystique, furnishes some fanciful details. A beautiful and learned Athenian girl is left impoverished on the death of her father, after her two wicked brothers steal her share of the estate. Finding her way to Constantinople, she is discovered by servants of Pulcheria, carrying out her imperial brother's instructions that she find him a wife. The emperor, enchanted by her beauty, marries her. She forgives her brothers, and everybody lives happily ever after.

Some of this is true. The girl who became the empress Aelia Eudocia did come from Athens, and was indeed beautiful and learned. However, she was not discovered by Pulcheria, but by a palace cabal anxious to undermine Pulcheria. Nor was the outcome entirely "happy ever after." The threatened Pulcheria moved out of the palace to an imperial residence in the suburbs, remote from the center of power. There she and her sisters continued their philanthropic activity in the monasteries, deepening loyalty to Pulcheria among the monks.

In any event, Theodosius now acted decisively. To have his appointee bishop condemned as a heretic was not only a humiliation to himself, it damaged the credibility of the New Rome. To counter the directive from the Old Rome and from Alexandria, he exercised his imperial prerogative and called an ecumenical council, summoning all the senior bishops to resolve the two central questions raised by Nestorius. First, could Mary be designated Theotokos, or could she not? Second, was Nestorius heretical in insisting she could not be so designated, or was he not? The council was set for the Feast of Pentecost, June 7, 431.

Nestorius assumed the council would be held in Constantinople, under the direct eye of his ally, the emperor, and easily controlled by the imperial troops. This proved calamitously in error. At the suggestion of Pulcheria, the council was set instead for Ephesus, where veneration of Mary was particularly passionate, where Mary herself, by popular acceptance (although not historical record), was assumed to have come to the end of her earthly life, where the whole Christian distinction of the city was bound up with her recognition as Mother of God,[7] and where Bishop Memnon of Ephesus saw Constantinople as usurping the respect due to his city whose Christian credentials went right back to the New Testament. Here, in the first basilica to be dedicated to Mary, would be held the

Nestorius assumed the council would be held in Constantinople, controlled by his ally, the emperor. But at Pulcheria's urging, it was set for Ephesus, where Mary was avidly venerated.

trial of the man popularly perceived as Mary's worst enemy. The selection of Ephesus evidences something else. Married or not, Theodosius was still listening to his big sister.

The emperor sent Count Irenaeus to Ephesus with a small company of bodyguards to protect Nestorius from the citizenry, and Count Candidian with a contingent of troops to protect the bishops from one another—both under strict orders to avoid theological debate. First to last, however, nothing unfolded as the emperor foresaw. The metropolitan bishops, he had said, should bring with them only those "eminent suffragan bishops" who could contribute to the debate. To Nestorius, this meant a modest entourage of sixteen, but he was counting on the support of the considerable contingent from the sprawling jurisdiction of his friend, John of Antioch.

But this was not how things worked out. First off, Cyril arrived promptly on the Egyptian grain fleet accompanied, most modern historians allege, by some fifty bishops, plus lower clergy, monks, farm boys and Egyptian sailors. As for the forty-three-member Antiochene delegation, it arrived very late indeed, held back both by mysterious causes (such as delay in the emperor's summons) and natural ones (such as flooding on the Orontes River).

And who should preside over the council? Count Candidian, the emperor's representative? But he had orders to avoid involvement in theological debate. The senior bishop present? But this was Nestorius, who early on in the proceedings was informed that he could not attend until summoned to stand trial for heresy.

7. Cyril's biographer, John A. McGuckin, reminds his readers that Ephesus, the city so devoted to the Mother of God, had in pagan times boasted the temple of the mother goddess Diana, or Artemis, a structure known as one of the seven wonders of the ancient world, where St. Paul ran afoul of the silversmiths (Acts 19:24 and following; see also, earlier volume, *The Veil Is Torn*, pages 156–159).

Cyril had a solution—he himself would preside as an unofficial designate of Pope Celestine. (Rome was sending only three lesser clergy.) But as some sixty neutral bishops vehemently protested, he was one of the chief disputants.

Nestorius, isolated in the house provided for him, was becoming more and more irritable. He alienated one influential neutral by his arrogant attitude, and another by treating him like a simpleton. Both announced they would now support Cyril. Word came from the Antiochenes that they would be delayed at least another week. That did it. Cyril took charge.

On a Sunday afternoon, he called the council into session for the following morning, Monday, June 22, 431. A four-bishop delegation was dispatched to Nestorius, summoning him to appear for his trial. He refused. All the delegates were not yet there, he said. This was the first of the three summonses required for a bishop under trial. While factional meetings were held throughout the night, Bishop Memnon prepared the Double Church for this momentous event. Count Candidian rushed from one group to another, warning them all that the meeting would be illegal.

Some hundred bishops nevertheless assembled, Cyril presiding. The Holy Spirit was invoked in prayer, the Gospels were centrally enthroned to symbolize the presence of Christ, and the Nicene Creed was read out. Then four bishops were dispatched to serve Nestorius with a second summons. This time, Count Candidian answered the door. Nestorius would respond, he said, "when all the bishops are assembled."

At this point, sixty-eight bishops who opposed the meeting walked in procession behind the count's troops to the church, to present a demand that proceedings be delayed until the Antiochenes arrived.[8] Candidian ordered those already assembled to disperse forthwith. He had in his possession an official *sacra* from the emperor, he said. Until it was read aloud before them, they could not legally meet.

Even dissenting bishops resented Candidian's order as high-handed bullying of the church by the state. Some shouted at him that he was lying—that the emperor in his document would have said no such thing. It most assuredly did, said the count. It did not, shouted the bishops. Furious, the count said he would prove his point by reading the letter aloud to them, which he then did. Fine, declared Cyril triumphantly, the official letter had now been read, so he declared the council legally in session.

The bishops then ordered Candidian and his soldiers to depart, since the document he had just read specified they were to take no part in theological proceedings. Hoodwinked and humiliated, the count stalked out, the bishops banging their staffs on the floor to indicate the council was now legally in session. There were then 158 in attendance.

A delegation went for a third time to Nestorius's residence, where they were met with open hostility by the imperial troops and told to wait. Wait they did, in the hot sun, all day. No Nestorius appeared. They returned to the church to report their failure. Cyril's letters carefully enunciating the case against Nestorius's theology were then read out and endorsed. Nestorius's replies were also read aloud, and then condemned. A motion was carried affirming the decision at Rome, and declaring Nestorius heretical and deposed. By now, more than forty of the sixty-eight dissenters had been persuaded to join Cyril's side, and the motion carried handily. Nestorius's support had dwindled to less than thirty.

All day, crowds had surrounded the church, awaiting the outcome. When the decision was announced, whoops and cheers filled the night, and torchlight parades began, led by women chanting hymns to the Theotokos. Never before had Nestorius understood the depth of the feelings he had offended, writes Cyril's biographer, the Orthodox historian John A. McGuckin (*St. Cyril of Alexandria: The Christological Controversy*, New York, 1994). The following day, a fiery notice was delivered to his heavily guarded residence:

> The holy synod gathered by God's grace in Ephesus, in accordance with the instructions of our most religious and Christ-loving emperors, to Nestorius, the new Judas: Know that because of your wicked preaching and disobeying the canons, on this twenty-second day of the present month of June, in accordance with the ecclesiastical precepts, you have been deposed by the holy synod and excluded from all ecclesiastical dignity.

Designated officials of the synod then proceeded to the city square to formally announce the decision. They found themselves barred by Candidian's troops, reinforced by the Ephesus garrison. But again Cyril moved shrewdly. He sent his couriers racing with the news to Constantinople, signaling his anti-Nestorian agitators to begin a celebration and urging Pulcheria to speak with her brother, Theodosius. His approval of the deposition was essential, but amid celebrating crowds he would find it that much harder to refuse.

Very late one June evening in 431, psalmody and candlelight suddenly brighten the dark street. The vindication of the Virgin Mary as Theotokos (Birth-giver of God) has been officially announced, and a vast crowd of approving women is walking joyously in procession through Ephesus, carrying an icon of the Virgin.

About four days later, John of Antioch and his forty-two bishops were escorted by Candidian's troops into Ephesus. Having listened to Nestorius's report on what had occurred, the outraged John refused even to meet a delegation from the council. Instead, he called a council of his own, which formally deposed Cyril and his local supporter, Bishop Memnon. This, said John, was the decision of the *real* Council of Ephesus (later known as the *Conciliabulum*, the Little Council).

When word of John's council arrived in Constantinople, the baffled emperor sent a magistrate to Ephesus to find out what exactly was going on, and meanwhile he told the crowds that Nestorius was still their bishop. This set off an explosion of popular rage, and an enormous procession of monks marched on the imperial palace. They were led by an aged archimandrite called Dalmatius, who had not emerged from his cell for forty-eight years. This was considered a masterstroke by Pulcheria; the emperor had great affection and respect for Dalmatius. The whole question was under inquiry, said Theodosius, which satisfied nobody. The crowd poured into the Great Church and refused to leave it. Night and day they stayed there, demanding that Nestorius be deposed and chanting praises for Pulcheria.

Early in July, when his investigator returned, Theodosius reached a decision: He would accept the actions of both councils. He pronounced Nestorius, Cyril and Memnon all deposed, and appointed a new military commander, Count John, to relieve Candidian at Ephesus. The crowd in the Great Church dispersed, angry that Cyril had been removed, but pleased that at least Nestorius was gone.

Cyril nonetheless carried on for four more council sessions, during which Bishop John and his Antiochenes were three times summoned to join it. Three

The earliest depictions of Mary invariably show her simply robed and holding the Christ child, a style continued in the fifth-century "Sinai Madonna" (1). But controversy over her role led some in that same century to depict her in regal earthly terms, as in the mural in Santa Maria Maggiore, Rome (2), in which she appears in imperial garb and jewels, sitting at the right hand of her enthroned child. Later eastern iconography (3) returned to and preserved the austerely spiritual earlier style, while western church art turned toward physical realism, as for example Correggio's sixteenth century "Madonna Campori" (4).

times they refused. How could he receive a summons, John demanded, from a council whose presiding bishop had been deposed? So the council excommunicated all the Antiochene bishops (but did not depose them), and finally adjourned Monday, July 24.

However, they were still under imperial order to stay in Ephesus. Candidian, not yet relieved of duty, cut back their food supplies and stopped all communication with the outside world. The wily Cyril nevertheless got out one message to the capital, concealed in a beggar's cane, informing the monk Dalmatius, and through him no doubt Pulcheria, that the bishops were in fact imprisoned under terrible conditions; some were actually dying. Early in August, Count John arrived, placed Nestorius, Cyril and Memnon under house arrest, and told the others to go home.

Cyril kept on lobbying, however, his agents distributing so many bribes that he almost bankrupted the Alexandrian church. Theodosius reached two more decisions. Probably swayed by Pulcheria, he affirmed the dismissal of Nestorius and ordered him back to his monastery at Antioch. At the same time, he summoned a colloquy of sixteen theologians, representing the churches of Antioch, Alexandria, Rome and others, to reconcile the rival views of Antioch and Alexandria. In two months they arrived at a compromise. John of Antioch would accept the term Theotokos; he would declare that while Christ had two natures, there was in him an essential unity of one person; and he would apologize for having held a rival council. Cyril and his supporters would agree to withdraw his twelve anathemas against Nestorius, because some of the points implied Apollinarianism, the doctrine that Jesus Christ was not fully human. Significantly, try as they would, neither side could convict the other of heresy.

With that, the three imprisoned bishops were released.

However, credit for bringing about final agreement between Cyril and John belongs to an aged and very diplomatic bishop, Paul of Emesa, who on the emperor's orders worked on this project in Antioch and Alexandria throughout the year 433. Among other things, Cyril came to realize that the charges of Apollinarianism against him, which he had regarded as absurd, must be answered.

His modifications were accepted by John and composed by the Antiochenes into a document known as the Formula for Reunion. It declared: "There has been a union of

An icon of the enthroned Theotokos and Child, which would serve as a model for eastern churches in the centuries to come, was placed high above the altar of Hagia Sophia in Constantinople. It has also been interpreted symbolically as a representation of the church bearing Jesus in its bosom. That it survived Hagia Sophia's later conversion to a mosque is astonishing. Situated directly above the Islamic prayer niche (lower corner), it must have been subject to energetic but unsuccessful efforts to have it painted over.

two natures; wherefore we confess one Christ, one Son, one Lord." Meanwhile John affirmed the deposing of Nestorius and proclaimed him a heretic. Each then told his followers that the other had conceded, but the fact was, observes the sixteenth-century Anglican theologian Richard Hooker, that they had always been "nearer to each other than either at the time would have admitted."

Again crowds filled the Great Church, this time to proclaim that "Mary the Virgin has deposed Nestorius the Jew . . . Christ on the cross has won the victory . . . Nestorius, the Jew, should be burnt." (Nestorius was not Jewish, but his theology was popularly believed to be influenced by Judaism. Pulcheria was notably anti-Jewish.) Count Irenaeus, Nestorius's military protector at Ephesus and a supporter as well, came in for further abuse. He was called "sorcerer . . . Hellene . . . a shameful creature." Pulcheria was proclaimed victorious. "Many years to the empress!" cried the crowd. "She has strengthened our faith! She is the orthodox one."

But elsewhere the issue was not settled. Some of Nestorius's followers continued to battle for his theology. Banned from the empire, they moved into Persia, where at first they suffered severe persecution but later won acceptance. Nestorius himself, far from remaining quiet in his monastery, conducted a pamphleteering war from Antioch.

This activity occasioned his removal to Petra, the caravan center in northern Arabia. Unsuppressed even there, he was moved to the penal colony in the Great Oasis of Egypt, a waterhole surrounded by desert. From that desolate place, he laid blame for his problems squarely on Pulcheria. There, too, he wrote his apologia, known as the *Bazaar of Heraclides*, and there in 451, he died, bearing his sufferings, many said, with "nobility of spirit." In a letter to Cyril, he assessed his plight as follows:

> I, who had [on my side] the chief men and the emperor and the episcopate of Constantinople, I, who had been long-suffering unto heretics, was harassed by you [Cyril] so as to be driven out; and you were bishop of Alexandria and you got hold of the church of Constantinople—a thing which the bishop of no other city whatsoever would have suffered, though one wished to judge him in judgment and not with violence. But I have endured all things while making use of persuasion and not of violence, to persuade the ignorant; and I looked for helpers, not for those who contend in fight and cannot be persuaded.

But the Christian world had not heard the end of either Nestorius or the issue that caused his downfall. His theology, or some semblance of it, became the basis of the Nestorian Church, which launched a Christian missionary endeavor that would carry the cross as far east as China in the ensuing four centuries. Meanwhile, at Constantinople, Alexandria and Rome, it soon became evident that the perplexing question—Who was Jesus?—was still open, and the battle to resolve it over the next twenty years would become sharp, violent and permanently divisive. ■

CHAPTER 7

The Chalcedon council answers the question but splits the church

A patriarch perishes in an ecclesiastical brawl, so pope and empress join to force the issue— permanently alienating the church in Egypt

Constantinople, in the year 439, was beset by shocking development. The fairytale romance and marriage of the emperor Theodosius II and the girl from Athens, Aelia Eudocia, was breaking up. By now, the empress Eudocia had given birth to two daughters. One, Flacilla, had died in 431; the other, Licinia, was married in 437 at age fifteen to Valentinian III, the western emperor. That same year, Eudocia undertook a pilgrimage to the Holy Land. She was much moved by her experiences there—so moved that when she returned to the capital it was announced that she would leave the imperial household and live as a holy woman in the Holy Land.

The official explanation attributed this entirely to religious commitment, a much admired motive. One unofficial explanation was that her husband, himself always infatuated with the ascetic life, had ceased all conjugal relations. An even less official explanation attributes her departure to a charge against her of adultery with a certain Paulinus, a boyhood friend of the emperor. Paulinus was subsequently executed, though Eudocia was not the given reason. In any event, Eudocia returned from the pilgrimage a changed woman, devoted to works of charity.[1] In 440, she went back to Palestine and established herself in regal splendor as a Christian philanthropist. (See sidebar page 194.)

1. Contemporary with Eudocia's pilgrimage to the Holy Land, though not connected to it, is a significant incident. On September 25, 438, a severe earthquake struck the city of Constantinople. As buildings toppled around them and fire spread, people fled to the city's outskirts, some taking refuge in the Hebdomon, Pulcheria's suburban palace. There, so the story goes, when the ground shook in an afterquake, a child in their midst was swept up into the air and then gently returned to earth, saying three times over a simple prayer: "Holy God, Holy Mighty, Holy Immortal, have mercy on us." The bishop who was with them repeated the prayer, and the quake was over. Theodosius and Pulcheria decreed that this threefold prayer be chanted throughout the Christian world. Known as the Trisagion, it is still repeated at every service in the Eastern Church.

The departure of Eudocia, however, did not entirely restore the emperor's sister Pulcheria to her former ascendancy. Instead, another rising figure in the imperial circle, a eunuch named Chrysaphius, with the title of grand chamberlain, had gained the ear of the emperor in all spheres of public policy. As a recent convert to Christianity, he took a particular interest in ecclesiastical affairs. It was he, according to some historians, whose diligent machinations to enhance his own influence with Theodosius probably broke up the emperor's marriage.

Chrysaphius's mentor in the faith was the aged Eutyches, the senior archimandrite of a Constantinople monastery and a passionate supporter of Cyril of Alexandria, and therefore frankly appalled at the reports still emerging from Antioch. It was by now 441, ten years after the Council of Ephesus, and eight after the Formula of Reunion. Nestorianism, or something very like it, was being promoted more vigorously than ever at Antioch. And the culprit (or so Eutyches saw it) was Theodoret, bishop of Cyrrhus (forty miles northeast of Antioch), widely recognized as the most persuasive and therefore dangerous of those who embraced the two-person Christology.

Moreover, there was evidence that some at Constantinople and even at Alexandria had also gone soft on the Christology question. When Proclus, who had preached so boldly for the Theotokos a decade earlier and was now bishop of Constantinople, launched a campaign to depose Theodoret for heresy, none other than the mighty Cyril himself urged Proclus to back off. The fight must have gone out of Cyril, some said, when he reached his late sixties. Seeking peace in the church, he was also appealing to his former allies in Antioch to work toward unity, not strife.

John of Antioch died in 441. His successor, Bishop Domnus, became a mere sycophant of Theodoret, at whose suggestion he appointed as bishop of Tyre the

Historians depict Dioscorus as a violent man whose mission, self-assigned, was the total extermination of two-person Christology at whatever cost to himself or the church.

same Irenaeus who had commanded Nestorius's bodyguard at Ephesus. Not only had Irenaeus supposedly been banished, he had also been married twice. Bishops, by tradition, were not to be married at all. This appointment was, in effect, a taunt aimed squarely at the credibility of the Council of Ephesus, which it was Theodoret's aim to repudiate. Historian R. V. Sellers (*The Council of Chalcedon*, London, 1953) calls the Irenaeus appointment Theodoret's "masterstroke."

On June 27, 444, just short of his seventieth birthday, Cyril died. He was succeeded by his archdeacon, Dioscorus—and now the major player in the last act of the christological drama has appeared. Dioscorus had none of Cyril's theological capability and all of Cyril's bullying inclinations. He cared fervently for his city and shared its contempt for upstart Constantinople. Just as passionately, he subscribed to Cyril's theology—not (as he saw him) the fallen Cyril of recent years who had so supinely compromised with the wily theological manipulators at Antioch, but the real Cyril, the Cyril who had hammered the entire church into accepting the declarations at Ephesus. Historians depict Dioscorus as a violent man whose self-assigned mission was the extermination, root and branch, of two-person Christology, wherever it appeared, at whatever cost to himself, to his enemies, or to the church.

Dioscorus swiftly cleaned up what he viewed as the mess the declining Cyril had left behind. He purged the Alexandrian establishment of all Cyril's supporters. He leagued with his old friend at the capital, the archimandrite Eutyches, through Eutyches to the grand chamberlain Chrysaphius, and through Chrysaphius, he hoped, to the emperor. It took four years, but by February 448 Dioscorus's connections paid off. Shown some of Theodoret's latest writings, Theodosius saw the whole unity of the empire imperiled. Certain of those writings must be burned, the emperor decreed. Theodoret himself—described as a "vexatious and turbulent busybody"—was to be confined to his own diocese. The consecration of Irenaeus as bishop of Tyre was to be revoked. This edict, read in the cathedral at Antioch, caused a riot.

Furthermore, one effect of the furor was to focus attention, not only on what Theodoret was teaching, but also upon the line being taken by his opponents. It became clear that the theology espoused by Eutyches and Dioscorus was as heretical in one direction as Nestorius's had been in the other. Nestorius had distinguished the human nature of Christ so thoroughly from the divine nature as to require two Christs. But according to the pronouncements of these current critics, after the union of the divine and human natures in Jesus there was but one nature, and that divine. Hence, God died on the cross; a man did not. Human-kind could only be redeemed through the cross, however, if both natures were present: the human nature suffering death, the divine nature prevailing over it. Cyril had avoided this pitfall in the days of his "decline" by conceding that both natures must have continued. Eutyches, and to a degree Dioscorus, seemed to have fallen straight into it.

Eutyches's extreme theology became evident to anyone who talked to him, and especially to his friend, Eusebius—the same Eusebius who had shouted out in the Great Church twenty years earlier that the preacher, Nestorius, was a heretic. Reluctantly, declared Eusebius, he had discovered another heretic: his friend Eutyches. His complaint to the patriarch put Eutyches on trial for heresy. But the patriarch was no longer Proclus; in 446, a gentle, timorous cleric named Flavian had succeeded to the

Unearthed in 1910, the silver Chalice of Antioch has acquired a near-legendary following as the Holy Grail—that is, the cup Jesus used at the Last Supper. Only seven and one-half inches high, it consists of a simple inner cup (the Grail) of plain design, and an outer goblet obviously designed to contain it. The latter is exquisitely worked with ornate representations of the Lord Jesus, biblical events and Christian symbols.

office. Three years later, it would prove the death of him.

After an exhaustive trial by Constantinople's home synod, Eutyches was found guilty and Flavian deposed him as archimandrite—which gave the scheming Dioscorus precisely the opportunity he was looking for. Using his connection through the eunuch Chrysaphius, he persuaded Theodosius to call a second Council of Ephesus to appeal the conviction of Eutyches. But far more was involved; his real aim was to stamp out every trace of sympathy for Nestorianism, beginning with the patriarch Flavian himself. This council, set for August 449, was destined for infamy. It would explode into an exhibition of human willfulness and raw brutality for which Christians would spend the next millennium and a half apologizing.

Guided by Eutyches and Chrysaphius, the emperor Theodosius laid out the council's procedure. Dioscorus would preside. Theodoret, by far the most skillful of the Antiochenes, would not be invited to attend. As an innovation, the senior Syrian archimandrite Barsauma, currently in the capital, would be invited to speak for the monasteries, hitherto unrepresented at church councils. He could bring other monks to assist him.

Two factors, however, Dioscorus did not take into account. One was the emperor's sister, who, though he didn't realize it, had more influence over the monasteries at Constantinople than did Barsauma, and more theological capability than Dioscorus himself. Pulcheria very quickly discerned that Eutyches, having virtually denied that the humanity of Christ persisted after the fusion of the divine and human natures, was indeed a heretic.

The other factor was the bishop of Rome, Pope Leo I, soon to be known as Leo the Great. Dioscorus may have assumed that Leo would be too preoccupied to think much about theology.

Following a path well-trodden over the centuries by visitors, merchants and not a few bishops, priests and monks, present-day tourists flock through the Gate of Persecution in the walls of ancient Ephesus. It is so named because of the carvings that once graced it, depicting the classic hero Achilles pursued by his foes.

Rome had been sacked once and was about to be sacked again; Gaul and Spain were already desolate and further endangered by the Huns; Britain had been abandoned to the Saxon horde; North Africa had been lost to the Vandals. But Leo did find time to think about this council, and the concordat he made with Pulcheria would bring Dioscorus's plans crashing down.

In response to a plea for help from Patriarch Flavian, Leo set forth a declaration known as the *Tome of Leo*. It was not intended as a complete christological theology, but as a refutation of the specific errors of Nestorius on the one hand and Eutyches on the other. Christ's manhood, said Leo, was permanent in him and did not change him. The human nature was not "absorbed" by the divine, but rather "each nature [works] in interaction with the other and does what appertains to it."

Leo concluded by describing Eutyches's Christology as "absurd."

On August 8, nearly 130 bishops assembled in the Double Church. It was the same one used by the council of 431, but the seating had been altered somewhat. Dioscorus, styled, a supreme guardian of the faith, was seated on a throne high above the other bishops. The Roman legate Julius, sat closest to him, clutching Leo's Tome. Hilary, a deacon and the second Roman legate, sat several places away from Julius so that the two could not confer. The next in position and precedence was Flavian, patriarch of Constantinople. Behind the bishops were crowds of Barsauma's monks, talking, restive, and generally ill-behaved.

Preliminaries completed, Dioscorus called for discussion of the heresy charge against Eutyches. Julius, the Roman legate, rose and announced that he had a communication from Pope Leo that should be read. Dioscorus received the letter, but refused to read it. After Eutyches had stated his defense of himself at considerable length, Julius again asked that Leo's letter be read. Again he was refused. A letter from the emperor, excoriating Nestorianism, was read instead. Then Dioscorus called for a vote. Some 111 bishops voted to restore Eutyches as head of his monastery. Again Julius asked to be heard; again he was ignored. So Leo's Tome was never read.

Then Dioscorus revealed the full scope of his plan. The emperor, he said, had required that the council assess a charge of heresy against the patriarch Flavian and against Eusebius, the accuser of Eutyches. This trial would now proceed.

LEO THE GREAT ON REFLECTING GOD'S IMAGE

Human beings were made after the image of God, that we might be imitators of our Maker. In us, as in a mirror, the character of the divine goodness should shine out. That he might find in us the character of his goodness, he gives us further, the capacity to do what he does, lighting lamps in our souls, and enkindling us with the fire of his love.

Dioscorus summoned the soldiers and forced wayward bishops to sign the condemnation. One objector, Flavian, was beaten, knocked down and kicked viciously by a pack of monks.

There was a roar of protest. To acquit Eutyches was one thing. To bring charges against Flavian and Eusebius was going entirely too far. Bishops stood in their places and shouted their objection.

Pandemonium broke out. Dioscorus summoned the soldiers, who swarmed into the church, swords unsheathed, and forced recalcitrant bishops to sign the condemnation. From the various accounts, a probable course of events can be pieced together. Flavian loudly objected to this summary procedure. He was then set upon by the soldiers and by Barsauma's monks, beaten, knocked down and kicked. Some reports say that Dioscorus himself took part in the beating, and actually put the boots to the old man.

Somehow, Flavian stumbled free of the melee and took refuge in the sanctuary of the church, where he was kept prisoner until the council ended, and

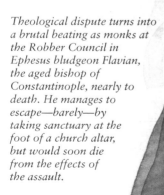

Theological dispute turns into a brutal beating as monks at the Robber Council in Ephesus bludgeon Flavian, the aged bishop of Constantinople, nearly to death. He manages to escape—barely—by taking sanctuary at the foot of a church altar, but would soon die from the effects of the assault.

then was to be escorted into exile. He died from his injuries a few days later. Several accounts say simply that he was "murdered."[2] The Roman deacon Hilary, who also vehemently objected to the charges, was assaulted and fled the building, leaving his baggage behind. Finding the port blocked to prevent his return to Italy, he fled along back roads to an outport and there took passage back to Rome, where in twelve years, he would become Leo's successor. The legate Julius also escaped, but there is no record of how.

In successive sessions, Dioscorus completed his agenda. Theodoret and other bishops who supported him were all deposed. One was Ibas of Edessa, who was strongly supported in Persian territory. His removal provided further grounds for the huge Nestorian movement that lay ahead. Another was Domnus of Antioch, who shrank from attending the meetings due to "a great bodily debility." He was tracked down at his Ephesus lodgings, and like the rest, was forced to concur. The council wound up by declaring Cyril's twelve anathemas (which Cyril himself had withdrawn) to be orthodox Christianity.

When the accounts of these proceedings reached Leo, he branded the Second Council of Ephesus as the *Latrocinium* or "Robber Council," the epithet by which it would be known to Christian history. Dioscorus himself he called "the Egyptian plunderer" and "the preacher of the devil's errors." But to his supporters, Dioscorus was "the apostolic preacher and Christ's true martyr."

Deacon Hilary had carried back to Rome a letter from Flavian, presumably written in captivity at Ephesus, appealing to Leo to rescue the eastern church from the heretical religion being preached by Dioscorus. In response, Leo mounted a concerted campaign to discredit and annul the Robber Council. He wrote to Theodosius, pleading for another such meeting, but in Italy, where it could include bishops from both east and west. He besought Pulcheria to influence her brother and the monasteries in the east. He urged the western emperor Valentinian III, his empress Licinia, and his mother Galla Placidia to prevail upon their kinsman, Theodosius, to repair the damage done "by the frenzy of one man." But Theodosius resisted all efforts. As far as he was concerned, the doctrinal questions had been settled by the Second Council of Ephesus. The case was closed.

Then occurred one of those coincidental events that shape history. Theodosius wrote his rejection to Leo on July 16, 450. Twelve days later, the emperor fell from his horse and shortly died of the injuries. But in that brief interim, he and his sister had reached an agreement. Since he had no male heir, she was to marry a Roman military commander named Marcian, aged sixty, well-supported by the army, though to honor her vow of virginity, the marriage would not be consummated. This simple plan had extraordinary consequences. "The history of Christian doctrine," writes historian R. V. Sellers, "followed a course which at that time none could have anticipated."

Pulcheria and Marcian were married within a few days, Pulcheria placing the crown on her husband's head. Their first act was to fire the troublesome eunuch Chrysaphius. Their second was to serve notice on the Huns that the huge bribes Theodosius had been paying them were over and they were now at war. Their third act was to order the body of Flavian brought back to the capital for state burial beside the great ecclesiastics of the past. This served notice on Dioscorus that his influence in the palace was at an end.

Next, Marcian called a council of the church to meet in October 451 at Nicea, a venue later changed to Chalcedon, across the Bosporus from the capital. Another eastern synod was not what Leo had wanted, but he knew this was the best he would get. So he endorsed the plan. Meanwhile, a home synod in Constantinople anathematized both Eutyches and Nestorius, and all bishops in the jurisdiction of Constantinople were required to accept the Tome of Leo.

Dioscorus and his Egyptian bishops disembarked on the Asian mainland, probably at Ephesus, declared themselves a synod, and excommunicated Leo of Rome. They then proceeded to Chalcedon, where more than five hundred bishops assembled in the Church of St. Euphemia, those supporting Dioscorus on one side, those supporting Leo on the other. A phalanx of imperial officials, constituting a commission, was seated before them all, to act as a legal authority and preserve order.

On October 8, when the Gospels were enthroned for the first session, the papal legates declared that if Dioscorus were seated, they would withdraw. The commissioners ruled that Dioscorus could be excluded only by act of the council, and until such a motion was passed he had the right to a seat. He sat down amidst his supporters. The papal legates remained. Then Theodoret was seated, amid a fusillade of abuse from Dioscorus's faction, excoriating him as "a Jew . . . a fighter against God . . . an insulter of Christ . . . he who anathematized the holy Cyril. . . ." From the other side came cries of "murderers . . . agitators."

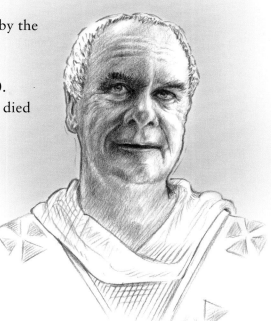

LEO THE GREAT ON 'LOVE YOUR NEIGHBOR'

Christian grace despairs of no one, and teaches that no one should be passed over. And rightly does it also tell us that enemies are to be loved and persecutors prayed for. For, as it daily grafts branches of wild olive from every nation into its holy olive tree, it makes friends of enemies, adopted children of strangers, and justified people out of sinners.

2. In a detailed and detective-like study, the twentieth-century British historian Henry Chadwick attempts to piece together from the various records, what actually happened to Patriarch Flavian (*The Exile and Death of Flavian of Constantinople: A Prologue to the Council of Chalcedon*, Journal of Theological Studies, 1955). He comes to the conclusion that the most commonly accepted account (given here) is probably the most reliable.

The Formula of Reunion, which had been reached by Cyril and John of Antioch back in 433, was then read and loudly cheered. Then the commissioners drew attention to a puzzling inconsistency. This same Formula of Reunion had been widely denounced at the Robber Council. Now it was being acclaimed. What had changed? One bishop after another arose and declared that he had erred. "We have failed. We ask for pardon."

Not Dioscorus, however. The council's third session took up the matter of his conduct, and the effect was to put the whole Robber Council on trial.

In stormy seas, Judaism sails on

Abuse flies from both sides, and occasional persecution sometimes becomes violent, as the Jews make clear that most will not convert, and that their faith is here to stay

With the era of Constantine in the fourth century, and the collapse of the western Roman Empire which followed, the Jews began their long trek through the Christian Middle Ages. The first two centuries of that journey would establish the pattern of the ensuing eleven. Sometimes they were tolerated. Often they were persecuted. But in the course of this they established one incontrovertible fact. They were not going to disappear. They were here to stay.

Christian leaders denounced them, often viciously, but their language was no more vitriolic than the language the Jews used in their own literature to describe Jesus and Christianity.[1] The Christian emperors were generally much more tolerant of them than were Christian bishops, and historian B. J. Kidd (*History of the Church*, Oxford, 1922) cites recurring evidence of this.

He notes, for instance, that the emperor Valentinian I and his brother Valens promulgated laws protecting synagogues and Jewish rites. Arcadius ordered that prices for goods sold by Jews be fixed by Jews, not Christians, and that their reigning "illustrious patriarchs" be treated with respect. Honorius forbade insults to Jewish synagogues or interference with the Jewish Sabbath.

Theodosius the Great, the man who made Christianity the empire's state religion, was also sympathetic, decreeing, among other measures, that the state not interfere in the internal discipline of Jewish communities. In 388, when Christians in Callinicum on the Euphrates burned down a synagogue, encouraged by their bishop to do so, Theodosius ordered him to rebuild it. But the emperor backed down and countermanded his order when Ambrose of Milan, his spiritual mentor, furiously objected. "The maintenance of the civil law is secondary to the religious interest," Theodosius explained.

Particularly strident condemnation of the Jews came from the sainted John Chrysostom, who was appalled when they sought to proselytize Christians at Antioch, and some Christians began to attend synagogue services. His language would make later generations of Christians shudder. Synagogues were "whorehouses," or "robbers' caves," or "places of refuge for unclean animals," he stormed, and charged that Jews "live for their bellies, seek greedily after earthly riches, and are no better than swine or goats in their dissipation and excessive longing." John did mellow somewhat with age, however. Upbraiding Christians for indolence in prayer and worship, he cited the exemplary devotion of religious Jews.

Anti-Jewish fervor frequently became violent, and one center of serious conflict was Palestine, where the Jewish community acquired an improbable ally. Following the breakdown of her marriage, (see page 187), the empress Eudocia, wife of Theodosius II and foe of his sister Pulcheria, left for Palestine to live the life of a devout woman, but with a difference. Rather than open a convent, she used her vast Holy Land estates to establish a palace suitable for herself as empress, and to enhance the grandeur of Jerusalem.

Since Pulcheria from childhood onward had expressed contempt for the Jews, Eudocia became their ally and gave them permission to worship again at the ruins of their ancient Temple. This set off a Zionist movement, with Jews from all over the empire flocking to the Holy City. When Syrian monks, in angry protest, ambushed and beat to death some Jewish pilgrims, Eudocia ordered them executed without trial. She had to release them when mobs besieged her palace, however, threatening to burn both it and her. The Christian historian Socrates did not conceal his scorn. Anti-Jewish violence, he wrote, "is utterly foreign to those who have the mind of Christ."

A similar rampage occurred in Alexandria, although

Four Alexandrians, protégés of Cyril, who subsequently would be persecuted by Dioscorus, began the case against him. As one supporter after another deserted his cause, Dioscorus stood firm. He would withdraw nothing he had written, he declared. He had not erred. He did not seek pardon. He had nothing to repent. With little further discussion, he was deposed. It was a banishment, notes British historian Trevor Jalland (*The Life and Times of St. Leo the Great*, London, 1941), that "seemed to purge the offenses of others whose guilt was probably not less than the actual victim."

Signs of the zodiac decorated the floor of the late fourth-century synagogue at Beth Alpha, Israel. Such motifs were not uncommon in synagogues of the Byzantine era.

this time the violence began on the Jewish side. A certain Hierax, aide to the patriarch Cyril, happened to attend a meeting where the imperial prefect, Orestes, was talking to some Jewish leaders. When these men identified Hierax as a troublemaker, Orestes ordered him thrashed on the spot. Cyril formally warned the Jews that such conduct would be punished. In response, Jewish extremists attacked Christian homes at night, killing several of the occupants.

Patriarch Cyril thereupon put himself at the head of a mob that seized a synagogue, drove Jews out of Alexandria, and opened their homes to looters. The emperor ordered that they be allowed back and that the bishop and prefect reach an agreement. But by then, the desert monks had stormed into Alexandria to stone the prefect for persecuting their bishop. A

crowd appeared, rescued the bleeding Orestes, drove off the monks, and then tortured and killed their leader. Cyril was dissuaded from burying him as a Christian martyr.

The strangest anti-Christian, pro-Jewish event of the era, however, was caused by neither Jews nor Christians, but by Julian, the emperor who succeeded Constantius II and who attempted to restore the pagan religion. To discredit Jesus Christ's prophecy that the Temple would be left without one stone atop another (Matt. 24:2), and to recruit the support of the Jews against the Christians, Julian resolved to rebuild the Temple.

But things immediately began to go wrong with this massive undertaking. Earthquakes disrupted the work. A huge portico toppled, killing several workmen, while others took refuge in a nearby church. The Christians also said crosses kept appearing mysteriously on the building stones. Then "balls of flame" began bursting out near the foundations, burning several workers to death. Julian abandoned the project.

It is hard to dismiss this entirely as legend or lies, writes historian Giuseppe Ricciotti (*Julian the Apostate*, Milwaukee, 1960). The pagan historian Ammianus, the Arian Philostorgius, and the Christians Socrates, Sozomen, Theodoret and Gregory of Nazianzus all recount the story. And although some modern scholars attribute the "balls of fire" to bitumen deposits around the Dead Sea, dislodged by the earthquakes, the Dead Sea is twenty-five miles distant and four thousand feet downhill.

God simply stopped the Temple project, said the Christians. However, he did not stop the Jews. They continued and often thrived, an embarrassment to the Christians—just as the continuing spread of faith in Jesus as Messiah was an embarrassment to the Jews. ∎

1. Certain verses in the Talmud, apparently dating from this period, appear to equate Gentiles with animals and to exempt Jews from all moral obligations to Gentiles. Rabbinical scholars contend that they are misinterpretations of the text, however, and that even if valid, would be in decided contradiction of other Talmudic teaching.

3. The word "subsistence" is an English rendering of the Greek word *hypostasis*, one of four terms that figured centrally in the debates of the first four church councils. The others were *ousia* (substance or essence), *physis* (nature) and *prosopon* (person). Much of the conflict that attended and followed the councils was caused by misunderstandings over the precise meaning of these terms, particularly when they were interpreted into what was assumed to be their Latin equivalents.

There were other holdouts. The Illyrian bishops balked at certain proposals advanced as the council's final definition of the faith, and fourteen Egyptian bishops refused to wholly concur in anything whatsoever because they said it would mean certain death when they returned to Alexandria. This was an omen of things to come. They were instructed to remain in Constantinople. Several archimandrites similarly demurred. But a hefty majority swore to the statement, representing as it did the outcome of more than a century of constant debate and occasional bloodshed. It declared:

> We all with one accord teach men to acknowledge one and the same Son, our Lord Jesus Christ, at once complete in Godhead and complete in manhood, truly God and truly man, consisting also of a reasoning soul and body; of one substance with the Father as regards his Godhead, and at the same time of one substance with us as regards his manhood; like us in all respects, apart from sin; as regards his Godhead, begotten of the Father before the ages, but yet as regards his manhood begotten for us men and for our salvation, of Mary the Virgin, the God-bearer; one and the same Christ, Son, Lord, only-begotten, recognized in two natures, without confusion, without change, without division, without separation; the distinction of natures being in no way annulled by the union, but rather the characteristics of each

The Turkish cities of Kadikoy (foreground) and Istanbul gaze at each other across the busy waters of the Bosporus. Kadikoy is now, as it was when it was known as Chalcedon, a suburb of the great city across the water, then called Constantinople. And now, unlike the era of the Roman Empire, the trip can be made faster. The Bosporus was traversed by a suspension bridge in 1974.

> nature being preserved and coming together to form one person and subsistence,[3] not as parted or separated into two persons, but one and the same Son and only-begotten God the Word, Lord Jesus Christ; even as the prophets from earliest times spoke of him, and our Lord Jesus Christ himself taught us, and the creed of our fathers has handed down to us.

This declaration, with few amendments, would remain the standard of Latin and Greek Christology from that time forward, surviving intact even through the Protestant Reformation in the sixteenth and seventeenth centuries. Martin Luther, though he never used the title, Theotokos, "willingly received" the Councils of Nicea, Constantinople, Ephesus and Chalcedon, and did use the term "Mother of God." John Calvin, theological ancestor of the Presbyterian,

Dutch Reformed and Christian Reformed Churches and of the English Puritan movement that founded the first American colonies, was consistent. He accepted the first four councils, and also wrote: "We cannot acknowledge the blessings brought us by Jesus without acknowledging at the same time how highly God honored and enriched Mary in choosing her for the Mother of God."

Writing on behalf of modern Evangelical Christians in *Touchstone* magazine (July/August 2003), the Protestant scholar Timothy George[4] used unequivocal language: "Evangelicals, no less than Roman Catholics and Orthodox believers," he declared, "stand in fundamental continuity with the 318 fathers of Nicea, the

Jewelry of the early Byzantine era reflects the preoccupation of Roman citizens with matters religious. Abstract or pagan designs were still in use, but such images as displayed by the rings at left— Christ, the Virgin Mary, saints, crosses and other symbols—became increasingly prevalent.

150 fathers of the First Council of Constantinople, and the canons of Ephesus, including the affirmation of the Theotokos and the condemnation of Pelagianism, as well as the definition of Chalcedon."

Since the Anglican Church accepts the first four Ecumenical Councils, it further accepts the title, Theotokos, although rarely uses it. Nevertheless, in the early nineteenth century, when one clergyman who did use it was threatened with expulsion, the archbishop of Canterbury declared that the state would protect him from censure.

Such Christian unanimity, however, by no means prevailed in the fifth century. When Bishop Juvenal returned to Jerusalem, he was declared a traitor to Cyril. Armed monks prevented his reentry into the city until a contingent of soldiers was called out to escort him to his church. Subsequently, the monks went on a rampage of looting, murder and the rape of "noblewomen." Marcian was for cracking down on them with Roman severity, but Pulcheria dissuaded him; in the end he left their punishment to God.

At Alexandria, a presbyter named Proterius, consecrated as successor to the deposed Dioscorus, was hideously murdered. Armenia refused to recognize Chalcedon, setting the Armenian Christians at odds with both Constantinople and Rome. Even at Rome, Chalcedon came in for severe criticism because of one of its nontheological decisions. Known as Canon 28, this affirmed the decision made at Second Ephesus that Constantinople would rank second to Rome and gain jurisdiction over the provinces of Thrace, Pontus and Asia. Constantinople approved Canon 28, Leo refused, and that question remained unresolved.[5]

Soon, therefore, Christendom would be split four ways. The traditionalists,

4. Timothy George is founding dean of the Beeson Divinity School, a Southern Baptist institution at Birmingham, Alabama. He is an executive editor of *Christianity Today* magazine, and has served on the editorial boards of *First Things* magazine, *Books and Culture*, and the *Harvard Theological Review*.

5. The Council of Nicea had conferred the status of patriarch upon the bishops of the three great sees of Rome, Alexandria and Antioch. The Council of Constantinople in 381 added Constantinople, and gave it second priority behind Rome. The Council of Ephesus designated the church in Cyprus as autocephalous, meaning autonomous, thus removing it from the jurisdiction of Antioch. It remains so to this day. The Council of Chalcedon, in addition to confirming the status of Constantinople, added Jerusalem as the fifth patriarchate.

6. In the twentieth century, the
Orthodox Church and the Coptic
Church in Egypt made significant
progress toward reconciliation. A
series of meetings culminated in four
agreed statements that may yet pave
the way for the restoration of full
communion. The Coptic Church is
also involved in discussions with the
Roman Catholic Church.

increasingly referring to themselves as "universalists" or "catholics," held sway in Rome, Constantinople, the future Balkans, the future Turkey, and a half-century later in the growing Frankish kingdom in the west. The other barbarian peoples still hewed to the religion of Arius, the Vandals very aggressively. Nestorian Christianity, a product of the backlash following the First Council of Ephesus (431), became increasingly alienated from Rome and Constantinople.

But the greatest rupture, borne of Chalcedon, ripped the church apart in Syria and Egypt. Over the next two centuries, the monks and many churches there would go into permanent schism with Rome and Constantinople, which labeled them "Monophysites," believers in a one-nature Jesus (*mono physis*), a term they have consistently rejected. In the seventh century this split, exacerbated by Constantinople's efforts to coerce conformity, would contribute to the worst disaster suffered by Christianity in its first two thousand years, the catastrophe of the Islamic conquests.[6]

Pulcheria survived Chalcedon by about twenty-two months. They were not happy ones. Surveying the wounds in the church, both eastern and western, she realized that her efforts to doctrinally purify Christianity were, if anything, farther than ever from fulfillment. A final collision with her sister-in-law no doubt also darkened her last days. (See sidebar, page 194.) Her death in July 453, at the age of fifty-four, struck the capital like a bombshell, for she had seemed so indestructible. That she had been a master of political manipulation was self-evident. That her manipulations were those of a devout servant of Christ was equally self-evident. She was buried in the mausoleum of Constantine, near the tomb of her grandfather, Theodosius the Great, and many regard her as his true successor. One objective she assuredly did achieve, however. Devotion to the Virgin Mary as the Theotokos, the God-bearer, would survive in the Eastern Churches until this day, and Catholics in the West would similarly sing *Ave Maria* right into the twenty-first century. Marcian, her husband, though nine years her senior, outlived Pulcheria by four years. He never did have to stand test for his defiance of Attila, because that rugged and aging Hun died in the same year as Pulcheria. But Marcian acquitted himself well. His internal financial reforms, his holding the line on the Persian front, and his steady hand at Chalcedon won him recognition as one of the greatest of the early eastern emperors. Both he and his wife were canonized in the east. ∎

LEO THE GREAT ON DESIRE

Let earthly desires not weigh down spirits that are summoned to raise themselves up.

CHAPTER 8

The cutthroat Franks improbable ancestors of Christian Europe

The treacherous wiles of two early matriarchs set the bloody stage of the first French monarchy, as fearless bishops plot the course to civilization

Over the relatively brief time covered by human history—a mere seven thousand years on a planet deemed to be four and a half billion years old—most people at most times have lived in a condition of barbarism, battling as tribes for territory, livelihood and existence itself.[1] Occasionally, however, something called a civilization occurs—in the valley of the Tigris and Euphrates or the Yangtze, for instance, or the Nile, or among the peaks of the Andes. Building on Greek culture, Rome had produced arguably the greatest of civilizations, but now, in the fifth Christian century, the western half of her empire was facing its doom. Civilizations exhibit two notable qualities. One is that they are not eternal. Every one of them comes to an end. The other is that they do not simply appear. They emerge from a particular tribe or place, subsequently rise through a long and fitful process until they reach an apex, then begin to fall back into squalor.

Such was the phenomenon experienced in the fifth century by the citizens of Gaul, the largest and most civilized Roman province of western Europe, as their cities and villages fell before yet another onslaught from beyond the Rhine. These invaders were a confederation of tribes known as the Franks, and within four generations they would drive out of Gaul not only the remaining vestiges of

1. This series assumes the traditional definition of history—that which is recorded after humanity acquired the ability to write and began to make note of its thoughts and observations. Everything before that it considers "prehistoric."

The spiritual heart of the Frankish nation was the Basilica of St. Martin at Tours, portrayed here in a fifth-century mosaic now in the Louvre, Paris. In the basilica was the tomb of Martin, the soldier-turned-bishop, and to that tomb came both kings and peasants with their petitions and offerings. (See sidebar page 208.)

Roman power, but every other barbarian challenger: Visigoths, Ostrogoths, Burgundians, Alamanni, Heruli, even the Huns.

The name Franks is thought to derive either from a Teutonic word meaning "formidable" or a Celtic word meaning "free," and both theories nicely accord with what is known of these people. The final demise of the western empire would be followed in Gaul by two sordid centuries under its new Frankish masters. Out of the almost unremitting treachery and blood-lust of their rule, however, would emerge another civilization. And it can be cogently argued that Gaul's fate would have been far worse under any of the barbarian nations they would defeat, and that the Franks themselves might never have become civilized at all were it not for one overwhelming factor. That factor was the Christian church.

Any suggestion that the Franks would be the ones to inherit and safeguard the traditions of Rome and the faith of Jesus Christ would have struck most Gallo-Romans as preposterous. Alone among the Germanic nations, the Frankish tribes outside Rome's boundaries were still resolutely pagan. Every other people that established itself in Roman Europe had by then adopted the religion of Arius. (See earlier volume, *By This Sign*, chapter 10.) But as historian W. H. C. Frend observes in *The Rise of Christianity* (Philadelphia, 1984), many Christian leaders saw paganism as a lesser threat than heresy. Thus Bishop Lupus of Troyes, he notes, actually supported Attila the Hun in the fifth century, in preference to Rome's Visigoth allies, who were Arian.

Up on the northern fringes of the crumbling empire, the Franks had stubbornly maintained their ancestral paganism. Its precise tenets are not known, but it must have resembled the beliefs of other Germanic and Nordic peoples. As such, it can hardly have been a cheerful faith. Worshipers of Thor and Wotan, for example, as reflected in Old Norse writing, saw life on earth as mirroring a cosmic battle between the gods of that fierce northern pantheon and the terrible, and more powerful, frost giants. Valor in war ranked as the highest virtue, qualifying a man to fight and feast with the gods, but ultimately, according to this supremely stoic religion, both men and gods would go down to defeat, with the frost giants destroying everything in one final, frightful cataclysm. The best course for a pious pagan was to get what he could out of life and hope to die heroically in battle.

The Romans first encountered assorted Frankish confederacies early in the third century. Time and again these tribes broke through the northern frontier and fought their way southward (once all the way to the Pyrenees), pillaging the countryside and burning walled cities. Time and again the legions forced them back. One particularly belligerent group was the Sicambrian or Salian confederacy,

Childeric, enraging his warriors by making free with their wives and daughters, took refuge in a royal court across the Rhine. He repaid his host by seducing his wife.

the latter name derived perhaps from *sal* (salt), because they seemed to originate in the North Sea region. From about 250, they inhabited an area the Romans knew as Toxandria (now in modern Belgium).

Not that they remained quietly there. The emperor Julian found it necessary to "pacify" them in 358. That is, he soundly thrashed them, confined them to Toxandria, and enlisted them as *federates*. But this arrangement did not last either. Led by one Clodio, the Sicambrian confederacy sacked and captured Cambrai in 428, thereby breaching the defenses along the Roman road through to Cologne and extending their territorial control into southern Gaul.

Clodio was succeeded by his son Merovec. The contemporary historian Priscus tells of seeing Merovec in Rome after his father's death: a very young man with thick blond hair that fell about his shoulders, who had come to ask the Roman general Aetius to support his claim to his father's throne.[2] Subsequently, Merovec is thought to have headed a contingent of Franks at the Battle of Chalons in 451, where Aetius turned back the vast forces of Attila the Hun just short of Paris. This was the crucial engagement that ended any Hunnish aspirations in Gaul. It may also have ended the aspirations of Merovec's elder brother, who is believed to have enlisted with Attila for the same reason that caused Merovec to fight for Aetius.

Merovec was succeeded by his son, Childeric, after an initial difficulty caused by that prince's profligate way with women. Childeric so enraged his warriors, by making free with their wives and daughters, that he had to take temporary refuge across the Rhine in Thuringia, territory held by another Frankish ruler. Childeric shortly contrived to return to his court at Tournai and to reclaim his throne, but he did not return alone.

2. Frankish warriors—tall, blond and big-boned—wore their hair clipped short like Romans. Only their royalty might wear their hair long, which caused them to be dubbed "the long-haired kings." Thus, if an heir was being deliberately rejected, his hair would be symbolically shorn. One conquered Frankish prince, thus shorn, defiantly noted that his hair would soon grow again—whereupon his enemy cut off his head.

The Merovingians combined a taste for violence with refined appreciation for delicate ornamentation, like this gold pin used for clasping a cloak.

3. A founding legend developed around the Merovingians. As preserved in a seventh-century source, it asserted that Merovec was sired by a centaur-like sea monster when his mother was bathing one day. Perhaps to add cachet by connecting the Frankish kingdom to classical times, the legend further claimed it was founded by two Trojan princes, after the fall of Troy.

4. After the collapse of the western empire in 476, the Roman cities between the Somme and Loire Rivers remained independent for about a decade, under the leadership of Syagrius, son of Aegidius, the region's last Roman commander. Gregory of Tours calls Syagrius *rex Romanorum*, but the kingdom of Syagrius, menaced by the Franks on one side and the Visigoths on the other, could not last long. Clovis defeated Syagrius's army in 486, and captured and killed him. The town of Soissons then became a favorite Merovingian capital.

Childeric had repaid his host's hospitality by seducing his wife, Basina, and she insisted upon following him home. Since Childeric was the strongest man she knew, declared the doughty Basina, she would live with him. If she knew any man stronger, she would have gone to him instead. Such were her terms of endearment. But no lover succeeded Childeric, and he firmly reinforced his reign over the Salian Franks, as well.

To this formidable couple was born an even more formidable son, whom they named Chlodovech, or Clovis in its Latinized form, who was destined to inaugurate a royal dynasty known as Merovingian after his grandfather Merovec.[3] Just fifteen when his father died in 481, he would, in the following thirty years, turn most of Gaul into a Frankish realm variously centered on Metz, Orleans, Paris, Soissons and Cologne. Furthermore, his sons and grandsons would extend this realm of Francia until it encompassed almost all of modern France, the Netherlands, Belgium, Switzerland, and much of Germany as far as the Elbe River. Thus was laid the foundation of a great modern nation whose name, derived from that of their people, would be France.

Clovis's own name, too, would be handed on right through to the nineteenth century. For by natural erosion the letter "C" would disappear, and Clovis would become Lovis or Louis, the name adopted by seventeen later kings of France. And on an even more fundamental level, some historians maintain, this pagan tribal chief would provide the groundwork for a Christian Europe.

With the end of the Roman Empire in northwest Europe plainly in sight, observes Russell Chamberlin in *Charlemagne, Emperor of the Western World* (London, 1986), Clovis had to make a firm choice. He could ally himself with what was left of Roman power, or he could attack it and grab the remains. "Being the kind of man he was," says Chamberlin, "he turned upon it and rended it."

Therefore, Clovis began his territorial expansion by conquering neighboring Soissons, Rome's last remaining foothold in Gaul,[4] and securing his father's conquests south to the Loire, and west to Armorica (roughly Brittany and Normandy). Then, he used his small but mobile army, estimated by some at six thousand or so men, to attach the small Frankish principalities to the northeast, including his father's temporary refuge, Thuringia.

Since Gallo-Roman citizens predominated in most of Gaul, Clovis's Salian invaders became a minority ruling a Christian majority. Even such individual Franks as had managed to settle in Gaul may by then have been converts. But Clovis, legend aside, was no mere barbarian ruffian. He undoubtedly spoke Latin, and possibly could even read it. He seems to have genuinely tried to govern with an even hand. He maintained (and at length codified) Salian tribal law for his Franks, while preserving Roman law for the Gallo-Romans. He affirmed his conquered subjects in possession of their property, and of their orthodox Christian faith. He brought at least some order to a countryside ravaged by bands of brigands. He apparently tried to limit plundering by his warriors, especially of churches, and in general treated the church with deference.

Three reasons can be advanced for this relatively enlightened governance.

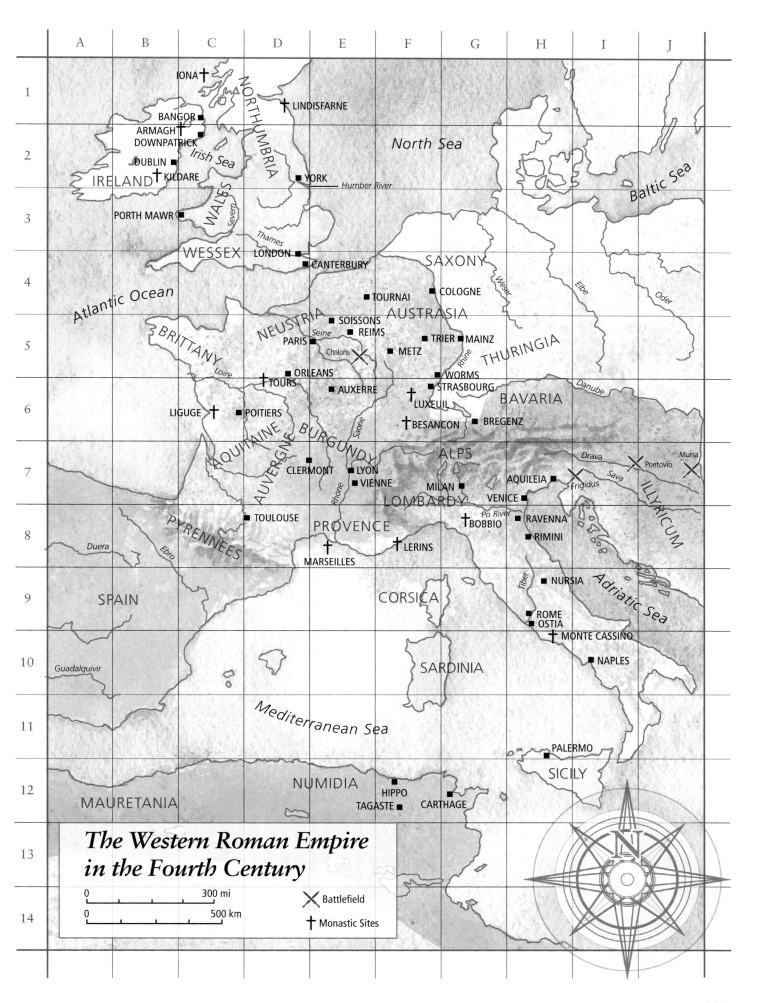

The Western Roman Empire
in the Fourth Century

First, the Franks had long observed the Romans with admiration. Second, it appears that Clovis aimed from the outset to rule a mighty kingdom, not a collection of tribes. And the third and most important factor was the Christian church, which survived intact in the aftermath of the empire. Because Gaul's well-established church preserved and propagated the faith, and because it also embodied all that remained of Roman administrative structure, it became the source of, quite literally, saving grace.

For the province of Gaul, when the pagan Franks came bursting through, was a realm already permeated by piety. Urban residents, from upper and middle-level aristocrats to the humblest laborer, flocked to their churches. The monastic movement was reaching into the countryside. (See sidebar, page 208.) Day and night the psalms were chanted in the monasteries and cathedral churches.

In Gaul's hundred or so dioceses, the conquerors encountered Christian bishops, many of whom were monks as well, living as monks despite the demands and distractions of episcopal office. Equal parts piety and practicality, these men usually came from the Gallo-Roman aristocracy, from families accustomed to exercising high office, both secular and ecclesiastical. Indeed, concludes Henri Daniel-Rops in *The Church in the Dark Ages* (London, 1963), a bishop in Clovis's day was simultaneously priest and prefect, and at his best, he was "order incarnate, the living conscience of his people."

Just such a one was Remigius, archbishop of Reims (and a monk). Son of a Gallic count, Remigius belonged to a family that had already produced five saints, and was himself revered as a miracle worker. He had been elected archbishop of Reims at age twenty-two, had organized missions to the Arians of Burgundy, and was now a seasoned administrator in his vigorous forties. In 481, as soon as the Frankish warriors raised Clovis on their shields and acclaimed him king in traditional tribal style, Remigius sent him a letter of congratulation—and admonition. "Show deference toward your bishops," he wrote. "Always turn to them for advice. And if you are in harmony with them, your land will prosper." Many further letters would follow.

While Clovis may have welcomed the help of the Christian establishment in keeping his new subjects loyal, he showed no immediate desire to embrace the faith himself. But the bishops were a devious lot. The marriage of Clovis to Clotilde, niece of King Gundobad of Burgundy, bears every mark of a deft collaboration between Remigius and a Burgundian colleague, Bishop Avitus of Vienne.

The Burgundian royal family was of Arian persuasion, but Clotilde, as both bishops well knew, had been raised devoutly orthodox. She set about converting her husband, with no apparent success and some reason for discouragement. Their first son, for instance, died shortly after his baptism. "My gods would have cured him!" exclaimed his wrathful father. Nonetheless, when their second child was born,

GREGORY OF TOURS ON THE DARKNESS OF HIS TIMES

Scarcely a day passed without someone being murdered, scarcely an hour without some quarrel or other, scarcely a minute without some person or other having cause for sorrow. Who could possibly set down in words all this violence, all this slaughter, all this evil?

Clovis, leader of the Sicambrian Franks (left), reluctantly strikes a bargain with the God of his Christian wife Clotilde, in an illustration by Alphonse Marie de Neuville (1836–1885). In return for victory over his dangerous enemies the Alamanni, Clovis promises, he will turn from his pagan beliefs and accept Jesus Christ. God obliged, and Clovis honored his pledge. The founder of Gaul's Merovingian dynasty was baptized at Reims Cathedral ca.500, along with about three thousand of his warriors. The painting of the baptism (below) by Joseph Paul Blanc (1846–1904) is in the Pantheon, Paris.

Clovis permitted him also to be baptized. (This infant, too, became ill, but after much prayer he survived.)

It was not until the king was hard-pressed by dangerous neighbors, the Alamanni of Alsace, that his wife's prayerful efforts took tangible effect. Toward the end of the fifth century, he met them in pitched battle on the Rhine. There was terrible slaughter, writes Gregory of Tours, nearly a hundred years later in his *History of the Franks*, and Clovis's army seemed about to be annihilated. In desperation, he raised his eyes to heaven and appealed to "Jesus Christ, you who Clotilde maintains to be the Son of the living God."

Gregory, a bishop himself, recounts in some detail the deal Clovis made with God: "If you will give me victory over my enemies, and if I may have evidence of that miraculous power which the people dedicated in your name say they have experienced, then I will believe in you and I will be baptized in your name." At that very moment, it was said, the Alamanni leader was killed, and with their chief dead, his warriors capitulated.

So Clovis kept his bargain, and the ceremony in Reims Cathedral was a magnificent one. The public square was hung with colored fabric, as was customary on great occasions, and the church with white. Candles gleamed, writes Gregory, and incense gave off such clouds of perfume that all present imagined themselves "transported to some perfumed paradise." Standing ready for Christian baptism were Clovis himself, by then styled "King of Gaul," along with his eldest son, Theuderic, and some three thousand warriors. (Theuderic, although the child of a casual liaison, was recognized as a legitimate heir. The Franks were not unduly concerned about legitimacy; a son was a son.)

The king was the first to approach the baptismal pool. "Bow your head, Sicamber," came the stern order of Archbishop Remigius. "Worship what you have hitherto destroyed, and destroy what you have hitherto worshiped!" To address Clovis so, a reference to the origins of the Franks, was like saying "Bow your head, barbarian." Remigius, who had supervised the instruction in the faith of this royal catechumen, well understood how difficult it is to plumb the depths of any human mind and heart.[5]

Later historians have cast doubt on the sincerity of Clovis's conversion. It was doubtless from "considerations of policy rather than from any profound

A Spain that was, and would be again

Artifacts of Spain's Visigoths evidence a civilization which the Muslims would supplant, but with a seven-hundred-year-long battle the Christians would regain the country

German Visigoths overran Spain in the fifth century, becoming for the next three hundred years the overlords of earlier peoples that had settled on the Iberian Peninsula. Its first recorded inhabitants, the Iberians, may have migrated from prehistoric Africa. They were followed by, and merged with, the Celts, many of whom embraced Christianity. When the Visigoths, who were Arian Christians themselves, arrived, they blended with the population as well, governing Spain until Islamic invaders fell upon the country in the eighth century. The Muslim Arabs occupied most of the region, renamed it Andalusia, and drove the surviving Christians into the mountainous north. Even now in Spain, however, numerous artifacts of Visigoth society keep turning up, of which the crown shown here is merely representative. During the succeeding seven hundred years, the Christians gradually pushed the Muslims out of the country, finally restoring it completely to Christianity in 1492—the same year that Columbus, sailing under the flag of once-Visigoth Spain, arrived in America. ■

The rule of the seventh-century king Recceswinth was one of consolidation and advance for the Visigoths of Spain. His crown, featuring strands that hung over the face, bore his name in gold and jewels (left). Among the oldest churches of the country is the seventh-century Basilica of San Juan Bautista de Banos (above) on the Balearic Islands.

conviction" that Clovis decided to be baptized, writes Christian Pfister of the University of Paris, in *The Cambridge Medieval History* (1923). After his conversion, notes historian J. P. Whitney of King's College, London, in the same volume, "the wars that spread his power took somewhat the character of crusades, and for three centuries this remained true of Frankish campaigns against the heathens. Broadly speaking, with the power of the Frankish kings went the power of the church, although the fellowship between the two was sometimes closer, sometimes looser."

Gallic bishops clearly approved of Clovis's attacks on the Arian Visigoth regimes in Spain and Aquitaine, which were oppressing their conquered orthodox

Clovis approached the baptismal pool. 'Bow your head,' came the stern voice of Remigius, 'Worship what you have hitherto destroyed, and destroy what you have hitherto worshiped!'

subjects. Even under more tolerant rulers, as in Burgundy, Christians were restive and unhappy. One of Bishop Avitus's letters to Clovis seems especially significant: "Your ancestors have opened the way for you to a great destiny. Your decision will open the way to a yet greater destiny for your descendants. Your faith is our victory." Avitus then urges Clovis to spread true Christianity in "distant lands." Not precisely an invitation to invade Arian Burgundy, perhaps, but it seems close.

At that time, however, Clovis still needed the help of the two brothers then ruling Burgundy, Clotilde's uncles, against the still dangerous Alamanni (who were also Arian). After wresting Alsace from the Alamanni, he next undertook a major campaign against the Visigoths of Aquitaine. Marching south, according to Gregory's *History of the Franks*, Clovis sent sumptuous gifts, including a horse, of which he was particularly fond, to the vitally important shrine of St. Martin at Tours, seeking the saint's approval.[6] At Vouille, near Poitiers, the Franks and their allies did indeed triumph, with Clovis himself killing the Visigoth ruler, Alaric II, in single combat. His kingdom now extended to the Pyrenees.

As he returned through Tours, he received from Constantinople the gratifying news that the eastern emperor had conferred upon him the honorary title of consul, thus recognizing, and in effect legitimizing, his conquests. He was now entitled to wear the purple tunic and mantle and a diadem, which he did with pride, as he proceeded in solemn procession to the church, scattering coins to the people. While there, so the story goes, Clovis also tried to buy back his beloved horse by offering a hundred gold coins for it. He was much impressed when the animal refused to move until he doubled the price. "Blessed Martin is a fine helper," was his comment, "and careful in business too!"

It must be acknowledged that Clovis acquired no obvious aura of holiness; the sparse accounts of his times chronicle lifelong ruthlessness and treachery. His last years, according to Gregory of Tours, were devoted to annexing assorted northern territories, mostly belonging to Frankish relatives of his, often by notably ignoble

5. At the point in the baptismal service when Bishop Remigius was to anoint Clovis with holy chrism, according to a legend first recorded in about the ninth century, he prayed, and a dove flew down with an *ampulla* of the sacred oil. *The Oxford Dictionary of the Christian Church* notes that a globular vessel known as the *Sainte Ampoule*, of a tin-like material and bearing a depiction of the Adoration of the Magi and Shepherds, was long preserved at Reims. Used in the coronation of French kings until the eighteenth century, it was smashed during the French Revolution.

6. Clovis's messengers, on their way to battle with the Visigoths in 507, entered the chapel of St. Martin at Tours just as Psalm 18 was being intoned there: "For thou hast girded me with strength unto the battle; thou hast subdued under me those that rose up against me." What could be a clearer prediction of victory? Henceforward, the fragment of St. Martin's cloak would be the Merovingians' most cherished relic, and their battle standard.

methods. He attached several smaller tribes by the simple expedient of assassinating their chiefs. He eliminated Sigibert the Lame, chief of the Ripuarian Franks at Cologne, by persuading Sigibert's son Cloderic to kill him, then arranging for Cloderic to be assassinated in turn. Clovis thereupon presented himself before the Ripuarians as the avenger of their ruler, and offered to take over. Preferring to back a winner, the Cologne tribesmen bought into this tale and signed on.

It all began with a shared cloak

How a Roman soldier decided to fight a different sort of battle, which one day would result in 4,000 French churches and 485 villages being named Martin

Even in skeptical twenty-first-century France, the influence of a certain long-dead monk remains inescapable. More than four thousand French churches bear his name, and so do 485 villages. St. Martin of Tours is now greatly honored and much loved right around the world, of course, and this process began very early. But it was in Gaul that the renowned fourth-century holy man carried on the heroic work that established him as the first patron saint of France, and made him a central figure of devotion for Clovis and the first dynasty of Frankish kings.

Martin was born in Pannonia (present-day Hungary), about 315. His father, a native Pannonian, rose to the rank of tribune in the Roman army. Although both Martin's parents were pagan, the boy became a devout Christian catechumen at age ten, and even aspired to take vows as a hermit. But his father "looked with an evil eye on his blessed actions," writes Martin's friend and biographer, the Aquitanian nobleman Sulpicius Severus; furthermore, the law required soldiers' sons to follow the paternal profession. When Martin turned fifteen, his father reported him to the military authorities.

Thus forcibly inducted, he served about five years in the imperial cavalry. Legend has it that he did his best even there to live an ascetic life, reversing roles with his orderly, a slave, by cleaning the man's footgear and serving his meals. Then, while his troop was fighting the Franks in northern Gaul, came the incident with which his name would henceforth be inextricably connected: the affair of the cloak.

On garrison duty at Amiens during the severe winter of 338–339, the young officer rode out on inspection one night, and at the city gate, happened to encounter an ill-clad beggar, who looked likely to freeze to death. Martin promptly removed his *chlamys*, the great white cloak worn by Roman lancers, and used his sword to slice it in two. Bestowing one half upon the shivering man, he rode on, clad in the remainder.[1]

That night in a dream, he beheld the Lord Jesus wearing half of the sundered garment, and heard him say, "Martin, still a catechumen, covered me with his cloak." The vision prompted him to seek baptism that Easter. However, Severus writes, after his baptism, Martin believed he must no longer fight and kill, and so applied for discharge from the army.

When his commandant (probably the emperor Julian) understandably discounted his request as simple cowardice, Martin countered with an offer to walk before his troop into battle on the morrow, completely unarmed. His offer was accepted—but the battle never happened. The Franks unexpectedly decided to negotiate, and Severus, for one, was in no doubt what power had arranged the truce.

Martin next sought out Hilary, bishop of Poitiers, a man known as "the Athanasius of the West" for his skilled and stubborn opposition to Arianism. These two might seem curious partners—Hilary, the sophisticated intellectual, and Martin, the passionate, ascetic ex-soldier—but they were matched in ardent faith and missionary zeal. Martin supported Hilary's anti-Arian campaign. Hilary gave Martin some land at Locociagus (Ligugé), then four miles outside Poitiers, where in 360 he founded the first Gallic monastery to operate on a recognized rule.

Ligugé was the first of three establishments considered integral to the development of early western monasticism. The second appeared fifty years later, on the barren, snake-ridden little island of Lérins (now St. Honorat) in the Mediterranean, off present-day Cannes. Its founder, a Gallo-Roman aristocrat named Honoratus, had studied the work and rule of Basil of Cappadocia, and Lérins is described by *The Oxford Dictionary of the Christian Church* as "the nursery of a long line of scholars and bishops."[2] (This monastery operated until 1788.)

The third and vital influence was provided by John Cassian, who came from Constantinople on an embassy to Pope Innocent I, and settled in southern Gaul. A keen observer of humankind, Cassian had lived as an ascetic in Egypt, and thought deeply about developments there. He found Gallic monastic habits deplorably lax and self-indulgent, tendencies he

He also took care that none of his kinsmen remained alive who could possibly challenge his sons' inheritance, Gregory writes, pensively musing late in his life, "How sad it is that I live among strangers like some solitary pilgrim, and have none of my own relations left to help me when disaster threatens." However, Gregory adds, this was "not because he grieved for their deaths, but because in his cunning way, he hoped to find some relative still in

resolved to avoid in the two monasteries he founded in 415 near Marseilles, one for men and one for women.

Like Basil in the east, Cassian aimed to balance the extreme asceticism of much eastern practice by means of communal living and practical work. He taught that work, whether labor in the fields or copying manuscripts in the scriptorium, is also of spiritual benefit. (Monkish labor would, not unnaturally, prove to be a source of other benefits, too.) Cassian's own great works were his *Conferences* and his *Institutes*. Written to provide detailed instructions for his own monasteries, these became the basis for many western rules, including that of Benedict of Nursia in the sixth century. (See also sidebar page 167.)

As for Martin, he was able to stay at Ligugé for only twelve years. Upon the death in 372 of the bishop of Tours, the townspeople overwhelmingly elected Martin as his successor. When he refused, they tricked him into coming to town, and in effect hijacked him. Bowing to necessity, he appointed a successor at Ligugé, and, to the great joy of the citizenry, moved to Tours. His episcopal colleagues, most of them scions of substantial Gallo-Roman families, were not so enthusiastic. Severus says many objected to his "despicable countenance," his "mean" clothing, and his "disgusting" hair.

The Gallic bishops had been presiding over a great blossoming of Christianity among the urban and literate members of Gaul's population, writes W. H. C. Frend, in *Town and Country in the Early Christian Centuries* (London, 1980). However, most country folk still worshiped the pagan gods and celebrated their festivals. To this situation, in the valleys of the Loire and the Seine, the new bishop Martin directed his efforts.

He must have been an energetic and convincing evangelist. Severus records miracle upon miracle, recounting how Martin brought dead men back to life, routinely healed illnesses, and directed the weather, permanently banishing hailstorms from one district. He expelled demons (one of which, in Severus's pungent description, exited "by means of a defluxion of the belly, leaving disgusting traces behind him"). He demolished heathen temples, sometimes wielding the ax himself and sometimes persuading the worshipers to do the job.

One pagan devotee offered to cut down a sacred pine tree if the bishop would stand in the line of fall. Martin agreeably did so, but when he raised his hand in blessing, the tree obediently changed direction.

The Roman officer Martin, on patrol duty at Amiens, cuts his cavalry cloak in half to share it with a shivering beggar. (Detail from a 1549 painting by Amalteo Pomponio.)

Thus through miracle, eloquence or prayer (or a combination of the same), churches and monasteries rapidly replaced pagan shrines and temples. By the end of the fourth century, Frend writes, the common people of much of Gaul were Christian.

Martin died at an outlying village in November 397, provoking an unseemly altercation over his body. Henri Gheon, in his biography *St. Martin of Tours* (New York, 1946), describes how a crowd from Poitiers, headed by Ligugé monks, passionately vied for possession with a mob of Tourainians, headed by monks from Marmoutier, Martin's later-established monastery.[3] Each claimed the honor of providing a gravesite. Each set guards on the building where the body lay.

But either the men of Tours were craftier, says Gheon, or St. Martin lulled the men of Poitiers to sleep. The Tourainians sneaked their saint out through

the land of the living, whom he could kill."

Yet it seems hardly reasonable to conclude that Clovis's conversion to the Christian faith was wholly—or even largely—based on "considerations of policy." Certainly he appears to have been, in his own eyes, a sincere enough believer. Gregory writes that when Bishop Remigius described to his royal convert the betrayal and Crucifixion of Jesus, Clovis was passionately affected. "Oh, if only I

a window and headed down the Vienne and Loire Rivers toward home. At dawn, the Poitiers contingent discovered the subterfuge—too late. Thousands of mourners of every age and class thereupon came to follow the barge along the towpath, and St. Martin was buried in his episcopal city, in the Cemetery of the Poor (his own preference, it was claimed).

Over his tomb, successive chapels and basilicas were built, and several times burned by Norman raiders. The body itself, often moved temporarily to safer locations,[4] remained intact until 1323, when King Charles the Fair had the head removed and enshrined in a special reliquary. In the sixteenth century, however, a Huguenot army swept into Tours, burned the relics, and melted down the reliquaries. Only two small pieces of St. Martin's physical remains survived, although this apparently did not diminish his miraculous powers.

Neither did it diminish his influence upon the rulers of France for upwards of a thousand years, nor the devotion of the common people in perpetuity. The beloved saint, it is said, kept right on healing every sort of illness from deafness to gout. His shrine at Tours became part of the great pilgrimage route from Compostela in Spain to Rome, and his cult spread far. In England alone, observes B. J. Kidd in *A History of the Christian Church*, no fewer than 151 pre-Reformation dedications to St. Martin attest to his popularity there. Moreover, he is a saint of undivided Christendom, recognized in both West and East as "equal to the apostles."

Severus's miracle-packed biography, which circulated widely, was doubtless part of the cause, as was his hero's adoption by Merovingian royalty. But what chiefly recommends St. Martin of Tours is the uncontestable fact that he stands as the ideal missionary bishop: single-hearted, fearless, and conspicuously holy. ∎

Soon after the death of Bishop Martin of Tours in 397, recognition of his sanctity spread far beyond Gaul. This depiction of his death, attended by an angel and two of his monks, is from an eleventh-century Spanish manuscript.

1. Martin's half-cloak reputedly survived and became a revered treasure of the Merovingian kings, who adopted him as Gaul's patron saint. Martin remains a patron saint of France, but from medieval times has had to share honors with Dionysius of Paris, a third-century martyr enshrined at the Abbey of St.-Denis, north of Paris. Later French kings carried into battle a sacred banner called the "Oriflamme of St. Denis" (from Latin *aurea flamma*, flame of gold).

2. The monastery founded by Honoratus at Lerins benefited significantly from scholarly refugees fleeing Frankish attacks on Trier, Mainz, Cologne and Reims, notes historian Katherine Scherman in *The Birth of France: Warriors, Bishops and Long-Haired Kings*. The beneficent character of its founder may also have added luster. Honoratus, a man of sunny personality, believed monks should be joyful, as expressed in Psalm 105.

3. Bishop or no, Martin the monk needed solitude. He therefore found a hideaway two miles outside Tours, up a steep cliff above the Loire River. However, eighty or so other God-seekers inevitably followed (Sulpicius Severus among them), to live in caves or huts, (silent except for prayer, on one meal a day.) This became a famous monastery called Marmoutier (from *Martini Monasterium*, or Martin's Monastery).

4. In the eighth century, when Martin's remains were taken for safekeeping to the Church of St. Germain at Auxerre, he became a temporary *post mortem* guest of another notable Gallic saint, the former Bishop Germanus of Auxerre. Historian Henri Gheon recounts how a man, afflicted with sores, reportedly was laid in the crypt between the two tombs. Healed only on Martin's side, he had to be turned round for a full cure. St. Germain was merely being courteous, embarrassed Auxerre citizens claimed.

had been there with my Franks!" he exclaimed. There were other indications. Passing near Tours on the way to war, for instance, he forbade his soldiers to seize anything from the inhabitants. When one man disobeyed, Clovis killed him on the spot. They could hardly expect to win this battle, he explained to his warriors, if they were going to offend St. Martin by pillaging his own special countryside.

In matters perhaps more convincing to a twenty-first-century mind, Katherine

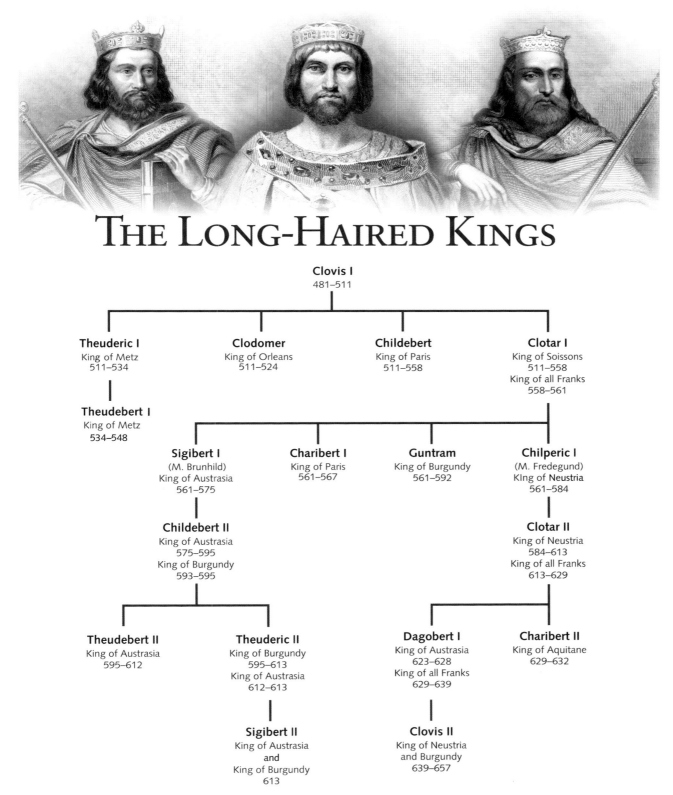

THE LONG-HAIRED KINGS

Clovis I
481–511

Theuderic I
King of Metz
511–534

Clodomer
King of Orleans
511–524

Childebert
King of Paris
511–558

Clotar I
King of Soissons
511–558
King of all Franks
558–561

Theudebert I
King of Metz
534–548

Sigibert I
(M. Brunhild)
King of Austrasia
561–575

Charibert I
King of Paris
561–567

Guntram
King of Burgundy
561–592

Chilperic I
(M. Fredegund)
KIng of Neustria
561–584

Childebert II
King of Austrasia
575–595
King of Burgundy
593–595

Clotar II
King of Neustria
584–613
King of all Franks
613–629

Theudebert II
King of Austrasia
595–612

Theuderic II
King of Burgundy
595–613
King of Austrasia
612–613

Dagobert I
King of Austrasia
623–628
King of all Franks
629–639

Charibert II
King of Aquitane
629–632

Sigibert II
King of Austrasia
and
King of Burgundy
613

Clovis II
King of Neustria
and Burgundy
639–657

Scherman, in *The Birth of France: Warriors, Bishops and Long-Haired Kings* (New York, 1987), emphasizes Clovis's even-handed treatment of his Gallo-Roman subjects, and the fact that he provided in Gaul quite orderly government. He appears to have completed the elimination of Arianism throughout his realm without undue cruelty. And he and Clotilde (who would be honored as a saint) encouraged Christian missions and established churches and monasteries, which were then the only real source of relief for the needy.

Clovis died in 511 in Paris, then his capital, and was buried in the church of St. Peter and St. Paul, which he and Clotilde had built there. His kingdom was divided, according to custom, among his four sons, and for the next half century, territorial warfare among them would scarcely ever cease. If no outside conquest was in prospect, one brother was usually marching against another one, or preparing to do so.

The first of Clovis's sons to die was Clodomer, killed in 524 in a campaign

Clovis's son Clodomer falls in battle in 524, and his brothers Childebert and Clotar covet his kingdom of Orleans. They resolve to kill Clodomer's three heirs, mere children, and divide Orleans between themselves. Servants save one little boy, but the other two die at the hands of their wicked uncles. When Childebert, originator of the plot, has an attack of scruples over one weeping child, the indignant Clotar urges him to get on with it: "Kill him or pass him to me!"

SMITH

against Burgundy, a campaign which he inaugurated by gratuitously murdering one of the two Burgundian rulers in advance, along with his wife and children. Clodomer's own death in the subsequent battle looked to some contemporaries like divine retribution, and more was to follow. Clodomer's three young sons, all of them less than ten years old, inherited his kingdom of Orleans, under the protection of their grandmother, Queen Clotilde. But two of their uncles resolved to divide Orleans between themselves, so they tricked grandmother Clotilde into turning the youngsters over to them, ostensibly to be readied for coronation.

The servants attending the children, growing suspicious, managed to snatch away one of the three to safety, but the wicked uncles seized the other two and stabbed them to death. Childebert, king of Paris, who had originated the plot, weakened at the last. He could not bring himself to actually murder the weeping child who was clinging to his knees and pleading for his life. His brother Clotar, having already dispatched the other boy, briskly vetoed such squeamishness.

King Childebert, who had conceived the plot, weakened at the last and could not bring himself to murder the weeping child. His brother Clotar, however, vetoed such squeamishness.

"Kill him or throw him to me," he ordered. "You started this, and we're going to finish it!" Which Clotar proceeded to do.[7]

Clotar, Clovis's fourth son, had inherited the kingdom of Soissons. He was the most ruthless of the four brothers, and the most successful in terms of longevity, acquired territory, and—of equal significance—progeny. He sired seven vigorous sons who all grew to manhood; to him and to his line would fall the entire Merovingian inheritance. Meanwhile, he hastened the process by appropriating chunks of his brothers' territory at every opportunity.

If divine retribution ever touched Clotar, it came in the form of his youngest and favorite son, Chramn, a vicious youth whose evil ways reputedly surpassed even Merovingian standards. Chramn actually menaced bishops and broke such sacred laws as that of sanctuary. He also kept trying to seize power from his father, but Clotar, hampered by an inexplicable and abiding tenderness, could not bring himself to punish him. But when Chramn finally went too far, by marching against him with a Breton army, Clotar's ruthless rage erupted. He ordered that this favorite son, together with his wife and small daughters, be locked in a shed, and the shed set on fire. After that, in sorrow and remorse, he went to Tours with gifts for St. Martin, to plead for the saint's intercession and God's forgiveness.

Clotar displays in most vivid form the characteristic Merovingian blend of savagery and sensibility, which may help account for his extreme fondness for women. He had one duly recognized queen, Ingund, who bore him five sons and one daughter. But he also had a longstanding relationship with Ingund's beautiful sister Arnegund, an arrangement apparently approved (or at least accepted) by

7. Clodoald, the royal child who escaped when his murderous uncles killed his older and younger brothers, was probably eight. Later, he is believed to have voluntarily cut his royal locks, to signify renunciation of his father's kingdom, and dedicated his life to God. Founder of a monastery and church near Paris, he was revered as St. Cloud. His saintly grandmother Clotilde, grief-stricken over her inadvertent part in the murder, spent the rest of her life at Bishop Martin's abbey at Tours, caring for the poor and suffering.

The uneasy coexistence of violence and piety among the Merovingian royals may have been assisted by portrayals such as these two carvings. Both are of Frankish provenance (fifth to sixth century). In both, Jesus Christ is a warrior, carrying spear and sword in his triumph over evil.

both women. Arnegund bore his son Chilperic. Another liaison was with the widow of his brother Clodomer (the one whose children he killed); she became the mother of Chramn. But his strangest relationship was with the lovely and virtuous Radegund, daughter of King Berthar of Thuringia, who had been seized at the age of eight when the Merovingians conquered her father's realm.

After the conquest, the royal brothers drew lots for this little girl, and Clotar won. For seven years she was nurtured and educated by pious women, after which Clotar (by then in his fifties) sought to claim her as wife. Radegund, however, was determined to dedicate her life to Jesus Christ. When Clotar insisted, she agreed to marry him, but only as an act of Christian charity. She also continued her pious vocation: abstemious eating, rigorous asceticism, tending the sickest villagers, and what historian Katharine Scherman calls her "flinty chastity."

Though Clotar complained about being "married to a nun," he put up with it fairly amiably, and Radegund too seems to have remained content to act as his queen—until he saw fit, that is, to kill her younger brother. (Nothing personal, of course, but this young man might easily have staged a coup in Thuringia.) Then she urgently besought her spiritual adviser, Bishop Medard of Soissons, to release her from her marriage and consecrate her a real nun—a request that posed for Medard the kind of dilemma not infrequently faced by Merovingian bishops. He wanted to respect Radegund's married state, dubious though it might be. Quite compelling, too, was the fact that some of her husband's henchmen appeared determined to drag him from his altar. But he also had to recognize the validity of her religious vocation.

Radegund herself resolved the situation. She placed her regal robe and jewels on the altar, herself donned the nun's habit, and again approached Medard, who at her earnest pleas, finally laid his hands on her and consecrated her a deaconess. Next, she searched for a site where she could found a monastery, and when Clotar proposed to force her to come home she enlisted the help of Germanus, the respected abbot of St. Symphorian in Autun. Soon to become bishop of Paris, Germanus already had influence with Merovingian royalty.

In the end Clotar renounced any claim on his beloved Radegund, donated generously to her convent, and faithfully protected it.[8]

Meanwhile, it was business as usual on the conquest front. In the mid-sixth century, the Merovingians gained the entire region of Provence and a large bribe as part of a deal with Witigis, the Ostrogoth ruler of Italy. In return, they were to help him fight off an attack by the eastern emperor at Constantinople (see page 268), but the Merovingians were again playing a double game. The

The saintly Radegund was a Burgundian princess taken captive as a child by the Merovingian king Clotar I, and carefully nurtured to marriageable age. Here she is being presented to Clotar, years later, as his bride. The illumination at left is from a tenth-century account of Radegund's life.

Byzantine historian Procopius recounts that they bided their time until they heard that the warring armies were both in bad shape. Then, "forgetting for the moment their oaths and the treaties they had made a little before with both sides (for this nation [the Franks] in matters of trust is the most treacherous in the world), they straightway gathered to the number of one hundred thousand under the leadership of Theudebert [Clotar's nephew, king of Austrasia 534–548], and marched into Italy."

After wreaking indiscriminate slaughter upon the wives and children of the Goth soldiers, Procopius writes, the Franks attacked the Goth army from behind, and routed it. Then they turned upon the Byzantine troops, who mistakenly welcomed them as allies, and defeated them too. At length, famine and malaria drove the Franks from the devastated land. They nevertheless continued to keep some footholds in northern Italy, which they would later have to defend against extensive attacks from Lombard invaders of both Italy and southern Gaul. The conquest of Provence, which included the important trading city of Massilia

8. Queen Radegund took refuge at the shrine of St. Hilary at Poitiers. Nearby she founded a convent, named Holy Cross after she was given a sliver of the true cross brought from the east. Her friend and admirer, the poet and hymnographer Venantius Fortunatus, was a frequent and honored resident. Holy Cross nuns followed a mild rule of religious exercises and literary studies—all except for Radegund herself, who reputedly continued her extreme austerities until her death in 587, at about age sixty-eight. Her friend Gregory of Tours buried her, and Venantius wrote her biography.

Ornamenting the instruments of war was a natural interest for Frankish culture. "Sigurd's Helmet" (above), with its ferocious combination of formed metal at the crown and the newer armament of mail protecting the jaw, may according to folklore have belonged to King Sigibert of Austrasia. The intricately patterned metal piece (below) is a mounting for a sixth-century Frankish sword.

(Marseilles) and its whole Mediterranean coastline, made Frankish Gaul larger than Roman Gaul had been.

As for Clovis's sons, Childebert died in 558, leaving Clotar as the last survivor of the four. Hastening the widow and her daughters into exile, Clotar took over Childebert's kingdom of Paris. He reigned as king of all Franks until he too died in 561, at age seventy-seven, of a high fever that developed after a day of hunting. Not that he was ready to go, notes Gregory, quoting his indignant deathbed protest against God: "What manner of King can be in charge of heaven, if he is prepared to finish off great monarchs like me in this fashion?"

Of Clotar's seven sons, four had survived the violence and debauchery of their young manhood: Chilperic, Sigibert, Charibert and Guntram were all ready and eager to take over. Chilperic inherited the northwestern kingdom, known as Neustria. To Sigibert went the northeast, Austrasia. Charibert got Paris and the southwest. Guntram inherited Burgundy. When Charibert died childless in 567, the other three amicably divided his lands. But amicability ended at that point, due in no small part to two fearsome royal women.

Members of this generation of Merovingians, although Christian every one, were as cruel, violent, treacherous and overall barbaric as their father and uncles, and degenerate to boot. If anything, they seem worse, perhaps because the heroic days of initial conquest were past, and the living easier. Or perhaps it is because we know (or think we know) more about them, for theirs was the era when Gregory of Tours, primary source for so much Merovingian history, was on the scene in person. As a firsthand witness, Gregory watched the closing years of the sixth century become a chaos of civil war, while between actual battles, the favored techniques of internecine conflict within the royal family involved daggers, poison and alleged witchcraft.

For commoners, taxes were a major terror; defaulters could be chained in prison and left there to rot. Meanwhile, bands of freelance invaders and local brigands menaced forester and farmer. Armies (whether Merovingian or newcomers) marched and countermarched across the land, despoiling it as they went. The innate greed and aggression of Clotar's sons would doubtless have been sufficient to keep their armies marching, but the murderous machinations of two of their queens raised the level of ferocity to ever greater heights. They were Fredegund, mistress and later wife of Chilperic of Neustria, and Brunhild, who was married to Sigibert of Austrasia. Fredegund, the more lethal of the two, was consumed with hatred for Brunhild, and Brunhild soon returned her wrath in full measure. She had good reason.

Brunhild was the educated and cultured daughter of the Visigoth king Athanagild. Although her family was Arian, she adopted orthodox Christianity and married Sigibert in a lavish ceremony at Metz. This caused Chilperic of Neustria to become furiously jealous. His own wife, Audovera, had borne him four children, but she was a mere run-of-the mill Frankish woman. Nothing would do but that Chilperic, too, must marry a Spanish princess, and he set his heart (or his ambitions) upon Brunhild's elder sister Galswintha. In due time, this marriage took place, and Galswintha brought Chilperic a satisfactorily substantial dowry.

Nothing else proved satisfactory, however, for lurking in the background at the Neustrian court was Fredegund. This woman was merely Chilperic's primary mistress (debauchery being one of his several vices), but she was a formidable

Chilperic sent his first wife, Audovera, to a convent and wed Fredegund. The move afforded her more scope than ever for sinister scheming, and in practical terms paid handsomely.

personality indeed. Queen Galswintha became a bitterly unhappy bride, complaining constantly of all the insults she had to bear, and one night her unhappiness came to a sad end. In the morning she was discovered strangled. Galswintha's sister Brunhild suspected, with good reason, that Fredegund was responsible, which would have been quite enough to ensure lifelong hatred. But there was more to come—much more—and much of it was directed at Brunhild.

Fredegund had venom to spare, and a firm hold on Chilperic. Shortly after Galswintha's death, he sent his first wife, Audovera, to a convent (and later had her killed), and married Fredegund. This afforded her more scope than ever for vicious scheming, and in practical terms, paid off handsomely. Until then, Chilperic had been doing very badly in the family wars, having lost most of his territory to Brunhild's husband Sigibert.[9] Now Fredegund took a hand, with spectacular results. To Sigibert's next victory celebration she sent two assassins who, just as the king was being raised in triumph on his warriors' shields, stabbed him with poisoned daggers.

Chilperic quickly marched on Paris to seize Sigibert's treasury, along with his widow and his five-year-old son. He did not get the boy, because an Austrasian duke quickly spirited him away to Metz, where he was proclaimed Childebert II. But the Austrasian nobles had no interest in rescuing their queen. Austrasia remained the most Germanic part of Gaul, and they had always resented this imperious Spanish lady as a pretentious and pushy foreigner. Besides, they aimed to appoint one of themselves to act for the boy king. So Brunhild ended up imprisoned by Chilperic in a convent at Rouen, and there a prince called Merovec, one of Chilperic's sons by Audovera, sought her out and married her.

This act assuredly contributed to Merovec's later murder, and also that of the man who performed the ceremony, Bishop Praetextatus of Rouen. Behind both

9. "It causes me great grief to have to describe these civil wars," Gregory writes. "When a year had passed, Chilperic once more sent messages to his brother Guntram. 'Come to me, dear brother,' said he. 'Let us meet to make peace, so that we can attack Sigibert, who is our enemy.' This was achieved; the two met and exchanged presents. Chilperic raised an army and marched as far as Reims, burning and destroying everything in his way. When Sigibert heard of this, he once more summoned the tribes from across the Rhine. . . ." And so it went in Frankland.

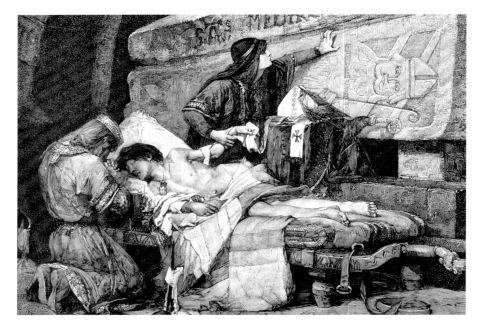

In this nineteenth-century French illustration, King Chilperic of Neustria and his queen, Fredegund, pray at the shrine of St. Medard at Soissons for the recovery of their son Clodebert, stricken in one of Gaul's recurrent plagues—perhaps a form of dysentery. Their prayers were in vain. The youth died, causing the malevolent Fredegund to embark on an extermination campaign against her stepsons, Chilperic's sons by other women. From Guizot's History of France.

killings was Fredegund. Insanely ambitious for her own progeny and pathologically jealous of her stepsons, she had long since persuaded her husband that his son was plotting against him. Chilperic had been easily persuaded—and, of course, it may have been true. He locked up Merovec, and not only cut his hair but had him tonsured a monk. But Merovec escaped, and was on the run when he contracted his brief marriage with Brunhild. In the end, however, he was trapped and killed.

As for Bishop Praetextatus, Fredegund first had him exiled on treason charges. Forced by the insistence of his devoted flock to let him return, she sent one of her hired killers to stab him before his altar. Never lacking in nerve, the queen actually dropped round before he expired, with a solicitous offer of medical assistance (also perhaps involving, it might be conjectured, a dab of poison). "God has decreed that I must be recalled from this world," was the bishop's stalwart reply. "As for you, who are the prime mover in these crimes, as long as you live, you will be accursed, for God will avenge my blood upon your head."[10]

Fredegund was nothing if not thorough, and not one of Audovera's offspring would survive. Theudebert, the eldest, fell fighting for his father against Uncle Sigibert. When two of Fredegund's own children died of dysentery, Fredegund accused Clovis, Audovera's third son, of causing their deaths through evil spells. She had Chilperic send him to a district where plague was raging, hoping that he, too, would be infected. When the young man uncooperatively remained healthy, writes Gregory of Tours, Fredegund brought further accusations: conspiracy to depose his father and "unforgivable remarks" about his stepmother.

So Chilperic turned poor Clovis over to Fredegund herself, bound and in rags. He was stabbed to death and buried with the knife still in his body, presumably to imply suicide. Nevertheless, a number of people were accused of having a hand in his death, and were tortured or burned alive. Nor did Audovera's daughter Basina fare very well. Forcibly consigned to the monastery founded by her late aunt, Radegund, she expressed her resentment by participating in a scandalous rebellion organized by some of its highborn inhabitants. But having nowhere else to go, Basina perforce repented and was allowed to return to Holy Cross Convent.

Fredegund had her own sorrows, of course. Of the five sons she bore Chilperic, four died in childhood of infectious disease. To explain this, or any other untoward event, she subscribed to two theories common then (and later, too, for that matter). Perhaps she or her husband had offended God or St. Martin. She could doubtless recall many things of which either one might have

10. Bishop Praetextatus never did mince words with Queen Fredegund, writes Gregory of Tours. The second time she threatened to exile him, he had the temerity to reply: "In exile and out of exile, I have always been a bishop . . . but when you give up your role as queen, you will be plunged into the abyss. . . . If you were to give up the boastful pride that burns within you, you might gain eternal life and be able to bring up to man's estate this young boy whose mother you are." The queen, Gregory adds, "bore his words ill."

disapproved. Alternately, disaster might be due to the evil activities of some enemy. This, in fact, was the explanation usually favored by Queen Fredegund of Neustria, and candidates were never lacking.

For the death of her fourth infant son, for example, she blamed the prefect Mummolus, a man who had thwarted some of her plans. And so, writes Gregory, she had "a number of Parisian housewives . . . tortured with the instruments and the cat," until they confessed they were witches and had "sacrificed" the baby prince to save the life of Mummolus. This statement, he adds, he found "quite incredible." After their confessions, the queen had "these poor wretches tortured in an even more inhuman way, cutting off the heads of some, burning others alive, and breaking the bones of the rest on the wheel." Then Mummolus himself was tortured to death.

Meanwhile, Fredegund's adversary Brunhild was, for the time being, getting on quite well. After Chilperic allowed her to return to her realm of Austrasia, a curious misjudgment, she took firm charge as regent. She controlled her restive aristocracy with a combination of military action, judicious assassination and sheer gall. Some nobles were loyal to her, and the rest were at least willing to protect her little son, Childebert II. Brunhild also enlisted as an ally her brother-in-law Guntram of Burgundy. (Among the four brothers, this monarch was the favorite of Gregory of Tours, who even referred to him on occasion as "Good King Guntram.") In 577, having no sons himself, Guntram "adopted" Childebert II as heir to Burgundy as well.

Brunhild was a competent ruler. She rebuilt some of Austrasia's Roman roads and other structures. She founded monasteries. She corresponded with Pope Gregory the Great in Rome, who was doing his best to maintain some liaison with the Gallic church. She became an important patron (if the later adversary) of the saintly Irish monk Columban, who arrived in Gaul about 590. After beguiling Childebert's court, Columban moved on to the wild Vosges Mountains (near the borders of Germany and Switzerland), where he established a mission to the Suevians in an abandoned Roman fort. Several dozen more monasteries followed. (See chapter 9.)

But over in Neustria, King Chilperic and Queen Fredegund were thriving too, and more dangerous than ever. They now controlled the whole western segment of the Merovingian realm, which included Tours. To the chagrin of Bishop Gregory and the sorrow of its citizens, the town became a center for plots and counterplots. The region suffered numerous attacks, Gregory writes, and Chilperic's avarice knew no bounds. He reinstated the tax demands on the churches, which his father Clotar I had remitted out of fear of St. Martin.[11] He used judicial fines to extort

11. King Clotar I, early in his reign, decided to tax churches one-third of their revenues. Most clerics acquiesced, but not Bishop Injuriosus of Tours. If the king seized what belonged to God, he told Clotar, "then the Lord will soon take your kingdom away from you, for it is criminal for you, who should be feeding the poor from your own granary, to fill your coffers with the alms which others give to them." Injuriosus then turned and stalked away, leaving Clotar so terrified that he hastily sent gifts after him, with pleas to pray that St. Martin would forgive him.

In Merovingian times, poison was reputedly a regular and recognized hazard in royal circles. It might be delivered on the point of a dagger (like this one, of Saxon fashioning), or on the lip of a goblet or drinking horn. (The horn depicted is a rare glass one of the period.) Such assassination attempts, however, seem to have failed more often than they succeeded.

12. By adopting and standing surety for both his surviving nephews—Brunhild's son Childebert II and Fredegund's son Clotar II, King Guntram inevitably involved himself in the vicious rivalry of the two women. He bore it philosophically. Gregory of Tours writes that Guntram once lauded young Childebert II as a wise man and an able one, then added as an amiable afterthought: "It is true enough that his mother Brunhild tried to kill me, but as far as I am concerned, that is a matter of small moment. God who snatched me from the hands of my other enemies, also delivered me from the snares of Brunhild."

money from the wealthy. He disallowed bequests to the church. He sold bishoprics to wealthy laymen.

Gregory was also irritated by Chilperic's intellectual pretensions and seriously disturbed by his heretical inclinations. The terms "Father" and "Son" as applied to the deity struck this Frankish monarch as ridiculously anthropomorphic, and he considered the third person of the Holy Trinity, the "Spirit" a quite unnecessary addition. Therefore, he ordered, the term Trinity must not be used in prayer. In vain, Gregory disputed these theories, the king merely brushing aside his arguments. At this time, too, Gregory was frequently drawn into the accusations and trials resulting from the intrigue that permeated the Neustrian court. This was usually to defend someone else, but once to defend himself (successfully) against a charge of slandering Queen Fredegund.

Chilperic died in 584—stabbed while out hunting. Why and by whom was never established, but there were myriad possibilities. An agent of Brunhild and her son Childebert II? A ruined noble bent on revenge? Fredegund herself? This last may seem far-fetched, but is not beyond possibility or even probability. After her husband's death, Fredegund took refuge with the endlessly patient Guntram, as her enemy Brunhild had done ten years earlier. At this point, a provocatively worded demand was presented to Guntram in the name of young Childebert II of Austrasia: "Hand over the murderess, the woman who garroted my aunt [Galswintha], the woman who killed first my father [Sigibert] and then my uncle [Chilperic], and who put my two cousins to the sword [Merovec and Clovis]." Guntram declined.

With all her sons and stepsons dead, the amazing Fredegund had managed to produce another male offspring, just four months old when his father died. The Neustrian nobles proclaimed the baby Clotar II, and induced his father's cities to pledge allegiance to the child and to King Guntram of Burgundy. Thus Guntram became the designated guardian of two underage kings, a responsibility which made him anxious about his own chances for survival.[12]

Living in Paris, Gregory says, the Burgundian monarch never went anywhere without a troop of armed guards, and at one Sunday Mass he actually addressed a plaintive plea to the congregation. "I ask you to remain loyal to me, instead of assassinating me, as only recently you assassinated my brothers. Give me two years to bring up these two nephews of mine, who are my adopted sons." Otherwise, if he should be killed while the boys were still small, there would be no one to protect the people. And so, Gregory adds, "the entire population prayed to God for his safety."

Fredegund was soon back to form, however, ruling Neustria as regent for little Clotar II. She had the advice and help of one Landeric, an able general who fought her battles, administered the royal estates, and functioned as her lover. Judging in part by the remarkable

GREGORY OF TOURS ON THE DEATH OF LITERACY

"What a poor period this is!" you hear it said. "If among all our people there is not one man to be found who can write a book about what is happening today, the pursuit of letters really is dead in us!"

power Fredegund exercised over her late husband and the Neustrian nobles, historian Scherman comments, she must have been both beautiful and possessed of a sexual allure irresistible to many men.

Even so, Fredegund's agents seem to have failed in at least half a dozen assassination attempts upon Brunhild and her son Childebert II, and finally upon Childebert's son Theudebert. Such failures boded ill for the hit man assigned to the job. One minor cleric, sent to ingratiate himself into Brunhild's household and kill her, was detected and expelled. When he returned to report failure, Fredegund had his hands and feet cut off. As her entry in the *Encyclopedia Britannica* succinctly observes: "Ruthlessly murderous and sadistically cruel, Fredegund can have few rivals in monstrousness."

A sore trial to her, however, was her daughter Rigunth, with whom nothing seemed to go right. Rigunth was betrothed to Recared, son of King Leuvegild of the Spanish Visigoths, and set out in the fateful year 584 with fifty carts of gold, silver and fancy clothing. Much of this treasure was allegedly stolen along the way by her extensive entourage. The rest disappeared when they stopped at Toulouse, where they got the news of Chilperic's assassination, and Rigunth took refuge in a church.

Some of her attendants struggled home to tell Fredegund, who naturally jailed and tortured them. The eventual return of Rigunth brought her little joy either. For one thing, Rigunth used to taunt her mother for being of servile origin, while she herself was a princess of the blood royal. One day the infuriated Fredegund slammed the lid of a heavy chest on her daughter's neck. Then she "leaned on it with all her might," says Gregory, until Rigunth's eyes were bulging, and servants intervened just in time to save her life.

After that, "there were never-ending outbursts of temper and even fisticuffs," of which "the main cause was Rigunth's habit of sleeping with all and sundry." Fredegund's "outbursts of temper" would end only with her (peaceful) death in 597. She was buried with other Merovingian royalty at St. Germain des Près in Paris. All these bodies disappeared during the French Revolution, writes historian Scherman. However, Fredegund's twelfth-century effigy, beside the high altar at the Cathedral of Saint Denis, "has an air of well-bred modesty."

So Brunhild had the satisfaction of outliving her implacable enemy. The terrible denouement of her own life was still sixteen years away, and she continued to hold her own against the Austrasian dukes. Childebert II duly grew up to rule his kingdom, and for a few years reigned over Burgundy as well—his legacy from King Guntram, who died in 592.

The relationship between Queen Fredegund and her unfortunate daughter Rigunth was a predictably stormy one. In this nineteenth-century French illustration, Fredegund has slammed a heavy chest lid on Rigunth's head and is trying unsuccessfully to throttle her. From Guizot's History of France.

Again, when Childebert II died at age twenty-five, Brunhild instantly took charge on behalf of his two young sons. She became regent for Theudebert II in Austrasia, and installed Theuderic II in Burgundy, with a loyal noble in charge. And again, according to the chronicles, all went well until Theudebert II married, and his lowborn but high-spirited young queen proved more than a match for his domineering grandmother.

The disgruntled Brunhild moved to the Burgundian court at Besançon, where Theuderic kept a number of concubines, and their several children, but had no official queen. At Besançon, Brunhild as dowager still held top rank, and Theuderic appreciated his grandmother's advice. But he was also much influenced by Brunhild's friend Columban, who had a monastery nearby at Annegray, and the autocratic Irish monk disapproved of loose marital liaisons. Columban prevailed upon Theuderic to take a bride, and he complied. Brunhild was aghast.

The story, as recorded in the seventh century (in *The Life of St. Columbanus by the Monk Jonas*), begins like this: "But the Old Serpent [i.e., the Devil] entered into his grandmother Brunhild, who was a second Jezebel, and aroused her pride against the holy man . . . for she feared that her power and honor would be lessened." Brunhild, perhaps to provoke a quarrel, brought to Columban two of Theuderic's sons and asked him to bless them. He indignantly refused. "Know that these boys will never bear the royal scepter," said he, "for they were begotten in sin." After that, says Jonas, "she began to persecute the neighboring monasteries."

As Brunhild perhaps intended, this led to escalating conflict between her grandson and the monk, and to expulsion from Burgundy of Columban and his Irish monks (although not the local men they had recruited), in 610.[13] But the end was rapidly approaching for the old queen, and for her grandsons, too. Fredegund's late-born son, Clotar II of Neustria, had been slicing off pieces of Burgundy, so Theuderic and Theudebert combined forces to defeat him. But then, instead of cementing this triumph, they turned upon each other, with Brunhild allegedly egging them on.

The monk Jonas claims that their adversary Clotar asked Columban which brother he should support. Neither, said the holy man, for in three years he himself would be master of all three kingdoms. And so it was. In 612 at the Battle of Zulpich, near Cologne, Theuderic defeated Theudebert, and according to some, had him decapitated then and there. Others claimed that Theudebert

The doughty dowager queen Brunhild of Austrasia is dispatched at last, in a manner gruesome even by Frankish standards, tied to the tail of a wild horse and thus kicked to death. Observing her execution is King Clotar II, who ordered it. He is the grandson of Brunhild's bitter enemy, Fredegund. An illustration from Guizot's History of France.

13. When Columban was expelled from Gaul, he was almost seventy, and had only five years to live. He and his companions nevertheless hiked over the Alps (in winter, it is said) and founded in northern Italy another monastery, Bobbio, which would powerfully influence the Christianization of Europe. So too, however, would the many monasteries previously established in Gaul, where the Gallic monks Columban had trained carried on. Columban's story in detail appears in the next chapter.

was betrayed into Brunhild's hands, and she had him murdered. In any event, a year later, Theuderic died of dysentery at age twenty-six. Alternately, according to one seventh-century account, Brunhild poisoned him so that she could rule through his small son Sigibert.

Certainly, she tried to do so. She proclaimed the boy king of Austrasia and Burgundy, as Sigibert II, but the poor youngster did not last the year. The Austrasian seigneurs conspired to rid themselves of their old bugbear, Brunhild, by offering both kingdoms to Clotar II of Neustria. Even Brunhild's Burgundian army capitulated as soon as Clotar's forces approached. Sigibert II and a younger brother were summarily executed, and then Clotar summoned Brunhild.

Dauntless to the end, this woman, in her late sixties, appeared in full regal style before Clotar and his troops, but this time, she could not prevail. The soldiers shouted for her execution. Clotar, accusing her of all manner of wickedness, sentenced her to three days of torture. Then to further humiliate her, Jonas

Flawed, credulous, self-seeking, ignorant or compromising as its members often must have been, the church of the Franks seemed nevertheless intent on glorifying and emulating God.

writes, he had her mounted on a camel "and so exhibited to all her enemies around about." Then they tied her to the tail of a wild horse; whipped into a frenzy, it kicked her to death. The year was 613.

After that, according to the seventh-century *Chronicle of Fredegar*, her executioners burned her body and scattered the ashes, obliterating every trace of the hated Queen Brunhild. What might have distressed her more, however, was the fact that her detested rival Fredegund had triumphed in every respect. The entire posterity of Sigibert I and Brunhild was no more. Of the Merovingian line, there remained only Fredegund's son and grandsons.[14]

Although Clotar II appeared to have united once more the kingdom of Clovis, this appearance was deceiving. In all three territories, the great landholders were asserting their power, foremost among them the two men who had carried the Austrasian proposal to Clotar II: Pepin of Landen and Arnulf, bishop of Metz. Reputedly pious Christians, as well as men of action, these two were about to found a new dynasty. In the course of the next century, it would parallel and maintain the continuity of the Merovingian line—and would then supersede it.

Pepin of Landen (the name derives from his estate in the Brabant region) was mayor of the palace in Austrasia. This title and function had developed as soon as Frankish chiefs came into possession of large and settled estates. They needed a *maior domus*—manager of the household—to run them. The job had expanded in scope ever since, especially during the tenure of child kings. But even adult monarchs found good use for the mayor of the palace, who acted as chief adviser and spokesman, and ideally was an accomplished general as well. Pepin was one of the best.

14. Concerning the unpleasant Neustrian royals and their progeny, Gregory records a vision of his own which, likely as it seemed, would not prove correct: "One night, when I lay sleeping in my bed . . . I saw an angel flying through the air. As he passed over the holy church, he cried in a loud voice: 'Woe and more woe! God has stricken Chilperic and all his sons . . . not a single one has survived ever to rule over his kingdom.'"

Arnulf, too, had served with distinction in the court of Theudebert II. In 614 he was consecrated bishop of Metz, at the behest of Clotar II (quite likely as part of the takeover plan). Arnulf and Pepin proceeded to stabilize Austrasia through the reign of Clotar's son Dagobert I (623–639), who was the last Merovingian to direct his own armies. Dagobert's successors began an ever-accelerating slide into indolence and debauchery, always carefully protected and maintained by capable mayors of the palace, who in time would produce the Carolingian dynasty.

Early in this process, Pepin of Landen's son Grimoald did make one misstep. After serving faithfully as mayor for Sigibert III until Sigibert's death in 656, Grimoald then tried to seize the Austrasian throne outright. He gave the young heir a haircut, shipped him to an Irish monastery, and attempted to make his own son king. The leading men of all three kingdoms swiftly combined to destroy them both.

But after that and into the eighth century, all the mayors of the palace took diligent care of the royal individuals whom French historians would dub the *rois fainéants* (do-nothing kings). Needing a facade of legitimacy, they maintained the true heir (or a convincing substitute) with all the appropriate trappings of Merovingian royalty: court protocol, long hair, beards and ceremonial ox-cart progressions through their domains. They actually enhanced the mystical aura. It was now that the legends about Merovec and classical Troy first appeared, probably to bolster the supposed authority of the sacred kings. (See footnote 3.) Theoretically, the mayors were mere agents; in reality, they were stealthily seizing royal power.

For some decades, the mayors fought each other as bloodily as ever the kings had, until out of the confusion there rose to prominence in public affairs a family, dubbed the Arnulfings, who were descendants of Arnulf and Pepin. Bishop Arnulf, before he took holy orders, had married a daughter of the count of Boulogne. One of their sons, Ansegis, married Begga, a daughter of Pepin of Landen. Their son, distinguished as Pepin of Heristal, rose to power in Austrasia, and with strong support from Neustrian nobles, unified the two realms. By the end of the seventh century, Pepin made himself master of most

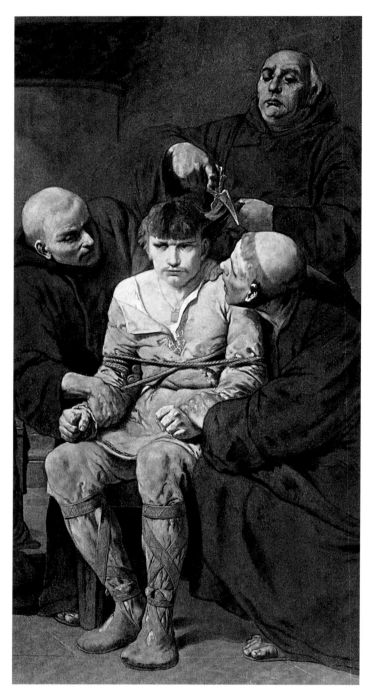

Among the Merovingian kings, the cutting of their long locks symbolically disqualified them as royalty. Occasionally this was voluntary, as when a youthful sixth-century prince named Clodoald cut his hair to renounce his inheritance and became a hermit later revered as St. Cloud. More often, it was distinctly involuntary. Illustrated here is the ritual shearing of a late Merovingian king, Childeric III, on orders of the ruling Mayor of the Palace. The illustration, by an unnamed artist, is in the Bettmann Archives, Iron Mountain, Pennsylvania.

of the kingdom of the Franks.

Within another two generations, recurrent periods of anarchy notwithstanding, descendants of Bishop Arnulf of Metz and Pepin of Landen would be the acknowledged and crowned monarchs of this kingdom. A little later still, one of their thrice-great-grandsons, known to history as Charlemagne, would expand it into a still vaster realm, which by later medieval times would be hailed as the Holy Roman Empire.

The term "empire" would not be a misnomer. The Franks had absorbed and applied all they could comprehend of the Roman structure, and by their very limitations had actually simplified and thereby improved it. Unstable and chancy the Merovingians may have seemed, but they had not done so badly. To last for two and a half centuries was an impressive achievement in those times. The appellation "holy" would be equally justified. The Franks had embraced the Christian faith whole and complete, and despite their many obvious flaws they preserved it, and spread it.

And for these accomplishments, both secular and spiritual, credit must go to the Gallic Church—its bishops, priests, monks, nuns, missionaries and ordinary believers. Flawed, credulous, self-seeking, ignorant or compromising as its members often must have been, the church of the Frankish kingdoms was clearly intent upon glorifying God and emulating its Lord. Through its labors on behalf of the homeless, the helpless, the sick and the dying—the people Jesus called "the least of these my brethren"—was established the tradition of social concern that one day would sharply distinguish western society from most others. Very many of these stalwart Christians were awarded the title "saint." History testifies that they earned it.

Out of the cruelty and turmoil, slowly and painfully, there emerged a semblance of order. When the Merovingians faded

GREGORY OF TOURS ON THE FRANKS

To this day, one is still amazed and astonished at the disasters that befell these people [the Franks]. After the preaching of the missionary bishops, the earlier generations were converted from their pagan temples and turned towards the churches. Now they plunder those same churches. Their forefathers endowed them; the sons tear them to pieces.

The long span of French royalty was inaugurated by the Merovingian line. The long-haired Kings and their consorts began the tradition of royal burial in the great churches of Paris, first at St. Germain des Près, later at St. Denis (shown here). During the French Revolution, the tombs and burial vaults were emptied and vandalized, but the royal effigies remain today in calm and stony repose.

into the past and were replaced by the Carolingian dynasty, the old Frankish warrior skill would again prove its worth. For in another dark hour, less than a century ahead, the swords of Islam would flame out of the Middle East, through North Africa, across the Gibraltar strait, through Spain, over the Pyrenees and well into France, crushing Christendom everywhere—and the Franks would be the ones to stop them cold. "If only my Franks had been there," tough old Clovis had cried when he heard the story of the Crucifixion. This time, they were. ■

CHAPTER 9

With Britain doomed, the faith takes root in barbarous Ireland

Patrick, the escaped slave, goes back to the land of his masters and launches the crusade that will carry the gospel to Scotland, England and Europe

Hobnailed army sandals shuffled and scraped across the shingled beach, bronze armor and iron blades clanked, and muffled grunts and curses could be heard over the lap of the surf, as file on file the Roman legionaries heaved themselves aboard weed-slimed, lumbering transport galleys. The year was 407. Though few people would have believed it at the time, and the horror of it would only gradually dawn, the last legion was leaving Britannia. Rome, after nearly four centuries of occupation, was abandoning its northernmost province to its fate, and its fate would not be pleasant.

These stolid veterans of a hundred border skirmishes were crossing the channel in support of the latest British candidate for an imperial crown, Constantine III, later called the "Usurper." Four years hence, his luck would run out, and he would be cornered, captured and beheaded by the almost equally hapless emperor Honorius. This was in fact the third revolt by a British general in the past decade, and it would be as short-lived as the first two.

None of the soldiers Constantine commandeered would ever return to Britain, leaving the island more vulnerable than ever to three perils: from the west, hideous half-naked pirates crossing the Irish Sea; from the east, ferociously insatiable Saxons crossing the North Sea; and from the north, the angry, tattooed

Picts, whom the Romans had never been able to subdue.[1] After three years of mounting calamity, representatives of Britain's fifteen-odd city-states met in desperation, overthrew the absent Constantine's provincial administrators and wrote to the emperor Honorius, humbly professing their loyalty and pleading for governors, troops and money to rebuild their defenses.

The appeal was futile. Honorius was himself in disarray. Other barbarian nations were running wild through Gaul and had crossed the Pyrenees. Spain was gone and North Africa imperiled. Three years after the last legion left Britain, Rome fell to the Goths, who stripped it of all movable wealth and forced the ill-starred Honorius to let them settle in southern Gaul. (See chapter 4.) Honorius, hunkering in his marsh-girded fortress of Ravenna in Italy, sent his dismaying answer: "The cities of Britain must look to their own defenses."

As the realization sank in that they were now completely on their own, fear gripped the Britons. The reality, however, would surpass their worst forebodings. They were living in the sunset before a night of deepening darkness that would last for more than two hundred years. For generation after generation, grandfathers would watch their grandsons withdraw into ever more desolate and ever more threatened homesteads.

These two hundred years are known as, the "Dark Ages," because they are all but opaque to historians. Since the invaders could not write, only a few sparse records survive of the entire period: an account by the Gallic bishop Germanus of Auxerre, for instance, and the writings of the monkish reformer Gildas.[2] But these were like stars that glow in a moonless sky; they can be seen, but throw little light. However, two other remnants shine brightly enough for some pattern of events to be discerned: the partly legendary record of a warrior king who would become the last defender of the western Roman empire; and the memoirs of an escaped slave who would passionately embrace Christianity and help lay the foundations of the new Christendom, rising in the ruins of the old.

But all this—and much else—was far from foreseeable in the fateful year 407. The Britain abandoned by the Romans was an agrarian society of about four million people, living between Hadrian's Wall in the north and the south coast. Perhaps one in ten spoke Latin and took part in civic life. The rest were peasants. Still largely pagan, Celtic-speaking and illiterate, they were the renters, laborers or slaves of Latin-speaking, highly civilized landowners. These aristocrats, living mostly in the fertile southern lowlands in fifty-room villas with heated mosaic floors, had grown rich supplying grain to the legions in Gaul. The northern frontier area had been dominated by the army, now evacuated. Britain's two dozen cities and military centers were decaying, industry having shrunk to a few local pottery factories.

A century after Constantine the Great, the British church, according to some historians, was locked in a struggle between urban bishops, concerned mainly with civic government and seemingly indifferent to the peasantry, and the evangelical followers of Martin of Tours, whose self-sufficient rural monasteries fervently preached the gospel throughout the countryside. This was a familiar

1. *Britannia* was the Roman name for the whole island. The particularly formidable inhabitants of the northern highlands were *Picti*, "painted ones," so-called from the tattoos of their warriors. *Scoti* was Roman slang for the Irish pirates who raided Britain's west coast. In the sixth century, Irish migrants settled in Scotland's southwest highlands, intermarried with Picts and produced today's Scots. The Cornish, Welsh, and Cumbrians (called *Cymry*, "citizens" in Celtic), resisted the Anglo-Saxon invasion for most of two centuries.

2. Such Roman sources as Prosper's *Roman Chronicle* provide some dates for British history in the fifth and sixth centuries, but the most complete narrative of the period is Gildas's *The Destruction of Britain*, written about 540, and the earlier *History of St. Germanus*, by the presbyter Constantius of Lyon (ca.480), supplies further detail. In the eighth century, a compiler named Nennius "made a heap of all I found" of earlier documents, particularly the *Kentish Chronicle* and a work identified as the *Chronographer*, covering approximately 425–460. In addition, there are many mutually confirming "lives" of the saints, poems, legends and folk songs.

The Celts: barbarous but always artistic

Celtic life in fourth-century Ireland had advanced little beyond Celtic life in Britain, when the Romans first conquered the southern part of the island four hundred years before. The illustration of the trio of Celts (1) is based on Roman descriptions of the skin-clad savages (from Cassell's History of England, *1875). But rudimentary as conditions may have been, primitive Celtic society was not without its refinements. For example, the swirling etchings on this Celtic monolith (2) in Scotland records events such as great battles, now lost in the mists of time. Such decorative arts flourished among the Celtic tribes. Jewelry, like these solid gold torques (3), was regularly worn by high-status individuals or used in votive offerings. As for their dwellings, Celts' domiciles were arranged in compounds called "crannogs" (from the word for "tree"). In this reconstruction in Ireland (4), the buildings are enclosed in a palisade built on stilts over artificial islands.*

conflict in Gaul as well, but in 396, irate British bishops had actually expelled one of Martin's missionary students for allegedly disrupting the populace. Nevertheless, within a generation, many a village church in Britain was being dedicated to St. Martin.

As the Roman provinces and city-states disintegrated, small local tyrannies and monarchies tried to replace them. The only concerted national endeavor, as one bishop recorded, had been the bloody overthrow of the administrators of Constantine III, some of whom lay unburied, their corpses torn limb from limb and picked over by beasts and birds. Over the next decade, the monk Gildas writes a century later, a conclave of British chieftains made and unmade "kings." In quick succession, these unfortunates "were anointed, then soon slain by those who

The only previous national effort had been the overthrow of the Roman administrators whose bodies lay unburied, torn limb from limb, and picked over by beasts and birds.

anointed them." But for a time, the various barbarians were slow to fully exploit the island's weakness, and in the north, a Roman leader, known as Coel Hen (historic model for the legendary Old King Cole) effectively checked the Picts.

Civilization steadily weakened nevertheless. Pillaging of farms became commonplace, as did ambushes on the highways, which were degenerating into mere tracks. Wood or leather receptacles gradually replaced professionally produced pottery. Crumbling stone buildings were patched with wood. Trade declined. Barter replaced money. Brute force replaced law. Since fewer and fewer people could read and write, all communication became direct and verbal. Eventually, no one would accurately remember what civilization had been like, and only its ruins bore witness to it.

A mere two decades after the departure of the legions, serious distress seems to have been manifest among the poor. In 428, Bishop Germanus of Auxerre, sent by Pope Celestine to deal with Pelagian tendencies in the British church, also felt it necessary to intercede for the common people against excessive taxation. On one count or the other (or more likely both), he earned the hostility of local bishops. But Germanus, an advocate by training and a onetime Roman administrator in Gaul, was not easily intimidated. When he returned to Britain in about 445, for instance, he was asked to lead the militia of southeastern Wales against a major Irish invasion, in an engagement that became famous as the "Alleluia Victory." Bishop Germanus positioned his troops on the slopes of a steep valley. As the enemy approached, he ordered them all to shout "Alleluia" in powerful concert, at full lung power. The noise echoing from hill to hill persuaded the attackers they were outnumbered and surrounded, and they precipitately fled.

Far more dangerous, however, were the Saxon invaders. Sidonius Apollinaris, statesman, author and bishop of Clermont in Gaul, vividly described them to a friend newly in command of a Gallic coastal squadron:

The Saxon is the most ferocious of all foes. He comes on you without warning. He never attacks when you expect it. Resistance only moves him to contempt; a rash opponent is soon put down. If he pursues, he overtakes; if he flies himself, he is never caught. Shipwrecks to him are no terror, only so much training. His acquaintance with the perils of the sea is intimate; he knows them as he knows himself. A storm puts his enemies off their guard, while the chance of taking the foe by surprise makes him gladly face every hazard of rough waters and broken rocks. . . . It is their custom, homeward bound, to abandon every tenth captive to the slow agony of a watery death, casting lots calmly among their doomed captives in execution of this shameful death sentence . . . they consider it a religious act to perpetrate this horrible slaughter.

Saxon raids led inevitably to Saxon settlement. It doubtless became common knowledge among the folk back home, writes E. A. Thompson in *Saint Germanus of Auxerre and the End of Roman Briton* (Suffolk, 1984), that Britain was a far richer country than their own waterlogged fields, and the post-Roman citizenry were far from outstanding as warriors. In short, says the *Anglo-Saxon Chronicle*, the Saxons became convinced of "the worthlessness of the Britons and the excellence of the land."

Their ambitions were notably advanced by a powerful British chief named Vortigern, who was likely backed by independent farmers of the western hills. About 425, much to the discomfiture of comfortable southern magnates, Vortigern established a tenuous sovereignty over Roman Britain. Subsequently, hard-pressed by the lean and hungry Saxons, he followed established Roman policy. He bought off some attackers, but he also—this time to the discomfiture of all Britain—settled whole contingents of Saxons as "federated" barbarians, to defend his east coast against seaborne attacks by the Picts.

It was a disastrous move. According to the historian Nennius, writing in the ninth century, "First came three keels [i.e., ships] full of Saxons driven into exile from Germany. In them were the brothers Horst and Hengest. Vortigern welcomed them and handed over to them what was then the island of Thanet, off the east coast." (Thanet has since become part of the mainland.) Gildas, in his *Destruction of Britain*, also condemns this move as "raw, hopeless stupidity. . . . Of their own free will, they invited in under their roof the enemy they feared worse than death." The initial Saxon trickle became a flood, and when the British finally took arms against Vortigern, he allied with these formidable freebooters against his own countrymen.

The immense fort at Portchester in England was just one of many built by the Romans in the dying days of their occupation of the island. The stronghold protected the merchant and military vessels sheltering in the expansive harbor. Later, Normans would take advantage of the stout walls and construct a castle within them (upper right corner of the enclosure).

The arrival of Saxons, Jutes and Angles in Britain is commemorated in this twelfth-century illumination from the Passion and Miracles of St. Edmund. *(The Pierpont Morgan Library, N.Y.)*

Saxon numbers steadily swelled, Vortigern's ability to pay them off steadily shrank, and by 442 they struck in force. No Germanic invasion of the western Empire, even that of the Huns, worked such slaughter and destruction as did the Saxon assault upon Britain. "All the greater towns fell to the enemy's battering rams; all their inhabitants, bishops, priests and people, were mown down together, while swords flashed and flames crackled," Gildas writes, the horror still vivid a hundred years later. "There was no burial save in the ruins of the houses or in the bellies of the beasts and birds." In 446, the British again appealed to Rome, to the accomplished general Aetius: "The barbarians push us to the sea, the sea pushes us to the barbarians," they pleaded "Between the two . . . we are either slain or drowned." The reply was the same. No help was available.

The Saxon population was yet too small to prevail. They could only raid, not conquer, the midlands. The British held London, separating the Saxon forces in southeastern Kent from their allies in eastern Anglia. By 452, after ten years of fighting, they had at least been checked, although their settlements were much stronger. Some time after 455, according to the chronicles, Hengest proposed a treaty, calling a peace conference, which his own delegates attended with daggers hidden in their shoes. "The Saxons, friendly in their words but wolfish in heart and deed, sat down to celebrate, each man next to his British neighbor," records the *Kentish Chronicle*. Then, when their leader gave the signal, "all three hundred [British] elders were slaughtered; the king [Vortigern] alone was taken alive and held prisoner."

With their foremost men dead, the Britons were leaderless. Vortigern survived, hated by all his nation, and wandered the land "till his heart broke and he died without honor." Soon "huge numbers of [Saxon] warriors" crossed over the sea to carry out murderous attacks on Britain. "Some of the wretched survivors were caught and slaughtered in heaps; others surrendered themselves to perpetual slavery," Gildas writes. "Others entrusted their lives to the rugged hills, the thick forests . . . until after some time the plunderers went home again." That "home" was the eastern third of the island, which the Saxons now increasingly shared with compatriot barbarians known as the Angles. Since the Angles were tougher and more durable even than they were, the territory acquired a new name. It became "Angle-Land," and evolved from there to, "England" and "English."[3]

The existing Celtic inhabitants of this area were almost totally obliterated, historian Thompson emphasizes, along with their society—and very quickly. How else, he contends, "could we account for the utter disappearance of the Celtic language from eastern England, and of the Christian religion? How could we account for the fact that only about a score of nouns made their way from British Celtic into Anglo-Saxon, and none at all from British Latin? Why did the Saxons fail to borrow as simple a device as the potter's wheel? Why did tens of thousands of Britons flee to the continent as early as the 460s? Why was it that the Britons who survived in the west of the island conceived a hatred of the Saxons that the passage of generations, and even of centuries, did little to abate? Why, in fact, did they refuse to preach the gospel to their tormentors even in the early eighth century, a fact which shocked Bede?"

3. The British first knew the Germanic invaders invariably as Saxons, but later historians distinguish between the Saxons from the mouth of the Elbe (who invaded Britain's southern shore and Thames estuary), the Jutes from the Frisian coast (who took southeastern Kent and the Isle of Wight), and the Angles from west-central Denmark (who settled the eastern bulge of Anglia). While the Saxons could be at least temporarily suppressed, the Angles proved impossible to defeat. Thus the invaders became known collectively as the Angle-ish, or English.

4. The flight of so many Romano-British soldiers to Britanny under Riothamus (or John Reith) may well have prevented the inhabitants of Britain from expelling the Saxons while expulsion was still possible. The emigrants probably thought of themselves as Roman provincials first, and only secondarily as British. But in Gaul, allied with the Roman remnant and later the Franks, they may have become a decisive factor in preventing the establishment of a Saxon kingdom in the Loire Valley.

The main exodus to the continent consisted of a veritable army of twelve thousand British men with their families. They fled to Gaul under the leadership of one Riothamus, where they became allies of that province's last Roman leader, Aegidius. They were settled in Armorica, which in consequence was renamed Brittany. They managed thereafter to hold Brittany more or less independently, and their Celtic language can still be heard there. Having lost hope in their former homeland, they never returned.[4] For them, Britannia was dead.

But Britannia was not dead. It still had some fight left, and it was helped by a change in the invaders. Over long years, they settled in with their families and put down roots. They now had something to lose. New waves of Saxon migrants arrived as settlers rather than pillagers. The first English towns began to appear. Moreover, against all odds, the British recovered from the slaughter, and a resistance movement took shape, centered in the future Wales.

At this point, there appears among the British an enchanted figure, mythical in most respects, yet fully historical in some. For a crucial half century, he would inspire Britannia's last defenders to block the continuing waves of invaders. He would also inspire the makers of the island's romantic mythologies for the next fourteen centuries. Hundreds of years later, his name and memory would be used to introduce into a still barbaric world a Christian concept called chivalry, imposing upon the strong the obligation to respect and care for the weak. The man himself was said to be a scion of Roman nobility, even remotely of the imperial purple. Legend designates him a monarch, and he is known to both history and romance as King Arthur.

Nennius's *History of Britain*, written nearly four hundred years after the Saxon invasions, is the only source of such scant details as exist about Arthur, but he is referred to in Welsh song and poetry from a much earlier date. For example, the majestic Welsh poem *Y Gododdin*, probably dating to the sixth century, describes the deeds of some distinguished warrior but then adds dismissively that he was "no Arthur."

An advantage that the British possessed was precisely the skill as horsemen to which the poem alludes, something the invader English could not easily counter. The earliest Welsh poetry sings constantly of mounted warriors, sword-wielding and scarlet-plumed, who contend with bands of unmounted spearmen. The English had no horses, and some were said to be ignorant even of how horses looked. The British, on the other hand, raised cavalry mounts on their beleaguered estates, and could move at four times the speed of infantry. They could not attack strong and prepared positions, but depended for their successes upon surprise. They could catch small raiding bands unawares, or—when the English tried to assemble larger armies—would raid their encampments. Between skirmishes, the Britons would recoup in walled towns or Iron Age hill forts, difficult to besiege in numbers sufficient to prevent a breakout by a concerted charge.

Nennius tells of twelve major battles in which Arthur triumphed. Although he names the sites of all twelve, scholars have never agreed on their locations. The decisive one, however, was called the Battle of Badon, which Gildas and Nennius

both describe as a siege. Likely the British cavalry, perhaps a thousand strong, were surrounded on the hilltop by many times their number of English infantry. After three days, when the English lines had been somewhat weakened by the need to send out foraging parties, Arthur's knights charged downhill, slaughtering (it is said) 960 of the besiegers at the first shock. Many or most of the rest—hungry, scattered and on foot in enemy territory—may have been cut down in the following days.

Arthur would die twenty years later, around 515, at the Battle of Camlann, a particularly bloody engagement in the endless border "peacekeeping," which he conducted for at least thirty years, and which continued to check the Saxon advance for twenty more.[5] But eventually, internecine strife once again engulfed the surviving British aristocracy. Having known nothing but fighting for three generations, after Arthur died, his countrymen apparently could not refrain from turning on one another. Moreover, it was becoming apparent that they would never be able to expel the English from the island.

Though he does not mention Arthur by name, Gildas looks back nostalgically on his era. He calls it a time when "rulers, public officers and private persons, bishops and clergy all kept to their proper station" and the "restraints of truth and justice" were respected. Gildas was writing around 540. By then, he said, all those qualities had been "shattered and overthrown." It is noteworthy that this nostalgia for a "golden era" did not end with Gildas. Throughout the medieval era, the name of Arthur was invoked to inspire honesty in human affairs and honor in battle, and in the nineteenth century the poet Tennyson would enlist

Arthur's defeat of the Saxons at Badon is depicted in this illustration. This nineteenth-century engraving is housed in the Bettmann Archives.

5. Frank D. Reno, in his *The Historic King Arthur* (McFarland & Co., 1996) offers a theory on the true identity of King Arthur. Arthur and the historic Riothamus are, he contends, one and the same, the name Riothamus being a title awarded Arthur for the battles he waged against the Saxons in Gaul. The reason the scenes of battles recorded by the historian Nennius can't all be located in England, says Reno, is that some of them were probably fought in Gaul.

The real and fabled king
Poems, movies, books celebrate Arthur's glorious story

Variations abound, but the central story of the King Arthur legend remains the same. He was born out of wedlock to the king of Britain, remaining ignorant of his heritage until he bested all challengers, aided by a magical sword. As king of Camelot, Arthur ruled with the help of the magician Merlin and the fabled Knights of the Round Table. All was not well, however. A favorite knight, Sir Lancelot, stole the heart of his beloved Queen Guinevere, and Arthur was eventually slain by his wicked sister Morgan le Fay and his jealous nephew Mordred. Versions of the story have been set down by writers including Geoffrey of Monmouth, Cretien de Troyes, Sir Thomas Malory, Alfred Lord Tennyson, Mark Twain, T. H. White and John Steinbeck. *Camelot*, the Broadway musical that was said to have inspired the late President John Kennedy, became one of dozens of movies about Arthur, ranging from the adventurous *First Knight* with Sean Connery to the flippant *Monty Python and the Holy Grail*. Richard Wagner based his operas, *Tristan und Isolde* and *Parsifal*, on stories long associated with Arthur and his knights. ∎

The Arthur legend has proven to be a rich source of inspiration for the arts, whether literature, movies or painting. (1) Arthur and Guinevere sang their way into the hearts of thousands in the 1960s Broadway musical and then movie Camelot. (2) Children's books on Arthur have been many and lavishly illustrated, like this one by Henry Gilbert. (3) An Aubrey Beardsley woodcut from a nineteenth-century edition of Sir Thomas Malory's epic poem, Le Morte d'Arthur. And (4) the painting of Arthur's death by J. M. Carrick (English, nineteenth century) is just one of hundreds on the subject.

(5) Tintagel Castle on the Cornish coast is known to have been constructed in the thirteenth century, but some claim it covers the site of the mythic Camelot. (6) Also in the thirteenth century, the nobility and merchants of Winchester hung their concept of the Round Table in the great hall of their city. Even by then, the historical Arthur had become legendary. (7) In a twelfth-century mosaic in the Cathedral of Otranto, Italy, he rides in pursuit of the Holy Grail.

6. Much is known of Patrick's character and attitude from his two surviving writings, his *Confession* and his *Appeal to the Soldiers of Coroticus*, but he provides no dates and few place-names. Some historians theorize an "early Patrick," born around 385, and a "later Patrick" who died in 495. This account follows the dates proposed by Patrick's twentieth-century biographer, E. A. Thompson (*Who Was St. Patrick?* New York, 1985). He concludes that Patrick was born ca.375, enslaved ca.393, freed ca.397, initially rejected as bishop to the Irish in 427, consecrated as bishop in 435 and died in 445 at the age of about seventy.

once again the memory of this ancient British king, to reaffirm the old values for yet another generation.

But Arthur's solidly historic contributions were far from negligible either. By blocking the Anglo-Saxon invaders, he prevented them from reaching the Irish Sea, and thus made possible the astonishing transformation now occurring on its farther shore. There, in Ireland, the Christian gospel was being embraced with astounding zeal. The succeeding two centuries would see Irish missionary monks voyage to Scotland, then south into Saxon England, and then across the channel to the future Belgium, France, Germany and The Netherlands, helping to draw them all into a Christendom so vastly expanded as to be scarcely imagined by their predecessors.

All this Christian expansion began with the man named Patrick, who leaves in his *Confession* a simple and heartfelt defense of his life's work, which was to evangelize the wild people of the island where he had been taken as a youthful captive and sold as a slave. "I, Patrick," he begins, "a most uneducated sinner and the least of all the faithful, most contemptible in the eyes of many, am the son of Calpurnius, a deacon, a grandson of Potitus, a priest, from the village of Bannaventa Burniae (thought by most scholars to have been somewhere in northwest England). He had an estate nearby where I was taken captive. I was then about sixteen years of age. I did not know the true God, and I was taken away to captivity in Ireland, like so many thousands of people. . . ."

Christian British viewed the Irish as demonic savages, who offered human sacrifices to fornicating idols—enemies not only of civilization, but of God himself. Patrick's family villa was likely within a day's march of the Irish Sea. Given his avowed ignorance of the faith, it is possible that his grandfather and father, like many aristocrats of the post-Constantinian empire, had themselves ordained for political advantage and clerical tax exemption. Nor is Patrick's written Latin very polished, which may mean the Irish pirates snatched him about 393, before he received the classical education still common to his class.[6]

The pirates sold him to a "king" in northwestern Ireland—that is, to a local strongman, probably the boss of a few dozen herdsmen and rustlers. There, this hitherto pampered son of Romano-British landowners lived for several years the lonely life of a shepherd slave, "chastised daily by hunger and nakedness." There, too, he placed himself in the hands of God, and through the brutality of his existence, he was sanctified. "The love of God came to me more and more, and my faith was strengthened. My spirit was so moved, that in a single day I would say as many as a hundred prayers, and almost as many at night . . . in the woods and on the mountains, I would get up for prayer before daylight, through snow, through frost, through rain, and I felt no harm."

Then one night, he recalls, he was suddenly awakened. A voice seemed to be speaking to him. "It is well," said the voice, "that you hunger. For soon you will go to your own country." A short while later it spoke again: "See, your ship is ready." He could only guess that this meant he was perhaps intended to escape. Although an escaped slave faced terrible punishment and even death, if captured, he sensed that he must obey the voice.

So he simply walked away, with no notion where exactly he was heading, but curiously felt no fear. A ship had been mentioned. This must mean the coast. But where on the coast? In Patrick's memory, he trekked about two hundred miles across hostile land, which must indicate that he was dodging here and there to escape capture, since no part of Ireland is more than eighty miles from the sea. Finally, he found a port where a ship was ready to sail, loaded with Irish wolfhounds and bound for Gaul.

At first, the captain angrily refused him passage, probably recognizing him as a fugitive, but when Patrick walked away, praying, the sailors called him back. "Come aboard," they said invitingly. He assumed they meant to sell him into slavery again, but the voice had said "a ship" and this was a ship. So he joined them.

Three days' sailing brought them to Gaul, likely the Brittany coast. The sailors, their hounds and Patrick set off on foot, trudging for twenty-eight days through what he describes as an "uninhabited wilderness." The notation has long baffled historians. Where in Gaul, or Britannia, could you walk for four weeks and encounter no living being? One explanation has occurred to some. They were in Gaul all right, and the Suevi and Vandals had recently passed that way, leaving nothing alive behind them.

Near starvation, the captain challenged Patrick—the Christian—to pray to his "great and all-powerful god" for food. Patrick advised his companions to turn trustingly to the Lord "who can do all things." When they did, he reports, their prayer was interrupted by a stampede of snorting animals, a herd of wild pigs, upon which they and the hounds feasted for two days. Something else may have happened at this time, though Patrick leaves few details of it. He speaks obscurely of being enslaved a second time (perhaps by the sailors). The voice returned, however,

In the lore that surrounds St. Patrick, the Rock of Cashel is the site of one of his many dramatic encounters. Steadying himself while baptizing King Aengus of Cashel, Patrick accidentally drives his spiked crosier through that chieftain's foot. The king makes not a murmur, and when Patrick, aghast, realizes what he has done, the king seems surprised at Patrick's concern. Given the story he had heard of a God whose feet were pierced, says the king, he assumed it was part of Christian initiation. In the twelfth century, the now-hallowed place became a Christian monastery atop the great rock.

With the Welsh coasts and Britain forever behind him, Patrick sets his eyes and energies to the mission before him: to evangelize the wild Irish.

SHUTTLEWORTH

assuring him that this time it would last only sixty days. So it turned out to be.

At this point in his *Confession*, Patrick jumps ahead. "Again after a few years, I was in Britain with my people," he relates, with no explanation of how he got there. If, as is certainly possible, he was redeemed from his new enslavement by Gallic Christians, he would probably have spent those "few years" within the Gallic church. Tours, home of the saintly Martin, lay up the Loire River, probably a three-week journey from the coast, and Martin's student, Amator, was now bishop of Auxerre, three weeks to the east.

In any event, once back at his ancestral villa in Britain, Patrick tried to settle down. Then came another dream. He saw "a man named Victoricus, coming as it were from Ireland, with countless letters." They were all marked "The Voice of the Irish." He heard voices crying out: "We ask you, boy, come and walk once more among us." Such dreams recurred, increasing in intensity. "He that has laid down his life for you," said one voice, "it is he that speaks in you."

To Patrick, all this could mean only one thing. In the service of Jesus Christ he must return to the land from which the voice of God had once led him away. He must go back to that fierce, coarse, villainous, conniving, quarrelsome, murderous—and yet unpredictably generous and crudely poetic—people called the Irish. If God could raise up children to Abraham out of the stones of the ground, as John the Baptist had said he could (Matt. 3:9, Luke 3:8), then no doubt God could raise up Christians even out of the Irish. But first Patrick must be trained to the task, and he appears to have returned to Gaul. His biographer Muirchu, writing after 650, reports that he studied for the priesthood under Germanus, he of the "Alleluia Victory." However it came about, by 427, Patrick was being prepared as missionary bishop to the Irish.

It remains one of the ironies of history that he was initially rejected for the job. He had once confessed to a friend some dire sin committed in his youth. Its nature is not specified, and some speculate that it was murder. In any event, when the friend reported this sin, the church vetoed Patrick as a bishop. Instead, Pope Celestine is thought to have consecrated the deacon Palladius as Ireland's

In the service of Christ, Patrick must go back to that fierce, villainous, conniving, murderous—and yet unpredictably generous and crudely poetic—people called the Irish.

first bishop. Palladius, who may previously have prevailed upon Celestine to send Germanus to Britain, was to contend once more with the Pelagian heresy there, and also to launch a mission to the Irish. Three church sites near Wicklow in the southeast have been identified as Palladius's work, but his success appears to have been minimal.

The same was not true of Patrick, although in all likelihood he first returned to the isle of his captivity as a deacon or priest, answering to an absentee bishop. Crossing the Irish Sea, probably from Porth Mawr in Wales, he established his first mission at Downpatrick, about twenty-five miles southeast of Belfast. Forty-five miles inland, he founded the powerful Christian center of Armagh, where he is said to have built a stone church, and which he used as a missionary base to begin the conversion of the whole island.

Thence by his own account, he traveled the island, baptizing "many thousands." Tradition says he built well over fifty churches, and that in the decade after his death the north alone had five bishops. Within his lifetime or shortly thereafter, the Irish slave trade ended, the warrior violence softened, and relatively peaceful relations began with the British across the sea.

Women, too, were soon caught up in the movement. A probable contemporary of Patrick was Brigid, descended from the chiefs of Faughart in County Louth. By tradition a beautiful young woman who spurned many offers of marriage, she became a nun and founded the famous Convent of *Cil-Dara* (The Oak), now

Kildare. This developed into two monasteries, one for men and one for women, both ruled by Brigid, who held the power of an abbot and virtually appointed the local bishop. Cil-Dara became a center of learning for all Ireland, celebrated in particular for artistic metalwork adorning the covers of ancient books. These intricate designs amazed researchers for centuries, although not the local people, who simply explained that an angel provided them. Widely beloved and revered as "Queen of the South, the Mary of the Gael," Brigid (or Bride, as she is sometimes styled) became Ireland's saintly patroness.

But it is to Patrick above all that the conversion of the island is credited. Reputedly a gentle man, he could also be stern. At one point, a British chieftain, Coroticus, was raiding Ireland's increasingly peaceful northeast, killing and enslaving Patrick's converts, possibly in their hundreds, with the "chrism still fragrant on their foreheads."[7] Patrick wrote to Coroticus, demanding that he release the slaves. When Coroticus made a jeering reply, Patrick penned his only other surviving work, *Epistle to the Soldiers of Coroticus*: "I beseech you, it is not right to pay court to such men, nor to take food or drink in their company . . . until they, by strict penance with shedding of tears, make amends before God and free the servants of God and the baptized handmaids of Christ, for whom He was crucified and died." He ends with an anguished query: "Is it a shameful thing in their eyes that we have been born in Ireland?" (He was not, of course, but his people were.) There is no known reply to Patrick's plea.

How Patrick could so swiftly set afoot the conversion to Christianity of this fierce people became and remains a historical mystery. The pagan Irish had long sacrificed human beings to their gods—children to their fertility gods, captives to their war gods. In times of crisis, smiling Druid priests joyfully strangled their victims. But this same people, in a span of barely a hundred years, would become zealous servants of Christ: renowned for their mercy and their care of the poor, the sick and the helpless; eager students of Latin and later Greek; diligent scribes spending their entire lives copying ancient manuscripts that would preserve the classics of antiquity for ages yet to come. What was it about this man that set this whole process in motion? History is clear that he did it. But how?

Various explanations are advanced: his warmth and undisguised love for suffering people; his earthiness, which particularly appealed to the earthy Irish; his seemingly supernatural generosity; his self-evident courage. He made it abundantly

7. The use of chrism, a mixture of olive oil and balsam or other perfumes, to anoint Christians after Baptism and at Confirmation, is attested to by several early fathers, including Tertullian, Ambrose and Theodoret. Its origins go back to the Old Testament in the consecration of priests and kings. Early adopted by Christians, it is extensively used today among Catholics and Orthodox, and also on occasion by other churches—Lutheran and Anglican, for example (the latter, most notably, in the coronation of the British monarch).

Pilgrims trudge the fourteen-mile path up Croagh Patrick, ascending over twenty-five-hundred feet from the sea in the misty distance. At the top of the mountain, according to the legend, Patrick banished snakes from the whole of the Emerald Isle.

clear that he was afraid of nothing, including the ferocious Irish themselves. "He transmuted their pagan virtues of loyalty, courage and generosity into the Christian equivalents of faith, hope and charity," writes Thomas Cahill in his story of the conversion of Ireland and its consequences (*How the Irish Saved Civilization*, New York, 1996). But Cahill regards this explanation as insufficient to account for such a spectacular conversion of such improbable converts. He attributes it instead to the pervasive horrors of the pagan Irish religion, whose gods reduced all men to a meaningless nothing. By contrast, he writes, for Patrick's new Irish Christians, "the magical world is no longer full of dread. Rather Christ has trodden all pathways before us, and by every crossroad and every tree the Word of God speaks out."

A further factor, which may have facilitated this spectacular development, is noted by the Jesuit historian John Ryan (*Irish Monasticism: Origins and Early Development*, Shannon, Ireland, 1931). The Irish custom was for every family to send two or three of its sons, while still children, to be raised by Druid priests and bards who instructed and indoctrinated them. When the Irish became Christians, they continued this practice—but now they sent their sons to monasteries, where the monks ran schools which, among other things, trained the boys to become monks. The result was an avalanche of young men into the monastic life.[8]

Patrick, with his reluctance to provide names and dates, is not helpful in solving the mystery of his own success. But Irish mythmakers and the weavers of Irish fairy tales more than compensated for this loss over ensuing centuries. Patrick becomes the man who banished all snakes from Ireland. His curse causes a Druid magician to be swept up into the air, then thrust to the earth and dashed to pieces. His old slave master, hearing of Patrick's return, barricades himself and all his treasure in his house, then ignites it into his funeral pyre. And when Patrick drives his crozier into the earth to steady himself while baptizing King Aengus of Cashel, he discovers to his distress that he has driven it through the king's foot. But as King Aengus explains to the apologetic saint, he had not flinched because he thought this was part of the ritual. It seemed altogether appropriate, after all, when he considered the magnificent story Patrick had told him of another King whose feet were pierced.

8. As in Egypt, Irish monasticism began when men, seeking some sacrifice equivalent to martyrdom, took to dedicating themselves as hermits. This was not so long-lasting in Ireland as in other locales, partly perhaps because the Irish were simply too sociable by nature. The hermit stage nevertheless lasted long enough for Kevin of Glendalough, who lived in a hole in the cliffside, to establish celebrity by standing stark naked for hours in the wintry water of a lake, and in summer by hurling himself into a clump of stinging nettles.

9. The Irish hymn "*Be Thou my Vision*" was translated from the Gaelic by Mary Elizabeth Byrne and published in the *Journal of the School of Irish Learning*, in 1905. It was put into verse by Eleanor Henrietta Hull, founder of the Irish Text Society and president of the Irish Literary Society.

Patrick and his successors also initiated another kind of conversion, as the poetry and hymnology of the Celtic monasteries make evident. He plainly knew he could never take warfare away from the Irish, any more than he could part them from their joy in the raw power manifest in nature's wild violence. But he could redirect it. In this transformation, his converts' real enemy becomes the enemy within them. Their weapons become those celebrated by St. Paul: "the shield of faith . . . the helmet of salvation . . . the sword of the spirit" (Eph. 6:16–17). And their king or chieftain becomes Jesus Christ. Thus the ancient Irish hymn, attributed to Dallan Forgaill in the eighth century (*Rob tu mo Bhoile, a Comdi cride*) echoes the passionate commitment of the warrior:

> Be Thou my Vision, O Lord of my heart;
> Naught be all else to me, save that Thou art.
> Thou my best Thought, by day or by night,
> Waking or sleeping, Thy presence my light.
>
> Be Thou my battle Shield, sword for the fight;
> Be Thou my dignity, Thou my delight;
> Thou my soul's shelter, Thou my high Tower:
> Raise Thou me heavenward, O Power of my power.
>
> Riches I heed not, nor man's empty praise,
> Thou mine inheritance, now and always,
> Thou and Thou only, first in my heart,
> High King of Heaven, my Treasure Thou art.[9]

The hymn is usually sung to a tune called *Slane*, of Irish folk origin. It was in 433, on Slane Hill near Tara, a few miles northwest of Dublin, that Patrick is said to have defied a royal edict by kindling a bonfire on Easter Eve. Tara's high king Logaire had decreed that no one might light a fire there, before Logaire himself did so to mark the pagan spring festival. So impressed was Logaire by Patrick's devotion (or perhaps by his defiance) that he let him continue his mission.

In *St. Patrick's Breastplate*, probably written several centuries after the saint's death, the power of God is made manifest in the might and majesty of nature:

> I bind unto myself today the virtues of the star lit heaven,
> The glorious sun's life-giving ray, the whiteness of the moon at even,
> The flashing of the lightning free, the whirling wind's tempestuous shocks
> The stable earth, the deep salt sea,
> Around the old eternal rocks.

In defiance of the king of Tara's orders, Patrick leads the Easter procession up Slane Hill to light the first bonfire of the feast. In the end, the bold act only served to endear the bishop to the king. (From Great Men and Famous Women: A Series of Pen and Pencil Sketches, New York, 1894.)

As the hymn goes on to eloquently declare, however, God's power is also proclaimed in the ministry of Jesus Christ—in "Confessors' faith, Apostles word," in God's hand that guides us, and his ear that hears us, and above all "in the strong Name of the Trinity." Finally, in the midst of this resounding celebration of God's strength and omnipotence, comes a tranquil meditation on the implications of the divine grace for every Christian soul:

> Christ be with me, Christ within me,
> Christ behind me, Christ before me,
> Christ beside me, Christ to win me,
> Christ to comfort and restore me.
>
> Christ beneath me, Christ above me,
> Christ in quiet, Christ in danger,
> Christ in hearts of all that love me.
> Christ in mouth of friend and stranger.[10]

In the century after Patrick, the Irish warriors who had given their lives for the clan became the Irish monks who gave their lives for Jesus Christ. Monasteries began appearing throughout the country, and whole communities grew around them. They ran schools for children, and not merely those of the gentry, where they were taught to read Irish and Latin, and were required to memorize the Psalter and the Bible at least in part. If they went on to become monks, they studied the classics of Latin, and in later centuries, Greek. Within an astonishingly short time, the island that had been arguably the most barbarous place in Europe was becoming the most literate. "As Roman lands went from peace to chaos," writes Cahill, "the land of Ireland was rushing even more rapidly from chaos to peace."

One consequence was a distinctive Irish church, run by abbots rather than bishops, or more frequently by abbot-bishops. In this monastic church, which typically recruited its clergy as children, Patrick's disciple and colleague Lomman trained the monk Foirtchern from boyhood. Similarly, Foirtchern trained Finnian of Clonard, and Finnian trained a boy prince of the Clan Conaill who is known to British history by his Latin name, Columba, but to Irish history as Columcille (pronounced: *kolmkilla*).

Columcille would become the greatest figure in Irish history after Patrick. His mentor Finnian, recognized as the most gifted tutor of all the early monastics, inculcated in him boundless faith and zeal for the Lord's work, and a powerful love of art. So strong, in fact, was this artistic impulse that the young Columcille spent months surreptitiously copying a magnificent Psalter, the possession of Finnian's monastery.

10. Although *St. Patrick's Breastplate* has several English translations, the one used here is the most familiar. It is by Cecil Frances Humphreys Alexander, an English-born nineteenth-century poet and essayist and the wife of an Irish Anglican priest, who is better known for three children's hymns: *All Things Bright and Beautiful*, *There is a Green Hill Far Away*, and the Christmas carol *Once in Royal David's City*.

Typical of the Celtic crosses that dot Ireland, the one at Kells marked the eastern door of Columcille's now-destroyed monastery. In the 1798 insurgence against British rule, it was used as a gallows from which to hang local rebels.

When everyone's Irish

Dublin and New York naturally mark St. Patrick's Day but so do Sao Paolo, Beijing, Hong Kong and Moscow

Irish soldiers in the English military organized the world's first St. Patrick's Day parade on March 17, 1762—not in Ireland, but in New York, where the annual march remains the largest of those now held worldwide. At right, green-hatted celebrants jam the Fifth Avenue parade route in 2001. Below, Fifth Avenue's centerline is painted green for a parade in the 1950s. Other cities across North America also enjoy Irish festivals, the biggest in Chicago, Boston and Montreal. Below right, a nun teaches two boys the Irish jig in St. Louis, Mo., in the 1960s. Though there is no reliable record of the day or year of Patrick's death, Dublin and Killarney always officially mark the date assigned by tradition, March 17, 461. But so do London, Paris (which boasts fifty Irish pubs), Rome, and more recently Sao Paulo, Tokyo, Singapore, Beijing, Hong Kong and Moscow. ∎

Beware the awful curse of the Irish . . .

May the devil damn you to the stone of dirges or to the well of ashes seven miles below hell, and may the devil break your bones. And all my calamity and harm and misfortune for a year on you.

Rain and fire, ill wind and snow and hard-frost follow her.

Your old frame dead and lifeless with never a stir. With none to wake your corpse, your limbs without a shroud!

Aeolus chase her into the harbors of Acheron Down. Nine times sicker than the Ulstermen's illness let her be. May this insect get an illness that Hippocrates cannot cure.

May the devil cut the head off you and make a day's work of your neck.

May fire and brimstone never fail to fall in showers on (name of town). May all the thieving fiends assail the thieving town of (name).

The anguished bankruptcy of the year to you.

May the devil take him by the heels and shake him.

The devil swallow him sideways.

but if they give you blessings, rejoice

May you live all the days of your life, and may the saddest day of your future be no worse than the happiest day of your past.

May there always be work for your hands to do.
May your purse always hold a coin or two. May the sun shine bright on your window pane. May the rainbow be certain to follow each rain. May the hand of a friend always be near you. And may God fill your heart with gladness to cheer you.

May you live as long as you want, and never want as long as you live.

May you live to be a hundred years, with one extra year to repent.

May your glass be ever full, may the roof over your head be always strong, and may you be in heaven half an hour before the devil knows you're dead.

May the Lord keep you in his hand, and never close his fist too tight.

May your home always be too small to hold all your friends.

May you have warm words on a cold evening, a full moon on a dark night, and the road downhill all the way to your door.

May you be poor in misfortune, rich in blessings.

May your pockets be heavy and your heart be light.

When this was discovered, Columcille was forced by the local king, Diarmait, to surrender his cherished copy. "As with every cow goes her calf," said the king, "so with every book goes its copy." It was a ruling Columcille did not forget.

As a young man, he traveled to Tours and visited the tomb of Martin, where he became infatuated with his monastic rule, and brought it back to Ireland. He is reputed by the age of forty-one to have founded forty-one Irish monasteries. When one of his monks was killed, however, by the same King Diarmait who had deprived him of the Psalter, he rounded up his kinsmen of the Clan Conaill, did battle against the king and avenged the dead monk with the lives of more than three thousand of Diarmait's men. So, anyway, the story goes.

The result is more than fable. The penalty if a monk took up arms was excommunication. Columcille's penance was deportation from his beloved Ireland to the country of the wild Picts, where he must win one Christian convert for every man of the three thousand his clansmen had killed. In other words, it was lifelong exile. Thus, in the year 564, he and twelve colleagues crossed the sea to the island of Iona, off the Scottish coast, eighty-five miles northwest of Glasgow. There he established the mission from which all Scotland and most of Saxon England would be converted to Christianity over the next century.

Here the exile, who at forty-one might have thought his life was almost over, discovered that it had scarcely begun. Pictish barbarians and the Irish immigrants known as the Scoti poured into his island monastery, eager to join it. When their number reached one hundred and fifty, he sent out thirteen of them to establish a second monastery. Thereafter, each thirteen newcomers occasioned another such mission. By Columcille's death at the end of the sixth century, Iona had spawned sixty new monastic communities scattered over Scotland and down into England.

The explanation lay in Columcille's extraordinary influence over people, particularly his habit of making the individual in need more important than his missionary program. Thus, when a woman laments that she has lost all love for her husband, he stops what he is doing, prays with her, and their prayers restore her love and her marriage. When he catches an impoverished thief robbing him, he reproves the man, then provides him with a store of food and instructs the abbot of a subsidiary monastery to make sure the man's future needs are met. When Irish Christians demand a ban on all poets, no doubt because of their persistent ridicule of people in authority, he returns to Ireland and saves the poets. Ireland, he declares, would not be Ireland without poets—it needed more of them, not less. He then hides in humiliation beneath his cowl as twelve hundred of them assemble to sing his praise.

Yet this same Columcille has been described as a "man of iron." He slept on a stone floor with a stone for his pillow. "His devotion to fasting and watches passed the bounds of credulity," writes John Ryan, "and he led his monks to do the same." In the early days at Iona, when the thirteen were very low on supplies and near starvation, one fell ill. The rest did without any food at all for three days in a special fast, which they were sure accounted for his recovery. Along

with the pre-Easter, forty-day Lenten abstinence, Columcille's monks appear to have emphasized and most stringently observed two other annual fasts, one before Christmas (now Advent in the West, the Nativity Fast in the East) and another after Pentecost (also customarily observed in the East, albeit more briefly).

Iona's founder finished his life with what could be called a good death. Sensing his strength departing, Columcille went to the fields, bade farewell to his comrades one by one, then retired to his cell and began copying the thirty-fourth Psalm. He stopped at the tenth verse. "They who seek the Lord," he wrote, "shall want no manner of thing that is good." That night, his fellow monks found him before the altar in their darkened church. They said his face reflected ecstasy, for he had exceeded at least tenfold his quota of three thousand converts. He then died before their eyes.

In bringing the faith to Scotland, Patrick's spiritual descendant Columcille followed his master by a span of some twelve decades. After yet another eighty years, a monk named Aidan, Columcille's spiritual descendant, brought Christianity to pagan England. But by now, the date was 635 and things were changing.[11] Oswald, prince of Northumbria, the northernmost English kingdom, had been sent by his family to Ireland to be educated by the monks, and had returned to rule his people as a Christian monarch. But his people were still pagan, so he appealed to Iona to send a mission to Northumbria, to operate with his royal blessing. Corman, the monk sent to Northumbria, returned to Iona after two years of futile effort and declared the pagan English to be hopelessly

barbarian. However, at a formal review of the failure, Aidan spoke up. Corman had been too tough with these people, he said; he had expected too much of them. All right, said the others, then you go.

So Aidan did, and King Oswald bestowed on the mission the island of Lindisfarne. Ten miles southeast of the present Berwick, near the English-Scottish border, Lindisfarne is just a few hundred yards from the mainland (actually connected to it at low tide), and was within sight of Oswald's castle at Bamburgh. Like Iona, it would become a Christian bastion, recruiting generations of monks and sending them as far south as the Humber, and even, some historians say, as the Thames. Aidan became an abbot-bishop, creating with King Oswald a union of church and state that furnished a model for all Saxon England. Aidan's conversion formula proved likewise successful. First, he believed, the Saxons must be won over to Christ. The stern rules of the Celtic monks could come later, which indeed they did. Lindisfarne, renamed Holy Island, became home to a whole succession of Anglo-Saxon saints.

The Christian phenomenon born in Ireland became known as the Celtic Church, and while some of its monks were working the conversion of Scotland and England, many others were gaining even greater renown on the continent. The leader of this endeavor was Columban (not to be confused with Columba, the Roman name of Columcille). Columban was born in Leinster, Ireland, in 543, about twenty years after Columcille, whom he would outlive by eighteen years. Columban was such a handsome young man, say his biographers, as to be irresistibly attractive to women—resulting in temptations to which he frequently succumbed. Finally, fearing for his immortal soul, he consulted a "holy woman" who gave him candid but unwelcome advice: "There is no safety for you, young man," she said, "except in flight."

11. Between King Arthur's time and the arrival of Irish monks in Saxon England, the British church produced another holy man who looms larger in myth than in history. This was David, or Dewy (ca.520–601), patron saint of the Welsh. David is believed to have assured victory to the Welsh troops on one occasion by having them wear in their hats a stalk of leek, a species of onion, thereby distinguishing themselves from the enemy English. For centuries, the Welsh have worn a leek on St. David's Day, March 1. Reputed bishop of Menevia, a chief embarkation point for Ireland, David was also an abbot of notable austerity. His monks pulled their own plows, dressed in hides, and lived on bread, cabbage and water.

The early Irish monks preferred the inaccessible cliffs of the seaside and its rocky islands for their flinty form of monasticism. But they eventually moved inland to more inhabited areas like Glendalough near Dublin (1), where St. Kevin founded his early sixth-century monastery. Their preference, however, was for the islands, preeminently Iona (2), in the Hebrides off the west coast of Scotland. Here, Columcille and his twelve disciples first set down roots in soil inhospitable to all else but faith. From there, their labors spread to the far southwestern shores of Ireland and Greater Skellig Island, with its unusual beehive stone dwellings and chapels (3). In 635, yet another of Columcille's disciples, Aidan, led his band of monks to a slightly more verdant island, Lindisfarne, on the other side of the Scottish mainland, which would act as his base in the evangelizing of England. A monument to Aidan (4) stands before the ruins of the original priory and the thirteenth-century church of St. Mary (5).

The myth that may not be mythical

Brendan, the monk, crossed the Atlantic in his leather boat, they said, and scholars scoffed, until a gutsy sailor proved it could be done

The twentieth-century leather curragh Brendan *confounds doubters by duplicating, in 1976, the legendary and supposedly impossible thirty-five-hundred mile Atlantic crossing of her saintly namesake.*

Brendan of Clonfert, sixth-century priest and monk from Ireland's Galway area, is a famous founder of monasteries and churches. What chiefly caught the medieval imagination, however, was his reputed missionary expedition across the Atlantic Ocean, to what was called "The Land Promised to the Saints," as described in the ninth-century saga *The Voyage of St. Brendan*.

On this voyage, said to have lasted seven years, the saint and his monks encountered many wonders. There was the Isle of Temptation, where one monk was tricked by Satan into stealing; celebration of the Easter Liturgy on the back of a whale; fallen angels who appeared as talking birds; an island of towering crystal occupied by silent monks; and a smoking mountain Brendan proclaimed to be hell. Equally amazing, they reached the Atlantic's farthest shore—and returned.

Over the centuries, this tale would become entirely incredible to enlightened scholars. By modern times Brendan's transatlantic trip had been entirely dismissed as myth—until, that is, a twentieth-century skipper duplicated it. Using primitive tools, wood, flax and ox hides sewn together, all available to the saint, Timothy Severin supervised the replication of a traditional Celtic

curragh, thirty-six-feet long, which he named *Brendan*.

Christened with a bottle of Irish whiskey and blessed by a bishop, *Brendan* departed for North America in May 1976. Fierce storms and extreme discomfort, as Severin writes in *The Brendan Voyage* (New York, 1978), made him and his four-man crew begin "to appreciate the lives of medieval sailors, who had to trust in God, keep patience and faith alive, and risk death by storm, starvation and thirst."

But by July they reached Iceland, closely accompanied by a procession of whales that at one point numbered one hundred and forty. They observed smoking mountains and crystal islands too, under less-fanciful names. The next spring, navigating through darkness and high waves (and among some of the saint's crystal islands), *Brendan* rounded the southern tip of Greenland, and landed on the Newfoundland coast, leather hull intact.

She had shown, Severin writes, "that the saga of her namesake was no mere splendid medieval fantasy, but a highly plausible tale." St. Brendan could indeed have crossed the Atlantic, before even the Norsemen, and a thousand years before Columbus. ∎

So Columban resolved to "retire from the world." His horrified mother objected, throwing herself across the doorstep to obstruct his departure, but he gently stepped over her, bade her farewell, and left for the monastery at Bangor on the coast of County Down. He would see neither his mother nor his home again. For about twenty years he lived as a monk, but at age forty sensed himself drawn to "preach the gospel in foreign lands," and after much persuasion, finally gained his abbot's permission to do so. With twelve companions, constituting the usual party of thirteen, he sailed for Saxon England, stayed there two fruitless years, and then in 585 landed on the French coast, penniless, friendless and starving.

Wandering inland, living on herbs, berries and the bark of young trees, they reached Burgundy, where the king, Guntram, gladly welcomed them. Both his people and his court, Guntram acknowledged, were sadly dissolute, bereft of both faith and morality. Burgundy needed Columban and his companions. They set themselves up in a half-ruined Roman fortress in the Vosges Mountains in eastern France, and people began seeking them out for healing, advice and a share in the grace that seemed to surround them. (So insistently did they want Columban in particular that he had to seek refuge in a nearby cave.) There were many recruits, and as their numbers grew, the king turned over to them a castle called Luxeuil. It would become a Christian bastion throughout the Middle Ages.

Although their work flourished and new monasteries began appearing, Columban and his monks were not universally popular. The Gallic bishops resented their widening influence, and in Frankish country, unlike Ireland, monastic abbots were subject to the local bishop. Eventually, the bishops met and condemned the Irish monks, charging, among other complaints, that they were celebrating Easter on what the Gallo-Romans considered the wrong date.[12] Another grievance was that the Irish allowed no outsider to enter the inner precincts of their monasteries, a prohibition that included the local bishop. The case was referred to the pope.

Matters grew worse. Guntram died and was succeeded by the youthful and profligate king Theodoric whose grandmother, the dowager queen Brunhild (see chapter 8), encouraged his debaucheries. Brunhild favored an assortment of concubines for Theodoric, rather than a legitimate queen who would inevitably challenge her own hold on him. When the young monarch appeared to be falling under Columban's spell, the old queen moved swiftly and had the monk arrested. He escaped, returned to his monastery, and was arrested again. This time, Brunhild (her grandson acquiescing as usual) ordered every Irish monk out of the country.

Held captive aboard a ship, they descended the Loire River and reached the sea, where their vessel foundered. The monks made their way cross-country,

12. Up to 525, Britain followed Rome, rather than Alexandria and the Eastern churches, in the long dispute over the dating of Easter, which varied according to what method was used in calculating the Paschal full moon in relation to the vernal equinox. The east used one system, and Rome another. But in 525 Rome adopted the eastern system, while the Celtic Church, which may not even have heard about this change, remained firmly attached to its traditional one. This dispute was finally resolved in principle at the Synod of Whitby in 664, after which various regions of the Celtic church, one by one, fell in line with the "new" Roman system.

As the Irish monk Columban traveled from the French coast to the Appenines of northern Italy, he left a string of monasteries. Near Bobbio, Italy, where he established the last of them, is this hermitage that bears his name.

once again friendless, penniless and hungry. This time, however, fortune smiled sooner. They were now in the western Frankish kingdom of Neustria, where the king, Lothar, an enemy of Brunhild, knew all about them and pleaded with them to stay. But once again, Columban felt called. They must bring the cross to the still-pagan tribes in the high mountain country to the south, he said. He and his monks ascended the Rhine River to its tributaries, and on the shore of Lake Zurich, preached the gospel to the Alamanni and Suevi—who responded by chasing them away.

At Bregenz on Lake Constance, however, they had better success. A monk named Gall, one of the original mission of thirteen, could speak the local language. The people listened, and the monastery at Bregenz was born. The tireless Columban next sought to push on to Milan in Italy, but Gall balked. He was sick and he had had enough. He insisted upon remaining in the Bregenz region, and there he would die. The monastery that bears his name is a visible legacy, and Gall is generally credited as the man who brought the alpine Suevi and Alamanni, later known as the Swiss, into the Christian faith. Another tradition makes him the author of a certain charming poem about a monk and his cat. (See sidebar.)

In Italy, the Lombard king Agilulf, who had also heard of the Irish, eagerly welcomed them and bestowed upon them property at Bobbio, between Milan and Genoa. On his way to the site, Columban stopped to preach at a town called Mombrione, whose citizens were so enchanted by him that they renamed the place San Colombano. Their work prospered at Bobbio, as elsewhere, but establishing this monastery was his last assignment. He died there in 615 in a cave—seeking as always in solitude the escape that the old nun had counseled.

The Catholic Encyclopedia describes Columban as "eager, passionate and dauntless," while noting that these same attributes could also make him "impetuous, even headstrong," the qualities which accounted for both his failures and his successes. Legends nevertheless abounded of his tranquility of spirit—how birds would fly down from the trees and land on his shoulders, how squirrels would nestle in the folds of his cowl. His heritage, however, was not just legend. He became the prototype for hundreds of Anglo-Saxon missionaries, who in the ensuing three centuries would help work the conversion of western Europe through a Christian amalgam of their Celtic and Anglo-Saxon heritage.

NUNN

Their names include Killian, Virgilius, Donatus, Wilfred, Willibrord, Swithbert and Winfrid (alternately Boniface), all of them canonized. "Almost all of Ireland, despising the sea, is migrating to our shores," wrote Heiric of Auxerre in 870, adding ruefully, "with a herd of philosophers."

It was this herd, however, along with Frankish monks from the continent, who in the coming centuries tamed the murderous instincts of the barbarian peoples, and laid down a Christian foundation upon which the extraordinary phenomenon known as Western culture would one day arise. So long as the foundation endured, so would this culture. Remove the foundation, however, or let it rot from within, and the whole structure would collapse. Such were the terms under which Western man ultimately would either prevail or perish. ■

Wherever they went, the Irish took their devotion to learning and the production of books and Bibles to enable that pursuit. Their illustrations in these manuscripts vary in style, but uniformly remain wonders of color and detailing. From left to right are pages from the Book of Kells *(ca.800), the* Linidisfarne Gospels *(ca.698) and the* Book of Durrow *(seventh century).*

A more mature, double-chinned Justinian gazes out from a mosaic at Ravenna, Italy. In the sixth century, a halo did not specifically indicate sanctity. Rather, it was a commonly accepted convention in portraiture denoting a person of good character or prestige, a condition one might claim for the man who managed to reign nearly forty years in turbulent times. So his look of satisfaction may have been entirely justified.

CHAPTER 10

The unlikely marriage that shaped the destiny of Europe and the faith

When the bachelor-emperor married an ex-prostitute, the capital was aghast, but together they prepared the city to defend Christianity for the next 900 years

While smoke and dust hung like a pall of death over Rome and its crumbling western empire, Constantinople, the New Rome on the Bosporus, presented a very different scene. In 457, with the demise of old Marcian, the late-in-life husband of the empress Pulcheria (see chapter 7), Constantinople was precisely one and one-third centuries old. Already, it was exhibiting the two qualities that would distinguish it throughout its long history. One was the internecine feuding of its court. The other was its virtual impregnability to attack, a fact the barbarian tribes were the first to discover. Constantine the Great, its founder, had recognized the near invincibility of this strategic location, and history would prove him right. The city would stand unconquered until the fifteenth century.

Five undistinguished emperors followed Marcian. Then, with the sixth, fate, fortune or possibly God favored the eastern empire with a new dynasty and new vigor. After Marcian came Leo I (457–474), who, as father-in-law of Marcian's granddaughter, could claim at least a tenuous family connection to the previous Theodosian Dynasty.[1] Leo held the barbarians and Persians at bay, then destroyed his credibility and the imperial solvency with a disastrous attempt to reclaim North Africa from the Vandals. (See sidebar, page 270.) His grandson, Leo II,

1. From Constantine onward until the fall of Constantinople in 1453, Byzantine emperors fall into thirteen dynasties as follows: The Constantinian (306–395), the Theodosian (395–457), the Dynasty of Leo (457–518), the Justinian (518–610), the Heraclian (610–717), the Isaurian (717–820), the Phrygian (820–867), the Macedonian (867–1057), prelude to the Comnenian (1057–1081), the Comnenian (1081–1185), the Dynasty of the Angeli (1185–1204), the Lascarid in Nicea (1204–1261), the Palaeologian (1259–1453).

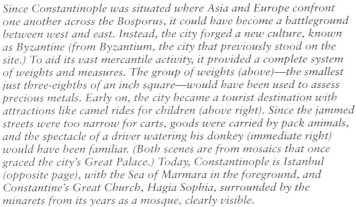

Since Constantinople was situated where Asia and Europe confront one another across the Bosporus, it could have become a battleground between west and east. Instead, the city forged a new culture, known as Byzantine (from Byzantium, the city that previously stood on the site.) To aid its vast mercantile activity, it provided a complete system of weights and measures. The group of weights (above)—the smallest just three-eighths of an inch square—would have been used to assess precious metals. Early on, the city became a tourist destination with attractions like camel rides for children (above right). Since the jammed streets were too narrow for carts, goods were carried by pack animals, and the spectacle of a driver watering his donkey (immediate right) would have been familiar. (Both scenes are from mosaics that once graced the city's Great Palace.) Today, Constantinople is Istanbul (opposite page), with the Sea of Marmara in the foreground, and Constantine's Great Church, Hagia Sophia, surrounded by the minarets from its years as a mosque, clearly visible.

ruled ten months, and died of natural causes. Verina, widow of Leo I, survived for another ten years, long enough to back her brother Basiliscus (475–476) against her son Zeno (474–491). But Zeno prevailed. He trapped his uncle Basiliscus's family in a church, promised not to execute them if they surrendered, then exiled them to Cappadocia where they were deliberately starved to death.

When Zeno died, his widow secured the succession of a prominent court official named Anastasius as emperor (491–518), and of herself as empress, by marrying him. Anastasius, in his twenty-seven-year reign, was noted for numerous achievements, but one in particular. He erected the "Long Walls," crossing the base of the peninsula upon which the New Rome was built. Against these walls, successive waves of barbarians in the centuries ahead would hurl themselves hopelessly and perish. Then, with the death of Anastasius, the Dynasty of Leo, as it came to be called, was over.

The Long Walls provided Constantinople with an outer defense line, but its inner defense line, at the western city limits, was formidable too. Built by Constantine the Great, it proved its worth in 378 when the Goths assailed the capital and were stopped by these inner walls. Anthemius, administrative head of government under Theodosius II, built a second line, and Anastasius's Long Walls became a third.

Safe behind them, the city flourished. Historian Glanville Downey takes readers on an imaginary tour of the early sixth-century city (*Constantinople in the Age of Justinian*, Oklahoma, 1960). Built on a hilly peninsula, it was surrounded on three sides by salt water: the Sea of Marmara to the south; the Bosporus, which divides Europe from Asia, to the east; and its harbor, the Golden Horn, one of the best anchorages in the ancient world, to the north.

At the promontory stood a high plateau, towering 140 feet above the sea. Here stood the palace, home of the emperor, and close by it the Hippodrome, part-time home of nearly everybody else. Here too stood Hagia Sophia (Holy Wisdom), known as the Great Church. It would soon be rebuilt, and its huge dome would rise 180 feet above the plateau.

If the visitor arrived by sea, his vessel would enter the Golden Horn; the narrow, four-mile-long harbor whose crescent shape protected it against storm winds from every direction. From there the visitor would probably be taken uphill to the Augusteum, a public square that served as the heart of the city and the heart of the empire. Facing onto the square was the Senate House. Nearby was the main gate to the Great Palace with its brick and marble buildings, its gardens, terraces on different levels, reception halls, summer pavilions, churches, a private stadium and an indoor riding school.

Running off the Augusteum toward the inner walls, was the *Mesê*, Middle Street, along which the city's development had extended, an avenue flanked by tall columns supporting stone roofs, and ornamented by statues of the emperors. Here too, often in booths between the columns and in side streets, were hundreds of shops offering every manner of merchandise known to the ancient world.

Along the Mesê by day thronged the citizenry in their thousands, plus the animals they led, rode, bought, sold or butchered, these contributing a braying, neighing, barking and bellowing to the cacophony of human voices. In the damp, chill winter, men and women wore a wool tunic, covered by a wool cloak. The women's tunics reached to the ground; the men's were varied, with workmen's extending to the knees, and gentlemen's to the ankle. Children's clothes replicated their parents'. The ancient Roman toga was gone, worn now only on ceremonial occasions.

Most people wore sandals, some low shoes of cloth or leather, some military boots that came to the calf and some went barefoot. The streets were too narrow for vehicles. Goods were usually transported by donkeys, camels or porters, picking their way between the jam of pedestrians and the occasional flock of sheep or geese being herded to market.

Water was delivered by aqueducts from the nearby hills and stored in cisterns all over town, or fed into the many public baths, or supplied free at drinking fountains located everywhere. An underground system drained sewage into the sea. Such hygiene, however, did not prevent recurrent dysentery, sometimes fatal, nor an outbreak of bubonic plague in 542 and 543, said to have peaked at ten thousand deaths in a single day, in a city with a six hundred thousand population.

The wealthy lived in brick houses that presented a blank wall to the street, broken only by bay windows on the second floor, from which the ladies of the house could watch the street scene and the neighbors. Courtyards in the rear

Was any city in the world ever more preoccupied with spectator sports than Constantinople? People took the chariot races so seriously that riots could erupt after a bad call by a referee.

might feature a fountain and gardens. The homes of the less wealthy were miniatures of those of the rich, but with smaller rooms, often accommodating more people. Then came the very poor, writes historian Downey, in the midst of this opulence, unemployed and in dire poverty. However, churches fed and clothed them, while the government distributed free bread; and both government and church operated hospitals and shelters for the poor and elderly.

The prevailing language by then was Greek, though the more learned or traveled knew Latin as well, and Latin was still the official language of the court. Mixed with these were scores of other languages spoken by slaves, Germans in the army stationed in the city, Persian merchants, and the curious incomprehensible tongues of the Huns, Avars and Slavs who were gradually infiltrating the general populace.

It was an "outdoors" city, with seaside strolls and meeting places where most social life took place. However, the center of nearly everyone's social interest was the Hippodrome, modeled on the Circus Maximus at Rome, which could accommodate sixty thousand people in its thirty tiers of seats. Since it was too long for the promontory hill, its southern extremity rested on an artificial foundation of stones piled high in the air. Down the center of the oval chariot course ran a narrow decorative island adorned with statues. Above these towered an eighty-four-foot obelisk of porphyry, brought from Egypt by Theodosius the Great, at its base a sculpture of the emperor presiding at the games.

It would be difficult to name any city in the world more preoccupied with what a later generation would call spectator sports. Constantinople's citizens, from the wealthiest to the most bitterly impoverished, took the chariot races so seriously that citywide riots could erupt after a bad call by a referee. Early in the city's development, a race most often involved four competitors, each identified by a color—the Blues, Greens, Reds and Whites—their fans sitting in the four sections reserved for them. Over the years, these groups hardened into distinct factions, called the *demes* (from *demos*, the people), and their activities extended far beyond the Hippodrome. They were in effect political parties, social clubs, labor unions, welfare agencies with cradle-to-grave programs, and finally theologies. Over time, the Greens and Blues absorbed the Reds and Whites, so that in Constantinople, your favorite team, your friends, your social standing, your politics and your theology would all be reflected by whether you were a Blue or a Green.

So, often, would your work. Thus in 447, the Blues and Greens provided sixteen thousand laborers for the construction and repair of the city's foundations, writes historian Byron C. Tsangadas (*Fortifications and Defense of Constantinople*, New York, 1980). Inscriptions on the walls still testify to their work. The two enlarged parties wielded major influence, and even the emperor would ally himself with one side or the other, after calculating the political benefit offered by each. Thus, the fortunes of either faction were very much tied to the patronage of the reigning emperor. If he leaned toward the Greens, the Greens got the government jobs. If a Blue emperor succeeded a Green, then the incumbents promptly changed in thousands of offices and positions, many of them highly lucrative.

Members of the factions adopted distinct styles of dress, with elaborate tunics and headdresses, haircuts, mustaches and beards. Their spokesmen engaged in public dialogue with the emperor's staff when at the Hippodrome, advancing their members' concerns. And some of their more unruly members took knives and clubs with them as they roamed the city streets at night, mugging anyone, especially of the other party, who crossed their paths. That form of lawlessness became so common that men of fashion kept two sets of pins and buckles: some of gold for daytime use, some of bronze if they had to leave home after dark.

In the late fifth century, the Blues and Greens became heavily involved in church politics. Whether you were Green or Blue, you would be Christian, of course, but if a Green, you would probably be a Monophysite Christian, bitterly opposed to the decisions of the Council of Chalcedon. If you were Blue, you would be orthodox, a word that meant "right faith," and you would be referred to as *Catholic* or

Justinian significantly expanded and embellished the Great Palace of the emperors in Constantinople. The mosaics he commissioned for the courtyard and audience hall alone covered over twenty-thousand square feet. Those that have survived, like this one of a villa garden (twenty-five-hundred square feet), are in the Mosaic Museum at Istanbul.

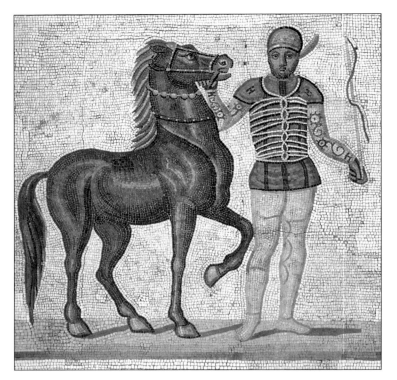

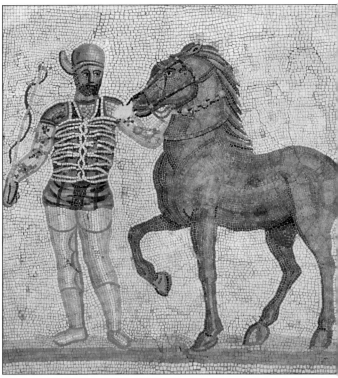

The charioteers of the Roman and later the Byzantine Empires were the sports stars of their time, and were suitably eccentric in dress and lifestyle. Tattoos cover the arms of both the Green driver (above) and Blue (right) in these depictions now in the National Roman Museum, Rome.

Chalcedonian, meaning that you affirmed the Chalcedon council, the assembly of bishops through which Marcian and Pulcheria had sought to end once and for all the dangerous wrangling in the church over the relationship between the divine and human elements in Jesus Christ. (See chapter 7.)

Far from ending it, however, Chalcedon had made it worse, and the conflict in the capital merely reflected a strife that engulfed the whole eastern empire, and preoccupied whatever emperor might occupy the imperial palace. In Alexandria, for example, Dioscorus, an evil villain in the eyes of the Council of Chalcedon, had been deposed as patriarch and banished into exile. But he was regarded as a valiant hero by most Christians in Egypt and they later canonized him. In his place as patriarch, the Chalcedonians, enjoying imperial favor, had named the gentle priest Proterius. The Copts, as the rural people of Egypt were called, greeted this news with a riot, and imperial troops drove many of them away from their homes. Similarly, in Jerusalem the Chalcedonian Juvenal had to be escorted by soldiers into his cathedral, inciting Monophysite monks to celebrate his arrival with a rampage of looting, riot and assault.

Thereafter, the Copts at Alexandria had elected a rival patriarch, one Timothy Aelurus. This translates as, Tim the Cat, and according to some sources was bestowed on him because he allegedly was given to certain nocturnal enterprises.[2] However that may be, Tim the Cat assembled a band of turbulent monks, took possession of a large church, and had himself consecrated patriarch of Alexandria. He was promptly expelled by imperial order, whereupon his adherents blamed the unfortunate Proterius, beat him to death, dragged his body through the streets, cut it up, burned it and threw the ashes into the air. The date was Good Friday, 458. The Eastern Churches venerate him as a martyr.

Leo I, by now emperor, sent Tim the Cat into exile and appointed to the Alexandrian see another man of the same name, Timothy Salophaciolus. Leo had hoped this man's dithering theological uncertainty would somehow endear him to both parties. It endeared him to neither, and due to his nervous vacillation, history regrettably remembers him as "Timothy of the Trembling Hat." Leo died in 474. His successors—Zeno, then Basiliscus, then Zeno again—merely sustained the chaos, because Zeno was Chalcedonian and Basiliscus Monophysite. By the time Zeno regained the throne, the patriarchs of Alexandria, Jerusalem and Antioch were all three in schism with Rome and Constantinople. Zeno concluded that something must be done, or the whole eastern church could disintegrate.

Consulting the patriarch of Constantinople, a suavely charming ecclesiastic named Acacius, Zeno came up with a plan. They would issue a clever document. It would placate the Monophysites by evading all the divisive issues raised by Chalcedon. It would unreservedly endorse the Nicene Creed, which was no longer seriously disputed; it would condemn Nestorius and the teachings of the monk Eutyches which had helped make Chalcedon necessary; it would endorse

The Copts elected a rival patriarch, known as Tim the Cat, who with a band of turbulent monks took possession of a church and had himself consecrated. He was promptly expelled.

the teachings of Cyril of Alexandria, and finally, it would totally ignore both the Council of Chalcedon and the Tome of [Pope] Leo. They called the document the Henoticon, meaning "the Instrument of Union." Instead, it became an instrument of conflict. How, people asked, could Rome and the pope possibly accept it? Rome did not matter, came the reply, because Rome was now being ruled by the Ostrogoths.

But Rome did matter. Ostrogoths or no Ostrogoths, Pope Felix II acted decisively. He sent two bishops to Constantinople with a summons to Patriarch Acacius to come to Rome and explain what was going on. Zeno and the smooth Acacius talked the two bishops around; both endorsed the Henoticon and refused to return to Rome. So Felix called a synod at Rome, which denounced and deposed the two bishops, denounced the Henoticon, and excommunicated and deposed Acacius. In response, Acacius excommunicated Pope Felix, and for the next thirty-five years the eastern church and the western were in schism. Zeno's successor, Anastasius I, upheld the Henoticon then declared himself a full-fledged Monophysite. By now, with the dynasty of Leo at an end, the west was largely a smoldering ruin from the viewpoint of fashionable Constantinople, while the east was schismatic and mired in Monophysitism from the viewpoint of Rome.

However, while the bishops battled, the charitable work of the church continued, whether Monophysite or Chalcedonian. At Alexandria, a group of Monophysite nuns ran a home for girls "in trouble," the kind of place churches would run all through the centuries and all over the world. To this home there

2. *The Dictionary of Christian Biography* explains that, "Tim the Cat" (alternatively, "Creeping Tim"), sometime patriarch of Alexandria, won his nickname from his practice of stealing through the cells of the monks at night, softly calling to the more gullible by name. When they asked who he was, he would announce: "I am an angel, sent to warn you to break off communion with Proterius, and to choose Timotheus (meaning himself) as your bishop." Historian Henry Chadwick (*The Church in Ancient Society*, Oxford, 2001) however, has another explanation for the nickname. He says Timothy Aelurus means, Timothy the Weasel, referring to his emaciated countenance.

came one day a very sad and disillusioned young woman named Theodora. She knew she could not long deceive these holy women, so she told them the truth. Since childhood, she had been a prostitute in the Hippodrome at Constantinople. Her sex shows had been the toast of the crowd. On a promise of luxurious living, a man had persuaded her to accompany him to North Africa, where he had dumped her. She was now trying desperately to get home

The empire that never was

The Ostrogoth Theodoric, who once cut a man in two with a single blow, dreamed that Romans and Goths could fashion a new realm, and he nearly succeeded

In 493, the Latin-speaking population of Italy cowered under the joint rule of two Germanic chieftains, Odovacar and Theodoric. The pair had come to a truce after battling each other to a draw at Ravenna, which by then had supplanted Rome as the Italian capital. On March 15 of that year, the truce and the war and Odovacar all came to an end at once. It happened during a banquet, memorable for an act of treachery and of butchery.

To solemnize the truce, Theodoric invited his erstwhile enemy to a dinner in the Palace of the Laurel Grove in the southeast quarter of the city. Odovacar arrived, and two suppliants appeared before him and knelt down, each grasping one of his hands, apparently to make a petition. Too late, the chieftain realized this was not why they were gripping him.

Theodoric strode forward and raised his broadsword. "Where is God?" cried his guest, defenseless but reportedly unafraid. "This is what you did to my friends!" roared the enraged Theodoric, referring to an earlier treachery against his personal bodyguards. With one blow, he split Odovacar from shoulder to crotch. As the corpse toppled, his royal killer gibed, "I think that weakling never had a bone in his body." Thus perished Odovacar, king of the Heruli, the man who had conquered the last Roman emperor in the west.

His murderer goes down in history as Theodoric the Great, a king whose ambiguities of both character and policy make general description of him difficult. Accomplished in war, he nevertheless provided Italy with the only stable peace its people enjoyed for many decades before and after his reign. Generous and patient, he would nevertheless deal savagely with betrayal. Though he could not write and had to use a gold stencil to sign the first four letters of his name on decrees, he placed the highest value on Roman learning. In an age when corruption was the norm, he acted vigorously to prevent his Germanic officers and Latin administrators from robbing his subjects. Finally, a personal believer in Arianism, he ruled with universally acknowledged impartiality between faiths and nationalities.

His Ostrogoths (meaning East Goths) were large-framed, fair-haired men who fought and farmed. Historical details about them are sparse. In the mid-fourth century, they were living in Pannonia, a Balkan province between Italy and Byzantium, under a king named Walamir. His brother Theodomir, Theodoric's father, willingly served as a common soldier before being crowned as co-ruler. He also remained loyal for life to Erelieva, Theodoric's mother, although their love remained unchurched. (Arian rulers sometimes left the formal marriage rite open, in case it was needed for a state alliance.)

Theodoric was born around 454, on the shores of Hungary's Plattensee, the largest lake in central Europe. His birth was deemed highly propitious. It coincided to the day with tidings that Walamir had destroyed the last army of the Huns, who had lorded it over the Goths for about seventy-five years. At age eight, Theodoric was sent to live at the Byzantine court, as an assurance that the Ostrogoths would honor their latest treaty. Jordanes, an Italian historian of Gothic descent, says the hostage princeling's face and charm won favor with Emperor Leo I.

For ten years, the youngster had a palace-eye-view of the western world's most sophisticated city. Commentators suggest that here he likely developed respect for *civilitas*—civilization. A Byzantine emperor displayed himself to the public in purple robe and shoes, his head encircled with a jewel-encrusted band of white linen, his person surrounded by eunuch clerks and glittering armored soldiers. To a child this pomp would present an overwhelming contrast to rough Goth procedure, where a man conducted his business, public and private, while armed.

Upon his return home, Theodoric immediately made a name for himself as a military campaigner—and none too soon. Two or three years later, his father died. In Germanic fashion, the Ostrogoth warriors assembled and proclaimed as monarch this twenty-year-old scion of their royal Amali clan. In coming years, he sometimes fought in alliance with the Byzantines, who in return made him annual payments and bestowed titles like "patrician" or "consul."

to Constantinople, earning money for the trip the only way she knew.

The nuns took her in, and in the following weeks a strange thing occurred. Quite clearly, they said, the Holy Spirit came upon this young woman, shining forth in her so that her whole manner and outlook astonishingly changed. She returned to the capital a very different person, avoided the Hippodrome crowd, and worked as a spinner of wool in a humble cottage near the palace, contenting herself to live in

When the payments lapsed, however, Theodoric retaliated. By 488, his troops were ravaging farmsteads within fourteen miles of the imperial capital.

Leo had been succeeded as emperor by Zeno. This imperial schemer feared the rising power of Odovacar, another Arian king (sometimes rendered in English as Odoacer), who, eleven years earlier, had seized power at Rome and Ravenna, deposing Romulus Augustulus, who is regarded as the last Roman emperor in the west.

So Zeno made a pact with Theodoric. If he could take Italy from Odovacar, he would have Constantinople's authority to rule it. Zeno, of course, had good reason to pit one heretic barbarian against another. Theodoric, for his part, understood that Italy was an easier target than Byzantium, because his troops could never breech the formidable walls of Constantinople.

In pursuit of the glittering prize represented by Rome, Ravenna and Italy, Theodoric's nation-army set out that autumn, with women, children, and all their possessions loaded on thousands of lumbering wagons. British historian Thomas Hodgkin, in his classic *Italy and her Invaders* (Oxford, 1896), estimates that the warriors alone numbered perhaps forty thousand. Much of their route lay through mountainous terrain, where food was scarce and enemies plentiful. At one point, a horde of Gepids, another Germanic tribe, almost broke the Gothic vanguard, until Theodoric personally led a desperate assault across marshy ground through a hail of arrows. This victory fortunately yielded a welcome windfall of supplies. Next summer, the barbaric invaders moved out of the Julian Alps into the fertile plain of northern Italy.

At that period, the bulk of Germanic mercenaries already recruited into Italy came from minor tribes. Odovacar, who was Hun and Scyrrian himself (though some highly reputable historians deny he had any Hun ancestry), was a chieftain among the Teutonic Heruli. His crucial opening battle with the Ostrogoths came near Verona. To make his hireling troops fight, Odovacar placed them with their backs to the swift current of the Adige; many of them died in it. Theodoric, purposely wearing distinctively bright garments, led repeated charges until his Goths broke through the enemy positions.

In 490, an army of Ostrogoths and their western cousins the Visigoths defeated Odovacar and his

Erected by his daughter in 526, Theodoric's tomb features a dome carved of a single stone, thirty-six feet in diameter. Inside is an empty sarcophagus—the king's body having been thrown into the marshes around Ravenna shortly after his interment in the monument.

Burgundian allies ten miles from Milan. Many of Italy's cities, perhaps impressed by the Ostrogoths' imperial commission and relatively restrained behavior, rebelled against Odovacar's garrisons. The vanquished general fled to Ravenna, which was nearly impregnable because of its surrounding swamps. Theodoric, after besieging his foe there for more than two years, agreed to a joint kingship as the price of peace—but that truce would end with the fatal banquet in 493.

For the next three decades, the new king of the Goths and Romans ruled with a competence that struck his contemporaries as nearly miraculous. His vision was clear. Roman and German together could restore the faded glory of the western empire. Roman roads and aqueducts were rebuilt, classical works of art protected, skilled artists patronized, churches erected, the ravaged state treasury restored. Merchants operated in peace, reportedly unafraid by day or night. Food prices plunged, greatly benefiting the poor. Justice was so consistently even-handed that western Christians willingly submitted a complex dispute over the papal succession to their Arian overlord. ■

Christ and accept whatever God might have in mind for her. The day came when she met again a man she had known in her former life, and by any reading of the historical records, he now fell hopelessly and irrevocably in love with her.

His name was Flavius Petrus Sabbatius, but he would soon become Justinian I, augustus of the New Rome, tireless, visionary, devout, deeply perceptive of human nature, about forty years of age, unmarried and now accepted as a

Perhaps because his own mother was not Arian, the king consistently favored religious toleration. He once told the Jews of Genoa: "We cannot legalize only one religion, for no one can be compelled to believe against his will."

Land was a crucial issue, the major source of wealth and power. The Ostrogoth soldiers appear to have been allotted one-third of the agricultural property, a massive incursion that seems to have triggered remarkably little protest from Latin landowners. In part, the redistribution process had already begun under Odovacar, and many potential fields may have lain fallow in the frequently ravaged countryside. Besides, the prospect of having a Gothic warrior as neighbor may have appealed to many Latins.

Theodoric's diplomatic skill in handling property rights is commemorated in one Solomon-like legend. A young man attempted to claim his inheritance after his father died. The widowed mother, wishing that the property be transferred to her new lover, denied that the lad was in fact her child. To resolve the impasse, Theodoric ordered the widow to marry the young claimant, shocking the woman into confessing that he was indeed her son.

Like the Franks in Gaul, the Ostrogoth sovereign perceived that he could best govern a new realm by using the administrative structure of the conquered Romans. His selection of Roman officials was particularly astute. His most important choice was Cassiodorus, a senator with a shrewd grasp of his civilization's devious ways, yet constantly upright and trustworthy himself.

The renowned scholar of the age was Boethius, a man whose talents ranged from clock design to a treatise on music that remained a definitive work throughout the Middle Ages. He also translated thirty books of Aristotle into Latin. The king appointed Boethius's two young sons as consuls, a signal honor, and frequently accepted his appeals on behalf of Romans suffering from miscreant royal officials.

However, Boethius came to a bad end. By 523,

After Ravenna fell to the Byzantines, all traces of Theodoric were removed or mutilated. In the mosaic of his palace, the king and his court were originally placed between the columns. Their images were rather clumsily removed, leaving dismembered hands and arms on the columns, such as the portion of an arm (inset).

Theodoric was aging, and worse still, lacked a mature son. At Byzantium, the new emperor Justin took to persecuting his Arian subjects as heretics, and on similar religious grounds, many Christians in Italy began yearning for a return to Byzantine rule. At this difficult time, Boethius apparently failed to report communication between a friend and Byzantium, a neglect Theodoric considered treacherous. He ordered Boethius put to death. While awaiting execution, the scholar had time to compose *The Consolation of Philosophy*, a famous book later translated into Saxon English by Alfred the Great. But the execution of Boethius signaled the final failure of the Ostrogoth monarch's attempt to unify Goth and Roman.

Following Theodoric's own death in 526, an imperial army successfully invaded Italy amid wild enthusiasm from the Latin population. But Byzantine tax collectors and soldiers proved to be rapacious parasites, whose grip did not hold. The peninsula fragmented irreversibly into petty principalities. Henceforth, Rome's role in world affairs would be exercised by its popes, whose religious dominion proved far more enduring than the statesmanship of barbarism's noblest monarch. ■

lifetime bachelor. That he should marry at all was considered unlikely. That he should marry a commoner was considered inconceivable. That he should marry a former prostitute from the Hippodrome was considered not only unthinkable but illegal. However, Justinian I was not a man to let such trifling obstacles stand in his way.

He was not, it is true, altogether self-made. He had gained the imperial crown through his uncle Justin. When Anastasius, last emperor of the old dynasty, died in 518, several men tried unsuccessfully to seize control. Justin, commander of the imperial guards, the Excubitors, prevailed, and at age sixty became Justin I. He appointed his nephew the Count of the Domestics.

Little is known of the nephew's youth. He was born around 483, in Illyricum, on the Adriatic's east coast, along the recruiting ground for the Roman army. Early on, he took the name Justinian as a sign of gratitude to his uncle, who sent him, in his twenties, to be educated in Constantinople. Justinian made good use of that education, lived in the palace, and soon became Justin's right-hand man and obvious successor. Not without a rival, however. Justin had given the highest

To a church home for girls came a very sad young lady named Theodora whose sex shows had been the toast of the crowd. The nuns took her in and a strange thing happened to her.

military command to a well-connected ex-rebel named Vitalian. In 520, Vitalian turned up dead, the victim of a brutal murder, commonly ascribed to both nephew and uncle. In any event, the path was now open for the former to succeed the latter.

Since Justin and Justinian backed the Blues, the police tended to leave them alone during street battles, and to come down hard on the Greens. The Blues got the good government jobs, and they knew they could depend on Justinian for funding. They kept him informed of affairs in the city, and were ready to assemble crowd support wherever Justinian needed it—in the unlikely event of a power struggle upon the death of his uncle, for instance.

Sometime in the early 520s, Justinian fell in love with the woman who— against every expectation, probability and imperial protocol—would become his wife. Theodora was by all accounts bright, charming, intelligent and beautiful. Her acceptance of Christ notwithstanding, she was as ambitious as Justinian himself. Unlike Justinian's early life, however, much is known about Theodora's. Some would say too much, because she and her husband were to be made victims of what is arguably the most famous published smear in history.

Justinian would reign as emperor from 527 to 565, and through much of this period, his inner circle would include an official historian named Procopius, whose glowing accounts of the regime's achievements fulfilled all the expecta-tions of a sixth-century public relations department. However, all the while, and in the strictest secrecy, Procopius was composing a very different portrayal of the imperial couple. It remained secret for more than a century after both they and he were dead. Not until the mid-seventh century was it discreetly published as *The Secret History*, and achieved a limited circulation.[3]

The book—consisting of thirty chapters, filling about two hundred pages in a modern volume—savagely scores Justinian and others. But its continuing notoriety is fueled most especially by its lurid tales of Theodora's early life. She began, writes Procopius, at the very bottom of the social ladder, in a family with no money or position. Her father was employed by the Greens to tend the bears that were kept to fight in the Hippodrome. He died when she was a young child and the Greens abandoned the family, leaving them destitute until the Blues gave Theodora's stepfather a job, and employed the young Theodora in bawdy circus farces.

Procopius spares his readers no detail of the empress's dark young life—her uninhibited exhibitionism, her "partying with ten young men or more," her night-long orgies, her shamelessness over these activities. He writes "with the neurotic lasciviousness of a prude," notes the British historian Robert Browning (*Justinian and Theodora*, London, 1987), who warns that Procopius hated and feared the empress, and that his source for the sordid stories "was mainly malicious tittle-tattle." However, even Procopius makes it evident that she very much wanted to escape this life, and that is why she became the official mistress of a bureaucrat named Hecebolus, who took her to North Africa and abandoned her.

Justinian had encountered Theodora in this earlier, unsavory life. Even then, he was apparently enchanted. She was already a popular entertainer, quick with one-liners and clever impersonations, smart, pretty, and uninhibited. But, the

In her lifetime, the empress Theodora (left, in a mutilated statue now at Milan) caused many a sensation in the gossipy halls of the capital. In 1884, the French dramatist and producer Victorien Sardou opened a play in Paris (poster, far right) that claimed to be based on her life at court, and starred the celebrated Sarah Bernhardt (center). Ever vigilant for the scandalous and the titillating, the theatergoers of the city attended in droves. By all accounts, they did not leave disappointed.

better social circles were strictly forbidden to her. Under the law, any gentleman who had sunk so low as to marry an actress would be barred as a senator. Any woman who took a stage role without her husband's permission could find herself quickly divorced.

However, Theodora, the devout Christian, would make a far more acceptable empress than Theodora the wanton actress, and the more discerning could see that she was just what Justinian needed. He was a socially distant man who could work alone on his official papers all night with little or no sleep. She was fifteen years his junior, witty, and gracious with people in groups large and small. Historian Browning observes another factor: "At crucial moments, his courage sometimes failed him, and he floundered in indecision. Theodora was his ideal complement. She never lost her head in a crisis." Before long, Justinian knew without any doubt that he wanted to marry her.

The obstacles were nevertheless real. Apart from her past, there was the problem of the venerable empress Euphemia, wife of his uncle Justin. Though she herself had been a concubine and slave before Justin bought and married her,

Theodora was exactly what Justinian needed. He was a socially distant man who could work alone all night with no sleep. She was fifteen years his junior, witty, and gracious with people.

she flatly rejected any suggestion that a marriage to an actress could take place. That woman? Moving into the palace? It was preposterous.

But not to Justinian. Deftly, he had his uncle confer upon Theodora the formal honor of the patriciate—the highest rank that could be bestowed upon a subject. Then in 524, Euphemia died. Neither Justinian nor Theodora grieved any more than good manners demanded, and his uncle signed an unprecedented piece of legislation. If an actress had truly rejected her former life, and had been granted high honor, she could marry any man of whatever rank. In the subsequent nine-hundred-year history of the empire, the law was applied only this once, and Justinian and Theodora were married in 525 in the Great Church.

In the same year, his emperor uncle gave Justinian the rank of caesar, and two years later made him co-emperor. On August 1, 527, Justin died, victim of an old, infected war wound on his foot. Justinian became sole emperor, with Theodora his empress. There were no other contestants. By then, writes the American historian John W. Barker (*Justinian and the Later Roman Empire*, Madison, 1966), Justinian had been effectually running the empire for nine years. "The Age of Justinian did not suddenly begin in 527. It had been a reality since 518."

It was to be an age marked by vast expansion of imperial territory and munificent building programs that produced an unprecedented number of forts, aqueducts and churches. It saw a complete reorganization of the documents and principles of the law, and a valiant but unsuccessful attempt to bring eastern and western Christians into unity. "His reign," says Barker, "was a crucial phase in the

3. Copies of Procopius's *Secret History* seem to have been rare throughout the whole Byzantine era. Gossip was not rare, however, and eleventh-century tourists in Constantinople were shown a little cottage where Theodora was said to have kept assignations with Justinian. Later, the eleventh-century monkish writer Amoin de Fleury recounts the adventures of a young Justinian and Belisarius with two prostitutes, named Antonina and Antonia. Justinian, he writes, fell in love with the latter. Eventually, in 1623, Niccolo Alemanni, the Vatican librarian, found a copy of the *Secret History*, and Procopius's work, by then eleven hundred years old, achieved a much wider readership.

transformation of the later Roman Empire into what we call the Byzantine Empire. . . . Justinian emerges as a pivotal figure in the development of the medieval European world out of the breakup of the ancient Mediterranean world."

Even as Justinian was being crowned, Roman troops were battling the Persian army on the Euphrates River. They were under the command of Belisarius, a tall, handsome and heroic native of what is now western Bulgaria, who would be recognized by military historians as one of the world's greatest generals (and in the *Secret History* as a gullible dimwit, deceived by his treacherous and promiscuous wife). Whatever the gossip and skepticism of Procopius, the fact remains that Belisarius enabled Justinian to stabilize the Persian frontier, the constant problem of Roman emperors. He won several key battles against the Persian king Khosrov I, and forced him to sign a treaty. When Khosrov broke it, and looted cities in Armenia, Syria and Mesopotamia, Belisarius pounded him into another treaty, this one a fifty-year truce, which held.

That gave Justinian the chance to attempt the goal to which he had aspired since the crown had first seemed within his reach—the recovery of the western empire. His first objective was to regain Vandal North Africa, the project that destroyed Leo I and bankrupted his treasury. Justinian put ninety-two warships

What Byzantium had regained was a crippled, war-torn Italy in need of massive rehabilitation. Such an effort was not possible and the ensuing destruction would leave Rome a ghost town.

and about five hundred other vessels under Belisarius's command in June 533. The big fleet met little resistance, landed its troops, and by March 534, North Africa had been retrieved for the empire.

On the Danube front, the Slavs[4] and Hunnic Bulgars staged continual raids into Dacia, Dalmatia and Thrace. A healthy contingent of Kotrigur Huns joined them in 559, and pushed south to Thermopylae and east as far as the Constantinople wall. Belisarius went in, rallied the civilian population, and pushed the barbarians back. Border battles continued, though, and in 561, when an energetic contingent of Avars (Asian relatives of the Huns) joined in the attack, Justinian paid them off. This removed the immediate threat, though many Slavs and Bulgars settled into ethnic enclaves within the Roman territory, not fighting but not assimilating either.

But Justinian's main target was Italy, which he had long wanted restored to the imperial fold. In the late fifth century, virtually the whole peninsula, Rome included, had fallen under the control of Theodoric, an Ostrogoth, who had embraced the religion of Arius. (See sidebar, page 262.) Justinian sent Belisarius and a fleet of ships to Sicily, where, in 540, they defeated Witigis, the new king of the Ostrogoths. Belisarius then recaptured the Italian capital of Ravenna, and re-established imperial rule.

But the recovery could not be sustained. In 541, the Ostrogoths named a new

4. This is the first substantial appearance in Christian history of the Slavic peoples, who, five hundred years hence, will be baptized into the faith and later carry the gospel all the way across Asia, over the Bering Sea, and into northwestern North America.

king, Totila, who within two years had regained Naples. Justinian sent Belisarius after him in 544, but by now, the imperial strength was waning and Belisarius was not adequately supplied. Totila soon controlled all but three Italian cities. The exhausted Belisarius was recalled to Constantinople, and Totila signaled a willingness to bargain.

This time, Justinian dispatched another general, the personable Narses, a eunuch, a first-rate strategist and a financial expert, with a reputation for honesty. Better supplied than Belisarius, Narses defeated Totila and killed him on the battlefield, so that by 562, the Byzantines held all of Italy once more.

What they had regained from the Ostrogoths, however, was a crippled, war-torn, poverty-stricken country in need of massive restoration. Such an effort was not forthcoming, and soon large areas of Italy would slip from the empire's hands and into a state of destitution that would briefly leave Rome itself a silent ghost town, its famed aqueducts wrecked, struggling to stay alive. Belisarius, meanwhile, returned to the capital, and soon found himself accused of sedition and placed under guard. He was quickly absolved, however, retired with dignity, and died in 565.

Early in his reign, Justinian launched the initiative that would carry his name into legal history, establishing a foundation in law that would enable Byzantine society to function efficiently for the next nine centuries. It is known as "the Code of Justinian," his revision of the entire Roman legal system, by then an accumulation of often contradictory laws, rescripts, regulations, traditions and precedents dating back five hundred years to the republic and beyond. The Justinian reforms were far more, however, than mere revision. His lawyers composed a textbook of Roman law called the *Institutes*, plus a careful selection of legal opinions from great legal scholars of the past called the *Digest*, and finally, a revised law code called the *Codex*. These three were fundamental to the history of both Byzantine and Western law.

The lawyer whom he enlisted to oversee the work was the pagan Tribonian. Aided by nine other jurists and scholars, Tribonian gathered related legislation from its myriad sources, deleted repetitions and inapplicable sections, resolved contradictions and assembled the result in rational order. In 535, they completed the job: twelve volumes containing 4,562 laws.

To Justinian also must go the credit (or blame) for ending the age-old dominance of Athens as the intellectual center of the Mediterranean world. In 529, he closed the Athenian schools. He had observed that the university professors there remained

The Barberini Ivory (top), now in the Louvre at Paris, is believed to depict Justinian, triumphant over his military foes and blessed by Christ. As he or his generals forced lost lands back into the empire, they would quite literally cement the reconciliation with building programs. After North Africa was returned to the fold by military conquest, Justinian ordered the construction of a new civil basilica at Sabrata, Libya, and had it decorated with a lavish floor (immediately above).

pagan, flatly refusing to bring their teaching into line with the Christian view of classical philosophy that was being developed and taught in Constantinople, Gaza and Alexandria. This new view was based upon the radical notion that the old, classical culture, which had held sway for so long, need not be abolished. Its ideals and wisdom—and its emphasis on eloquence—could be used, once its pagan elements were eliminated, in the education of Christians. At that point, writes historian Downey, the culture of Constantinople "supplanted that of Athens."

The most serious crisis in Justinian's reign did not come on the military front, nor the theological, nor the intellectual. It came on the civil front, and while the

The case of the vanishing Vandals

The Arian Vandals raged into North Africa and unleashed fury on its Christians, but left little historic legacy—except a universal word for wanton destruction

The Vandals were terrorists. They outclassed even the Huns in terms of damage, and rivaled the Saxons in their savagery toward Roman civilization. First in Gaul, then Spain and North Africa, this Germanic tribe wrought unprecedented havoc, and finally in 455, their seaborne warriors conquered Rome itself. Yet after that triumph, the Vandals vanished as a people within a century. Today, their name is no more than a word in most Western languages, a word meaning pointless, vicious destruction.

Like other Germanic peoples, the Vandals adopted the Arian faith during the fourth century while living beyond the Roman frontiers. Their war bands, very brave and persistent in attack, consisted mainly of unarmored infantry wielding light spears and leather-sheathed wicker shields. Only the better-off tribesmen could afford swords, armor and horses. In 406 they burst through the Roman frontier, along with other tribes, and for three years, looted and burned their way through Gaul.

At the hands of the Franks, however, the Vandals suffered a major defeat. Uniting behind their king, Gunderic, they therefore crossed the Pyrenees into Spain, where they found another civilization, prostrate and virtually defenseless. Wanton destruction ensued. In Spain, they acquired ports and ships, and soon their galleys were roaming the western Mediterranean.

Gunderic was succeeded by his half brother Gaiseric, the crippled son of an unknown concubine and reputedly a man of exceptional cunning. In 429, Gaiseric crossed the nine-mile Strait of Gibraltar into North Africa. His host is estimated to have numbered eighty thousand, with a fifth to a quarter being fighting men. Here they found a bonanza: the gleaming cities and lush fields of Roman Africa, not yet ravaged by any invader. The Vandals fell upon Africa with their accustomed savagery.

The resident Roman count was Boniface, accused at the imperial court of intriguing to use his six provinces in a bid to seize the imperial crown, and of inviting Gaiseric into the region as a potential ally. If this is so, Boniface made a terrible error. The Vandals first seized land near Tingi (Tangier), then quickly conquered all of Mauritania, creating terror with their indiscriminate slaughter. Boniface retreated to the strongly fortified town of Hippo.

Behind its walls, the renowned bishop Augustine prayed for relief. Three months into the siege, he died. Hippo held out for eleven more months, hoping for relief from a Byzantine fleet. The fleet did reach Carthage, but it brought no relief for Hippo. The Romans ceded the city to Gaiseric without a fight, in exchange for keeping Carthage. But the Vandals later captured that city anyway, along with much of the fleet.

Settling down, Vandal leaders carved out huge estates. Gaiseric is said to have taken his Arian faith very seriously, and to have loathed the orthodox Christian church. He therefore sought to impose Arianism on his conquered subjects by maiming, decapitating, branding or hanging any who did not comply. The major churches were seized for Arian use. Christian priests were enslaved, and made to carry loads usually reserved for camels. Bishops were burned alive for refusing to disclose the whereabouts of hidden church treasures.

The brutality extended to all ages and all classes. Victor of Vita, a priest, tells of children being held by the feet upside down "and cut . . . in two from their bottoms to the tops of their heads." When stone houses did not burn easily, Victor writes, "[Vandals] smashed the roofs to pieces and leveled the beautiful walls to the ground, so that the former beauty of the towns cannot be deduced from what they look like now. And there are very many cities with few or no inhabitants, for after these events, the ones that survive lie desolate.

generals had a key part in it, the determining role was played by his wife. The source of the crisis was the conflict between the Blues and the Greens. Due to Justinian's favorable treatment of the Blues, they became bolder, defying any authority figure that stood in their way. Finally, Justinian had to prohibit violent demonstrations and commit the government to equal treatment of the two factions.

The Blue extremists resented this. Street fights escalated. In January 532, after several people were killed, thugs from both sides were charged with murder. Two of them, one Green and one Blue, were sentenced to hang. But the nooses failed to kill them, and spectators swarmed onto the scaffold and carried them to a

In an illustration of the 455 event, the Vandals of North Africa conquer Rome. History, however, offers no evidence of battles such as the one pictured. The city's riches were simply handed over in return for the safety of its citizens.

"Some had their mouths forced open with poles and stakes, and disgusting filth was put in their jaws so that they would tell the truth about their money. They tortured others by twisting cords around their foreheads and shins until they snapped."

Some Vandal women were so impressed by the fortitude of persecuted Christians as to consider conversion. When Gaiseric heard this, he stationed torturers outside his victims' remaining churches. According to Victor: "When they saw a woman or man who looked like one of their race going there, they were straightaway to thrust tooth-edged stakes at

that person's head and gather all the hair in them. Pulling tightly, they took off all the skin from a person's head, as well as the hair. Some people, when this happened, immediately lost their eyes, while others died from the pain. After this punishment, the women, their heads stripped of skin, were paraded through the street, with heralds going before them, so that the whole town could see."

Now Carthage, destroyed as a Phoenician city almost six centuries earlier, again posed a deadly threat to Rome. The Vandal navy prowled the Mediterranean, harassing and robbing coastal towns almost at will. Rome, meanwhile, was in chaos, its ruling families enmeshed in murderous intrigues over power. When Gaiseric's fleet appeared off Ostia in 455, Romans clogged the gates in abject panic to escape. Furious citizens recognized the emperor Maximus among the refugees and stoned him to death. His reign had lasted seventy days.

No armed defense was even attempted. Instead, Pope Leo I met Gaiseric with an appeal: Take what you want, but do not burn or torture. For two weeks, the invaders plundered palaces, churches and mansions. Among their prizes were the empress Licinia and her two daughters. Gaiseric married one daughter, named Eudocia, to his son Huneric, and eventually freed the other two imperial women. The union of Huneric and Eudocia produced a son, Hilderic, the next to the last king of the Vandals. In 472, Eudocia escaped from her husband, and sought refuge in Jerusalem, where she passed the remainder of her life.

Gaiseric died in 477. He never did succeed in breaking the spirit of North Africa's catholic Christians. Under his successors, religious persecution recurred sporadically until 534, when an eastern army under Belisarius reconquered North Africa. Gelimer, the last Vandal king, was paraded as a captive through Byzantium, and then settled in luxury on a government estate in Galatia. He was even offered the high status of patrician but refused, because he would not deny his Arian heritage. In due course the Vandals were absorbed into the North African population, and as a people entirely disappear from history. ∎

church, where they claimed sanctuary.[5] Guards were posted around the church. Justinian, attending a race in the Hippodrome, was mobbed by members of both parties, loudly demanding pardon for the offenders. The emperor made no response. The crowd began chanting, *"Nika! Nika!"* the Greek word for "conquer." That began the Nika Revolt.

Soon mobs moved in on the jail, set all the prisoners free, and torched the building. Now frenzied, they set other fires. That night and the next day, more buildings were burned. Justinian opened the Hippodrome, hoping the races would distract them. They did not. The rebels next demanded that three hated bureaucrats be dismissed. Justinian dithered, then abruptly fired all three. His capitulation made things worse. Mobs roamed the streets, burning and looting. His Senate opponents began calling for his ouster. Justinian barricaded himself in the palace and sent for Belisarius and another commander, Mundus, who assembled troops, but failed to disperse the mob.

On January 18, five days after the riots began, Justinian appeared before the angry throng in the Hippodrome, and swore he would grant a general amnesty. But the chanting and stomping continued after the emperor withdrew. His

Justinian, panicking, decided to run for it, but found himself confronted with an immovable obstacle. It was his wife. For her, she said, 'royal rank is the best burial garment.'

senatorial opponents thereupon presented to the crowd one Hypatius, a nephew of the late Anastasius I, who was hailed as the new emperor.

The emperor, panicking, decided to make a run for it. He ordered boats filled with provisions, gold and jewels. Then suddenly, he found himself confronted with an immovable obstacle. It was Theodora. All the wily survival instincts she had acquired from childhood onward, all the hair's-breadth dangers she had survived, all the lessons learned when she lived on the permanent edge of death, surged into the impassioned pronouncement she now made to her husband.

Procopius, in his *Secret History* for once gives her credit, recording a convincing version of what she said: "Emperor, if you still want to escape, there is no problem. We have plenty of money; the sea is there; here are the ships. Nevertheless, consider. Once you've managed to save yourself, might you not gladly exchange your safety for death? As for me, I cherish an old expression. Royal rank is the best burial garment."

That did it. Justinian decided to fight. Meanwhile, in the Hippodrome, the mob had convinced Hypatius that Justinian was gone, and that he should accept the role of emperor. He did, though reluctantly, apparently after failing to get word to Justinian.

It was time to strike. Belisarius and Mundus led their well-armed troops into the Hippodrome from two sides, and when they saw that the rioters were not going to be still, they swung into them with clubs and swords. The unarmed mob

5. The right of sanctuary was rooted in the idea that sacred things should be inviolable. It was recognized in the Code of Theodosius, and reaffirmed in the Code of Justinian. Leo the Great added papal authority for it about 460. It meant that any fleeing criminal could not be arrested if he could reach the sanctuary of a church. This right of asylum was originally confined to the church itself, though later some churches were permitted to extend it to the property around them, marked off by "sanctuary crosses."

The concentration of early Byzantine buildings at Ravenna, and in particular the mosaics within them, led UNESCO to declare the city a World Heritage Site. In its heyday, the city's population was an uneasy mix of Arian and Christian elements, and each tried to outdo the other in the construction of buildings and in their decoration. There were two baptisteries, and two basilicas dedicated to St. Apollinaris, the martyred first bishop of the city, each strikingly similar in design and decoration. The mosaics, such as those in Sant' Apollinare Nuovo (1), are considered some of the finest in the world. But the glories within are seldom betrayed by the rude exteriors, as for example the rough brick walls of the Arian Baptistery (2). The Church of San Vitale (3) is a striking octagonal departure from the long-naved basilicas most popular in churches of the era. But even it can only be properly appreciated when the visitor passes to its breathtaking interior (4).

was overpowered. The soldiers slaughtered all who could not escape. Estimates of the death toll stagger the imagination, ranging to thirty thousand and upward. If even a fifth of such a number perished, the whole vast complex would have been drenched in blood, with bodies piled three and four deep on the bleachers.

Hypatius and the aristocrats who had tried to make him emperor were arrested and hauled before Justinian. Hypatius pleaded for mercy, saying he had been forced, and he had tried to get things under control. But Justinian opted for strong measures, and ordered Hypatius and his brother to be executed and dumped into the ocean. The scheming aristocrats were exiled and their property seized. Some years later, the emperor would restore some of the impounded properties and make provisions for the care of Hypatius's family and that of his brother. But the effect of the Nika Revolt was to remove or silence all possible opposition, leaving Justinian unencumbered, powerful and free to take any action he wished.

It had also pulverized the capital city. The burials must have taken weeks. Thousands were missing from work. Broad swaths of ash lay where important buildings once stood. But Justinian's response was prompt and vigorous. He launched an extravagant redevelopment program, hiring the best artisans and

An appalling situation arose, and the imperial troops found themselves trying to forcibly drag away from the altar of a church an invited guest, Pope Vigilius of Rome

workmen to create striking new buildings and public spaces. Its scope and scale were unprecedented. "It is no coincidence that Justinian's most ambitious steps were taken only after the Nika outbreak," writes Barker. "The last obstacles to his bold schemes were now removed. It is from the quelling of this revolt that we can most decisively date the full-scale blossoming of the era of Justinian."

The industrious Procopius recorded it all in his non-secret history, producing six books on these public works, which were not confined to the capital alone. Forts, bridges, roads, aqueducts, reservoirs, courthouses and other official buildings, warehouses, and massive cisterns were constructed in Mesopotamia, Syria, Armenia, the Crimea, the Black Sea coast, the Balkan peninsula and Greece, Asia Minor and Palestine, Egypt and Africa.

Included in the program, as well, were dozens of monasteries and churches. Many still stand, including Justinian's masterpiece, erected to replace a structure that burned to the ground during the Nika Revolt. It was the new *Hagia Sophia*, Holy Wisdom, known as "the Great Church," which would serve Christendom until 1453, when the Muslim Turks converted it into a mosque. (See sidebar pages 278 and 279.) He also rebuilt the Church of the Holy Apostles, considered second in importance only to Hagia Sophia, which would serve as the architectural inspiration for the renowned Basilica of St. Mark in Venice.

However, building churches was one thing. Uniting the Christians who used them was quite something else, and here Justinian was no more successful than his predecessors. If anything, he widened the divide, not only between Chalcedonian and Monophysite Christians, but also between the Greek-speaking east and the Latin-speaking west. And in the course of his efforts, appalling situations arose. At one point, for example, his troops found themselves trying to drag away from the altar of a Constantinople church an invited guest, none other than Pope Vigilius of Rome. They subsequently kept him prisoner until he escaped by climbing over a back fence.

Things did not reach such an impasse quickly, however. They arose out of Justinian's attempt to restore the west to the empire and to unite his whole realm under one faith. To do this, he needed both the Chalcedonians and the Monophysites. The Chalcedonians were entrenched in the west, and their support was essential for the regaining of North Africa, Spain and particularly Italy. The Monophysites, who were very strong in rural Syria and Egypt, might at any time provide some dangerous independence movement with religious credentials. However, his own household represented a certain ecumenism, for while he was a Chalcedonian, his wife had never forgotten the kind and holy nuns who had rescued her at Alexandria. Theodora was a passionate Monophysite.[6]

It will be recalled that when Justinian's uncle became emperor, the eastern and western churches were in schism, the pope at Rome and the patriarch at Constantinople having excommunicated each other. Throughout the first years of his reign, Justinian sought to unobtrusively undermine the Monophysite hold on the east by appointing Chalcedonian bishops to the major sees. The policy seemed to work, and Monophysite Christianity appeared to decline—but then came Baradaeus.

A Monophysite monk from Mesopotamia of intense evangelistic zeal, Baradaeus was consecrated bishop through the influence of Theodora, and promptly began a sweeping Monophysite revival.[7] He had particular appeal for the Arabs of the south, who were Monophysite Christians, allies of the empire, and a major factor in keeping Persia in check. Justinian could not risk losing their support. He therefore decided that if he could not suppress the Monophysites, he must win them over to Chalcedon. Or alternatively, he must sufficiently diminish the decisions of Chalcedon to make that council acceptable to the Monophysites.

His attempted solution became known as the Three Chapters. It referred to the writings of three theologians—Theodore of Mopsuestia, Theodoret of Cyrrhus and Ibas of Edessa, all supporters of the heretic Nestorius (arch-foe of the Monophysites), and all dead. These are the "three" condemned by Justinian's Three Chapters. What makes things confusing is that accepting the Chapters meant rejecting the three theologians and vice versa. If the rest of the church met in council and supported the Chapters, therefore, this would appear to repudiate the Nestorians and thereby reconcile the Monophysites and restore them to the fold. Such, anyway, was his hope.

The problem was that the west would very probably see the repudiation of

6. Recalling her escape from life as a prostitute, Theodora, after she became empress, called all of Constantinople's brothel-keepers to the palace, condemned them for the evil they inflicted upon women, and ordered them to find another line of work. When they told her that they had invested five gold solidi in acquiring each of the girls, she gave each one the total amount he had spent. Then she called in the women, and gave them each a gold solidus and a new dress, and told them to go home to their parents.

7. Theodora arranged the consecration to the episcopacy of the monk Baradaeus at the request of the Arab chief (sometimes called king) Harith of the Ghassanids, a northern Arabian people. The Beni Ghassan (sons of Ghassan), as they became known, were Monophysite Christians. Unlike nearly all other Arab tribes, they refused conversion to Islam, and remained Christian throughout the entire Muslim occupation. One of their descendants became Byzantine emperor. The people as a whole eventually migrated to Georgia in the Caucasus Mountains, and have remained Christian to this day.

Like Constantine before him, Justinian was a builder, and the Nika Revolt and the devastation it left provided ample tracts of newly vacant land for him to indulge his passion. Chief among Justinian's legacies were the churches that he constructed, or as in the case of Hagia Eirene (Holy Peace, depicted on the right), that he reconstructed, in the imperial city. The monograms of Justinian and Theodora still grace the capitols of its columns, as does the huge cross above the altar. Though never converted to a mosque, it was for a time a Turkish arsenal, and today it is regularly used for concerts. More utilitarian and hidden from most eyes, the great cistern built in his reign (above) covers 2.4 acres, has a capacity of twenty-one-million gallons, and is supported by 336 marble columns. In the 1990s, walkways, atmospheric lighting and even a café were installed to cater to tourists.

the three theologians as an implicit repudiation of Chalcedon, which had restored Theodoret as a bishop and accepted some of the writing of Ibas. What was required, therefore, was the installation of a pope who would ratify the Chapters on his own authority, compelling the west to concur. But how could such a pope be found? Theodora knew just the man.

His name was Vigilius. He was Rome's official legate in Constantinople, an individual of high ambition and low resolve, whom Theodora had somehow persuaded to return to Rome to work for the Monophysite cause there. In Italy, the war with the Goths was in full sway. With the help of Belisarius and his wife (the latter acting as agent for Theodora), Vigilius became pope.[8] By then, he realized, however, that the western bishops were almost unanimously opposed to the Three Chapters. He therefore balked at signing, whereupon the emperor's agents abducted him, and hustled him onto a ship. They kept him captive for a time in Sicily, then transported him as a distinguished prisoner to

Constantinople, where he received a royal welcome from Justinian and Theodora at the dockside.

This amiability didn't last, however. With Vigilius still flatly refusing to approve the Three Chapters, the mood chilled. Then he changed his mind and it warmed again, and Justinian announced his plan for a church council to approve the Chapters. When it was disclosed that scarcely a single western bishop would attend, however, Vigilius again reversed himself, defied the emperor, and took sanctuary in the Church of St. Peter in Ormisda. A squad of palace guards, disregarding the rules of sanctuary, broke into the church, and found him clinging to the altar. Two men grabbed his legs, another his beard, and pulled. But Vigilius hung on, the altar toppled, and the frightened guards hastily left.

A few days later, imperial officials persuaded Vigilius to return to his designated residence. There, he once more became a closely watched prisoner, but one night he discovered an unguarded exit, jumped a back fence, and made his way to Chalcedon across the Bosporus. He took refuge in St. Euphemia's, the same church in which the controversial Council of Chalcedon had been held a century before.

By now, however, the Goths had been defeated in Italy, the empire was in control, and the support of the western church was far less essential. Justinian proceeded with the council. Composed almost exclusively of eastern bishops, it met on May 5, 553. Vigilius boycotted the meeting, the patriarch of Constantinople presided, and the Three Chapters were quickly approved. Prevailed upon to sign the council's decision, Vigilius at first refused, then changed his mind one final time, and signed. He was sent home, but died en route of a kidney disease.

Pope Vigilius's signature was by no means sufficient to gain the concurrence of the whole western church. But his successors, more decisive and persuasive men, continued to support this final act of his. In due time, the Second Council of Constantinople of 553 gained recognition as the Fifth Ecumenical Council of the Christian church (after Nicea in 325, First Constantinople in 381, Ephesus in 431 and Chalcedon in 451).

However, Justinian's grand objective, the reconciliation of the Monophysite

8. Vigilius took an odd route to the papacy. Serving as a papal envoy in Constantinople, he was offered the papacy by the empress Theodora, provided that as pope he disallow the Council of Chalcedon. Vigilius accepted, and when the reigning pope died, he went to Rome and was consecrated. But another pope had already been consecrated, so there were two. Vigilius persuaded the Byzantine general at Rome to banish the other one, who subsequently died in exile. However, for some time there were two popes, meaning that Vigilius must have been consecrated unlawfully. "It is therefore difficult to see," says *The Dictionary of Christian Biography*, "how Vigilius ever became lawful pope at all."

Justinian's masterpiece

Under his watchful eye, magnificent Hagia Sophia came into being, and to this day it dominates Istanbul

The Church of the Holy Wisdom, known best by its Greek name *Hagia Sophia*, still stands high above the Turkish city of Istanbul as it stood high above the Christian city of Constantinople for nine centuries. Its designer, Anthemius of Tralles, may have been the premier architect and engineer of his time, but the emperor Justinian closely supervised construction. He had studied architecture and competently sorted out problems that arose during the five-year project.

The original design was structurally faulty, however, and the huge dome perched atop the colonnades and galleries collapsed in 558. A new and higher windowed dome was designed and put in place, flanked by pillars and smaller domes, the soaring interior elaborately decorated. In 562, Justinian once again consecrated the church. The new dome has held ever since.

Hagia Sophia was turned into a mosque in 1453, after Constantinople fell to the Turks. Its mosaics were plastered over, and minarets and other Islamic touches were added to the exterior. The magnificent building, its original gold mosaics largely restored, now serves as a popular Turkish museum. ■

Photographs of the interior of Hagia Sophia give only a limited sense of the counterpoint of light and dark, the interplay of the surfaces in the basilica (above). The Great Church of the Holy Wisdom in modern Istanbul is a building meant to be appreciated by standing in it, and most effectively by worshiping in it. Using new techniques, Justinian and his architects meant to give the 110-foot dome the appearance of floating in light, cascading down on the east and west sides in a series of half-domes. To eliminate the need for heavy supports in the interior, the massive piers under the dome had to be supported by four great rectangular buttresses, two of which are visible in the photo (1) on the opposite page, and with the half-domes (2). In the estimation of some critics, exterior elegance was sacrificed for the sake of interior grandeur. Cross-sections of the Great Church (3) show the complex of huge spaces opened up inside by Justinian's engineering innovations. Even so, in size it ranks down the list, after St. Peter's in Rome, the cathedrals at Seville and Milan, and even perhaps a new church in Belgrade. Hagia Sophia's interior was later embellished with hundreds of mosaics, including one in which Justinian offers a model of his masterpiece to God (4). Among the last icons to be installed was that of the Deisis (5), Mary and John the Baptist worshiping Jesus.

Christians, proved a partial success at best.[9] What the Monophysites wanted was repudiation of Chalcedon, nothing less. Mere gestures to this effect did not interest them. On the other hand, the west knew very well that if the church began discrediting its councils, then no creed could be considered stable, no doctrine as ultimately true.

Theodora died in 548 of symptoms that suggest cancer. Justinian, sixty-six, was grief-stricken, and never quite recovered from the loss of his beloved wife. Though he made a desultory attempt to find another (see sidebar, page 20), he spent most of his last years studying theology and practicing a self-denying, ascetic lifestyle. He died in 565, at the age of eighty-three, after an official reign of thirty-eight years. Because he had come to be regarded as a tyrant, there was little public display of sorrow. His nephew, Justin II, took the throne amid great

The glories of the reign of Justinian and Theodora were the inspiration for famous mosaics in the church of San Vitale in Ravenna, in which the two, on opposite sides of the church, process toward the altar. In his parade, the emperor carries a bowl (perhaps for offering the Eucharistic bread). Behind and to his right is his famous general Belisarius. In the lead is Maximian, the archbishop of the city—and significantly the only figure to be identified in the mosaic. Justinian's eyes look straightforward, across the church to his empress, whose eyes are demurely and piously directed toward the altar. Theirs was a marriage in keeping with the best romances of history, one that closed one age and ushered in the flowering of the Byzantine Christian culture.

acclaim for what would turn out to be an undistinguished career, and Justinian was entombed in the new Church of the Holy Apostles.

In restoring the west to the empire he had failed, and in securing the unity of Christendom, he had doubly failed. Yet in one regard he would later prove to have achieved a crucial success. About five years after the death of Justinian, there was born in the dusty commercial center of Mecca, near the western coast of the Arabian Peninsula, a man named Mohammed. With the fierce fervor of a new creed and a new cause that mandated war and sanctified conquest, his disciples would swiftly crush the armies of both Persia and the New Rome.

In the ensuing century, they would subjugate, through military conquest, fully two-thirds of Christendom. In western Europe, they would be finally stopped by the Franks. Thrusting northward by sea, they would reach Constantinople, and there, too, meet defeat. Justinian had done his work well. He had readied the city for the nine-hundred-year siege that lay ahead, when it would guard and preserve all Europe for the faith of Jesus Christ. ■

9. One legacy of the emperor Justinian's efforts to resolve the Monophysite controversy is the hymn called *Monogenes* (only-begotten), which is sung to this day in most Eastern churches as a component of the Divine Liturgy of St. John Chrysostom. It was written in 528, either by Justinian himself or by Patriarch Severus of Antioch, his guest at the time. But no matter who wrote the *Monogenes*, that year Justinian ordered it used throughout the empire. It begins: "Only-begotten Son and immortal Word of God, who for our salvation willed to be incarnate of the Holy Theotokos and ever-virgin Mary, who without change became man. . . ."

ARTISTS FOR THIS VOLUME

With this volume, a new team of artists joins the series. All five artists for this book are western Canadians.

RICHARD CONNOR, of Edmonton, a graduate of Alberta College of Art and Design, has worked as an illustrator and designer in a number of art studios in England and Canada, and is now a freelance architectural illustrator for companies across western Canada.

JAMIE HOLLOWAY, of Edmonton, whose character sketches grace the margins of this book, has worked as an illustrator for Alberta advertising and government agencies.

JIM NUNN, born in Fort Macleod, Alberta, is a longtime Edmonton resident who has worked as a commercial artist and architectural illustrator throughout his thirty-five-year career. He is also an accomplished landscape artist, working in acrylics, and has done a number of portraits in pastels.

DALE SHUTTLEWORTH, who lives outside Edmonton in the resort area of Pigeon Lake, took his first watercolor class at age nine and later taught watercolor himself. He has been self-employed as a commercial artist for forty years, with most of his work in architectural illustration and rendering.

JOHN SMITH, of Edmonton, is a graduate of Alberta College of Art and Design and a senior illustrator, designer and art director in his own firm, Artsmith Communications, with major government, institutional and commercial clients. He is also a design instructor at Grant MacEwan Community College, Edmonton.

BIBLIOGRAPHY

Ammianus Marcellinus. *The Roman History of Ammianus Marcellinus*. London: G. Bell, 1911.

The Anglo-Saxon Chronicle. sunsite.berkeley.edu/OMACL/Anglo/.

Anson, Peter F. *The Call of the Desert*. London: S.P.C.K.,1964.

Aprem, Mar. *Council of Ephesus of 431*. Trichur: Mar Narsai, 1978.

Aprem, Mar. *The Nestorian Fathers*. Trichur: Mar Narsai, 1976.

Attwater, Donald. *St. John Chrysostom, Pastor and Preacher*. London: Harvill, 1959.

Augustine. *City of God*. Edinburgh: T. & T. Clark, 1871.

Augustine. *Confessions*. Harmondsworth, Middlesex: Penguin Books, 1961.

Augustine. *Confessions*. www.fordham.edu/halsall/basis/confessions-bod.html.

Barnes, Harry Elmer. *The History of Western Civilization*. NY: Harcourt, Brace, 1935.

Barnes, Timothy David. *Athanasius and Constantius: Theology and Politics in the Constantinian Empire*. Cambridge, MA: Harvard University, 1993.

Basil, of Caesarea. *The Long Rules*. Boston: Daughters of St. Paul, 1950.

Baur, Chrysostomus. *John Chrysostom and His Time*. Vaduz: Büchervertriebsanstalt, 1988.

Baynes, N. H. "Rome and Armenia in the Fourth Century." In *English Historical Review* 25 (1910): 625-43.

Benedict, *The Rule of St. Benedict*. Garden City, NY: Image Books, 1975.

Boissonnade, P. *Life and Work in Medieval Europe*. London: Routledge & Kegan, 1927.

Bowersock, G. W. *Julian, the Apostate*. London: Duckworth, 1978.

Brown, Peter. *Augustine of Hippo: A Biography*. London: Faber, 1967.

Brown, Peter. *The Body and Society: Men, Women and Sexual Renunciation in Early Christianity*. NY: Columbia University, 1988.

Brown, Peter. *The Cult of the Saints*. Chicago: University of Chicago, 1983.

Browning, Robert. *Justinian and Theodora*. London: Thames and Hudson, 1987.

Bury, J. B. *The Invasion of Europe by the Barbarians*. London: Macmillan, 1928.

Bush, Robert Wheler. *St. Athanasius: His Life and Times*. NY: E. & J. B. Young, 1888.

Butler, Alban. *Lives of the Saints*. London: Burns & Oates, 1956.

Cahill, Thomas. *How the Irish Saved Civilization: The Untold Story of Ireland's Heroic Role from the Fall of Rome to the Rise of Medieval Europe*. NY: Nan A. Talese, Doubleday, ca.1995.

The Cambridge Medieval History. NY: Macmillan, 1911-36.

The Carmen de Providentia Dei Attributed to Prosper of Aquitaine. Washington: Catholic University of America, 1964.

Cassian, John. *Institutes of the Coenobia, and the Remedies for the Eight Principal Faults*. www.osb.org/lectio/cassian/inst/index.html.

Cassiodorus, Senator. *The Letters of Cassiodorus: Being a Condensed Translation of the Variae Epistolae of Magnus Aurelius Cassiodorus Senator*. London: Henry Frowde, 1886.

Catholic Encyclopedia: An International Work of Reference on the Constitution, Doctrine, Discipline, and History of the Catholic Church. NY: Appleton, 1907-1910. www.newadvent.org/cathen/.

Chadwick, Henry. *The Church in Ancient Society: From Galilee to Gregory the Great*. NY: Oxford University, 2001.

Chamberlin, Russell. *Charlemagne: Emperor of the Western World*. London: Grafton, 1986.

Chapman, John. *Saint Benedict and the Sixth Century*. Westport, Conn., Greenwood, 1971.

Cleland, D. J. "Salvian and the Vandals." In *Studia Patristica* 10 (1970): 270-4.

Cross, F. L. *The Oxford Dictionary of the Christian Church*. London: Oxford University Press, 1974.

Daniel-Rops, Henri. *The Church in the Dark Ages*. London: Dent, 1963.

Daniel-Rops, Henri. *The Church of Apostles and Martyrs*. NY: Image Books, 1962.

De Clercq, Victor Cyril. *Ossius of Cordova: A Contribution to the History of the Constantinian Period*. Washington, D.C.: Catholic University of America, 1954.

Downey, Glanville. *Constantinople in the Age of Justinian*. Norman: University of Oklahoma, 1960.

Downey, Glanville. *A History of Antioch in Syria: From Seleucus to the Arab Conquest*. Princeton, NJ: Princeton University, 1961.

Drew, Katherine Fischer. *The Barbarian Invasions: Catalyst of a New Order*. NY: Holt, Rinehart and Winston, 1970.

Duchesne, Louis. *The Early History of the Christian Church*. 3 vols. London: J. Murray, 1909-1924.

Dudden, F. Homes. *The Life and Times of St. Ambrose*. Oxford: Clarendon, 1935.

Eerdman's Handbook to the History of Christianity. Grand Rapids, MI: Eerdmans, 1977.

Egeria. *Diary of a Pilgrimage*. NY: Newman, 1970.

Eno, Robert B. "Christian Reaction to the Barbarian Invasions and the Sermons of Quodvultideus." In *Preaching in the Patristic Age: Studies in Honor of Walter J. Burghardt, S. J*. Edited by David G. Hunter, 139-61. NY: Paulist, 1989.

Fisher, D. J. V. *The Anglo-Saxon Age, c. 400-1042*. London: Longman, 1973.

Fox, Robin Lane. *Pagans and Christians*. NY: Knopf, 1987.

Frend, W. H. C. *The Donatist Church: A Movement of Protest in Roman North Africa*. Oxford: Clarendon, 1952.

Frend, W. H. C. *Martyrdom and Persecution in the Early Church: A Study of a Conflict from the Maccabees to Donatus*. Oxford: Blackwell, 1965.

Frend, W. H. C. "Popular Religion and Christological Controversy in the Fifth Century." In *Popular Belief And Practice* 8 (1972): 19-29.

Frend, W. H. C. *The Rise of Christianity*. Philadelphia, PA: Fortress, 1984.

Frend, W. H. C. *Town and Country in the Early Christian Centuries*. London: Variorum, 1980.

Fülöp-Miller, René. *The Saints that Moved the World: Anthony, Augustine, Francis, Ignatius, Theresa*. Salem, NH: Ayer, 1984.

Gibbon, Edward. *Decline and Fall of the Roman Empire*. www.ccel.org.

Gildas. *The Ruin of Britain, and Other Works*. Totowa, NJ: Rowman and Littlefield, 1978.

Goffart, Walter A. *The Narrators of Barbarian History (A.D. 550-800): Jordanes, Gregory of Tours, Bede, and Paul the Deacon.* Princeton, NJ: Princeton University, 1988.

Gonzalez-Salinero, Raul. "The Anti-Judaism of Quodvultdeus in the Vandal and Catholic Context of the 5th Century in North Africa." In *Revue Des Etudes Juives* 155 (1996): 447-59.

Gordon, Colin Douglas. *The Age of Attila; Fifth-Century Byzantium and the Barbarians.* Ann Arbor: University of Michigan, 1960.

Gregory, Bishop of Tours. *The History of the Franks.* Harmondsworth, Middlesex: Penguin Books, 1974.

Griggs, C. Wilfred. *Early Egyptian Christianity: from its Origins to 451 C. E.* Leiden, NY: E. J. Brill, 1990.

Handmaids of the Lord: Contemporary Descriptions of Feminine Asceticism in the First Six Christian Centuries. translated and edited by Joan M. Petersen. Kalamazoo, MI: Cistercian Publications, 1996.

Hanson, Richard P. C. *The Search for the Christian Doctrine of God: The Arian Controversy 318-381.* Edinburgh: T. & T. Clark, 1988.

Heather, Peter. "The Crossing of the Danube and the Gothic Conversion." In *Greek, Roman, and Byzantine Studies* 27, no. 3 (Autumn 1986): 289-318.

Heather, Peter. "The Huns and the End of the Roman Empire in Western Europe." In *English Historical Review* 110 (1995): 4-41.

Hefele, Charles J. *A History of the Christian Councils.* Edinburgh: T. & T. Clark, 1894.

Hodgkin, Thomas. *Theodoric the Goth: The Barbarian Champion of Civilization.* NY: Putnam, 1909.

Holsapple, Lloyd B. *Constantine the Great.* NY: Sheed & Ward, 1942.

Holum, Kenneth G. *Theodosian Empresses: Women and Imperial Dominion in Late Antiquity.* Berkeley: University of California, 1982.

Jalland, Trevor Gervase. *The Life and Times of St. Leo the Great.* London: S.P.C.K., 1941.

Johnson, Paul. *The History of Christianity.* NY: Atheneum, 1976.

Jonas. *The Life of St. Columban.* www.fordham.edu/halsall/basis/columban.html.

Jones, A. H. M. *The Decline of the Ancient World.* London: Longmans, Green, 1966.

Jones, A. H. M. *The Later Roman Empire, 284-602: A Social, Economic and Administrative Survey.* Oxford: Blackwell, 1964.

Kelly, J. N. D. *Jerome: His Life, Writings, and Controversies.* NY: Harper & Row, 1975.

Kidd, B. J. *A History of the Church to AD 461.* Oxford: Clarendon, 1922.

L'Huillier, Peter. *The Church of the Ancient Councils: The Disciplinary Work of the First Four Ecumenical Councils.* Crestwood, NY: St. Vladimir's Seminary, 1996.

Lang, David Marsh. *Armenia, Cradle of Civilization.* Boston: Allen & Unwin, 1978.

Larson, C. W. R. "Theodosius and the Thessalonian Massacre Revisited - Yet Again." In *Studia Patristica* 10 (1970): 297-301.

Liebeschuetz, J. H. W. G. *From Diocletian to the Arab Conquest: Change in the Late Roman Empire.* Aldershot, UK: Variorum, 1990.

Limberis, Vasiliki. "The Council of Ephesos." In *Ephesos Metropolis of Asia: An Interdisciplinary Approach to its Archaeology, Religion, and Culture,* 322-40. Valley Forge, PA: Trinity, 1995.

Livermore, H. V., *The Origins of Spain and Portugal.* George Allen & Unwin: London, 1971.

MacArthur, John Stewart. *Chalcedon.* NY: Macmillan, 1931.

MacMullen, Ramsay. *Christianizing the Roman Empire: A.D. 100-400.* New Haven: Yale University, 1984.

Macpherson, Robin. *Rome in Involution: Cassiodorus' Variae in Their Literary and Historical Setting.* Poznań: Wydawn. Nauk. Uniwersytetu im. Adama Mickiewicza w Poznaniu, 1989.

Maier, Harry. "The Meanings of Nicaea: Interpretation in Fifth-Century Christological Controversies." In *Consensus* 16 (1990): 9-25.

Mänchen-Helfen, Otto. *The World of the Huns; Studies in Their History and Culture.* Berkeley: University of California, 1973.

Markus, R. A. *The End of Ancient Christianity.* NY: Cambridge University, 1990.

Matt, Leonard von and Stephanus Hilpisch. *Saint Benedict.* Chicago: H. Regnery, 1961.

McGovern, William Montgomery. *The Early Empires of Central Asia: A Study of the Scythians and the Huns and the Part They Played in World History, with Special Reference to the Chinese Sources.* Chapel Hill, NC: University of North Carolina, 1939.

McGuckin, John Anthony. *St. Cyril of Alexandria: The Christological Controversy: its History, Theology, and Texts.* Leiden, NY: E. J. Brill, 1994.

Moffett, Samuel Hugh. *A History of Christianity in Asia.* Vol. 1, *Beginnings to 1500.* San Francisco: Harper, 1992.

Mohler, James A. *The Heresy of Monasticism: The Christian Monks: Types and Anti-Types; an Historical Survey.* Staten Island, NY: Alba House, 1971.

Morris, John. *The Age of Arthur: A History of the British Isles from 350 to 650.* London: Weidenfeld and Nicolson, 1973.

Moses, of Khoren. *History of the Armenians.* Cambridge: Harvard University, 1978.

Neill, Stephen. *A History of Christianity in India, 1707-1858.* NY: Cambridge University, 1985.

Newark, Timothy. *The Barbarians: Warriors & Wars of the Dark Ages.* Poole, Dorset: Blandford, 1985.

The Nicene and Post-Nicene Fathers. www.ccel.org. Used for the writings of many of the fathers treated in this volume.

O'Donnell, James Joseph. *Cassiodorus.* ccat.sas.upenn.edu/jod/texts/cassbook/toc.html.

O'Flynn, John M. *Generalissimos of the Western Roman Empire.* Edmonton, Canada: University of Alberta, 1983.

Oost, Stewart Irvin. *Galla Placidia Augusta; A Biographical Essay.* Chicago: University of Chicago, 1968.

Orosius, Paulus. *Seven books of History Against the Pagans: The Apology of Paulus Orosius.* NY: Columbia University, 1936.

Palanque, J. R. *The Church in the Christian Roman Empire.* London: Garden City, 1949.

Palladius. *Dialogue on the Life of St. John Chrysostom.* NY: Newman, 1985.

Paredi, Angelo. *Saint Ambrose: His Life and Times.* Notre Dame, Ind.: University of Notre Dame, 1964.

Pettersen, Alvyn. *Athanasius.* Harrisburg, PA: Morehouse, 1995.

Procopius, of Caesarea. *Procopius.* Cambridge, MA: Harvard University, 1914-1940.

Queffélec, Henri. *Saint Anthony of the Desert.* NY: Dutton, 1954.

Reno, Frank D. *The Historic King Arthur: Authenticating the Celtic Hero of Post-Roman Britain.* Jefferson, NC: McFarland & Co., ca.1996.

Ricciotti, Giuseppe. *Julian the Apostate.* Milwaukee: Bruce, 1960.

Ryan, John. *Irish Monasticism; Origins and Early Development.* Shannon: Irish University, 1972.

Salisbury, Joyce E. *Iberian Popular Religion, 600 B.C. to 700 A.D.: Celts, Romans, and Visigoths.* NY: E. Mellen, 1985.

Salvian. *On the Government of God.* NY: Columbia University, 1930.

Sayers, Dorothy. *The Mind of the Maker.* NY: Harper Collins, 1987.

Scherman, Katherine. *The Birth of France: Warriors, Bishops, and Long-Haired Kings.* NY: Paragon House, 1989.

Sellers, Robert Victor. *The Council of Chalcedon: A Historical and Doctrinal Survey.* London: S.P.C.K., 1961.

Smith, John Holland. *Constantine the Great.* London: Hamish Hamilton, 1971.

Smith, William, and Henry Wace. *A Dictionary of Christian Biography, Literature, Sects and Doctrines.* London: J. Murray, 1877-87.

Swan, Laura. *The Forgotten Desert Mothers: Sayings, Lives, and Stories of Early Christian Women.* NY: Paulist, 2001.

Thomas, Charles. *Christianity in Roman Britain to AD 500.* Berkeley: University of California, 1981.

Thompson, E. A. *The Goths in Spain.* Oxford: Clarendon, 1969.

Thompson, E. A. *A History of Attila and the Huns.* Oxford: Clarendon, 1948.

Thompson, E. A., "Peasant Revolts in Late Roman Gaul and Spain." In *Past and Present* 2 (1959): 11-23.

Thompson, E. A. *Romans and Barbarians: The Decline of the Western Empire.* Madison: University of Wisconsin, 1982.

Thompson, E. A. *Saint Germanus of Auxerre and the End of Roman Britain.* Woodbridge: Boydell, 1984.

Thompson, E. A. *The Visigoths in the Time of Ulfila.* Oxford: Clarendon, 1966.

Thompson, E. A. *Who was Saint Patrick?* NY: St. Martin's, 1986.

Tsangadas, Bryon C. P. *The Fortifications and Defense of Constantinople.* Boulder: East European Monographs, 1980.

Victor, of Vita. *History of the Vandal Persecution.* Liverpool: Liverpool University, 1992.

Victor, Sextus Aurelius. *Liber de Caesaribus of Sextus Aurelius Victor.* Liverpool: Liverpool University, 1994.

Wallace-Hadrill, J. M. *The Barbarian West, 400-1000.* Oxford: Malden, MA: Blackwell, 1996.

Ward-Perkins, Bryan. *From Classical Antiquity to the Middle Ages: Urban Public Building in Northern and Central Italy, AD 300-850.* NY: Oxford University, 1984.

Wilken, Robert. "Tradition, Exegesis, and the Christological Controversies." In *Church History* 34 (1965): 123-45.

Williams, Stephen, and Gerard Friell. *Theodosius: The Empire at Bay.* London: B. T. Batsford, 1994.

Wolfram, Herwig. *The Roman Empire and its Germanic peoples.* Berkeley, CA: University of California, 1997.

Zosimus. *A New History.* Sydney: Australian Association for Byzantine Studies, 1982.

PHOTOGRAPHIC CREDITS

The editor wishes to acknowledge the sources that provided photographic images for this volume. Permission to reproduce has been sought in all cases. (**Bold** = supplier *Italics* = source.)

Art Resource, NY: 122-23 ©*Alinari*; 253 center ©*Art Resource*; 42 ©*Cameraphoto Arte, Venice*; 236(4) ©*Fine Art Photographic Library, London*; 77 top, 88, 106 left, 91, 197, 216 both, 229(3)(4), 256 above, 278(4) ©*Werner Forman*; 278(3) ©*Foto Marburg*; 46 upper right, 46 lower left, 202, 205 below ©*Giraudon*; 195 ©*The Jewish Museum*, NY; 17 bottom, 56, 64, 75(6), 89 left, 102 top, 121 below, 141, 153, 154, 184(1), 219 both, 237(7), 254, 259, 263, 269 top, 276 right ©*Erich Lessing*; 232 ©*The Pierpont Morgan Library*; 200, 214 right ©*Réunion des Musées Nationaux*; 146 left ©*A.M. Rosati*; 50, 72 both, 73, 86, 95, 102 below, 106 right, 133, 136, 140 below, 148, 151, 156, 159, 162, 164, 166, 179 top, 184(3), 185, 210, 256 above right, 257 right, 266 left, 273(1)(3), 280 both ©*Scala*; 190 ©*SEF*; 150, 253 right ©*Snark*; 105 right, 236(2) ©*Victoria and Alberta Museum, London*. **Aurora Glass**, Savannah, Georgia: 12, 67, courtesy Jon Erickson. ©**British Museum**, London: 90 both. **CORBIS/Magmaphoto.com**: 17 top, 124, 170, 206 left, 214 right, 225 ©*Archivo Iconografica, S.A.*; 74(2) ©*Johannes Armineh*; 278(2) ©*Yann Arthus-Bertrand*; 41, 74(1) ©*Dave Bartuff*; 248(3) ©*Tom Bean*; 229(2) ©*Niall Benvie*; 47(2), 127 left, 144, 205 left, 224, 235, 236(1), 244, 246 left, 246 top ©*Bettmann*; 62, 105 left ©*Jonathan Blair*; 211 all ©*Stefano Blanchetti*; 169(3) ©*David Butow*; 118(2) ©*Michelle Chaplow*; 209 ©*Elio Ciol*; 70, 161, 266 center ©*Corbis/Sygma*; 264 ©*Gerard Degeorge*; 260 both ©*Araldo de Luca*; 218, 221, 222 ©*Leonard de Selva*; 273(2) ©*Eric Dluhosch*; 206 right ©*Owen Franken*; 96 left ©*Philippe Giraud*; 231 ©*Jason Hawkes*; 179 below, 180 top, 180 left ©*Chris Heller*; 273(4) ©*Angelo Hornak*; 99 ©*Dave G. Houser*; 96 right, 169(1) ©*Hulton-Deutsch Collection*; 74(3) *Andrea Jemolo*; 93 ©*Mimmo Jodice*; 237(5) ©*Bob Krist*; 46 upper left, 186, 196, 276 left ©*Paul H. Kuiper*; 257 ©*Danny Lehman*; 278(5), 279 ©*Lawrence Manning*; 46 below center, 189 ©*Francis G. Mayer*; 79 ©*Buddy Mays*; 77 bottom, 249(4) ©*Michael Nicholson*; 69, 180 right, 237(6), 278(1) ©*Richard T. Nowitz*; 215 ©*Gianni Dagli Orti*; 75(5) ©*Christine Osborne*; 21, 246 right ©*Reuters NewMedia Inc.*; 169(2) ©*Fluvio Roiter*; 75(4)©*Hans Georg Roth*; 119(3), 243, 245, 248(1) ©*Michael St. Maur Sheil*; 135 ©*Ted Spiegel*; 236(3), 252 ©*Stapleton Collection*; 127 right ©*Vince Streano*; 266 right ©*Swim Ink*; 89 right ©*Vanni Archive*; 46 upper left, 226 ©*Gian Berto Vanni*; 50 right ©*Ruggero Vanni*; 15 below, 140 top ©*Sandro Vannini*; 131, 249(5) ©*Patrick Ward*; 248(2) ©*Wild Country*; 119(4), 146 right, 269 below ©*Roger Wood*; 15 left ©*Michael S. Yamashita*; 239 ©*Felix Zaska*. ©**Holy Transfiguration Monastery**, Brookline, MA: 22, 61 all. ©**The Metropolitan Museum of Art**, NY, bequest of Darius Ogden Mills: 17 middle. ©**Tim Severin**: 250. ©**Warner Press, Inc.**, Anderson, IN, by permission: 46 lower right.

INDEX

Entries in red indicate map page numbers and reference coordinates.

For additional copies of this book, or others in this series:

Write: **Box 530** • **Pembina, ND 58271**   or   **10333 - 178 St** • **Edmonton, AB T5S 1R5 Canada**

Call toll-free in North America: **1-800-853-5402**
On line: **www.christianhistoryproject.com**

Ideal for homeschoolers, an excellent companion text for
Bible study groups, and an invaluable resource for every home library.
The Christians is also a perfect gift for children and grandchildren.

Each volume of *The Christians* can be previewed
on a risk–free, fully returnable basis, for two weeks.
Call **1-800-853-5402** to have your order processed immediately.

The.
Christians

A unique new series of books about the real people and events of 2000 years of Christian faith